The Battle of the Frogs and Fairford's Flies

The Battle of the Frogs and Fairford's Flies

Miracles and the Pulp Press During the English Revolution

Jerome Friedman

St. Martin's Press
New York

Published in Great Britain as
Miracles and the Pulp Press during the English Revolution

First published in the United States of America 1993
Printed in the United States of America

ISBN 0-312-09125-7 (cloth)
ISBN 0-312-10170-8 (paper)

Library of Congress Cataloging-in-Publication Data

Friedman, Jerome.
    The battle of the frogs and Fairford's flies : miracles and the pulp press
    during the English Revolution / Jerome Friedman.
    Includes bibliographical references and index.
    ISBN 0-312-09125-7
    1. Great Britain—History—Puritan Revolution, 1642-1660
    Historiography. 2. English prose literature—Early modern, 1500-1700—
    History and criticism. 3. Popular literature-Publishing—
    Great Britain—History—17th century.
    4. Literature and society—Great Britain—History—17th century.
    5. Pamphlets-Publishing—Great Britain—History—17th century.
    6. Books and reading—Great Britain—History—17th century.
    7. Great Britain--Popular culture—History—17th century.
    8. Journalism—Great Britain—History—17th century. I. Title.
DA403.F75 1993
941.06—dc20   92-38575
                                                                    CIP

*This book is dedicated to Dr. Judith Sealander:
my very best wife, my very best friend, and my very best colleague.*

Contents

Part I
How England Fell

Part II
Religion in Fallen England

Part III
Sin and Society in Fallen England

Part IV
England Redeemed

List of Illustrations

Acknowledgements

I owe much to many people for their help and support in preparing this book. Many people read different chapters, and their suggestions and criticisms have been incorporated into the final version of the text. In this regard, special thanks to Dr. Christine Worobec, of Kent State University, who is not only a wonderful colleague but a fine friend. I am deeply indebted to Dr. Judith Sealander, of Bowling Green State University, for reading both versions of this manuscript and for making so many important additions, both times.

I am indebted to many institutions and agencies for their general financial support during the years this book was written. Dr. Eugene P. Wenninger, Dean of Research and Sponsored Programs at Kent State University, provided financial aid, travel grants, and authorized leaves of absence. A generous travel grant from the American Philosophical Society permitted me to visit archives and acquire source material otherwise beyond my reach.

Finally, my deep thanks and appreciation to Ms. Laura Heymann and Mr. Simon Winder of St. Martin's Press, who saw this project through from beginning to end.

Preface

Historian Norman Hamson, in a review of recent studies on the French Revolution, has argued that scholars often fail "to see that peasant society was largely motivated by a conception of the world that had little in common with the enlightened abstractions of the revolutionary legislators" and rarely consider that 95 percent of the population at that time ascribed different meaning to political change, indeed, entertained dissimilar beliefs about the basic construction of the universe.[1] Hamson's criticism could be applied to the histories of other revolutions as well. Scholars often prefer to study the writings of exciting, erudite vocal minorities through whose eyes, scholars believe, an age as a whole can be understood. In the case of the English Revolution, historians have generally used the views of eloquent parliamentary constitutionalists, Puritan theologians or social-gospel Leveller radicals to reflect the sentiments of the entire society.[2] However, that larger society was one that these minorities rejected and that rejected them. Literate, urbane academics rarely appreciate the need to study the seemingly unchanging, often superstitious views of the less educated, even though revolutions have often succeeded because the traditional views of such persons were accommodated.

This volume will examine the newsbooks and pulp press from 1640 to 1660 to assess how ordinary English people conceived of the English Revolution. There are various sources for newsbooks and pamphlet literature for the revolutionary period.[3] The over 300 titles in this study were located in the Wing Collection, the Short Title Catalogue, and the McAlpine Collection, as well as collections of pamphlets at the libraries of Harvard and Yale universities, Haverford College, and the Folger, Clark, Newberry, and Huntington libraries. Other pamphlets are from collections in the libraries at Oxford and Cambridge universities, the Bodleian Society, the library of the Society of Friends, and the John Rylands Library in Great Britain. But most important of all is the magnificent collection of pamphlets that the George Thomason Collection of the British Museum comprises. This collection of over 22,000 entries is the single largest collection of manuscripts for the period from 1640 to 1660. George Thomason was a book collector and bookseller during these tumultuous years. He was of Presbyterian sympathy and supported the Parliament until 1647, when power began to shift to the New Model Army. Fortunately, University Microfilms Incorporated in Ann Arbor, Michigan, has now completely filmed this vast collection, which is now available at several university libraries in this country. The collection includes a great number of anonymous pamphlets and individual works by authors from George Abbot to Richard Zouche. The collection also contains several hundred works in Hebrew and other Oriental languages and includes works on almost any religious or social topic from Adamites to prostitution, Jews, or strange apparitions; all manner of state papers; and the largest collection of newspapers and newsbooks in existence.

The materials published between 1640 and 1660, the time frame of this study, are important for at least two reasons. First, censorship was weaker at that time than during the fifty years before and after this period, when strong government and powerful ecclesiastical offices were more able to control the press. Second, the events surrounding the English Revolution were unique. They constituted an unprecedented crisis in English society that neither existing institutions, erudite intellectuals, nor the government could explain to the satisfaction of large numbers of people. This dissatisfaction found a ready voice in the newsbooks and pulp press of the age.

This volume is not a study of the causes of the English civil war nor of its constituencies. The catchphrases of constitutional law, revolutionary political slogans, radical sectarianism, or the Puritan religious invectives that the elites of each side hurled at the other in polemical tracts will not be discussed; neither will sermons or other forms of didactic materials. The fine literature of the age will find no space here and neither will most examples of "popular literature" such as pleasant histories. These subjects have been extensively studied by others and, in any event, hardly touched the lives or consciousness of the overwhelming number of Englishmen. It may be unfortunate, but most people in most ages are simply uninterested in these erudite forms of expression. Rather, several hundred newsbook accounts of ghosts, apparitions, miraculous events, witches and witchcraft, ancient prophecy, popular heroes, master criminals, sects and religious cults, monsters, and peculiar natural occurrences are the center of this study. Accounts of religious charlatans and scurrilous sectarian literature about other Protestants, Jews, Roman Catholics, and Jesuits abound. Works praising the medicinal and recreational values of tobacco, marijuana, liquor, and liberated sexuality proliferated in this age of Puritan reform. These short newsbooks, the seventeenth-century equivalent of modern yellow journalism and supermarket tabloids, were pamphlets ranging in length from four or five to forty pages. However, in the seventeenth century, distinctions among qualities of journalism rarely existed. Few readers distinguished between legitimate and sensational newswriting; to most the reporting of witchcraft felony and other descriptions of the destruction of life and property were one and the same.

Newsbook and pulp literature is never polite or refined, but its circulation dwarfed that of more serious publications during the interregnum as well as today. Moreover, examination of this crude material will clarify the emotional images, gut sentiments, and intellectual architecture by which ordinary Englishmen on both sides of the civil war understood contemporary events. The images and views of the rebellion that emerge from this literature may seem less historically significant than Whig parliamentary arguments, less dynamic than Leveller demands for democratic-type reforms, and less amusing than literary farces. On the other hand, they provide an insight into the mindset and images through which both sides in this conflict attempted to argue their cases, express their hopes, and vent their hatreds. Some scholars have concluded that most popular prose, especially the literature in Pepys's library, was wholly removed from the political conflict of the day. The several hundred pamphlets dealt with in this study will more than adequately prove just the opposite. In fact, there was something of a preoccupation with the fact of revolution in contemporary newsbooks. Not all Englishmen thought about politics with the same frame of reference but, as Hamson has pointed out, one can not dismiss the thought of the unsophisticated, rural or urban ill-educated readers simply because they expressed themselves in different terms. Indeed, it is likely that even educated Englishmen shared the unsophisticated, enchanted views of life and society that appealed to their social inferiors. For the largest number of Englishmen, the important questions were: Would God punish England for killing Charles? Was the recent poor weather related to God's punishment? Were the witchcraft trials of the same years somehow involved? Why were there so many monstrous births in Puritan households? In a word, the pulp press and common newsbooks tell us much about how Englishmen actually conceived of the revolution, not only if they were for or against it, but also about the ideas and concepts that determined how catastrophic events might be evaluated.

Accounts of apparitions, prodigies, criminals, monsters, whores, drugs, bizarre religious sects, ancient prophecies, and a host of other vulgar subjects should not be rejected as a source of information about a society simply because the ideas are gauche and of low quality. Otherwise, we might similarly wish to dismiss the huge literature on the subject of witchcraft even though, it too, does so much to explain how Englishmen thought. Moreover, all of these publications appeared during the civil war, often as a form of propaganda that attempted to win popular support to one side or another through the manipulation of fear or humor. This sort of propaganda continues to be used for purposes of persuasion in modern civil wars, during times of trouble and social unrest and even during elections in modern democratic states. Most recently, the manipulation of images was of central importance in Iraq's war against the world, where incredible visions of the Satanic West were balanced against equally incredible and offensive images of murderous and devious Arabs. In the seventeenth century, "Libertarian" Roundheads, "lascivious" sectarians, Parliamentary "Committee Men" and "Caterpillars" came in for the same type of abuse.

The great number of pamphlets that were published—one London publisher had an inventory of ninety thousand pamphlets—alone justifies their study. Unfortunately, like many archeological and anthropological finds, some important information about these publications does not exist. The authors were often anonymous or used assumed names, and publication dates were sometimes inaccurate. Both authors and publishers frequently had good reason to keep their identities unknown during a time of conflict and censorship. Knowing who, in fact, read these materials demands guesswork as well. In any event, the great volume of such publications certainly indicates a larger readership than the smaller amount of fine poetry, drama, and prose published, all of which reached very few people (who remain equally unknown to us today) but which are often used as mirrors of the age.

Some readers will be dismayed that these simple stories are often dealt with in a straightforward, often literal fashion rather than subjecting them to deconstructionist, reductionist, imagist, or symbolic methods of interpretation. I have made little attempt to discover subplots, alter-plots, subvocalizations and nonappearing personalities, techniques through which many modern critics are able to introduce words, ideas, and themes the original authors carelessly left unexpressed. Sensational literature, then as now, gloried in the impact of the literal word and the direct, graphic woodcut art that often adorned these pamphlets. Ordinary people *believed* in witchcraft and in all sorts of other perhaps unfortunate ideas. Tampering with the simple text adds little to this appreciation. And if sophisticated prose and poetry may be made to speak in voices their authors never heard, there is something patently silly about using the same technique for the seventeenth-century equivalents of *People* magazine and the *National Enquirer*. The medieval fourfold method of Scriptural interpretation had its place in the scholastic Middle Ages, but modern historians should permit a seventeenth-century author to tell his own tale without critics providing allegorical, anagogical, or tropological interpretations of what is obviously a simple story about simple truths.

Studying vulgar media images can turn history on its head. Rather than discovering those factors that explain why many Englishmen wanted to reform society, here we see a world fearful of all change. For the authors of these pamphlets, it is continuity and not reform that provides the overriding texture of the good society. Indeed, during turbulent times of revolution throughout history, the idea of change often elicited fear. Hence, rather than exploring the most eloquent or the most creative thoughts of the age, this volume is content to describe such depressingly classic ideas as gender hatred, fear of the unknown, mindless reverence for authority, blame of the weak, and victimization of the innocent. Unlike more ephemeral, revolutionary ideas of what might come about but does not yet exist, these more mundane views remain from one generation to the next, constituting the legacy of the past that we are.

These pamphlets explain little about Puritan views of predestination but rather show why and how Englishmen came to fear the cancer of sectarianism, devious Jews, seditious Catholics, and totally impossible Turks. They reveal few signs of the Puritan ethic but include humorous descriptions of alcohol, drugs, prostitutes, and sexual practices identified by less austere Englishmen as one of the benefits of restored monarchy. They show how ordinary Englishmen benefited from and welcomed magic but feared witches.

If the well-ordered world of the Newtonian grid finds no discussion in these pages, the miraculous, monster-inhabited world of devilish chaos and venereal disease so feared by Englishmen will. And if these pages have little to add about Oliver Cromwell, in so many ways the great personality of the age, they will have much to say about James Hind, an enormously popular Robin Hood–like hero (and crook) whose popularity and strident royalism was a reminder of Charles in France.

Most important of all, if these simple ideas, embroidered on a cloth of folk belief and laced with superstition and magic, do not indicate why the revolution began, they may tell us a great deal about why the revolution failed. Finally, while these pages speak little about Charles I's removal by the few, they reveal volumes about Charles II's enthusiastic and popular welcome by the many.

Strange Newes from
SCOTLAND,

OR,

A ſtrange Relation of a terrible and prodigious Monſter, borne to the amazement of all thoſe that were ſpectators, in the Kingdome of *Scotland*, in a Village neere *Edenborough*, call'd *Hadenſworth, Septem.* 14. 1647. and the words the ſaid Monſter ſpake at its birth:

Printed according the Originall Relation ſent over to a great Divine hereafter mentioned.

♦ ♦ ♦

1

Censorship, Popular Publication, and the Pulp Press

When William Caxton, the first English printer, set up his press in 1476, nobody could have predicted printing would become so popular so quickly.[1] Few people could read, paper production was complicated and costly, and printing equipment was expensive. Nevertheless, the printing press found avid supporters. The monarchy used the new art to advance its own cause and meet the needs of a growing government bureaucracy through the publication of proclamations, ordinances, decrees, and law codes. The church had legitimate publishing needs of its own, including new ecclesiastical ordinances, catechisms, confessions, and articles of faith, all of which the church saw as essential in the Reformation religious conflict.

Yet authorities actively discouraged use of the press as a vehicle for popular education. The religious debate tearing Europe into warring camps was itself largely possible because printing enabled readers in many parts of Europe to read Martin Luther's attacks upon church abuses. Even more, the same press that proved so effective against Rome could be used against political authority at home, who did not fail to notice that inflammatory pamphlets helped to incite the German Peasant Rebellion in the mid-1520s. Because governments everywhere watching developments in Germany saw in the printing press both benefits and threats, the sixteenth century saw the rapid expansion of both the printing industry and government censorship. Indeed, from the inception of printing, publication and censorship were twin activities revolving about a single axis of political authority.[2]

A list of prohibited books first appeared in England in 1529. The first government licensing system followed a year later. All printers were required to seek a permit from the royal court, and later from the Court of Star Chamber, to publish each and every pamphlet or other publication. Since governing authorities believed that placing the word of God into commoners' hands might also lead to unrest and dissension, officials restricted the publication of Scripture, and especially of the vernacular Bible. By 1538, a royal proclamation against "naughty printed books" extended the system of licensing for all types of printing to the Privy Council and the Archbishop of Canterbury.

In 1557 Mary Tudor chartered the English Stationers' Company to enable the government to control what Englishmen read.[3] The Stationers' Company had been founded in 1403 from older societies of scriveners, limners, bookbinders and stationers. It applied for a charter and publication privileges as early as 1534, and Mary finally agreed to grant the monopoly so that this agency could oversee, and control, all aspects of bookselling and publication. Every title published was to be listed in its register and no books, pamphlets, newsbooks, or broadsides without a license would be printed. Elizabeth enforced these same policies and added new elements of control: The printing of all domestic news was prohibited unless it was unrelated to national affairs.[4] In 1586 the Star Chamber affirmed that all publications had to be licensed and confirmed the power of the Stationers' Company to search for and seize illicitly printed materials. Publication was limited and only ninety-seven small hand presses were authorized.

The early Stuarts, seeking to rule without parliamentary opposition and facing a growing number of literate people, clearly wanted to control public opinion. A large ecclesiastical and government bureaucracy effectively stifled popular publication as well as popular forms of religious expression. In 1637 Archbishop Laud limited the number of master printers to twenty-three and created a complicated system of licensing. Those printing without a license would be whipped and pilloried.

Censorship continued during the early years of the civil wars. Legislation in 1643 and 1647 affirmed earlier attempts to control the press and on September 20, 1649, Parliament enacted a very detailed set of regulations restricting the right of publication to the city of London and to university presses at Oxford and Cambridge. The new regulations permitted the presses at York and Finsbury to continue to print the Bible but withdrew official approval for all newsbooks, enlarged the powers of the licensors, and required all printers to post a bond of £300 to guarantee their compliance. Through these laws the authorities hoped to curtail the spread of antigovernment opinion and stifle royalist propaganda efforts.

Oliver Cromwell was also concerned how his own policies would be received outside of London: Newspapers were prohibited from reporting the beheading of King Charles and subsequently were often encouraged not to report other sensitive news.[5]

Like many other programs during this period, implementation fell short of the goal.[6] Despite Elizabeth's restrictions, for instance, the humorous and scandalous Martin Marprelate tracts of 1588 and 1589, which laughed at sanctimonious Puritanism and enflamed the divisions within the Church of England, were widely circulated. Similarly, the revolutionary Parliament found it difficult to control the press during the early years of its conflict with the king, and the results were quickly apparent. Where only two newspapers were published in London in 1642, two years later over a dozen appeared regularly. The number would continue to grow.[7] And despite a succession of laws against the publication of blasphemy and Cromwell's best efforts to suppress army radicalism, no religious or political opinion, however extreme, failed to secure a publisher. Every radical constituency found a willing printer if only because many publishers simply and flagrantly flouted licensing laws and other government controls. Authors used initials or remained anonymous; printers used false imprints; publishers gave spurious identification. Even a cursory perusal of the listings in the Thomason Collection of the British Museum will indicate how few publishers of pamphlets and newsbooks even sought permits. This informal assessment is further underscored by recent scholarship. *The Cambridge Bibliography of English Literature* lists 350 titles of newsbooks that appeared from 1641 to 1659 despite active attempts by revolutionary authorities to curtail the publication of newspapers and newsbooks.[8] The numbers of informal, one-time newsbooks and pamphlets, the subject of this study, increased even more dramatically: George Thomason collected 22 pamphlets in 1640, over 717 pamphlets in 1641, 1,966 in 1642, and for the period ending in 1660, a total of over 22,000 pamphlets, newspapers, and newsbooks.[9]

Many factors made controlling the free expression of ideas difficult, especially during years of revolution. First, the confusing events of the civil war made news very desirable to more people than ever before. Second, the percentage of literate Londoners had increased as the demands of an urban merchant economy made reading skills vital to more people. Third, by 1640 setting up a small hand press demanded only a modest capital outlay, and the machinery could be easily concealed from government officials. Moreover, publishing was not particularly labor-intensive. Two men working eight hours on a hand press, for instance, could produce 1,000 folio sheets.[10] As a result, where twenty-five printing houses existed in 1640, over sixty were in operation by 1649.

None of this was lost upon Charles II. The Printing Act of 1662 restricted the printing of books to a small number of master printers of the Stationers' Company, the two universities, and the Archbishop of York and, further, limited the number of apprentices kept by each institution. No new publishing houses would be created until the total number had fallen to twenty, which was to be the permanent number of publishers in the future.

Newsbooks, however, were something else again. When Charles returned to power in 1660 he had appointed Sir John Berkenhead to suppress all existing newsbooks. In 1663 Sir Roger L'Estrange became Surveyor of the Press. Sir Roger had very definite ideas about his role and the dangers posed by a public that possessed information about government policies. He noted, "I think it makes the Multitude too familiar with the actions and counsels of their superiors, too pragmatic and censorious, and gives them not only an itch but a kind of colorable right and license to be meddling with the government."[11]

Rather than attempting to close the spigot of ink—essentially the failed policy of the past—Charles chose a far more sophisticated approach to newsbook censorship. The king understood the value of disseminating information and appointed Henry Muddiman to supervise the publication of two authorized newsbooks: the *Kingdome's Intelligencer*, which appeared on Mondays, and the *Mercurius Publicus*, which appeared on Thursdays. These newsbooks were designed to place the right sort of censored ideas and news before those seeking newsbooks. The government facilitated their success through free postage.[12] For the next several years Muddiman controlled the publication of all news effectively, but, even more, he was soon able to turn his staff of reporters into a spy network, providing the monarchy with local information vital to a controversial government.

Of the various factors making censorship difficult, both during the civil war and after, the single most important was the increasing rate of literacy. But determining literacy rates is a difficult enterprise. Students of traditional political history and fine literature have often identified low levels of literacy and the lack of published materials as factors that make it difficult to assess the views of more than a small group of educated social elites. Recent scholarship, however, has demonstrated that literacy was quite widespread, a fact that explains why and how a wealth of cheap pamphlet literature that expressed ordinary folks' sentiments about life, religion, government, and especially about the English Revolution, could find its way into print.

Until recently, educated opinion estimated that by 1640, approximately 30 percent of males and 11 percent of females were literate.[13] But these figures may be far too low: Many people who were unable to write could read.[14] In fact, recent work on literacy in the English countryside indicates that the number of individuals able to read increased steadily throughout the second half of the sixteenth century and the seventeenth century.[15] An important study of the village of Terling in Essex has underscored the degree to which reading ability was a rapidly growing skill.[16] In the period from 1580 to 1609, for instance, literacy among yeomen stood at 44 percent, among craftsmen at 25 percent, and among laborers at zero. A century later literacy among these same classes had risen to 83 percent, 68 percent, and 36 percent, respectively. Literacy rates were even higher in small towns than in villages like Terling and higher still in cities. One can assume that in London, the place of publication and the major market for almost all cheap pamphlets, literacy was common.

Even the illiterate benefited from the new technology of printing. The literate could and did read aloud in public places such as taverns and alehouses to those who could not read. Thomas Nashe noted how newsbook stories were common alehouse talk, and Peter Clark has written convincingly about the alehouse as the center of an alternate, lower-class culture, a development dependent on significant numbers of literate persons.[17] Indeed, Lawrence Clarkson has described how the literate and illiterate came together to discuss new publications and radical ideas, and the radical publisher Giles Calvert met with radical Puritans, Levellers, and Ranters in secluded alehouses along Coleman Street and elsewhere in London.[18]

The fact that pamphlets could reach large numbers of people was not lost upon other contemporary publishers. This was probably what motivated George Horton to publish several relatively nonpartisan newsbooks during the civil wars intended for the unsophisticated reader. *The Perfect Weekly Account* of January 24, 1649, reported: "In these days the meanest sort of people are not only able to write, but to argue and discourse on matters of the highest concernment and thereupon do desire that such things which are most remarkable may be truly committed to writing and made public."[19] In turn, because almost all pamphlets were published in London, they accentuated the great importance of that city.[20] It was already a large job market during a period of agricultural retraction, and from 1500 to 1700 the city's population increased tenfold to reach over 500,000 people. The new press was already proving itself to be commercially valuable to merchants, as seen by the steady increase in advertising space. Indeed, the first newsbook devoted entirely to advertising, *The Public Adviser*, appeared in 1657.[21]

London's importance was far greater than statistics would indicate, however, because it was the seat of royal power and, in the mid-seventeenth century, the focus of revolution and change. Consequently, London publishers exerted an enormous influence throughout the countryside because their product constituted a continual source of ideas explaining the complex events of the day. Indeed, one astute provincial observer correctly characterized this flow of news materials from London as "the sea of news from which smaller rivulets often flow to us in the country."[22]

The sheer volume of what was published underscores the existence of a large number of readers. Besides the 350 newsbooks alluded to earlier, other publications costing from one to sixpence included almanacs, ballads, single sheet broadsides, chapbooks, and jestbooks, all of which reached deep into the English countryside.[23] Bible stories were always popular, and in an age of Puritan dissent there certainly were treatises about all aspects of religion. Other than sectarian tracts, polemics, counter-polemics, and a great many theological treatises, many modest devotional pieces admonished the reader to repent, mend his ways and be the good person God required. An updated version of Arthur Dent's *The Poor Man's Plain Path-way to Heaven* (1603) reached its fifty-seventh printing in the 1670s, a fact that surely indicates that many young apprentices were spiritual—or perhaps that they were not but hoped to be or, at least, thought that one seeking social respectability should be. It is clear that they could read.

Almanacs sold briskly to an upscale market. By 1640 sales had reached 400,000 copies—one quarter of all households.[24] Some estimates maintain that over 2,000 almanacs involving over 200 authors appeared during the seventeenth century. Almanacs gave useful advice about gardening, church festivals, folk medicine, and seasonal time tables for the rising and setting of the sun. They also presented astrological prognostications of coming events as well as weather predictions. Like the *Farmer's Almanac* of more recent times, seventeenth-century almanacs proved popular with shopkeepers, artisans, and others for whom practical information was important. Their purchasers also included a growing percentage of the general population that believed, like more recent purchasers of multi-volume encyclopedia sets, that the possession of hard information was a mark of intellectual sophistication and a harbinger of social success.

Ballads, often printed as broadsides, were published in huge numbers and were even more significant than almanacs in presenting news of the day.[25] These nine-by-twelve-inch folio sheets, printed on one side, were the most popular printed format in England, and by 1641, 300 ballad sellers hawked their wares on London street corners alone. Ballads were frequently drinking songs, with verses based upon the deeds of bygone heroes such as Robin Hood, King Arthur, or personalities of the day. Ballads often poked fun at the personal deeds and misdeeds of those in power and posed salacious queries about those who, then as now, hid a personal immorality behind a public veil of sanctity. Their creators, "pot-poets" or street balladeers, acted as intermediaries between the newly literate and the world of culture and learning.

For many urban patricians the very idea that news of the powerful might become the property of the common poor was distasteful. They found something disreputable about commoners being able to read about the misdeeds of their social betters and judged those writing and selling these publications to be gossip-mongering low-lives, in a class with vagabonds and thieves. In fact, although artisans, servants, and laborers were the intended audience for most ballads, the songs also appealed to wealthy merchants and other people of means. Indeed, both almanacs and ballads demanded some level of sophistication since the former assumed the importance of practical information and some familiarity with the political events of the day while ballads were written in verse and often made use of classical literary images. Yet, while often biting or witty, ballads rarely expressed complex ideas.

Newspapers could provide a vehicle for developing opinions about events of the day and enjoyed an avid sophisticated readership in London. But they were largely short-run affairs since they faced stiff censorship if they opposed the new government's account of events. Newsbooks and pamphlets, on the other hand, provided a more subversive way to express antigovernment sentiment since they sold as individual issues and were almost impossible to censor. Consequently, during the interregnum, the early pamphlet, or chapbook, replaced the ballad as the prime medium of popular literary consumption and even surpassed the almanac in gross sales.

The pamphlet was little more than the ballad broadside printed on both sides of the page, folded over several times to produce four or eight pages, and bound together with a single long stitch.[26] Ink and paper were of poor quality, and crude art woodcuts were used over and over again. Indeed, to keep costs as low as possible (to better compete with ballads), the pamphlet was often printed on even poorer "pulp" quality paper than broadsides. Although they were longer than ballads, pamphlets were written in a simpler, spoken prose style and represented an attempt to reach the widest social and cultural common denominators. These publications may have been directed at the intellectually modest, but they were read both upstairs and downstairs. Indeed, while new and cheaper forms of printing made pamphlets available to the meanest fishmonger's apprentice, it would be a mistake to assume that more educated Englishmen did not share in this literature as well. Prostitution, witchcraft, alcohol, drugs, and popular prophecy were topics with universal appeal, and almost everyone accepted the veracity of prodigies and apparitions.

The pamphlet could be read easily in one sitting or started and then put into one's pocket for reading later. Because they were so cheap, a penny or two for most, pamphlets were an affordable commodity that could be passed on to others, much as urban commuters now leave newspapers in buses and trains.

Pamphlet authors often remained anonymous. The minority who can be identified were commoners: Thomas Deloney (1543-1600) was a weaver, Martin Parker (d. 1656) kept an alehouse; and John Taylor (1580-1653), the most prolific of them all, was a Thames waterman and later a tavern owner in both Oxford and London. Thomas Spigurnell started life as an apprentice bookbinder but practiced peddling, ballad singing, and keeping an alehouse and may have even been ordained after some fashion.[27] During the civil war years and interregnum, anonymous royalists wrote pamphlets for propaganda purposes in order to put the new government in a poor light. Like ballads, most pamphlets were published in London and hawked elsewhere in England by "chapmen"; for this reason the term "chapbook literature" has come to describe the cheap pulp pamphlet press of later centuries as well.

By the mid-seventeenth century the pulp pamphlet overtook ballads and almanacs as the medium of popular choice. The inventory of one London publisher, Charles Tias, consisted of 90,000 pamphlets at the time of his death in 1664.[28] In terms of the politics of the day, most pamphlets avoided overt political allegiance and thereby avoided censorship as well. Yet pamphlets describing the recent appearance of witches, monsters, and apparitions, all of which the English took seriously as divine signs and linked with the revolution, provided another means of expressing doubt about events of the day.[29] As a result, despite the censorship of newspapers, the two tumultuous decades of the English Revolution witnessed a virtual tidal wave of cheap newsbook and pamphlet publications, antigovernment as well as antiroyalist, directed at London's large audience of common but literate laborers, artisans, and shopkeepers. The literary quality of some publications, as we shall see, would seem to indicate a more educated and sophisticated readership as well. By the end of the century, 10,000 chapmen had made their way across England selling their pamphlets, as well as a variety of household goods, at fairs, in taverns, to small shopkeepers, and from house to house. While scholars have studied Puritan and Anglican theological pamphlets and the many political treatises that also proliferated at this time, the far larger volume of cheap pamphlet literature that expressed popular dread about the civil war conflict remains largely neglected.

Chapbooks covered a greater diversity of interests than ballads or almanacs and attempted to appeal to many audiences, from the most educated to the most vulgar. Each pamphlet dealt with one subject in greater detail than was possible in ballads; separate publications discussed religion, diet, medicine, cosmetics, news reports, political ideas, or almost any other topic for which there was a market. By reading a series of these chapbooks, even the poorly schooled artisan could acquire a smattering of education, and even the meanest laborer could use them to form opinions about the issues of the day, important or otherwise.

The literary themes found in secular popular prose usually emphasized the importance of romantic and mythical heroes such as Robin Hood and King Arthur and expressed a nostalgic longing for the simpler times of yesteryear. To an extent, this was the slightly removed secular cousin of accounts of traditional popular religious piety. Much as Bible stories told of unusually wonderful religious persons, the secular popular expression described nonbiblical popular heroes. While one wrote of sainthood and piety, the other explicated knighthood and chivalry. Accounts of St. George fighting monsters, savages, and giants were popular and combined the best of both tendencies. A romantic twist might be added by having the hero fall in love with an exotic princess from some strange land. Then, as now, Our Hero fought for Good against all the Forces of Darkness, in this world and the next.

This undisguised hero worship, while seemingly childlike, prepared the reader before the English Revolution to view contemporary authority with the same respect accorded these mythical heroes, who, in turn, were predicated upon biblical heroes. The king, for instance, was God's representative on earth, capable of performing miracles. Indeed, his blood, like Christ's blood, was able to heal the infirm and redeem the spiritually impoverished. One common story line recounted how the king dressed in common clothes in order to circulate among his subjects and discover their degree of happiness with his rule. These stories would further describe how the king lived with, and worked for, peasants or artisans and how, because he lacked manual skills, he was often lewdly insulted and abused by those ignorant of his identity. Through all his torments, the king patiently tolerated the ill treatment. When the king's identity was eventually disclosed, his hitherto peasant peers were apologetic, contrite, and terrified, but then relieved to learn that the king would not have them punished. Indeed, in recognition of the peasant's "true honesty and purity of heart"—despite his more obvious crudeness and lewd behavior—the king would reward him with land, wealth, and titles. Christ, of course, dressed as a commoner, served in a mean capacity, suffered indignities, and forgave his malefactors whom he then blessed with unmerited grace much as the king in these stories gave the lewd peasant unmerited status and wealth. Many of these accounts continued to urge obedience to the king even when his policies or ministers were bad, even after he had been executed. The value of myth to enhance political authority and the ability of chapbook stories to contribute to this myth may explain why many readers saw in these stories an explanation for the social hierarchy about them and why this sort of story was rarely censored.

As times changed, the new commercial economy produced its own contemporary popular heroes, although the socially conservative tone remained.[30] Despite the fact that new heroes were simple folk, they, too, received familiar mythical treatment. John Hawkwood was a poor London tailor's apprentice, and Tom Hickathrift, whose enormous strength enabled him to slay giants, was the son of a day laborer; both made good. Female readers could find a heroine in Long Meg, a young woman who came to London to seek employment and was forced to fight and compete in the rough world of tough men that awaited her. These and other stories reflected the hopes of the poor to better themselves. This universal theme was best expressed in Thomas Deloney's stories about Jack of Newberry, a poor lad who struck it rich in the garment trade and eventually employed thousands of other young men. Jack's message to his erstwhile mates was as simple as it has proven enduring: Hard work, honesty, and courage will be rewarded in this great age of opportunity.

Despite social myths that provided some comfort, the rigors of the world, monarchy, and commercial capitalism were often hurtful to ordinary people. Consequently, much popular literature consisted of stories that attempted to put a happy face on contemporary exploitative commercial and political social relations. All the popular heroes mentioned above emphasized their outstanding loyalty to the king and, like Robin Hood, placed blame for ineffective rule on the shoulders of the king's evil advisers. In his helplessness the commoner sought some measure of solace in a literature that made God, king, landlord, guildmaster, and employer seem more decent than was obviously apparent. In other words, simple stories helped to explain the social hierarchy. However, chapbooks rarely accorded similar mythical treatment to noblemen and local landlords as they did to kings. It was probably easier to maintain illusions about the power of the distant monarch than about the power of authority close at hand. Perhaps this also underscored the king's unique role as an earthly representative of divine order and enabled English kings to claim the title of supreme governor of the church since the time of Henry VIII.

On the lighter side, romantic love was another important theme. Ardent lovers, passionate suitors, false females, broken promises, betrayal, and insanity crowded the pages of chapbooks. Some stories idealized love, while others decried it and presented marriage as the worst fate to befall an innocent young man.

Seventeenth-century popular literature finds a parallel in modern paperback romances and heroic adventure stories. Moreover, this literature appeals to much the same socially conservative audience, who continues to demand both distraction from reality as well as a happy ending. Indeed, popular literature in all ages attempts to explain to the common and ordinary person how simple truths are still valid in the face of an increasingly complicated world. By identifying with the hero of the story, the reader affirms old-fashioned values in a world conceived of as increasingly crass, unscrupulous, irreligious, and immoral. This naive sense of hope in the face of cruel reality involved a strong element of wish fulfillment and unites seventeenth-century chapbook literature with more modern representatives of the same genre.

Popular writing changed with the civil war and the execution of the king. Rather than expressing hope and optimism that all was as it should be, new vulgar newsbook journalists paraded before the public horrible images of how everything was bad—and getting worse. Increasing numbers of pamphlets told of the appearance of witches, monsters, and apparitions, whose existence the average English reader took seriously, linked with the revolution, and interpreted as evidence of wrong actions taken by their social betters. Indeed, the interregnum witnessed a virtual tidal wave of cheap and crude pamphlets covering every conceivable topic from blasphemous religion to pornography, from reports of apparitions and monsters to odes describing the beneficial affects of opium and marijuana, from hysterical reports of impious Ranters to accounts of scandalous religious charlatans claiming they were Jesus, Mary, and a host of other biblical personalities returned from the dead. Ancient prophetic writings, with much to contribute to an understanding of the revolution, appeared for both the king and the Parliament. Most of these topics may seem historically innocuous compared to political issues, economic conditions, or the many other subjects analyzed so well by scholars. Yet they express how the course of the revolution was perceived by common Londoners, indeed, the terms by which the revolution was understood. Of course, it is difficult to penetrate the minds of other people at other times. But the sheer volume of this literature necessitates that the effort be made. Considering the great fear of witches during these years of change and the enormous pulp literature describing them to an avid public, the huge and fantastic sectarian polemical literature of the times that described theological rivals in obscene terms, one can hardly come to the conclusion that these publications did not enjoy a wide distribution. Had such alarmist publications remained unread, their numbers would have declined during the two decades of turmoil. But in fact, the number of such publications increased by a greater factor than that of any other type of publication. These are the materials treated in this volume.

There are important distinctions between popular literature and pulp journalism. Popular literature, which expresses mythic hope, and the vulgar imagination of pulp newsbooks, which express fear, may seem like opposites. Both, however, appeal to overlapping audiences; the former indicates a love of continuity while the latter expresses a fear of change. Yet, where popular literature concentrated upon classic and nostalgic themes, pulp literature was sensational and contemporary. All seventeenth-century reports of monsters, witches, criminals, and bizarre religious sects, for instance, were characterized by an adamant emphasis upon the dangers inherent in the immediate present.

The same dichotomy exists today. Paperback romances or Norman Rockwell paintings stress an old-fashioned notion of social relationships, representing the quintessential expression of popular nostalgia for what no longer exists, indeed, may never have existed. On the other hand, reports of UFO sightings, new terrorist conspiracies, and insidious, chemically induced monstrous births capture the quick of the pulp press and express the reader's dread that the object of his fear does, in fact, exist. Where popular literature emphasizes continuity of values with the past and attempts to interpret the present on the basis of the mythical heroes of bygone ages, pulp pamphlets warn of an uncertain future in a world that is out of control.

Fear and hope often stand hand in hand. Once revolutionary change became too erratic, and its fruits too unsuccessful, a fascination with fear may have replaced a tendency toward hope. In a word, the execution of the king, the destruction of the church, and the tearing apart of the social system was not only shocking, but frightening. As we shall see over and over again in the pamphlets treated later, large segments of the population perceived these actions as a rebellion against God's order. The subsequent inability of the revolutionary government to rule was therefore a sign of divine displeasure. The continuing religious dislocations, the wars with Holland, the rise in prices, and the starvation reported in many parts of England were all seen as additional signs of England's terrible deed. As one pamphlet explained, Englishmen had rebelled against God's orderly universe, and now all of the universe was rebelling against England.

Pulp newsbook journalism envisioned the present as the first step into a fear-filled future. By pointing to some conspiracy of evil, it attempted to provide an explanation for the anticipated collapse of everything familiar and dear to the reader. Seventeenth-century pamphlets pointed to heinous Jesuits, seditious Catholics, crafty Jews, warring Turks, blasphemous sectarians, and libertine-hedonists as constituting one great cabal responsible for England's woes. The reader's anxiety about the present was important because it provided the fundamental ground for conspiracy theorists' claims that all reasonable people should dread the future. Even a simple story recounting a tragic turn in someone else's life was an ominous indication of the evil lurking beneath the surface of seemingly everyday incidents. In turn, newsbook authors wanted the reader to know that he, too, was in danger of being trapped by an identical set of circumstances.

Every seemingly innocent event was really an indication of something more sinister. Just as God was the unseen force behind benevolent nature, nature gone awry was an indication of terrible evil forces now in control of events. In turn, disturbing social developments were indications of some cosmic disease, and thus individual feelings of anxiety could be converted into a sense of national dread.

As an example, in 1657 Nathaniel Butler's homosexual murder of his friend, Jonathan West, became an instant source of newsbook copy. After several pamphlets discussed every detail of each young man's background—the motives, deeds, character, and history—the last newsbook devoted to this lurid subject drew the logical conclusion. Hitting upon what earlier writers had missed altogether, the author of *The Penitent Murderer* (1657) explained that "we hear and fear 'tis true that [Catholic] priests and Jesuits (those Romish Locusts) do swarm amongst us in the city and suburbs." And after a long tirade, the pamphlet ended with the prayer to the mayor of London "to put forth your power to the utmost for the discovering and suppressing of them."[31] The message driven home to the reader was that Butler had been led to become a homosexual murderer, but he was innocent compared to the evil and unnatural papist influences forcing him to his evil deeds. In turn, every other Englishman was similarly at risk.[32]

To cater to this increasing fear that all was out of balance in England, that divine retribution was forthcoming and was already perceptible in every storm and peculiar natural occurrence, London publishers provided readers with a steady diet of reports from the hinterland of strange phenomena and peculiar events indicating a shift in moral poles of the universe. Sensational reports of heinous monsters, devious Jews, murderous Catholics, thrill-seeking libertines, conjuring witches, and monster-induced demons took the form of letters from alleged cousins and brothers still back in a small town. This was a convenient point of identification for many readers since so many Londoners still had kin living in rural villages all over England. Moreover, it may have seemed reasonable to readers then, as now, that someone in a remote corner of the country or world might be the cause of some evil for the remainder of society to endure. Rumors and fictitious allegations were more believable than fact because they were reflections of the reader's own innate system of values and fears rather than the true but confusing occurrences in a world gone awry. These accounts were so popular and sold so well that publishers soon began copying each other's stories and probably even resorted to making them up altogether. In a word, pulp newsbooks about monsters, apparitions, and a host of other manifestations of evil informed readers— or confirmed their fears—that God was angry with revolutionary England and demonstrated that important new forces were now at work in the world. As the crisis in governance deepened, so too did the sense of panic expressed in these publications. If little in these chapbooks was concerned with actual political ideology or internecine religious polemic, it is because, as we shall see, the chapbooks were predicated upon the belief that cosmic signs of disaster were more indicative of the state of conflict. What did law, reason, causation, and logic mean when God clearly punished one side or the other with monstrous births?

The shift from popular to pulp literature during the interregnum was dramatic. Pulp pamphlets devoted no space to King Arthur and Robin Hood as examples of enlightened and wise leadership and wrote instead of Captain James Hind, Richard Hannam, and other criminals successfully mocking the social order. While Puritans wished to argue about the signs of the "true church," pulp newsbooks focused on religious charlatans such as John and Joan Robins or William Franklin and Mary Gadbury, who convinced thousands that they were Jesus and Mary, come again to free their souls and liberate their wallets. Puritans may have longed for England before the imposition of the Norman Yoke, but pulp literature was disturbed, frightened, and enthralled with descriptions of witches, how they were tortured, and how special witch-hunters searched a witch's private parts for suck marks. Modern scholars have written about revolutionary constituencies, demographic loyalties to one side or the other, and the effects of class and geography upon political leanings. But these newsbooks reflected a more common sentiment: the fear that society's bottom had fallen out.

Another, lighter side to pulp literature focused upon "life in the creature," as contemporaries would have phrased it. It is possible that life in the flesh was the solace soothing the existence of ordinary Englishmen frightened by regicidal Roundheads and Puritans preaching the awesome doctrine of predestination. Humorous appraisals of prostitution, alcohol, tobacco, and marijuana abounded in stories with prostitutes and street rogues as central characters. The limitation on these many pleasures and liberties was Puritan "reform." Already on the eve of the civil war, Parliament had condemned "the swarming of lascivious, idle, unprofitable books and pamphlets . . . all in disgrace of religion and to the increase of all vice."[33] These publications indicate that many Englishmen entertained serious reservations about revolutionary "Caterpillars," parliamentary "Committee Men," and sanctimonious Puritan pious puffery. Indeed, there was also dirty gossip about the illustrious leaders of the revolution. This mockery is testimony, then, as now, that many were cynical about political and social change and held political reformers and their many programs—about whom so much is always written—in mild contempt, if they thought about them at all.

This volume concerns the pulp newsbooks published during the years of revolution and is divided into separate chapters according to the varied phenomena described. Rather than describing separate themes and then citing in endnotes the titles of the several pamphlets that support this point, the more usual method of scholarship, I have chosen to deal with pamphlets individually. Not only does this provide a greater sense of the language used and how contemporaries understood causation, it makes for better scholarship. With the more usual method, one often finds when looking into cited titles that the pamphlet text actually says just the opposite of what the scholar claims.

The revolution itself is not a separate topic, yet each chapter, in its own way and through a different type of manifestation of the times, expresses the fear and the horror of those who believed they were witnessing England falling to a sad state. So much has been written about politics and government, ecclesiastical history and orthodox and sectarian religious belief, diplomacy, economic affairs, fine and popular literature, and a host of other important topics that the pervasive sense of dread underlying so much of popular sentiment and so common in plebeian publications has been largely ignored. Yet it was this sense of dread and mockery of the revolution that led to the warm welcome accorded Charles II as he made his way to London. Hence, if these chapters tell little about the course of the revolution or about the process of revolutionary change, they may add to our understanding of those more inert forces and ideas that often cause revolutionary change to fail. This tour through the English sense of dread, however, demands a discussion of the shattering impact of Charles's execution on the ordinary Englishman's worldview.

Part I
How England Fell

THE
World turn'd upside down:
OR,
A briefe description of the ridiculous Fashions
of these distracted Times.

By T.J. a well-willer to King, Parliament and Kingdom.

London : Printed for *John Smith.* 1647.

Jan: 28

♦ ♦ ♦

2

Order Within the Universe: The Rebellion Against Charles

"EVERY DAY BRINGETH FORTH SOME NEW HORROR."

—*The Most Strange and Wonderful Apparition
of Blood in a Pool at Garreton (1647)*

The modern mind, comforted by post-Enlightenment rationalism, finds the possible existence of a hidden realm of the miraculous both emotionally frightening and intellectually disturbing. If it were—true that unseen powers lay within seemingly dead stones or that trees possessed the will to act or that inclement weather was the result of malicious spirits, the resources of reason would seem meager indeed. We lull ourselves with the soothing belief that the world is mundane and ordinary, that one need not fear Mother Nature. In the seventeenth century, however, people were convinced of the very opposite set of premises. Indeed, the reasonable person of three centuries ago would have condemned our most fundamental ideas of the universe as willful blindness and ignorance. Every rural Englishman knew that strange forces were at work in the universe and that, in the words of one newsbook, "only the heathen philosophers had nothing but natural causes." Nature was not benevolent, for physical existence was the vehicle through which hidden, often confusing, forces manifested themselves. Rivers, trees, animals, and even manufactured goods contained sometimes malevolent spirits.

This outlook on life may prove surprising to the modern reader, although it was common before the twentieth century. In his magnificent study, *Religion and the Decline of Magic,* Keith Thomas demonstrates that most seventeenth-century Englishmen had a totemistic view of the world. They believed human life and nature were subject to malevolent spirits inhabiting trees, rivers, hedges, and even peculiar-looking rocks, clouds, and storms.[1] Every village child learned how mysterious life was, and the experienced and wizened knew how best to cope with so potentially dangerous an existence—how to walk in the forest, and how to know which stones in a riverbed were accepting of people and would not cause them to drown. Since life was enchanted, many people carried amulets and talismen: love charms, good luck pieces, or other special objects intended for the amelioration of some specific spirit. Other people practiced strange ritual behavior or recited long series of benedictions, rhyming couplets, or special words known to chase evil spirits.

There was, however, a beneficial aspect to nature's magic. Some individuals, every town's cunning woman or wise man, understood how to coax special powers from tree bark, herbs, roots, and flowers. Lynn Thorndike and James Frazer have each discussed these enchanted forces in great detail, and Carlo Ginzburg has described a parallel world of Italian peasants in the Friuli, where those born to the cawl would awake in the middle of the night to do battle with unnameable spirits wishing to harm the community.[2]

Medieval Christianity accommodated an enchanted cosmology within its own theurgy. The modern mind may distinguish between magic and religion but during the later Middle Ages magic and religion were inextricably bound together. Wine turned into blood and bread became the body of Jesus Christ, Moses had performed miracles before Pharoah's magicians, and Joshua had made the sun stand still. The physical world was an expression of God's will and relics, pilgrimages, the magical mass, and the celebration of saints' days were all important elements of normal medieval life. Saints acted as shamans, sacraments as charms and talismen.[3] Equivalent ideas of enchantment and superstition existed within the Jewish community. Indeed, during the early middle ages Judaism and Christianity competed with each other for converts on the basis of whose leaders might produce the most interesting miracles.[4]

White magic found its antithesis in black magic and witchcraft. Precisely because the world was an expression of spirits and forces, both good and ill, the fear of witchcraft spread easily throughout the population, both among the ill-educated *and* among the educated and sophisticated. The witch-hunt craze, for example, reached its zenith during the years of the English Revolution.[5] Hence, understanding why many Englishmen were terrified by the civil war demands an appreciation of the magical parameters of the world as Englishmen understood them. Most contemporaries were probably less devoted to the various ideologies historians have since discovered and instead conceived of the confusing events around them in the same wondrous or miraculous terms that made the witch craze possible.

What was clear in the past (and largely has been lost in the modern world) is the sense that the world was enchanted, a condition that attributed power to inanimate objects through which one came to terms with nature. Life was perceived as essentially magical and largely beyond one's control. In much the same fashion that young children today, confronting a world they can neither understand nor control, do not step on sidewalk cracks for fear that something terrible might subsequently result, adults, too, often practiced a variety of personal rituals. Rural villagers and others attempted to fortify their lives through rituals, sayings, habits, and other forms of behavior involving some parts of nature to gain a sense of control over the rest. Over time, an endless array of ritual behavior accompanied every aspect of life—every celebration, every public event and private deed in life—in order to protect oneself from malevolence. And much as religion provided ritual objects for the sanctifying of one's religious life, daily life also had its special tokens, be they rabbit's feet, peculiar-looking pieces of wood, or polished quartz crystals. While it may seem objectively incomprehensible to attribute power to a material object, some of this lore has come through the centuries in the form of absent-minded rituals such as knocking wood, throwing salt over one's shoulder, or, more ominous, swearing off the evil eye. Despite transistors and satellite communication via microwaves, simple shamanism continues to characterize the faith of most people in most of the world.

Enchantment was initially born in a rural society, where the causes and effects of natural forces were more locally identified. Thus, it was believed that wind resulted from the shaking of trees; an understanding of larger forces constituting weather systems was not available, but just about everyone had had the opportunity to watch trees shake and feel the resulting wind. Reasonably, trees possessed the will to act, as did boulders, rivers, and other seemingly benign aspects of existence.

The rise of urbanism in early modern Europe first transformed and then eventually weakened the grip of a purely agricultural-based shamanism on the imagination. A new resident of London would find fewer obvious natural forces at work in city streets. The special trees in the forest, the special boulders in the creek, and the important places where local saints had performed miracles were not apparent. Still, mercantile urbanism was only an overlay on an older understanding of existence. Who could believe that enchanted forces so evident in the village were less powerful within the world at large? Moreover, newsbooks provided detailed accounts of the same strange forces at work in foreign lands, while the city itself seemed to possess an infinite number of peculiar people involved in even more peculiar forms of behavior.

Given the fact that one could hardly keep track of all the events occurring in a city with hundreds of thousands of people, enchanted forces could take on more forms than were evident in the hamlet. Hence, if the rural village was enchanted, the city was the repository of the amazing, and the world at large was even more miraculous than the city. With so much peculiar news from distant places and with sailors bringing home wondrous stories, souvenirs, and diseases from foreign countries they had actually visited, newsbooks, too, popularized the notion that the world was even more wonder-filled than the city, which, in turn, was more amazing than the hamlet. Hence, we have the new Londoner's dilemma: The urban world was subject to the same sort of enchanted definition as rural areas, but discovering such forces in the city and gauging their power was more difficult.

Today's sensational media informs readers about black holes, pulsars, UFOs, Bigfoot, an apparition of Jesus on a water tank in Findlay, Ohio, and a lady in Illinois who gave birth to an infant able to play the piano immediately. Although the modern reader discriminates between the tabloid press and more legitimate news reporting, many reasonable people are still willing to believe almost anything at all about life in space, indeed, about life on other continents. Such distinctions were less obvious in the seventeenth century, when the divisions between superstition and faith, and between reality and illusion, were less clear. Judging from the large number of newsbooks dealing with unusual phenomena (cases of witchcraft were reported in the press), the author of *The Most Wonderful and True Relation of Master John Macklin* of 1657 noted that "this age wherein we live hath been an age full of wonders and none have been more remarkable than in our own land" (p. 1). Literacy and trade brought new ideas from foreign shores and extended the Englishman's knowledge of enchanted forces from England's hamlets to the world at large.

For the seventeenth-century mind lacking a comprehensive, causal view of nature, even the most mundane activity could be invested with meaning. By definition, if shaking trees produced wind, all other events similarly resulted from an act of will on the part of some agency, divine or otherwise. Consequently, all occurrences were unique, even miraculous. A two-headed cow, some heavenly apparition, a strange celestial noise, unusual rain, and even a perfectly normal baby were similar for each was the result of a special action by God, by Satan, or by any number of minor powers inhabiting the architecture of the world. Yet despite the mind-numbing plethora of forces affecting humanity and the world, there was an overall pattern expressed in the regularity of nature.

To better understand the chaotic appearance of events and occurren-ces, we might consider the stories in two very popular newsbooks. In the chapbook *Strange and Fearful News From Plaisto in the Parish of Westham* (1645) the author tells us that in Plaisto, just four miles from London, there lived "one Paul Fox, a silk weaver, a man of an honest life and conversation and hath a wife and children and dwelt there many years" (p. 3). For the period of one month Fox's house was haunted, and many thousands of people were able to testify to the events that occurred there. First, a sword danced about the room. After Fox locked it up in a different part of the house, it came through the door and continued to dance about. Thereafter, a cane upended and also danced about (pp. 2-3). On one occasion, a boulder weighing fifty pounds came bouncing up the stairs and did so again after being returned to the garden, where it had previously sat for decades (p. 5). On another occasion, money tied in a cloth handkerchief escaped and flew about the room (p. 6). More wor-risome, Fox heard a rapping at the door and a hollow voice calling out of the darkness, "I must dwell here." To emphasize the point, the spirit threw bricks and canes about the house and cut up many yards of Fox's silk fabrics (p. 4). When Fox moved to another address, the spirit fol-lowed him and continued to destroy his fabrics. Finally, Fox returned to his old house, and the spirit followed him there, too. Despite his "honesty and good conversation," Paul Fox continued to be plagued by this spirit.

The author tells us that thousands of people and even some noted scholars witnessed these terrible occurrences. Some claimed that the spirit was related to past events. Others thought it was an omen for the future. Fortunately for Fox, witches did not seem to be involved and the spirit might not even have been evil—it scattered some books from a shelf but left the Bible and other "good books" standing in place (pp. 7-8).

Strange News From Plaisto must have had an impact because two years later another piece appeared that attempted to better the earlier work. On the very first page of *The Most Strange and Wonderfull Apparition of Blood in a Pool at Garreton* (1647), the anonymous author tells us that "the sword at *Plaisto* flourishing without hands and the great stone clam-bering up the stairs and whatsoever there are strange or wonderful but are sluggish miracles compared to *this*" (p. 2). Where Plaisto represents "for the most part some knavish lights and as it were the hocus pocus of a spirit, in this which now shall be represented unto you, the immediate anger of God in great character is most apparently to be read" (p. 2). In short, this was not merely a curious story but a pointed expression of God's anger.

The story was very simple. For four days the pond water in the town of Garreton in Leicestershire grew ever more dark. Most people believed that the water had turned to blood. When the cattle would not drink there anymore, the townsfolk drained the pond and scooped up the residue of sludge remaining on the pond bottom. People came from all over to see this strange water—or blood—and many dipped cloths into the blood for souvenirs. The author was not sure what it all meant. On the one hand, the cattle would no longer drink there, but the fish salvaged from the drained pond tasted fine. As in Plaisto, "philosophers" were called in to give a natural reason for these strange events, but, the author complained, "it subtracteth something from the greatness of the wonder" (p. 6). The author himself was very humble, declaring, "I will not presume to give you the interpretation of it nor say it is suitable to the present condition of these bleeding times" (p. 6). But he did wish to note that "the four days wherein the water every day seemed to increase in the redness of its color doth signify the four years of the [civil] war." In short, "We now liveth in the evening of time and in the last age of the world wherein all things begin to suffer a change" (p. 2). Neither author thought it unusual that objects would dance, that boulders would bounce up stairs, that a spirit might destroy Fox's cloth, or that Garreton's water might turn to blood, especially in "these bleeding times" of the civil war conflict. Indeed, the factual and the hypothetical were perceived as intertwined; four days of bloody water could easily symbolize four years of civil war. This was nature, not witchcraft.

The pamphlet *The True Relation of Two Wonderfull Sleepers* (1646) nicely demonstrates the close relationship between the ordinary and the unusual. The author told about John Underwood, a man of forty who lived on Gravell Lane, who reportedly had been asleep for over nine days, sleeping "so soundly that they who have seen him tell me you may hear him in the next room" (p. 8). An even better story concerned "Elizabeth Jefkins in the Old Bailey, a woman of unblemished conversation . . . laborious in her calling, pious to God, tender to her husband . . . and loving to all her neighbors" (p. 3). On Monday, June 25 of that year, with neither apparent reason nor cause, Mrs. Jefkins fell asleep and remained asleep. Her good husband did everything any loving spouse would do but could not wake her. He even tried all the usual magic formulae; he threw water in her face and put a key in her mouth "to unlock the senses," but nothing seemed to work. She remained asleep. Neighbors were called in, and they, too, tried their skills, "but no force, no art could prevail to awaken the women, only when they did pinch her hand she would express a little groan and such a one as it appeared that she neither much felt nor cared for the pain" (p. 5). Elizabeth Jefkins remained in this stuporous sleep until Saturday, August 1, when a physician bled her from the nose, after which she soon died.

While no explanation for such unusual sleep was provided, the key to the mystery apparently did not lie in some secret evil buried within the personalities of those involved. One was a good father and provider, the other a good spouse, neighbor, and a pious woman. Nor was this condition the result of magic. After all, a key had been placed in Elizabeth Jefkins's mouth, which always worked against magic. The pamphlet, therefore, was a warning that this same condition might affect anyone at all. Indeed, by way of introducing his main story about the sleepers, the author tells us what would seem to be a totally unrelated story of "a youth the last winter who, looking up to a sun dial to observe by the hand thereof of what time of day, [when] an icicle of great bigness fell undiscovered with the pointed end of it on the one side of his neck and killed him immediately upon the place" (p. 2). Random icicles and prolonged sleep were just two expressions of nature's tyranny over mankind. The prudent person should watch for the former every day of winter and fear the latter every night of his life.

A deeper meaning lay hidden within seemingly random incidents. After all, if the mind dreamed during normal sleep, certainly unusual sleep must produce unusual dreams. But then, dreaming was always perceived as very mysterious. In 1641 the author of a chapbook entitled *The Divine Dreamer* concluded, "I am of the opinion . . . [that the] soul in sleeping may foresee things to come for the soul, which of itself is divine and celestial . . . is at free liberty and best performeth her actions when the body sleepeth, not being busied with any other matters" (p. 20). In the case of John Underwood, about whom we have already read, we learn that people from the community "came every day in crowds unto him, expecting when he awaketh to hear some wonderful intelligence" (p. 8). Hence, in addition to random falling icicles and the sleep from which one might never wake, even a passive activity like dreaming indicated that beneath the exterior of curious events lay another realm of strange mystery. Omens, portents, prodigies, and apparitions were the important bands that tied these two worlds together.

Not all strange occurrences were dangerous and frightening. Take the case of a gentleman who lived an amazing 116 years. The newsbook *The Most Wonderful and True Relation of Master John Macklin* (1657) tells us about this local minister who, at the age of 116, "was miraculously restored to a youthful vigor and complexion, new hair growing upon his head, new teeth in his mouth and his eyes restored to a most clear and perfect sight after the use of spectacles for almost forty years together" (title page). Since the natural causes for growth were only dimly understood, it was no less reasonable to suppose that an old man might grow into a child than a child into an old man. The former was less usual, to be sure, but therein lay its significance.

Early death by icicle and unusually long life followed by renewed youth would seem to be opposites, but they were not, as the next story will indicate. In *Immortality in Mortality Magnified* (1647), two dead bodies were discovered in a basement. No one in the neighborhood knew of a recent death at that address, but an examination of parish records indicated that thirty-four years earlier, in "the year 1613 it was found that in that very place . . . one Mr. Pountney, Merchant . . . both he and his own brother, dying shortly one after the other, were buried in the same chancel." Curiously, while one of the two bodies disintegrated into dust, the other seemed almost alive, with "all his limbs and ligaments, his hair, both of head, beard and other usual places, all as firmly growing, or rather fixed, as it was when he was first buried" (p. 4). So fresh was the body that "it pleased the honorable spectators . . . to have a view of the internal parts and to that end two men sufficiently experienced in the art of surgery were sent for to open him which they did." When the body was opened before a large and curious audience of onlookers, it was discovered that "his entrails with his bowels were as supple and moist as if he had been but newly departed from this life" (p. 7). The author could offer no explanation, but we are assured that thousands of people have visited and observed the dead body, "including Sir Walter Earl and the Worshipful Alderman Foulk with hundreds more of credit" (p. 6).

That one dead body disintegrated while the other remained as fresh as life was mysterious only in a world where natural phenomena must follow definite rules. However, in a world where every occurrence was unique, even the most seemingly fundamental laws of nature such as decay and aging might be abrogated. In this light, even returning from the dead, though not common, was no less reasonable an expectation than birth. Such was the case with a young woman named Anne Greene, the subject of the chapbook entitled *A Wonder of Wonders* (1650).

According to the author, Anne Greene was a maid in the Read household in Oxford. She became pregnant and delivered a child, which she allegedly then murdered and attempted to hide in a pile of rubbish. The small body was discovered, however, and Anne was taken to the local justice of the peace, where she admitted having had sexual intercourse and carrying the child but not having killed it. Despite her plea of innocence, "after a short trial she was convicted for her life and received sentence to be hanged on Oxford gallows which was accordingly performed" (p. 2). At the gallows, "a soldier standing by gave her four or five blows on the breast with the butt end of his musket" (p. 4). To assure a swift death, "her kinsman took hold of her feet and hung with all the weight and force of his body on them that so he might the sooner rid her of her pain . . . and having hung half an hour she was cut down" (p. 4). With no pulse in her vein and no breath in her mouth, the body itself soon grew cold and hard.

Rather than being buried immediately, Anne's body was given to Dr. Petty for an autopsy. When Anne's corpse was placed upon a long table, "she began to breathe, which was no small terror or admiration to all that were present." Dr. Petty bled her, applied oils, and gave her special liquids and foods, and after sleeping for fourteen hours Anne awoke, praised God, and cursed the judge and jury for her terrible treatment. She became the talk of the town, and we are assured that "diverse both in city and country frequent hourly to behold her." The pamphlet concluded with the observation that "she is miraculously recovered . . . but her neck is very sore" (p. 6). What happened to Anne could happen to anyone, although most people did not return from the dead. Still, there was something special about Anne's particular experience.

It would seem that Anne Greene's return from the dead was very big news. Another newsbook supplied important additional details. *News From the Dead, or, A True and Exact Narration of the Miraculous Deliverance of Anne Greene* (1650) was written "by a scholar in Oxford" shortly after the previous pamphlet appeared. This supportive account reveals that an attractive Anne was a maid in the Read household, where she was "often solicited by fair promises and other amorous enticements of Mr. Jeffrey Read, grand child to the said Sir Thomas [Read], a youth about sixteen or seventeen years of age" (p. 1). After constantly badgering Anne to have sex with him, "at last she consented to satisfy his unlawful pleasure." She soon discovered that she was pregnant, and when the child was prematurely stillborn, Anne tried to hide the dead body lest she be convicted of infanticide, a common contemporary form of birth control. The small corpse was discovered, and though Anne was too simple to keep her secret from the law, she had no intention of making public the name of the child's father. Indeed, since the justice of the peace was a cousin of the Read family, she hoped her silence would result in favorable treatment. In fact, things went badly for that very reason. Sir Thomas, Jeffrey's aged grandfather, led the prosecution, and Anne was condemned to death. At the gallows she told those assembled to witness her execution about "the lewdness of the family wherein she lately lived" and begged God for a sign to prove her innocence. Having received her justice, Anne was then dispatched from this life.

This newsbook devoted considerable space to describing the nature of Dr. Petty's excellent care, which involved many long days of constant attention. The abundance of medical details, the care with which this information is explained, and the considerable attention devoted to describing Anne's feelings may indicate that the author of this account was possibly an assistant to Dr. Petty. Anne recovered from her brush with death, but the Read family attempted to have the hanging performed yet again in challenge to English law. "There is yet one thing more which hath been taken notice of by some as to the maid's defense," the newsbook author added. "Her Grand Prosecutor, Sir Thomas Read, died within three days after her execution, even almost as soon as the possibility of her reviving could be well confirmed to him" (p. 9). The world was miraculous and wonderful, the author believed, and God loved even the most modest of mortals. What appeared to be the hangman's failure to do a proper job was in fact God's intervention in the affairs of men. Anne Greene had called upon God to give the world a sign of her innocence, and He did just that when he returned her life and took that of Sir Thomas Read instead. The morals of the other stories are not as clear. Why one body in the basement decayed while the other did not was only mysterious because the lives of the two brothers were unknown to the casual observer. This was unfortunate, for beneath this mystery lay some special message for Londoners. Similarly, John Macklin's renewed youth was indicative of something, but what? And if Elizabeth Jefkins had not been bled by her physician and died, would she have told of amazing things and places visited by her spirit while she slept so long and so deeply?

Placed within the perspective of the pamphlets previously discussed, the story of Anne Greene exposes another layer of reality beneath seemingly random chance: an unseen but tightly conceived divine plan. Every action in the world, even the most mundane, represented a separate act of divine will or satanic interference. Newton's formulae, which indicated a well-ordered universe, would eventually prove helpful for it further simplified nature, made it orderly, convenient, and predictable. It would be decades, however, before theories about the regularity of natural existence were widely known and accepted. For the next century and more, enchantment would continue to provide most people with the most acceptable ideas to explain causation.

Anne Greene's dramatic story serves to introduce another level in the riddle of existence: God's unfailing punishment of the wicked and reward of the virtuous. Hence, curious events may have important moral overtones, which encourage the layman to steadfastly maintain his notion of social right and wrong despite pragmatic evidence to the contrary. The sophisticated and worldly often dismiss such sentiments as childish or silly, but the prevalence of such stories must indicate something about the human need for moral affirmation. The desire to have God intervene to help the innocent and punish the wicked may represent a powerful hope that, after all, there is some meaning to life. On the other hand, such stories also indicate that morality, like nature itself, is complex, seemingly random but actually orderly. Such stories come in a variety of forms, but a good example can be found in *A Strange and Wonderful Example of God's Judgments,* written in October 1645, when England was sorely in need of divine intervention.

James Braithwaight was a tailor in Shoreditch Parish. He had a wife and three children and is described in the pamphlet as "a man of a very loose life and conversation, given to many ill vices . . . [especially] drinking, swearing, cursing, and lying" (p. 2). Though never a model of virtue at any time, "when he was in his drink, upon every petty occasion he would often break forth into these or other like words, 'I pray God that the dogs may tear my flesh into pieces and pick my bones, if I do not such and such a thing'" (p. 2). Despite such terrible oaths, always sworn in great sincerity and solemnity, "he very seldom performed anything he vowed or cursed himself for if it were not performed" (p. 3).

His neighbors thought Mr. Braithwaight a boor. Eventually, to the general relief of all, he died. But, as a bad penny keeps turning up, on the day following Braithwaight's burial, the grave digger "found a great heap of mould cast up and lying loose on the side of the grave . . . and looking into the hole out of which the mould was cast up, he saw a great part of the carcass of the said James all torn and eaten" (p. 4). The authorities buried the body again, but "the next day the earth was scratched up again and the body uncovered, torn and eaten as before, but no dog found in the church yard" (p. 4).

After conducting a community-wide search for an errant dog or a wolf, the authorities buried the body yet a third time, deeper than before, and placed another coffin on top of that of James B. Despite these precautions, "the next day . . . they found the earth digged away again, and that the dogs had gotten quite under the coffin that lay uppermost, not offering to claw or break it, but got to the corpse of James Braithwaight underneath and had eaten, torn, and mangled it more than before" (p. 5). The author could offer his curious reader no concise explanation concerning the physical details involved, but he could see the proper moral conclusion clear as day. The last page presented a moral as obvious as it was wholesome: "Let everyone take head of rash vows, false oaths or imprecations." The author had also warned on the first page "that oftentimes men were punished in the same way that they themselves offended" (p. 1). This had also been the case when Sir Thomas Read tried to have Anne Greene executed and in the end was himself taken by God.

One year later, in October 1646, another pamphlet described the life, death, and strange burial of Joan Bridges. *A Strange and Wonderful Relation of the Burying of Joan Bridges of Rochester* probably appealed to the same audience as the previous chapbook and stressed the infallible logic by which the wicked received their just rewards. According to this edifying tale, Joan came from a good family and lived with her sister and brother-in-law. She was well considered by her associates and "she carried a civil deportment to all and was esteemed of amongst the best" (p. 3). The treatise does not explain why Joan became depressed or whether she was a spinster living under poor conditions with an unwilling family, but "she became expert in drink and was often times a great adventurer in that commodity than tendered her reputation, much less became her sex." Slowly sinking into the morass of alcohol, sin, and sex, Joan soon became an embarrassment to all who knew her. She was always intoxicated, and on one occasion she returned home late and so inebriated that she could be put to bed only with great difficulty. Joan remained in her wicked drunken stupor all the next day, and when it proved impossible to wake her the following morning, she was pronounced dead and was buried in the local churchyard.

Every night, dogs would howl and dig at Joan's grave until finally, believing something was amiss, the community disinterred the body from the bowels of the earth. When her coffin was opened, a crowd of neighbors was horrified to discover that "her face was rubbed off, her nose by the low roof of her prison house was beat flat with her cheeks, the strings which tied her toes together had torn the skin from the bone. . . . Her hands . . . became her executioners, ripping open her very bowels. Her left hand sticking in her belly and her right hand having raised the skin and flesh from her side" (p. 4). Clearly, Joan had been buried alive but was too drunk to realize what was happening to her at the time. In the words of the previous pamphlet, "God is pleased to punish sin in its own kind, that the party himself might be the more humbled and brought to see his own wickedness" (p. 2). Poor Joan had come to realize her own wickedness, but, alas, too late. Anne Greene came back from the dead, but Anne was guiltless while Joan was a distasteful drunk.

Other newsbooks also expressed the popular hope that God punished the wicked through seemingly natural, but actually mysterious, means. *A Blazing Star Seen in the West* (1642) told the sad but gratifying tale of Master Adam Fisher's daughter. In the early evening of November 14 in Totnes in Devonshire, this young lady visited some friends and unwisely remained long after dark. Her friends begged her to stay the night, but she did not wish to remain until morning for fear that her absence might alarm her father (pp. A2a-b).

Not long after she left her friends, Miss Fisher heard a horse galloping behind her and was soon stopped by Mr. Ralph Ashley, an alleged friend of her father's. He warned her about the many soldiers in the neighborhood and so took her on his horse, promising to carry her home. But rather than doing as he promised, Ashley took the young girl to a secluded spot, and "then presently he laid his hands on her and began to woo her to grant his desire." Despite her protests and her forlorn cries into the empty night, "he went about to ravish her, taking a grievous oath that no power on heaven or earth could save her from his lust" (p. A3b). The young virgin pled for her virtue, and when this proved unhelpful to her cause, she began to pray, but "he continued cursing and swearing that her prayers were in vain." God was not deaf to her pleas, however, and at that very moment, "a fearful comet burst out into the air." Miss Fisher was so struck with fear that she swooned, but the evil Ashley "took a great oath, swearing, God Damme, alive or dead he would enjoy her" (p. A3b). At the very instant of Ashley's last curse, "a stream of fire struck from the comet in the perfect shape and exact resemblance of a flaming sword so that he fell down staggering . . . blaspheming and belching forth many damnable imprecations" (p. A4a).

Fortunately for Miss Fisher, shepherds happening to be in the area took her limp body to her father's house, where eventually she made a full recovery. The author tells us that the story should serve as "a precedent for all those that are customary blasphemers and live after the lusts of their flesh . . . and except we repent we shall likewise perish" (p. A4b). We have already noted how sinners were punished in the manner of their sin, but consider the following stories, which indicate how God orchestrated all of nature towards moral truth and punishment.

The newsbook *A True Relation of the Most Horrid and Barbarous Murders, Committed by Abigail Hill* (1658) described a nursemaid's terribly irrational murders of young children in her care and included several other instances of murder as well. One story charged that Ralph Puckey from Norfolk committed a murder and attempted to conceal it. Unfortunately for Puckey, nature itself conspired against his unnatural act, for crows would follow him wherever he went and make terrible noises as they flew about his head. Now, the newsbook author explained, "the guilt of the murder was extraordinary . . . and he believed that the crows did particularly reprove him for his murder" (p. 6). Finally, Puckey could stand the birds no longer and took himself "before a justice to whom he confessed his long concealed murder and said moreover that if his tongue should deny it, yet his conscience would proclaim it" (p. 5). Puckey put himself back in tune with nature, and "having confessed it, he seemed to be at great ease, having discharged himself of a burden that did greatly oppress him and seemed to be worse than death unto him" (p. 6). Even better, the birds soon disappeared, although Pucky was executed shortly thereafter.

The same newsbook described a man who killed his brother and took the dead man's land for himself. To conceal his deed, the murderer told everyone that his brother had died while traveling abroad and secretly proceeded to bury his brother on his own land. No one suspected the evil deed, and the murder would have gone undetected were it not for the truthful forces of nature. The murderer was constantly pursued by two ravens that followed him wherever he went. He tried to shoot them and even offered a reward to anyone who could kill them, but every attempt failed, and "at last his hope and heart fainted and raving with despair, he confessed the murder he had committed." Because no one suspected him of so foul a deed, "his words, at first, were taken as proceeding from a man that had lost his senses and his health"(p. 8). When his brother's dead body was finally interred in a properly sanctified grave, "the two ravens (having done the business in which the divine providence did employ them) did fly away and they were seen no more about the houses" (p. 8).

If the reader was not impressed by this display of divine justice, the chapbook *The Good Angel of Stamford* (1659) was sure to please. This pamphlet told the story of Samuel Waller, who for thirteen years suffered from consumption. His condition grew progressively worse, and for "the last four years [Waller] lay bed-ridden and so weak that he could not turn himself therein without help" (p. 1).

On Whitsunday of 1659, Waller's wife left London for a short visit with country relatives, and he was left alone to look after his own needs. On one particularly rainy day Waller heard a knock at the door and with pain and difficulty admitted an old man, who asked of him, "Friend, I pray thee, give an old pilgrim a cup of thy small beer" (p. 2). Waller did so, and while the old man paced about the room slowly drinking his beer, he was able to observe that his guest was well dressed, "tall and ancient, his hair white as wool curled up with a white broad beard. He has a fresh complexion and wore a fashionable hat with a little narrow band, his coat and hose both of a purple color, his stockings pure white and a pair of new black leather shoes tied with a ribbon of the same color his clothes were" (p. 5). In short, the visitor was a well-to-do and respectable man. Curiously, however, Waller noted that "though it rained when he came in to the said Samuel Waller house . . . all day, yet he had not one spot of wet or dirt upon him" (p. 5).

When the old man finished his beer, he said to Waller, "Friend, I perceive thou art not well," whereupon Waller told his visitor the story of his illness. He told of the many doctors he had visited, how he was too poor to seek additional medical advice and how the doctors believed that his condition was now too serious to treat. At this point the old man gave Waller a prescription consisting of various herbs along with instructions for their preparation and use. The pilgrim promised that by following this regimen, Waller would be healthy again within six weeks. The old man departed; Waller followed his prescription, and within six weeks he was in full health. So amazed were all of Waller's friends and associates by his complete recovery that "there was a meeting of ministers . . . who concluded that this apparition was the good angel" (p. 6). Virtue invited its own reward much as murderers invited screeching ravens to drive them to confess their sins. Events may seem random, but only to those ignorant of the full story.

As these newsbook stories illustrate, natural order and moral truth were divinely ordained constants that provided for regularity of life in a world filled with heinous and evil forces. In society at large, divinely appointed kings and the true church kept society on its moorings. God, king, and paternity were the three pillars upholding the cosmic, temporal, and social orders. It was incumbent upon all subjects to respect the authority of all three agencies. Disturbing the social and religious order was possible, but terrible punishments usually rained down upon the offenders. Long before the divine right of kings became a political reality, monarchy enjoyed a special role within the English concept of cosmic order. Hence, during the civil war, Parliament was at a disadvantage. Royalists had the best miraculous stories because the institution of monarchy, unlike Parliament, was an emblem of God on earth.[6] Once Charles I had been executed, this became abundantly clear. But even before this, newsbooks noted that Parliament's rebellion had already yielded rotten fruit. As early as 1641 the author of the chapbook *A Strange Wonder, or, The City's Amazement* (1641) saw God's anger with Parliament manifest itself in the form of merciless weather and the flooding of the Thames on February 4 of that year. The author was not alone in his belief, noting, "Not long since was published an idle pamphlet entitled News From Hell," which envisioned demonic powers at work in the flood, and "no sooner was that breviary of tales and collection of idle falsity public, extinct and quenched men having both seen and read their fill, but behold comes *News From Heaven*" (p. 1). In short, the same mundane flood was alternately a sign of heavenly disapproval or devilish deceit. This writer, however, subtitled his chapbook "True News From Heaven," noting on the second page that "we think that his wonders stand for cyphers" (p. 2). A page later he again emphasized that "God himself cryeth, 'My wonders shall fill the earth.'"

There was nothing unusual in the belief that physical events on earth indicated God's judgments. Scripture noted that God gave Noah the sign of the rainbow, made the sun stand still for Joshua, and inflicted a dozen plagues upon Egypt's house. But rarely were the events of mankind so violent, troubling, and curious than the period beginning with the civil wars. These events included "blazing stars, the deaths of great princes and potentates, immoderate winds, plagues and pestilence, intemperate rains, rot, murren [sic] among beasts and cattle, the unexpected sudden and causeless swelling of rivers, dearth and famine, the disorderly and changeable ebbing and flowing of the tide, blood and dissension" (p. 2). England's usually wet and windy weather surely provided much opportunity for dreadful, albeit natural, surmise. Yet the many published accounts of such activity during these years indicate that many imaginations ran wild, seeing in every storm and peculiar event a significant expression of God's anger, Satan's power, or the work of demons, angels, and witches.

The situation was worse after Charles's death. Scholars have reasoned that Cromwell may have had to execute Charles in order to provide stability, but in so doing he eliminated from the world the one foundation of order that most Englishmen understood. And because the king was of divine importance, his removal, even for the best of reasons, would prove troubling to God. This, in turn, would be reflected in nature, and it was likely believed that the turmoil England experienced during the interregnum was a measure of God's anger and a penalty for having killed Charles.

Directly after the execution, the pamphlet *The Life and Death Of King Charles the Martyr, Paralleled with Our Saviour* appeared. Those in favor of the revolution feared this sort of publication because it reinforced how many Englishmen felt about the institution of monarchy, Charles I's faults not withstanding. Throughout the pamphlet the author drew parallels between Jesus and Charles to demonstrate how the condemnation of one was equivalent to the condemnation of the other. The author explained, "As Christ was above the law, being the Son of God, so he [Charles] was above the censure of human law, he being a king . . . As he was a king, he represented God's person here on earth and as he was a good king (full of grace) he was a most lively image of Christ" (p. 3). Moreover, Puritan rejection of Charles was compared with the Jews' rejection of Jesus. "As our saviour was rejected by his own people," the author explained, "so when our Sovereign's affliction grew great, some of his servants betrayed him like Judas, others denied him and almost all forsook him" (p. 4). The end was also the same in both cases. "At last, our Saviour suffered death, so did our Sovereign, at the very same hour of the day" (p. 6).

If Charles was a Christ figure, the analogy was troubling for England's future—for instance, how God treated His chosen people (the Jews) after they rejected Jesus and how He treated Pharaoh for rejecting Moses and how He rejected Adam and Eve before them. Even worse, there were already signs of doom. The author noted that "when our Saviour suffered there were terrible signs and wonders and darkness over all the land. So during the time of our Sovereign's martyrdom, there were strange signs seen in the sky, in diverse places in the kingdom" (p. 6). In short, in killing Charles, "they have overthrown the order of God and nature, dissolved the bonds of human society . . . Never such a tragedy was acted by any subjects in the Christian world since the first constitution of monarchy as this unparalleled murder" (p. 2).

Despite his defeat by Parliament and subsequent execution, Charles remained a magical figure. Pamphlets about him continued to describe him in miraculous terms. Indeed, precisely because he had been executed,

Charles could play an even greater Christlike role in his death for those mourning him and for other Englishmen who may have opposed Charles's policies but still venerated monarchy as a divine institution. As an example, God's enduring love for Charles I is amply demonstrated in *A Miracle of Miracles Wrought by the Blood of King Charles the First,* written a few months after Charles's execution, which described the curing and redemptive powers of the "dead king's blood.

According to the story, "a maid dwelling and living now in Detford, four miles distant from London, daughter to Mrs. Bailie . . . about the age of fourteen or fifteen years" (p. 2) suffered with a terrible skin problem, "which . . . putrified and corrupted not only unseen parts of her body but her face and eyes insomuch that she became blind therewith" (p. 2). Her mother took her to all the physicians her poor wallet would allow but none could cure her or even explain why nature had victimized the young girl, "and thus was the poor silly soul left past all hopes of recovery . . . blind in her sight, forsaken by the physicians, left off by acquaintances" (p. 3).

Now it so happened that Master John Lane, a draper from the Old Change district of London, had "a handkerchief about him which had been dipped in the king's blood on the day that he was beheaded" (p. 5). Being a monarchist and a fine fellow, he gave this poor girl a piece of the cloth and "applied it to her sores and, wiping the eyes with the bloody side of the handkerchief, [she] hath through heaven's providence recovered her eye sight and is become lusty and strong" (p. 5). Roundheads might scoff, but the "many hundreds of people coming daily to see her both from London and other places" (p. 5) was more than ample proof of the order and justice monarchy represented in the face of cruel nature.

Had the story ended here it might have been one more account of God's love for his innocent sheep and the king's role in the natural order of things. But the real point of this exercise was to indicate "what a precious jewel we lost." Pointing to Charles's many virtues, perhaps more obvious through hindsight, the author noted that "while the king lived, he was so gracious that when there was a numberless company of poor distressed people, he would appoint them a time to give them money and visit them and . . . he scorned not to touch the poorest creatures' sores and handle their wounds and do them good while the corruption of their diseases ran upon his princely fingers and by the virtue of the same they had their perfect cure" (pp. 6-7). Comparing Charles to Job and Jesus, the author cried, "How many times hath Charles I, the Lord's anointed, been not only touched but buffeted, kicked and spurned at?" (p. 8).

While his opponents "hoped to wash their hands in His heart's blood," Charles was all virtue. "He was a Solomon for wisdom, a David for courage and a Job for patience. He was a forgiver of injuries, a lover of religion and a hater of lewdness, a friend to his enemies, a maintainer of truth, Defender of the Faith, a protector of his subjects and a help to the poor" (p. 8). The author never explained how Charles had been so misunderstood during his lifetime. Perhaps, like Jesus, Charles had been doing God's bidding in an evil society now under the control of leveling Satanic Puritans, devilish Jesuitical Papists, or even both. But more than any of his other virtues, Charles possessed a divine element. His blood, like Jesus' blood, was miraculous. But if Charles was now gone, where did this leave England?

After Charles's execution the number of chapbooks fearing that this disaster would lead to terrible natural disasters increased. The pamphlet *Strange News From the North,* published in June 1650, was convinced that God was angered with England for taking Charles's sanctified life and that the first signs of divine displeasure already had been posted. The author reminded the reader of other recent occasions where sinful actions against Charles had elicited a negative divine response: "I formerly related to you how shortly after the Scots march into England in the aid of our Parliament, it rained blood and covered the Church and Church yard of Bewcastle in Cumberland" (p. 1). He also mentions the appearance "of three sins the day before Edgehill battle" and most telling of all, "a little before [General] Hambolton with his army came into England, two armies were in Yorkshire seen in the air visibly, discharging and shooting one against the other" (pp. 1-2).

Strange News From the North also mentioned "the many and marvelous signs and sights . . . the Lord warning us, as it were thereby, not only of our late troubles but of the continuance thereof" (p. 1). In fateful January alone "we have had very strange and fearful storms . . . and for a month after the storms, the sheep thereabouts ran madding about and would not keep in their pastures." Even worse, "when found and brought home, [they] were so wild and heated, as if they had been chased with a hundred Mastiff dogs" (p. 2). Many people took note of this strange behavior, and "people were so astonished therewith, as for a long time they had little other discourse than of the strangeness of the storm" (p. 2). Elsewhere, too, others observed the peculiar events transpiring on that very same day: "I see a relation of three suns lately seen in Manchester, but sure it is that in the beginning of March last there were seen at one time in Cumberland and Westmerland three glorious suns, to the admiration and great astonishment of many thousands of the beholders" (p. 2). Additionally, "upon the 11 of April last about five of the clock in the afternoon, in the counties of Cumberland and Westmerland we had a general earthquake. The people were so frighted therewith that they forsook their houses and some houses were so shaken that their chimneys fell down" (p. 3). The author assured the reader of the truth of these accounts, noting that "some may doubt and question the verity of these things. Be confident I have related nothing but what I know to be true" (p. 3).

All of this turmoil was just the beginning. The next decade of the English Revolution would provide ample proof that God was angry with England. Just a few years earlier, in 1647, T. J.'s *The World Turned Upside Down, or, A Brief Description of the Ridiculous Fashions of These Distracted Times* expressed the feelings of many confused Englishmen. The author called himself "a well willer to King, Parliament, and the Kingdom" and wrote:

> And if 'twere possible our father's old
> Should live again and tread upon this mould
> And see all things confused, overthrown,
> They would not know this country for their own.

Further, the author expressed the fear that England's condition could not be altered for the better:

> For England hath no likelihood or show
> Of what it was but seventy years ago.
> Religion, manners, life and the shapes of men,
> Are much unlike the people that were then.
>
> Nay, England's face and language is estranged,
> That all is Metamorphis'd chop'd and chang'd.
> For like as on the Poles of the World is whorl'd
> So is this Land the Bedlam of the World. (p. 4)

The general message offered by T. J. and the other authors was simple: As a result of Charles's removal, when man had rebelled against nature, this same nature, now a reflection of God's anger, was in rebellion against man. Little did T. J. realize how far England had fallen from God's good grace. *A Warning Piece to the World* (1655) stated the problem in succinct terms: "Before God sends any plague to a nation, he first gives them a warning, sometimes by apparitions, sometimes by visions, sometimes by monstrous births, sometimes by sects, schisms and divisions, sometimes by thunder and lightening, unnatural tides etc. and innumerable ways that the Lord can use to forewarn us of an approaching judgment" (p. 4). England's problem was simple: God was not sending just one of these signs to warn England, but all of them, and all at once.

A DECLARATION,

Of a strange and Wonderfull MONSTER:

Born in KIRKHAM Parish in LANCASHIRE (the Childe
of Mrs. *Haughton*, a Popish Gentlewoman) the face of it upon the breast,
and without a head (after the mother had wished rather to bear a
Childe without a head then a Roundhead) and had curst the
PARLIAMNET.

Attested by Mr. FLEETWOOD, Minister of the same Pa-
rish, under his own hand; and Mrs. *Gattaker* the Mid-wife, and divers
other eye-witnesses: Whose testimony was brought up by a *Member* of the House of Commons.

*Appointed to be printed according to Order: And desired to be published in all the
Counties, Cities, Townes, and Parishes in England: Being the same
Copies that were presented to the Parliament.*

march 3   London, Printed by *Jane Coe*. 1646.   1645

♦ ♦ ♦

3

Signs of the Times: Portents, Prodigies, and Other Indications of God's Unhappiness with England

"SUCH PRODIGIOUS AND WONDERFUL THINGS HAVE APPEARED AS NO AGE BEFORE HAVE EVER SEEN OR HEARD OF."

—A Warning Piece to the World (1655)

When God wished to demonstrate his displeasure with Egypt's pharaoh, he sent Moses to curse Egypt with ten plagues, each of which was worse than the former. It was reasonable, therefore, that God would express his dissatisfaction with England through similar signs. However fanciful belief in omens, portents, and prodigies may seem today, it was primarily through these images that earlier Englishmen perceived the conflict engulfing them.

The range of anomalies constituting omens and portents was extensive.[1] Apparitions included ghosts, spirits, and other unusual celestial beings but also included strange noises, images, comets, and unusual star formations in both the day- and nighttime skies. Neither a cloud nor a drum were apparitions, for instance, but a cloud that looked like a drum would certainly qualify. Similarly, leaves falling into the shape of a horse would be an apparition as would the image of Jesus on a water tank in Ohio.

Less mysterious but more horrible were prodigies: fantastic freaks of nature or monsters. Like apparitions, prodigies constituted divine warnings and therefore constituted the wise man's guide to God's appraisal of human society. A monstrously deformed child with no arms and two heads certainly indicated God's anger in a very tangible form. Should God's omens and portents go unheeded, as was the case in Egypt, they could be followed by something worse. Hence, when almost anything unusual appeared, was discovered, or was born, prudence required discovering how and why God had be angered. Almost any divergence from the perceived norm was a sign of trouble, and although some individuals were more competent at reading the signs than others, everyone had an opinion. And if no evil in particular was obvious, that in itself was a cause for alarm and worry. When an otherwise perfect goat was born with an extra leg, it was, like leaves forming the shape of a horse, a divine warning. Leaves were leaves and goats were goats, but extremely unusual configurations of either constituted signs of worse to come. Only those without eyes and ears would foolishly reject the importance of these signs, but only those with good sense could understand them. During the civil war, when little worked out as hoped, it was believed that apparitions and prodigies indicated God's displeasure with events in England. As *A Warning Piece to the World* (1655) put it, "There are innumerable ways that the Lord can use to forewarn us of an approaching judgment" (p. 4).

One example of the popular anxiety an apparition could incite was described in William Lilly's *The Starry Messenger, or, An Interpretation of Strange Apparitions* (1644). Lilly was the foremost parliamentary astrologer of the day and wrote a large number of treatises concerning the celestial view of the civil war.[2] In this pamphlet Lilly hoped to quell popular dread about the appearance of three suns in the heavens on November 19, 1644, King Charles's birthday. Some saw this as a trinitarian proof of God's love for Charles. Others maintained that the three suns represented the divine unity of England, Scotland, and Ireland even in England's hour of difficulty. Most observers believed that significant heavenly sign on Charles's birthday indicated God's displeasure with the king's opponents and that the apparition was a warning sign to Parliament, for "such prodigies, comets, etc., do never show themselves but as precursors of mischief" (p. 1). But, Lilly protested, apparitions could also be beneficial. He asked, "What greater benefit did ever happen to mankind than in the birth of our savior Jesus Christ and yet was his coming manifested to us by a star or comet" (p. 1). Similarly, "When God Almighty had drowned the world, in confirmation he would do so no more, he produced a rainbow and made it appear at all times and seasons in a constant and natural form and manner" (p. 19). More recently, "We have seen in our age that if the comet in 1618 did design out ill to the Austrian family, as indeed it did, yet the Swedes did thereupon thrive" (p. 1).

Lilly was a man of considerable education. He was aware of, and rejected, naturalistic explanations for apparitions in general and for the three suns in particular, noting that "many philosophers are of the opinion that these false suns . . . do especially appear when many subtle moist clouds are betwixt us and the sun. Others, that they are round clouds shining like the sun or that they are images of the sun in a thick and neighboring cloud in the form of a mirror" (p. 10). These explanations, however, did not apply in this instance because "when these three suns were seen, it was a very fair sunshine-day, a very clear day, no clouds, vapors, fogs or mists appearing" (p. 10). In any event, natural interpretation of apparitions refused to consider that God himself had chosen to manifest his will in this fashion. Lilly explained that since the infinite God of creation was removed from the finite universe, apparitions were a means of communication between God and man. He wrote, "I am clearly of opinion [that] these sights as well as many others, were caused by those tutelary angels who [act] by God's permission and under him" (p. 11). Later in his pamphlet he again stated that apparitions were significant because in each case "the Angels were willing we should discern something, else why was it made visible? There was no necessity of it" (pp. 19-20).

Nothing could be clearer: Apparitions were divine occurrences, produced by angels to enlighten. They could indicate God's pleasure as well as his anger. It was clear to Lilly that the appearance of three suns was a bad omen for Charles I and signaled the Almighty's approval of Parliament: "The heavens never sent forth any great signs which have not a particular relation to some great personage" (Letter to Reader). And since the apparition appeared on Charles's birthday, it was clear to whom the message was directed. "That some very great man, what king, prince, duke or the like . . . shall, I say, come to some untimely end" (p. 21). All of Charles's supporters should have taken note, for the heavens "absolutely study nothing but divisions and the suppression of monarchy" (p. 18).

Most newsbook authors were less theoretical than Lilly. Robert Ellit's *The New Years Wonder* (1642) claimed that on January 1, 1642, between 3:00 and 4:00 P.M. in Kenton, three countrymen saw a troop of horses coming at them at full speed. "But coming near unto them, they of a sudden sunk into the earth which turned to their more greater fear and amazement than at their first advancing" (p. 5). On the night of January 4, many people in a nearby city heard "the doleful and hideous groans of dying men . . . crying revenge and some again to ease them of their pain by friendly killing them" (p. 6). So frightened were local townsfolk by these noises that pregnant women miscarried while others hid in corners or under blankets. Those sufficiently brave to peek out their windows testified to seeing a troop of mounted horsemen ride into the night sky

(p. 7). The next night armed troops were seen in battle with the sound of carbines and the cries of the dying. "All night it lasted in this hideous manner but at the break of day all as they formerly in the twinkling of an eye did vanish. But since hath no more been seen which caused the inhabitants of Kenton to forsake their town and get new habitations for themselves" (pp. 7-8). The actual veracity of the sightings was beyond question. Ellit claimed to have been an "eye witness unto this" event which, in turn, was "Certified under the hands of William Wood, Esquire and Justice of the Peace in the said County, Samuel Marshall, preacher of God's Word in Kenton and other persons of quality" (last page).

Troops certainly provided familiar sights and sounds in revolutionary England, and this apparition may have been no more than an elaboration on the sounds of an active siege at a nearby castle. Nonetheless, *The New Years Wonder* and many other pamphlets chose an explanation more in keeping with their authors' system of enchanted logic. In such a system, these peculiar events revealed the spirits of the unquiet souls of those dying without benefit of clergy or the rituals of the old church.

Other authors were more ambivalent. *A Sign from Heaven, or, A Fearful and Terrible Noise Heard in the Air* (1642) described an event in Alborow in Suffolk, on Thursday, August 4, between 4:00 and 5:00 in the afternoon. For ninety minutes, people heard the sounds of beating drums, a long peal of small shot, and many rounds of cannon fire (pp. 2-3). When the noises stopped abruptly, a peculiar eight-inch stone fell from the heavens. This stone, discovered by Captain Johnson and Master Thompson, was later taken to the town square and put on display so that others might see it. Though the stone may have been nothing more mysterious than disfigured ordnance, the author was convinced that it was of great spiritual importance and wondered "what fiery impressions were seen in the air in sundry places in Germany both before the Battle of Prague and about the time of the coming in of the most victorious King of Sweden towards the Battle of Leipzig and Nordlingen and upon sundry other occasions?" (p. 4). The publisher's fears for the future were made evident by the addition of a two-page poem entitled "A Prophecy of Merlin's, concerning Hull in Yorkshire," which presented a dire warning of terrible things to come.[3]

Severe weather disturbances were also seen as spiritual manifestations of God's will and became obvious points of conjecture on the civil war. Within a month's time four pamphlets discussed the inclement weather in the English Channel on May 21, 1646. While all of the pamphlets were similar, each presented itself as the only viable account of strange apparitions. *Signs From Heaven, or, Several Apparitions Seen and Heard in the Air in the Counties of Cambridge and Norfolk,* published by T. Forcet of Old Fish Street on the same day of the occurrences, tells how thunder, lightning, and hailstones in unusual shapes appeared all along England's eastern coast (p. 5). Even more unusual, observers claimed to see a lightning ball and clouds in the shapes of spears and spires fighting while drums beat. Coastal weather in winter was normally unstable, but on this occasion severe thunder and ball and dagger lighting were actually perceived as three men, representing England, Ireland, and Scotland, fighting each other in the air (pp. 1-4).

On June 16 the treatise *Good News From Oxford,* printed by Jane Coe, also presented an account of these same storms as well as "the particulars of the seven visions seen at Grevanhage, the 21st of May last" (title page). The list of visions included: a battle between a lion and a dragon (representing Charles and Parliament?); a king with three crowns (Charles); a multitude of heads and bodies (civil war); a man on a horse killing himself (Charles?); a mighty fleet of ships (Spain?) and a great cloud (the Protestant wind of 1588?). In a second section, Coe presented an account of the surrender of Sherburne House and other particulars of the military conflict then in progress.

Not wishing to be outdone, T. Forcet, the printer from Old Fish Street, returned to amplify his original story. Two days later, on June 18, he published *Several Apparitions Seen in the Air at the Hague,* which consisted of the account of apparitions reported by Jane Coe as well as similar sightings observed over Cambridge and Norfolk. In a word, he republished his May 21 pamphlet and added Jane Coe's revelations. The market was still not exhausted, however, and on July 14, B. Alsop published *Sad News From the Eastern Parts,* yet another presentation of these same occurrences, including several pages of new interpretation. The lion, for instance, represented either Holland, Germany, or France, while the dragon represented Turkey. The king with three crowns represented the united monarchy in London, and the great navy belonged to France. The heap of heads, somehow, referred to the Turks, and the horseman shooting himself could represent anyone. After so many descriptions by others, this last chapbook felt confident in presenting three, generally valid, overall interpretations. First, "the Turk may be converted and become a Christian brother." Second, "the sweet gale of God's spirit, through the Gospel, shall quiet and comfort all again." But the most important interpretation of all was that the great cloud "is a presage of the great sorrow which shall remain for a time after so much bloodshed and calamity caused by these wars" (p. 6).

For the duration of the conflict between Charles and Parliament, the interpretations of apparitions were as vague and unsettled as the events they allegedly mirrored. However, after the fighting stopped, celestial manifestations seemed less confusing. For instance, in *A True Relation of the Strange Apparitions Seen in the Air on Monday, February 25, 1649,* Ellis Bradshaw reported that in Bolton, in Lancaster County, between 10:00 in the morning and noon, a white circle appeared around the sun in an otherwise cloudless and clear sky. Additionally, two rainbows appeared overhead, one near the sun and the other near the horizon (p. 3). Despite the diversity of signs, Bradshaw did not believe this apparition to be very difficult to interpret. He wrote, "It is observable that these two rainbows were . . . like two fallen arches and that with their backs together so that their four ends were at the furthest distance each from the others . . . which may well signify that such who have covenanted together shall desert each other in regard to mutual assistance" (p. 4). For Bradshaw the opposing arches symbolized the broken covenant between king and Parliament; he observed, "Thus our covenant engagement is parted into two, like the two rainbows, and is wrested and turned for everyman's ends" (p. 8).

All was in disarray with no agreement about even the most fundamental descriptions of the crisis. Bradshaw observed that "one accounts it a breaking off of Parliament which another accounts but a necessary restraint from enslaving the kingdom." More ominous yet, "One calls that murder while another accounts it a judicial execution of a grand murderer" (p. 5). Hence, despite remaining political tensions between Charles and Parliament, apparitions were easier to understand when military matters were more decisive. Thus, after the fighting ceased and political events were more settled, some apparitions were understood as celebrating significant events of the civil war and their anniversaries as if that actual historical conclusion had been God's intention all along. The short 1654 pamphlet *More Warning Yet, Being a True Relation of a Strange and Most Dreadful Apparition* describes how three soldiers stationed at the garrison at Hull witnessed two armies battling in the skies on September 3. *More Warning* considered this significant because September 3 was the day England defeated the Scots at the battles of Dunbar and Worcester. Additionally, this date was the anniversary of "the day appointed for the sitting of this Parliament" (p. 1). Clearly, the heavens could maintain a parliamentary calendar as well as royalist aspirations. That God would favor Parliament in 1654 was obvious since Parliament controlled England at that time and Charles did not. On the other hand,

England's inability to create a stable system of governance must also have been indicative of some divine wish.

Removing the country's rightful ruler had been sinful. As government replaced government, many people believed that England would never solve its political problems. God sent repeated signs to England. *A Warning Piece to the World* (1655) noted in frustration, "What unnatural tides have we had within these few years? What monstrous fishes? . . . What lamentable fires? . . . What unusual storms of hail have we had? What incessant showers of rain?" (p. 5). England should have repented for killing Charles, "yet for these assured signs of God's heavy displeasure, we, like deaf adders, stop our ears against the voice of the charmer, wrap ourselves in a soft blanket . . . and lie snug in our sins, dreadless and fearless of that vengeance that is ready to surprise us" (p. 5).

Once the monarchy was restored in 1661, new apparitions appeared, proving how Charles's fight had been righteous all along. The short pamphlet *The Just Devil of Woodstock, or, A Narrative of the Several Apparitions, the Frights and Punishments Inflicted upon the Rumpish Commissioners,* published in January 1660, argued that as early as 1649 various apparitions had proven the goodness of Charles's cause. According to the story, the Rump Parliament sent commissioners to assess the value of Charles's property near Woodstock on October 16, 1649, who had been plagued by a series of mishaps and ghostly apparitions for the duration of their stay. No apparitions had ever appeared in the area before nor after that time, and the author makes clear that they represented God's displeasure with Cromwell's actions. The author refers to these apparitions as the deeds of a "just devil" that represented God's desire to maintain Stuart property and sustain the family in times of adversity. Puritanism is mocked when the frightened commissioners turn to Pastor Hoffman, the local Presbyterian minister, to seek God's help against the devil plaguing them. Because any non-Anglican minister was a fraud in the author's eyes and therefore helpless in the face of divine apparitions, "when they came to fetch him to go with them, Mr. Hoffman answered that he would not lodge there one night for £500 and being asked to pray with them, he held up his hands and said that he would not meddle upon any terms" (p. 10). In 1660, it was easy to report a favorable heavenly assessment of Charles's cause from as early as 1649. We should remember, however, that in 1649 the heavens were in fact more supportive of Parliament's cause.

Despite swings in interpretation, for Bradshaw, Jane Coe, Mr. Forcet of Old Fish Street, and other pamphleteers, there was nothing illogical about viewing political events from within an enchanted context. Each level of understanding reinforced the other; to separate them was to assume that God did not care about human events. Hence, new apparitions could explain the latest turn in political developments even if earlier apparitions had given the very opposite meaning. Indeed, seventeenth-century observers marveled at the wisdom of those able to provide shifting interpretations of an apparition's importance.

In addition to apparitions, God made his intentions known to mankind more directly through the manifestation of physical prodigies, most importantly amazing freaks of nature and monstrous human births. While both types of deformity reflected God's anger, they were not identical. Fantastic freaks of nature were an emblem of the deformity of the times in general, an indication that nature itself was out of tilt. Monstrous human births were usually a divine punishment for the sins of a particular family entertaining blasphemous beliefs or practices. Pamphlets describing both types of prodigies proliferated during the years of the English Revolution.

The pamphlet *The Marine Mercury, or A True Relation of the Strange Appearance of a Man-Fish . . . Having a Musket in One Hand a Petition in the Other* (1642) is an example of the sort of amazing freak of nature that might serve civil war ends. In this publication, Charles's position was clearly supported by the appearance of a divinely inspired freak man-fish. According to six sailors, whose names appear on the title page of the chapbook, the man-fish "was very terrible, having broad eyes, hair black and curled, his breast armed with shining scales . . . having a musket in one hand and a large paper in the other hand" (p. A2b). The author explained that men-fish were very rare and "at first sight they were much dismayed but afterward, they, taking heart (some of them having none at first sights) made them the more adventurous." Despite their initial wariness, "after they had passed some words with this man-fish, he seemed rather an angel sent to guard this kingdom than an enemy to hurt us." Indeed, this divine angel/freak "told them he came inspired by providence for the good and flourishing state of this kingdom and the armed hand he advanced was the intelligence of all the dangers and plots of foreign princes against us" (p. A3a). The man-fish explained that he would now swim off to confront Parliament. Indeed, there was good reason to believe that "the kingdom may be easily recovered from the bloody rebels" (p. A3b). If this story did not warm the hearts of Charles's supporters, the last page of the newsbook described how subsequently "Sir Simon Heartley with his company gave battle to a company of rebels and slew 500, took four colors and routed 1500." In other words, human events and God's signs were of one cloth.

A few months later, in July 1642, a similar story appeared, entitled *A Relation of a Terrible Monster Taken by a Fisherman near Wollage.* It is likely that this fish story was inspired by the former one. According to the author, on July 15, between 4:00 and 5:00 in the morning, Thomas West, fishing above Wollage, threw his net in the water, and when he drew it out "he sees in the net a fiend, not a fish; at the least a monster, not an ordinary creature" (p. 1). The prodigy West withdrew from his net was not a man-fish but a *toad-fish,* which "is called a toad-fish and with good reason for the head and eyes, when it lies upon its belly, do perfectly resemble a toad. But, here lies the wonder, turn him up, or but a little raise his head and you shall behold the perfect breast and chest of a man . . . [with] two as perfect hands as any man whatsoever . . . his mouth [is] very broad, with three ranks of sharp teeth . . . yet is its mouth the very emblem of a toad, as likewise its eyes." In size, "he is in length five feet, in breadth a yard over, having on each side two huge fins . . . his tail a foot in length, as it were all of whalebone" (p. 2). In short, this was no ordinary toad-fish. When a nearby woman saw it, she "started from it with a shriek, crying 'Oh the devil in the shape of a great fish,' [she] swooned and was fain to be carried out" (p. 2). It was "a creature . . . at which human blood may rise, I never saw with my eye nor desire to see again."

Having established the freak's demeanor, *A Relation of a Terrible Monster* pondered its significance. The pamphlet stated that "unnatural accidents, though dumb, do, notwithstanding, speak the supernatural intentions and purposes of the divine powers" and reminded the reader that in 1515 a whale had come ashore at Dieppe a little before Francis I was taken prisoner at the battle of Pavia. The author prayed that "God in his mercy grant that this ugly monster may not for our sins prove the like to us" (p. 3). Surely a similar occurrence could not bode well for Charles. Indeed, the second part of the chapbook, entitled " A Relation of a Bloody Encounter Between the Lord Faulconbridge and Sir Henry Hotham," indicated that the Duke of Richmond was hurt at that engagement, and Lord Faulconbridge, like Francis I before him, was taken prisoner. It would seem that the appearance of the toad-fish augured Lord Faulconbridge's capture. Once again, human events and God's signs were woven together. This time, however, the prodigy appeared in support of Parliament whereas the previous one was royalist.

The pamphlet *The Most Strange and Wonderful Apparitions of Blood* (1645) also told of a freak of nature that reflected revolutionary conflict.

A good and kindly woman delivered in 1645 what "seemed to be, as it were, two children, the one arising from the upper monstrous part of the other, the first child out of which the other did proceed, [and] had neither head nor feet but was only content with thighs and two stumps for legs. Neither had it any arms but two imperfect branches came from the shoulders of it which had no hands at all" (p. 7). The child emerging from the stump of the first one was "perfect in every limb, it was but little but very lovely to behold." This pamphlet wondered whether the birth of a perfect child out of the monstrous stump of another was similar to revolutionary England being born from the corpse of the old monarchy.

The "evil condition of the times" could also account for the birth of other freaks. *Signs and Wonders from Heaven with a True Relation of a Monster Born in Ratcliffe Highway* (1645) told of two strange births. On July 28, Mistress Hart of Ratcliffe gave birth to a hermaphrodite with neither nose, arms, legs, nor hands and with one ear protruding from its neck. According to the testimony of Mistress Bullock, the midwife, Mistress Hart was religious, honest, and loved by all. Was England, with both a powerful Parliament and a king, a hermaphrodite? No less horrible, in Lombard Street in London, a goldsmith's cat gave birth to a monstrous kitten that was part human. While it had eight feet, two tails, and no head at all, its paws were like the hands of a child (pp. 4-5). The author concluded that the conflict between Charles and Parliament was a great sin and that God had turned nature upside down to repay those who would overturn monarchy. He asked, "Has not nature altered her course so much, that women framed of pure flesh and blood bringeth forth ugly and deformed monsters and contrariwise, beasts bring forth human shapes contrary to their kind?" (p. 2). Man had overturned God's order, and now God overturned the pattern of nature.

If amazing freaks of nature were emblems of the political and social debasement of the day, most accounts of monsters reflected the frightful religious conflict between Anglicans and Puritans and between the many sects and orientations dividing the latter. The two anomalies were related; according the William Lilly. "Usually, after the appearing of such prodigies, such lawless and unaccustomed monsters appear" (*The Starry Messenger*, p. 19) and many contemporaries believed that the current religious turmoil was best perceived through the recent proliferation of monsters, much as apparitions characterized the conflict between Charles and Parliament.

Monstrosity, a divine scarlet letter, was God's way of manifesting the secret evil within as it passed from parent to child. Just as a pure Mary conceived a pure Jesus, blasphemous parents produced monstrous children. Pamphlet after pamphlet noted that monsters were "exposed to public view to the infinite amazement of the beholders and to the great grief of the parents," and *Strange Newes from Scotland* (1647) had the monster exclaim to all present, "I am deformed for the sin of my parents" (p. 3). Even more, since monstrosity was an indication of guilt, one need feel no sympathy for the stricken, and it was therefore possible to blame the victim for the crime. From a simple religious perspective, the greatest revolutionary-age religious evil lay in supporting the wrong religious orientation. Hence, through accounts of monsters born to one's opponents, one could establish that they were of evil seed and the product of blasphemous parents. In turn, their monstrous children would themselves produce yet another generation of monsters.

Each sin had its penalty; monstrosity was usually related to blasphemy. The chapbook *A Strange and Lamentable Accident That Happened Lately at Mears Ashby in Northamptonshire* (1642) by a local Anglican priest named John Locke, presented a story of a child born without a head. According to Locke, heresy and blasphemy caused the appearance of monsters. He reminded his readers that "in the third year of Queen Elizabeth of blessed memory, when as in Moore and Geofferey, two of the devil's agents, published their prodigious and heretical tenets, to the allurement of many faithful and constant believers. The year after [there] were many monstrous births" (p. A3b). In his own day Locke was particularly concerned about the ungodly rebellion against king and church that "made [England] a laughing stock and a scorn to all nations." The perpetrators of this evil were Puritan Roundheads, and Locke observed, "I fear me we may have too many of these unfavorable and wheeling Rotundities frequent among us." The essence of his story, therefore, was that terrible Puritan views gave birth to terrible monstrous offspring.

According to the pastor, Mary Wilmore of Mears Ashby in Nottinghamshire gave birth to a monster. It seems that when she was still pregnant, a Puritan minister convinced Mary to reject the Anglican church. "It is reported she should say, 'I had rather my child should be born without a head than to have a head to be signed with the sign of the cross" (p. A3b). Predictably, Locke reported, "It pleased God about a month later, she was accordingly delivered of a monster . . . a child without a head, to the shame of the parents."

Puritan monster stories tended to view this anomaly from the same orientation found in Anglican newsbooks. Hence, whatever the importance of covenantal thought, double supralapsarian predestination, and an endless variety of Presbyterian ecclesiastical ideas that historians use to distinguish Puritans from Anglicans, both agreed about monsters. In the pamphlet *A Declaration of a Strange and Wonderful Monster, Born in Kirkham Parish in Leicestershire* (1645) the author explained that in Leicester, "The people that live there are . . . for the most part very bad. No part of England hath had so many witches, none fuller of papists" (p. 4). Among the evils perpetrated by these people include the fact that "they were the chief instruments in seeking to have that wicked *Book of Allowances for Sports on the Lord's Day* to be published." As a result, "the godly people amongst them have suffered very much under their reproaches and wicked malice."

Of the many "bad" people living in Kirkham parish, the Haughtons were probably the worse. According to the author, "they were of a very bitter disposition against godly people. Papists they were both and divertive [*sic*] against honest Protestants" (p. 5). Among other sins committed by the elder Mrs. Haughton was the fact that "she took her cat and said it must be a Roundhead . . . and caused the ears to be cut off, called her cat Prynn (instead of pussy) . . . and she hath often said that she hoped to see the Church flourish again (meaning the Popish church), all Roundheads subdued, and she hath done much for the relief of poor papists in those parts" (p. 5). If naming the family cat after the powerful Presbyterian leader William Prynn was an offense, the daughter-in-law was no better than the mother. "She hath been often heard to curse vs. Mr. Prynn . . . and the other Roundheads, also to revile the Parliament and say that she thought that the king and the bishops were the righter part of us . . . and that the Puritans and Independents deserve all to be hanged" (p. 6).

When Mrs. Haughton's daughter-in-law was pregnant, she was reported to have said in the presence of many people, "I pray God that rather than I shall be a Roundhead or bear a Roundhead, I may bring forth a child without a head." The result was, of course, "to provoke God to show such a testimony of his displeasure against her by causing her to bring forth a monster" (p. 6). The last page of the pamphlet was the usual letter attesting to the truth of this story, signed by Mr. Fleetwood, minister of that parish, and Mrs. Gattaker, the midwife delivering the infant. The cover page cited additional eyewitnesses. Both Anglican and Puritan parents produced deformed children seemingly because monstrosity, rather than theology, was the most visible sign that each set of parents were of the wrong church.

The internecine sectarian warfare within Puritan ranks also employed images of monstrosity. Of the many antisectarian monster stories appearing during these years, one of the best was the Presbyterian anti-Baptist newsbook *Strange News From Scotland* (1647). The author tells us that on September 24, 1647, a horrible monster was born to Baptist parents in the Scottish village of Hadensworth, near Edinburgh. The child had two heads, one male with long hair and one female with a smooth face, with donkey ears and a single eye set in the middle of each face. It had two short necks and a tree-trunklike body with arms protruding from various places, each of which had hands with talons. It possessed both male and female "secret parts" along with the legs and feet of oxen (p. 2). Those present at the birth were truly horrified, "in so much that it struck into a quaking terror all those that were eye-witnesses of this horned production." Others reacted by "taking themselves to prayers, and others . . . to flight and the rest standing amazed as if they had beholden a gorgon . . . and [were] suddenly metamorphosed into stone" (pp. 2-3). So grotesque was this monster that nature itself was repulsed, "and the heavens proclaimed its entrance into the world with a loud peal of thunder seconded with such frequent flashes of lightning" (p. 3).

Unlike other monsters, this one was able to speak, and upon being born, "the monster, with a hoarse but loud voice was able to speak these words, being ever after silent. 'I am deformed for the sins of my parents.'" The mother then explained to all assembled, "This judgment is questionless fallen upon me for my sins which are many and grievous . . . I have often wished that . . . rather than any child born of my body should receive these Christian rites . . . at their baptism, I confess that I did vehemently desire . . . to see the utter ruin and subversion of all church and state government" (p. 4). Before dying, she begged her friends and neighbors "to make your peace before your sins call to heaven for vengeance." This pamphlet's anonymous author, evidently quite moved by his own story, explained that those responsible for influencing this poor woman were "the ministry who were not of our faction" and "heretical factious fellows who go in sheep's clothing but are naught but ravenous wolves." He asked readers to "take this dying woman's counsel into their consideration before it be too late, calling to heaven for mercy before their sins call to heaven for judgment" (p. 5). For those doubting the details of this sobering tale, the veracity of the story "was certified by the minister of the Parish, a man of gravity and good estimation amongst his neighbors and of good repute generally, as also by the church-wardens of the same parish and other people of good quality and esteem, and the relation sent hither to a friend of his, one Mr. Obadiah Slingsby, a pious and a painful minister of God's word" (p. 1).

Even worse than the Baptists were the Ranters, about whom so many popular pamphlets were written. From a conservative viewpoint, Ranters held first place in the most-hated-by-God category of the Englishman's informal ranking of religious groupings and hence was the sect most subject to monstrous births. The story of one unfortunate Ranter, Mary Adams, was told in the pamphlet *The Ranter's Monster* (1652). Mary Adams came from a good and religious home in Tillingham in Essex. Unfortunately, when still quite young, Mary became rebellious and joined first the Anabaptists and then the Familists "and immediately turned Ranter, holding an opinion that there was no God, no heaven, no hell, but that creation came by Providence [and] that woman was made to be a helper for man and that it was no sin to lay with any man whether bachelor, widower or married by a thing lawful and abjured thereunto by nature" (p. 5). Reasonably, Mary became pregnant.

Despite *The Ranter's Monster's* claim that Mary lost all faith in God and religion, it asserted that Mary also "said she was the virgin Mary and that she was conceived with child by the Holy Ghost and how all the gospel that had been taught heretofore was false and that which was within her she said was the true messiah" (p. 3). Because of Mary's strange views, her erstwhile minister, Mr. Hadley, had pregnant Mary incarcerated, and after eight days of difficult labor, she gave birth to a monster. "It had neither hands nor feet," we are told, "but claws like a toad in the place where the hands should have been and every part was odious to behold" (p. 4). Mary, too, met with a sad fate: "She rotted and was consumed as she lay, being from head to foot as full of botches, blains, boils and stinking scabs as ever one could stand by another" (p. 4). The message was clear: Rantism was a monstrous life and led to monstrous children.

God was able to punish those of the wrong religion even when the did not produce monstrous offspring. Take the case of the Stichberry family, described in a pamphlet entitled *Wonderfull News, or, a True Relation of a Churchwarden in the Town of Toscester* (1642). For many Englishmen religious orientation was less a question of reasoned religious argument than a belief system incorporating religious totems and relics.

Robert Stichberry was the churchwarden in Toscester and a low-church Puritan as well. One day, while painting a window in the church, "he with some other of his accomplices did batter and utterly break and deface the same leaving it as a sad spectacle" (pp. A2a-b). When the townsfolk asked Mr. Stichberry to repair the window, he refused, "and so it lies as they left it." Stichberry was not the only rotter in the family. Anne

Stichberry, the churchwarden's sister, was also a Puritan defacer of God's glory, "affecting not the Book of Common Prayer but making, for these two years past almost, a scorn thereof" (p. A2b). So great was her hatred of God's true service, "at the last she tore it out with her hands."

God would not long permit the Stichberry family to mock his true church, and "Stichberry himself in short time after fell extremely mad, raving in a most fearful and strange case . . . insomuch that five or six men could hardly rule him, and so continued in that most extraordinary manner howling and making a noise until he died" (p. A2b). His sister's fate was no better: "Her hands that tore the same [prayer book] began presently in a most strange manner to rot the flesh flying from the bones and so continueth to this present, rotting in a most fearful and loathsome manner" (p. A3a). Indeed, her rotting flesh was so disgusting that "by the neighbors she is removed a mile out of town where she remains, lamenting much that she hath done so wretched and wicked a deed."

None associating with the Stichberrys could be innocent. Indeed, God punished Stichberry's wife for good measure. Though innocent, apparently, of any offensive deed, she "was exceedingly tormented on a sudden in her limbs, raging and crying most fearfully with the extreme anguish and pain she did endure . . . and so she died in that extremity" (p. A2b). The pamphlet's conclusion was as obvious as it was pious: "It is not good to attempt anything against sacred places or to vilify those things which have any past of holy Writ in them." To do so was to encourage God's wrath, and the author gleefully noted that God "suffereth no sin to go unpunished."

The same shamanistic logic appeared in the newsbook *A Strange and Lamentable Accident That Happened Lately at Mears Ashby in Northamptonshire* (1642) by John Locke, the local Anglican priest discussed earlier. Locke observed that Puritan abuse of Anglican ritual objects always met with divine punishment. Locke noted a Puritan who had "profaned the Lord's table by pissing upon it . . . [and] not long after the divine justice found him out for he was taken with a disease that rotted his bowels" (pp. A2a-b). Since it was only 1642 and it would be almost two decades until God's order would be reestablished, no one heeded Mr. Locke, and Puritans, no doubt, continued to urinate on God's table. Locke was confident that God would avenge all those callously urinating on His table and rejecting His true church, and he ended his short treatise by calling upon all true Christians "to suffer us not to exercise ourselves in the works of the flesh as hatreds, emulations, contentions, heresies, seditions, needless and unprofitable questions which tend to

rebellion and discord, breeding ungodliness and making dissension"
(p. A4a).

Apparitions, prodigies, and other signs from God were self-reinforcing
symbols, and each side in the conflict used them as tangible proof of
God's support. The problem was, of course, that each side had so many
proofs. How could a set of monstrous children on one side indicate a
truth contradicted by a set of monstrous children on the other side?
Something more was needed to sway Englishmen to one side or the other
of the civil war or even for individuals to convince themselves of the
meaning of events. What if it were possible, for instance, to prove that
Parliament's victory, or that of the king, had been predicted many centuries earlier by wise seers? Prophecy, after all, had deep roots in medieval England, as we will see in the next chapter.

Strange and Miraculous *NEWES* from

TVRKIE.

Sent to our *English* Ambaſſadour reſident at *Conſtantinople.*

Of a Woman which was ſeene in the Firmament with a
Book in her hand at *Medina Talnabi* where *Mahomets* Tombe is.

Alſo ſeverall Viſions of Armed men appearing in the Ayre
for one and twenty dayes together.

With a Propheticall interpretation made by a Mahumetan
Prieſt, who loſt his life in the maintenance thereof.

LONDON,
Printed for *Hugh Perrey* neere *Ivy-Bridge* in the *Strand,*
June 13. 1642.

♦ ♦ ♦

4

Ancient Prophecies

"WHEN CHARLES SHALL BE KING OF THE ENGLISH,
HE SHALL BE THE LAST KING OF THE BRITAINS."

—*Twelve Strange Prophecies (1648)*

Predicting the future is an important enterprise in many traditional societies. Whether it be through tossing bones, reading the entrails of pigeons, contemplating clouds, seeing visions from drug-induced trances, or applying numerological techniques to holy words, those individuals capable of "divining" the future can influence their peers, especially during difficult times such as during a civil war. Despite post-Enlightenment rationalism, astrology, numerology, fortune-telling, and dream analysis remain popular methods of predicting the future. Certainly for the medieval mind, there were no doubts about the veracity or value of prophetic prediction or of more general forms of prognostication.[1]

It was obvious from Scripture that God spoke to special people so that special messages might become known to all humanity. Ezekiel saw the wheel, the compressed image of the future in a form that only he understood, while Amos and others warned of impending doom in terms clear to everyone. The Old Testament prophecies of the Messiah were certainly important because without them, Jesus might have been hard-pressed to prove his identity.

As the New Testament replaced the Old Testament, the latter was reduced to the venerable status of introductory message, preamble, or prophecy. In turn, even the New Testament possessed prophetic messages of Jesus' imminent return. When Christ did not quickly return, a variety of prophetic formulae were substituted in his place. Some assumed Jesus was waiting for the year 1000 to usher in the thousand-year millennium. Thereafter, other formulae were developed. Joachim believed that there had been an Age of the Father, an Age of the Son, and an Age of the Spirit, the culmination of which would see the second coming. Others claimed that the fulfillment of the age—"time, times and half a time"— was not yet complete or that 1,260 years, or the equivalent in years of the days Jesus wandered in the wilderness, must pass before his return. When Jesus did not return in 1260, that number was added to an additional base date to compute the initiation of the millennium. Sixteenth-century prophets of change often added 250, the year of Diocletian's persecutions, to 1260. The result, 1510, seemed to explain the significance of the Reformation, and social/religious radicals from Holland to Bohemia believed Jesus' return was imminent.[2] For restitutionists like Michael Servetus, 325, the date of the Council of Nicaea and the establishment of Christianity in the Roman Empire by Constantine, was added to 1260. He believed, therefore, that the millennium would commence in 1585. Subsequent scholars substituted later dates as earlier ones passed without event.

The book of Revelation provided yet another approach to telling the future because it, too, describes how the future of the world will come about. Although it uses complex and mystifying images, throughout the medieval period people read major political events of the day against the background of complicated Scriptural patterns of the future. The times were scoured for hints about which contemporary personality, such as Charles V or Francis I, was the great bear, the eagle, the dragon, or the little horn and which of the seven seals had been opened, and when the Fifth Monarchy would commence.

Another prominent Reformation theme in seventeenth-century popular prophecy concerned the anti-Christ, often identified with Rome. All attacks upon Rome were conceived as assaults upon Satan himself. Hence, the Protestant Reformation had surely dealt a hammer blow in this continuing conflict, but in subsequent troubling times, such as the English Revolution, many thoughtful people envisioned their own travails as part of this battle as well. In *Brightman's Predictions and Prophecies* (1641) and again in *Reverend Mr. Brightman's Judgments* (1642) the author wished to demonstrate how Daniel, Ezekiel, and John predicted the current events of his day. Brightman attempted to trace the progress of the Reformation in Germany, Scotland, and Holland and then hook England's fate onto those prophetic events that had already transpired.

In addition to Scriptural prophecy, which England shared with the rest of Europe, the British enjoyed a separate tradition of prophetic speculation concerning their national identity and destiny. The separate mythic personalities of Merlin Ambrosius, Merlin Sylvestris, and Myrddin Emrys each supplemented the figures of Arthurian mythology. While these different personae reflected somewhat different mythical traditions, they shared a common mentality and cultural orientation. Geoffrey of Monmouth, the codifier of these prophetic traditions, provided Latin translations for the original Welsh texts. His *History of the Kings of Britain* became the foundation for much subsequent English prophetic speculation.[3] Later personalities and events for which ancient prophecies were sought included Evil King John, the Great Plague, and the War of the Roses. The violent introduction of the Tudor dynasty coupled with the English Reformation provided yet additional material for English prophetic speculation.[4] Some prophecies, for instance, attempted to explain the curious sequence by which Tudor children came to the throne, while others predicted when England would be free of the hated Norman yoke.

A belief that these old prophetic writings predicted contemporary events led them to be venerated. Sometimes the prophetic imagery was easily understood. Other times interpretation required the additional tools of astrology, numerology, or new prophetic formulae to extract the greatest meaning. In this way, the same ancient prophecy might be made to speak to a variety of times and conditions that, in themselves, meant very little. The effect was to console the reader that the distressing event, be it an assassination or a plague, was indeed part of a larger divine plan. The ancient prophet was, in a name, a soothsayer who explained disturbing events to troubled people in disquieting times. This characteristic was especially important during the years of the civil war, when both Anglicans and Puritans sought to bring prodigies and apparitions to prove the truth of their side.

Almost any major catastrophe or natural disaster might be interpreted to indicate that God wished some general alteration, but events surrounding governance were especially meaningful because monarchy was a quasi-divine institution. Hence, a king's unusual fall from power, an early death, and most certainly a revolution, were signals that God had initiated a new phase in history. Scholars would then ponder whether the event could be read into the known pattern of Scriptural prophecy or through a series of ancient prophecies attributed to Merlin and others. The judgments of these scholars could have significant political repercussions, and thus English rulers long tried to restrict the publication of prophecies.[5] In 1402 and 1406 Henry IV passed laws against prophecy as did Henry VIII in 1541, Edward VI in 1549 and 1552, and Elizabeth in

1562 and 1580. The essence of this legislation forbade predicting coming bloodshed, the loss of life, or other disturbances. Offenders were liable to a fine of £10 and a year's imprisonment. Repeat offenders faced life imprisonment and forfeiture of all worldly goods.

No sooner had civil war broken out against the Stuarts than publishers rediscovered a host of allegedly lost ancient prophecies that threw light on the present situation. Indeed, as the weather became more violent, as apparitions seemed more ominous, as reports of monstrous births became commonplace, England was awash in prophecies. Many Englishmen came to believe that their time of troubles had great cosmic meaning, that they may have been predicted in the book of Revelation and/or other ancient texts and would usher in the end of the world.

The problem lay in identifying with whom God was angry. In 1640, this was still not yet apparent. The papal anti-Christ was always an obvious target. *Certain Prophecies Presented Before the Kings Majesty by Scholars of Trinity College* (1642) noted that the Pope "shall not only be subject to ruine and destruction, but that most certainly it is to be pulled down . . . and the great swarms of popish priests, friars, monks, and cardinals and the whole popish hierarchy and pontifical clergy which like filthy locusts springing out of smoke fly together in so great heaps, in the west shall be blown away with an east wind" (pp. 3-4). But this had been predicted for decades, and in any event, there certainly were more direct roads to Rome than through London.

Equally widespread was the notion that the world was finally coming to an end. This, too, was an immediate reaction whenever something terrible happened. For instance, *The Wonderfull Works of God Declared by a Strange Prophecy of a Maid* (1641) saw England's local troubles heralding no less than the end of the world. "Good neighbors and friends," the prophetic maid told her neighbors, "be thankful to God that he hath certified you by sundry signs how the end of the world is at hand at the day of rest coming to rejoice us. Our charge shall be taken away and our travail shall have an end" (p. 4). Contemporary events "were but warnings sent us to mollify our hard hearts and to admonish us from that detestable pride which is here maintained" (p. 4). "If you do not amend and turn to God," the maid warned, "he will forthwith send you a general alteration and such a one as not only men but birds of the air and all living creatures shall tremble at his wrath, wars shall greatly grieve the earth, and shall destroy countries" (p. 5). This pamphlet was not at all consoling.

Neither was the pamphlet *The Wonderful Works of God Declared by a Strange Prophecie* (1641) very consoling. Before James Turner's dead sixteen-year-old sister could be buried, "even as one awakening from a slumber, [she] raised up herself and with a mild and cheerful contenance spoke unto her mother as followeth . . . 'I am sent as a messenger unto you and within five days I shall return again to the place I [just] came from where I shall live in all peace'" (p. 3).

Having established her prophetic status, Miss Turner turned to her message, surely of considerable general interest in the confused days of 1641. "God, he will forthwith send you a general alteration," she predicted, "and such a one as not only men but birds in the air and all living creatures shall tremble at his wrath" (p. 5). Even worse, "wars shall greatly grieve the earth and shall destroy countries and many people, men shall be most grievously chased from their houses and miserably murdered." It was probably reassuring to many conservative Englishmen that the pamphlet ended with the young maid being returned to her coffin for her second death, where "she was desirous to receive the sacrament and Christian communion of the Church of England" (p. 6). Then again, once the old church had been dismantled, this affirmation of Anglicanism may have been a cause for alarm.

Neither the end of the world nor the fall of the anti-Christ seemed to describe England's problems adequately. For one thing, neither occurred even though English troubles became more complex and confusing. It would have been comforting if the only question was determining whether God hated Charles or Parliament. Unlike other times of civil disturbance, however, the events of the interregnum were particularly confusing. There was not one but two civil wars; the king was not killed in battle but captured, tried for treason, and executed. The Parliament during the civil wars was not the Parliament after Charles's execution, and the position of Lord Protector was most peculiar, being neither king, nor dictator, nor very protective. Even worse, prophecies for England had to be squared with those for Scotland and Ireland since all three countries were jointly involved in these troubled times but were on different sides of the conflict. The restoration of monarchy after the revolution further complicated matters. Could it be that God toppled Charles only to topple Oliver Cromwell as well? Was the Church of England destroyed by Presbyterianism so that the latter could be replaced by the former? And what role did Holland play, let alone Scotland and Ireland? Whatever the value of traditional apocalyptic themes and ideas, none seemed to fit England's situation. Revolutionary uncertainty required prophecies keyed to the events of the day, prophecies that demonstrated how the very worst events everyone feared were in fact sanctioned by God and would lead to better times in the future. In short, the public wanted to know the happy ending.

English readers did not have long to wait. During the next few years the names "Mother Shipton," "Humphrey Tindall," "Ignatius," "Brightman," "William Lilly," "Christopher Syms," "Arise Evans" and perhaps a dozen others appeared before the public as new sources of information about the confusing times. There were prophets of doom, astrological prognosticators, numerologists, and both general and specific apocalypticians. Old mythic/prophetic personalities emerged from the distant past, including the "White King," the "Dreadful Deadman," and the "Chicken of the Eagle," all of whose messages contained the keys to England's future, once they were properly understood. But the public's appetite for newer, more complex, and more varied explanations was not easily satisfied, and the *Two Strange Prophecies* of 1642 gave way to the *Four Severall Strange Prophecies* of the same year. *Seven Severall Strange Prophecies* appeared a year later, in 1643, only to be followed by *Nine Notable Prophecies* in 1644. The *Twelve Strange Prophecies* of 1648 was a compilation that included the prophecies of Mother Shipton, the Blind Man, Ignatius, Sybill, Merlin, Ortwell Bins, Brightman and Gistheis, and John Saltmarsh. A year later *Fourteen Strange Prophecies* appeared for readers desiring a copy of every prophecy published to that time.

Indeed, publishers found that any old text, properly done up, might further excite public speculation. As an example, consider the pamphlet *Doomesday, or, The Great Day of the Lord's Judgment* (1647). At first glance, it seems like one more very traditional prognostication of England's present woes leading to doom and gloom. "Was there ever such a time of trouble as there is now since there was a nation upon the earth?" the compiler asked and then wondered whether "these troubles foretell the near approach of the day of judgment" (p. 5). After describing all the terrible possibilities, the pamphlet ended with the warning, "The day of doom is even now at hand and that the second coming of Christ is each day and hour to be expected" (p. 6). Where this publication is special, however, was in reaching these conclusions from "the prophecy of *Geofrey Chaucer,* who flourished in the days of King Richard the Second" (p. 3). Indeed, not only had Chaucer's words become a basis for prognostication, but even a contemporary's doodle on Chaucer was raised to the level of augury. Chaucer's pregnant lines were:

> When faith failes in Priest's sawes
> And Lords hests are taken for lawes
> Then shall the Isle of Brittanie
> Be brought into great miserie.

And the scholarly doodle was:

When Chaucer's prophecy shall be
Found true by the folk of Brittanie
When England walls and Scotland shall
Have pure religion 'mongst them all
Then low the Pope shall tumble down
And F. shall wear his triple crown. (p. 2)

Discovering the identity of "F" was a problem, but the pamphlet asked, "And have not our eyes seen the same fulfilled? What greater misery can come to a nation than to be at variance among themselves, mutually to sheath their swords in each others bowels, to batter down cities on one another's heads, to have their Sovereign in arms against them, to have all the calamities of war at once heavy upon them, and this hath this poor Kingdom of England till of late undergone. Therefore the fulfilling of Chaucer's Prophecy none but a madman will deny" (p. 4). Actually, neither Chaucer nor the secondary doodler were quite so bleak, but events were so frightening and so little understood that any very old text might have been interpreted to indicate that the present time of woe had been predicted in one sense or another. One could take comfort knowing that "F" lurked somewhere in the wings and would soon save the situation.

Most ancient prophecies attempted to demonstrate that Charles's fall from power was part of a larger divine plan. Hence, Parliament possessed the power of the sword, to be sure, but also legitimate political sovereignty and God's trust. If this did not make confusing developments any more explicable, it did lower the fever of popular anxiety. The most influential prognosticators were "Parliamentary Prophets," who interpreted the ancient prophecies in support of Parliament and the revolution. William Lilly was the most important of these.

The first major ancient prophet whose works appeared during the civil war was Mother Shipton with the publication of *The Prophecy of Mother Shipton* (1641). Mother Shipton was published again in the *Two Strange Prophecies* (1642) and once again that year in *A True Copy of a Prophecy Which Was Found in an Old Ancient House . . . Where Unto Is Added Mother Shipton's Prophecies.* Her prophecies, only a few pages long in all, were an instant success and acted as a bridge between those prophecies indicating a general coming alteration that applied to all Christendom and prophetic interpretations specifically for the English civil wars.[6]

Ursula Shipton's prophecies had been made during the reign of Henry VIII; they were then temporarily lost but had been rediscovered at the time of the civil wars. In her second prophecy, Mother Shipton had predicted that Wolsey would see but not enter into York with Henry VIII because he would die on the way. When Wolsey initially heard this prediction of his death, he dispatched the Duke of Suffolk, the Lord Percy, and the Lord Darcy to question Shipton and then burn her at the stake for heresy or witchcraft. Rather than being intimidated, Mother Shipton threw her cape and her stick into the fire to demonstrate that she, like her possessions, would not burn. Each of her intended prosecutors was eventually won over to her side; the account has each of them ask for his own personal prophecy.

The essence of Mother Shipton's words, spoken so long ago, illuminated the crisis of the times. According to her first prophecy, "a Scot shall govern there and if a plot prevent him not, sure then his sway shall continue till many a day . . . to sixteen joined twenty three" (p. 5). In her second prophecy, Mother Shipton spoke about the course of the civil war. She predicted that "the time will come when England shall tremble and quake for fear of a 'dead man' that shall be heard to speak, then will the dragon give the bull a great snap. And when the one is down, they will go to London town" (p. 7). She warned, "Then there will be a great battle between England and Scotland, and they will be pacified for a time. And when they come to Brammamore, they fight and are again pacified for a time. Then there will be a great battle at Knapesmore and they will be pacified for a while. Then there will be a great battle between England and Scotland at Stokenmore. Then will Ravens sit on the cross and drink as much blood of nobles as of the commons, then woe is me, for London shall be destroyed for ever after" (p. 7). There would also be sudden changes in religion. "In July month of the same year," she explained, "Saturn conjoines with Jupiter, perhaps false prophets shall arise, and Mohamet shall show his prize, and sure much alteration shall happen in religion" (p. 5).

After this long period of fighting, peace would return. "There shall never be warfare again, nor any more Kings or Queens but the kingdom shall be governed by three Lords and then York shall be London." This veiled reference to a possible oligarchy and the overturning of Tudor tradition was followed by an equally elliptic prophecy that predicted the outcome of the conflict. Mother Shipton saw "a man sitting upon Saint James Church hill weeping his fill. And after that a ship come sailing up the Thames till it come against London and the master of the ship shall weep and then the mariners shall ask him why he weepeth, being he hath made so good a voyage and he shall say, "What a goodly city this was, none in the world comparable to it and now there is scarce left any house that can give us drink for our money."

Mother Shipton's prophecies seemed to describe England's experiences well. In the 1650s people noticed that in addition to wars with Scotland she had also predicted a bloody war between king and Parliament, an alteration in religion, the end of monarchy and rule by an oligarchy, and the attempt to proscribe strong alcohol. And a decade later still, her words would be reinterpreted as having predicted the return of Charles II, the mariner, who came from abroad to mourn a ruined city. The images of the bull and the dragon—perhaps Parliament, or the king, and the army?—and the dead man (Charles I?), remained unidentified for the moment but would find their interpretations in a very short time.

The impact of these few pages was so great that Mother Shipton's prophecies were published an additional twenty times before Charles II returned to London, and few noticed that she had been unknown until her rediscovery in 1641. Popular acceptance of this remarkable prophecy also served as a sled to carry additional prophetic pamphlets into print since it was now obvious that the voice of the past could help alleviate the contemporary sense of dread. It was clear that God had a message for Englishmen, and Mother Shipton, it was believed, knew what it was, and at a profit to publishers. Moreover, her prophecy was more consoling than the appearance of portents and prodigies. Whereas the latter seemed to indicate God's anger with England, prophecies might justify the Puritan's actions.

If Mother Shipton helped explain the gravity of the crisis, her words did not provide clear political direction. This would fall to William Lilly, certainly the most significant of the many astrologer/prophets of the interregnum.[7] Lilly's works in favor of parliament were best-sellers. In them, he charted the course of popular prophecy for the age as a whole, but even more important, he provided the revolution with the popular images and mythic appeal dour Puritanism lacked. Other interpreters, such as Edward Calvers, Christopher Syms, and Arise Evans, supported the king. Reasonably, monarchist prognostication was less successful throughout the interregnum, but once Charles II was restored in 1660, prophecies, and the fortunes of their interpreters, were turned upside down. All prognosticators, however, agreed on one point: Portents and prodigies were important but the significance of the revolution was best appreciated according to mythic images established by wise seers of the past.

Lilly was born into a middle-class family in Diseworth in 1602. He was well educated and claimed to be able to read Greek, Latin, and Hebrew but never seems to have settled into a regular occupation. Fortunately, he was able to marry a woman of means. As a young man he expressed interest in the occult and magic and learned astrology from Arise Evans during the 1630s. This would change his life. From 1644, when he took for himself the name Merlinus Anglicus Junior, until the time of his death in 1681, Lilly produced thirty-six annual astrological almanacs. He also wrote a score of astrological pamphlets, and his *Christian Astrology* of 1647 was the most influential seventeenth-century English treatise on the subject of religion and astrology. It was Lilly's unique ability to blend astrology and prophecy that made him so influential. In part due to Lilly's influence, a formal Society of Astrologers was founded in 1649, more than a decade before the founding of the Royal Society.

From the earliest times people had read the stars; even the New Testament noted the importance of the Star of Bethlehem at Jesus' birth. Astrology had been successfully employed to explain the Protestant Reformation of the previous century, and it escaped no one that the terrible Thirty Years War followed the appearance of a comet in 1618. The confusing events of the English Revolution renewed popular interest in astrology as a potential tool to divine God's intentions for England. The royalist astrologer George Wharton wrote almanacs predicting the eventual success of Charles I, and, later, John Gadbury made similar astrological prognostications for Charles II. But Lilly's parliamentary prophecies dominated the interregnum.

William Lilly wrote two types of prognostications: astrological and narrative prophetic. The first type was published in almanacs and annual surveys of astrological and other heavenly occurrences. These complex works appealed primarily to sophisticated devotees of astrology who understood the intricacies of astrological charting. Still, it is remarkable how even these more difficult works were structured to influence common readers. Each consisted of a logical premise such as the importance of a recent heavenly occurrence—an eclipse or an apparition—followed by astrological charts sufficiently complicated to impress the reader. Following the charts Lilly included a verbal explanation of the astrology involved and, finally, a well-written interpretation that demonstrated first how the stars were fully in agreement with contemporary events, indeed, had even predicted them, and then how these events were similar to those surrounding previous astrological occurrences. In other words, Lilly used current scientific jargon to impress the reader with the objective basis of his analysis and predictions and then described the events of the present in terms of past astrology. Because Lilly supported parliament and presented interpretations that consistently supported the revolution, the effect was to make even the most troubling of events seem less troubling. As an example, his pamphlet *Starry Messenger,* discussed in the previous chapter, analyzed the significance of three suns appearing on Charles' birthday. Similarly, in *Supernatural Sights and Apparitions Seen in London June 30, 1644* (1644) Lilly tried to explain weather disturbances against the background of the imminent conjunction of Jupiter and Mars predicted for July 26, 1644.

After elaborating upon the astrological importance of this conjunction and how it had accompanied several major previous changes, Lilly turned to explaining its meaning for London. His conclusions were similar to those written in his other astrological writings. "It doth premonstrate [*sic*] the captivity of some king, Prince or Commander," he wrote (p. 13). Even more, "I say it expresseth a great and notorious defection of many Nobleman, Gentlemen, Men, Countries and towns from His Majesty" (p. 15). And elsewhere, "Oh the unexpected treason, treachery and unlikely failings that this figure portends to the kings of Europe and what infinite sufferers they shall be by means of policies and underhand subtleties of their bosom favorites" (p. 9). Still, Lilly wrote, some things must be held back because "should I write the whole truth, I might be deemed partial" (letter to reader).

Unsaid, but obvious, was Lilly's sense that the stars, like apparitions, were just too vague to offer real guidance in interpreting the meaning of the civil wars. Therein lay the value of ancient prophecy, Lilly's second and more successful method of prognostication. It was in these ancient writings that Lilly discovered the details and explanations of the world changes he saw in the stars. Additionally, there was reason to believe that discussions of ancient prophecy would reach a larger audience than astrology alone. Astrology demanded some technical skills on the part of the reader. A prophecy was a story whose interpretation could be attempted by anyone. By combining astrology with ancient prophecy, Lilly created a political orchestration of revolutionary events founded upon the credibility of astrology. Along the way, Lilly also made some lucky but politically astute predictions of developments that actually came about and provided the popular justification of the revolution in taverns, alehouses, salons, and everywhere else Londoners met to discuss events of the day. His interpretations were singularly important in demonstrating that God hated Charles, loved Cromwell, and wished the revolution to initiate a crusade against all monarchy.

If Mother Shipton's words made current political change credible in terms of ancient writings, Lilly successfully made Parliament's political cause into a legitimate expression of the venerated prophetic past. Whether Lilly wrote from political idealism, ego gratification, or for reasons of financial gain has never been established. But Lilly's gifts as a propagandist and publicist were first-rate.

Lilly came to appreciate the value of prophecy soon after the beginning of the civil war. In the introductory letter to *The Prophecy of the White King And Dreadfull Dead-man Explained* (1644), perhaps the most read of Lilly's works, he described how he came to make prophetic interpretations about the civil wars. He told how his appraisal of the conjunction of Saturn and Mars in 1639 led him to predict that "monarchy shall be eclipsed and darkened. Soldier glut thee with blood enough. Courtiers be well advised that a storm is coming" (p. 4). In April 1640, while recuperating in the country from a high fever, he predicted, "You at kingdom shall see thousands of armed men amongst you" (p. 2). He came to believe that the coming time of troubles would be very tumultuous and that the result would be the total reorganization of society from which England would emerge stronger than ever. "England, England, England," he wrote, "thou shalt flourish again and again . . . and when the fullness of time comes, or near 1700, thy shalt have a principle hand with thy sister of Scotland and some northern people in performing and concluding the mightiest action Europe ever beheld since the birth of our Saviour" (p. 5). In the meantime, however, the stars indicated there would be a period of turmoil and grief.

Lilly discovered the details of this period of grief in Merlin's traditional "Prophecy of the White King." The myth itself was very short but perplexing. After the demise of the Mighty Lion, the tragic White King emerges as the king of Britain but is subsequently destroyed in a great battle in which he enlists foreigners to fight against the people of England. After his fall, another mystical personality, the Chicken of the Eagle, who will make his nest "in the highest rock of Britain," will emerge as a successor hero and rule in peace thereafter.

Unlike Mother Shipton's words, the prophecy of the White King was well known before the revolution. Indeed, in 1625 the Earl of Pembroke attempted to persuade Charles to wear royal purple at his coronation rather than white satin. Charles was warned that two earlier monarchs, Richard II and Henry VI, wore white at their coronations, and both fulfilled the terms of the prophecy with violent deaths. Charles Stuart was stubborn and wore white.[8] When troubles with Scotland and Parliament led to fighting, few considered these events within the context of the prophecy. Then in 1643 the anonymous pamphlet *The Prophecy of a White King of Brittaine* purporting to be a copy of an ancient manuscript rediscovered in the library of Sir Robert Cotton, was published, reintroducing the idea that Charles was the White King. The pamphlet only offered the perplexing text itself and provided no further interpretation although the introduction mentioned the folly of tempting fate by wearing white at coronations. A year later, in 1644, Lilly, who was unknown to the wider public in 1643, wrote a major commentary of the prophecy and in the process provided Parliament with a propaganda tool of the first magnitude, laying the foundation for his reputation as revolutionary England's foremost interpreter of ancient prophecy.

In his *Prophecy of the White King* Lilly noted that it was unknown which Merlin was the true author but that the prophecy was originally written in Welsh and translated into Latin by Geoffrey of Monmouth. It was translated into English in about the time of Edward IV, and it was this text that Lilly would use. After reiterating the essence of the prophecy, Lilly turned to identifying the key personalities of the text. Though Lilly never explicitly named the Stuart monarch, in several pages of detailed commentary (pp. 11-19) he made abundantly clear why only Charles I could fit the description of the ill-fated White King. This association was really quite daring. Charles was still alive, still king, and according to the prophecy and Lilly's own interpretation, the White King must die. Indeed, Lilly was so bold as to offer that "'tis more than probable to me he evades captivity of his person until a little or immediately before his death" (p. 12).

Lilly predicted that after the death of the White King, England would go through a period of anarchy. He wrote that the text "intimates a kind of interregnum, as if his regal power should be executed by others for some years in his so long absence" (p. 13). In fact, this was actually Lilly's own extrapolation, to which he added: "Now begins a comedy, the White King once departed this life, the fury of the nation being prettily satisfied . . . [there comes] a serious consultation or debate of the states of the kingdom whether they shall again admit of monarchy by reason of the general hatred the people had to the White King, so that here appears an extreme unwillingness to accept the kingly title" (pp. 17-18).

Though the sad fate of the White King was not yet complete, Lilly wrote, "I am of the opinion this tragedy (if such shall ever be) is not yet acted," adding that "it shall absolutely be apparent, if not in some measure completed before or near 1666." A decade later it would appear as if

Lilly had predicted Charles's final and late capture by the English, his execution, and the resulting interregnum and the initiation of the Protectorate.

Determining the identity of the Chicken of the Eagle, the eventual ruler and seeming savior of Britain, could have proven even more controversial than identifying the White King. Still, it was Lilly's incredible luck that, in retrospect, his words seemed to have been corroborated by the unfolding of events. While he could not name the Chicken of the Eagle, he was able to describe the nature of this person in terms that in a few short years could be, indeed, would be, applied to Oliver Cromwell.

First, the Chicken of the Eagle "will show himself a cock of the game, and when grown to years will show himself no fool" (p. 15). Second, "the Chicken of the Eagle shall build his nest in the highest rock of all Britain," that is, he will assume ultimate authority but not necessarily the title of king. Third "having settled the Church and Commonwealth of the Britains in unity," his rule would prove materially beneficial to all Englishmen. Indeed, he will be a model of middle-class virtue, one who will have brought "the oppressed people to a reasonable flourishing condition, enabled the merchant to traffic securely in all ports, contenenced the laborious tradesman in the way of his vocation, exactly performed what a gracious Prince ought to perform for his subjects' good." Fourth, in the prime of his rule, "he then must prepare for another world . . . in his best years he unwillingly leaves the world." And again, "He shall neither live till he is old nor die young. When this Chicken of the Eagle having pacified this kingdom is dead, the nobility and gentry will suffer no injury to be done to any man" (p. 9). Fifth, "No more shall this Chicken of the Eagle have in himself or new acquisition of a realm, any stable hopes of the long enjoying thereof or leaving a numerous or happy offspring. Of this issue the prophet maketh no mention at all" (p. 18).

Considered within the context of 1644, Lilly could have been referring to any great leader. Considered through the hindsight of just a few years, readers were convinced that Lilly had known that a Cromwellian hero would emerge and lead England to the historical sunrise, die too soon, and never provide a true successor to himself.

Lilly bolstered these predictions by providing explanations for two other prophecies also included in this booklet. The "Prophecy of the Dreadfull Deadman" was, for Lilly, a variant on the personality of the White King. It was included in John Harvey's *A Discoursive Probleme Concerning Prophecies,* an early collection of prophecies published in 1588 but allegedly written at the time of Henry VIII. According to the prophecy, after a period of military conflict that sees England destroyed by seven kings of Europe, "shall come a Dreadfull Deadman and with him a royal 'Y' of the best blood in the world, and he shall have the crown and shall set England on the right way and put out all the heresies" (p. 20).

Mother Shipton had also mentioned a dead man, though in ambivalent terms, not indicating whether the dead man himself or "Y" would be responsible for England's subsequent good fortune. Lilly turned the story upside down and concluded that the Dreadful Deadman was actually the White King. He portrayed the Dreadful Deadman as "some dejected fugitive prince or one lost in the eye of the world and in the love and affection of his people . . . and then . . . deprived of government." He was removed by his subjects because he "intends nothing but confusion to thy long continued happiness, thy laws, thy liberties" (p. 21). Lilly interpreted this prophecy so that the dead man, like the White King, depended upon foreign troops to his own detriment. "The Deadman shall make a dead piece of work in trusting to his alien friends," Lilly wrote, "little dreaming that no one helps him for love." And as in the case of the White King, Lilly believed he could see in "Y" a future savior who, like Merlin's Chicken of the Eagle, was not himself a king yet "pacifies and sets the English in the right way and banisheth all heresies and novel sects for at that time both Church and State will be out of order. The English will honor this worthy man, and will they not have cause?" When Cromwell assumed power, people remembered that Lilly had written, "See how God in his wrath takes a crown from one and bestows it on another; this will seem strange but so it will be" (p. 22).

Lilly also found that the obscure "Prophecy of the Sibylla Tiburtina" could be interpreted toward his desired ends. This allegedly ancient text was said to have been discovered in 1520, chiseled into the Swiss mountainside. By comparing it to the prophecy by Ambrose Merlin, Lilly concluded that "towards the end of the British monarchy, the common people shall disturb all law and civil government and exceed their former bounds, and condemn and despise their superiors . . . and shall cause much lamentation and weeping amongst themselves and others and this is the issue of unruly tumults" (p. 27).

Lilly came to believe that the civil war was a watershed in English history. Indeed, "all or most of our ancient English, Welsh and Saxon prophecies had relation to Charles Stuart, the late King of England, unto his reign, his actions, life and death, and unto the now present times wherein we live and unto no other preceding king or times whatsoever."[9]

Lilly was a Roundhead and may have written *The Prophecy of a White King of Brittaine* in order to bolster popular sentiment for Parliament. In an open letter attached to *White King* Lilly soothed the reader's fears, noting that "we have not had on the Parliament's side one victory of any consequence but in our hearts we first despaired of the success" (p. 6). Indeed, Lilly believed that God had preordained Parliament's triumph. He wrote, "It is a comfort to be promised victory beforehand. It may encourage us to stand stoutly for our defense, our country's rights and privileges. Let us procure a union amongst us at this time and a constant resolution to unite with the Parliament at Westminister." The identification of Charles I as the failed White King and the Dreadful Deadman surely enabled Englishmen to bear the dislocations of the hour until the Chicken of the Eagle would emerge from within the ranks of good Englishmen. And Lilly's voice was certainly heard: This single pamphlet sold over 1,800 copies in three days and was reprinted thereafter several times. A large number of copies of editions of his work were printed; a publisher's bill indicates that the work went through three rapid printings for a total of 4,500 copies.[10]

Lilly's popularity was probably very gratifying to his publisher, but Presbyterians in Parliament, for whom Scripture was the sole source of all truth, considered astrology a pagan study.[11] Their doubts were not ill founded, although prophetic interpreters did not hesitate to claim the ancient writings were divine in some sense. In *Ignatius His Prophecy Concerning These Times* (1642) the anonymous author stated that "prophecy is the key of heaven . . . prophecy is a divine inspiration that discloseth the mystery of heavenly things, determined to be acted on earth, suggested by the divine providence of God" (preface). Other ancient prophecies expressed similar ideas, and Englishmen of all classes accepted their veracity as an extension of Scriptural prophecy. But Lilly alone stridently applied this divinity to political prognostication.[12] Indeed, Lilly had not been shy in this regard. In *White King* he commingled his political views with his astrological and prophetic findings and claimed the latter represented divine will.

In a pamphlet of the same year, *England's Prophetical Merline Foretelling to All Nations of Europe until 1663* (1644), Lilly had explained that "God doth not always speak unto men in express words and syllables but many times extraordinarily, admonishing us by motions and apparitions of the heavenly bodies (which are the works of his own fingers) is sufficiently testified" (p. 31). A year later Lilly was more circumspect. In *A Collection of Ancient and Modern Prophesies Concerning these Present*

Times with Modest Observations Thereon (1645), Lilly avoided referring to ancient prophets as divine and observed, "Whether any or all of these men whose prophecies I relate had so divine a knowledge, I can not maintain." Later he added, "Nor do I equalize them with those in sacred Writ: no, I do not so" (p. A3b). How then could mere mortals see the future? Lilly explained that "there is a certain art known to few men which doth so . . . that he may on a sudden be brought out of the fog of ignorance to the light of wisdom" (p. A3a). Even more, "though they died many ages since, yet was their eyesight admirable while they then saw the miserable times and sad actions of this present King and Kingdom and have delivered it not in enigmatic sentences but in words at large, significant and of easy understanding." Moreover, these prophets spoke the truth because "the strange harmony and direct consent I see betwixt these and my astrological judgments." We recall that a year earlier Lilly explained that the stars were moved by the fingers of God. It is doubtful whether Lilly's explanations satisfied the fears of the devout, especially when, a page later, he wrote of Merlin and Mother Shipton, "This is the mighty hand of God. A few years will tell you more, a very few" (p. A4b).

In *The World's Catastrophe or Europe's Many Mutations until 1666* (1647) Lilly again argued that stars are "but signs sent from the Supreme Cause and from our Saviour Christ for the abomination of the world" (p. 11) and called down abomination upon the heads of Europe's kings. As Lilly became more and more convinced that the ancient prophets manifested God's will, his enthusiasm for Parliament's cause developed into opposition to all monarchy. In turn, Lilly believed that all ancient prophecies were also opposed to monarchy as was God himself since His starry heavens provided Lilly's ultimate proof. Indeed, Lilly began to describe the emergence of a new England and new Europe in apocalyptic terms and envisioned that "these things shall be . . . more fierce after 1650 yet shall they be most terrible and vigorous after the year 1660" (p. 34).

Two years later, in 1649, in his *A Peculiar Prognostication,* Lilly again envisioned the destruction of monarchy. Of Turkey he wrote, "I conceive this year Constantinople will be much hindered by the head-strong Janisaries" (p. 5) and in western Europe, "I mention France wherein I find as much willingness in the people to rise and follow our steps in England, as ever any were to eat, when pitifully hungry, [what] the vial of wrath is preparing for that kingdom." Two years later, in his *Monarchy and No Monarchy in England* (1651), he again asserted that England should no longer have a monarchy. He wrote, "England shall no more be governed by Kings, [or] . . . by and of the issue or race of the late King" (p. 66). In writing about events to 1659, he wrote in *The World's Catastrophe,* "There shall almost be a destruction of monarchies especially . . . we conceive not only the destruction of the Turks but also . . . all the kings and potentates of the earth shall be hurt . . . all you kings of Spain and France, you princes and potentates of Italy behold and dread the sign sent from God" (p. 33). There will come a period of "rebellions, treasons, desolations, sudden and utter ruin and mischief of all kinds, so that all men living . . . shall be naturally inclined to the shedding of blood." Lilly believed the civil war was a battle against social injustice, and he championed the rights of yeomen and soldiers and hoped for the end of taxes on the poor.[13] A century later these same republican views would find political rather than astrological justification, but at the moment, the seventeenth century was still enchanted. Miracles, not political theory and argument, lay at the basis of popular public discourse.

Lilly was so successful in marshaling public support for Parliament that in 1648 it awarded him a gift of £50 and an annual pension of £100. The money was a good investment. In 1651, Lilly's propagandistic and highly antimonarchical *Several Observations on the Life and Death of King Charles I* supplemented his *Monarchy and No Monarchy.* One member of Parliament said, "His writings have kept up the spirit of the soldiery, the honest people of this realm, and many of us Parliament men."[14] This success explains why Tudor governments had prohibited the dissemination of prophecies and why, in the end, it was only a question of time before Parliament took the same action against Lilly. Believing that Parliament harbored secret Presbyterians, in 1652 Lilly wrote in his almanac, *Merlinus Anglicis,* that "Parliament now grows odious unto all good men" and that without further reform, the army should overthrow Parliament. On October 25, 1652, Lilly was arrested, and after thirteen days of detention and questioning, he was released but henceforth silenced.

Lilly was not the only prophetic interpreter whose work may have served political ends. The spiritual writer Elizabeth Poole, whose two works of 1649 both bear the title *An Alarum of War, Given to the Army,* gained prominence in military circles. Poole was less a prognosticator, however, than a highly spiritual moralist in the Old Testament tradition of Amos. For her the events of the civil war years were signs that God would wreak havoc upon the unjust. In the preface to the reader she wrote, "I am come to prostrate my neck and all the glory of my flesh to the wrath and malice of men, knowing . . . that all men must be done away . . . for flesh must be consummed that we might live in the spirit" (p. A2a). Poole hoped the army might be that scourging rod for sinful England and noted, "The manner of the cure of the land which I received by faith, and was often to declare to the army was that they must set themselves as in the presence of the Lord, to act for her cure, according to the rule of the gift of faith." It was this highly charged faith in the army that probably led to Cromwell and Henry Ireton's rather intense interest in her.[15] On the other hand, Poole feared that executing Charles might antagonize God. "Bring him to his trial that he may be convicted in his conscience," she warned in *A Vision* (1648), "but touch not his person" (p. 6).

By the time Charles I was executed, and Lilly's influence on other prognosticators and publishers was most widespread, it certainly made sense to consider Cromwell the Chicken of the Eagle. The anonymous pamphlet *The Lord Merlin's Prophecy Concerning the King of Scots* (1651) emphasized that Charles I would be England's last king. According to Merlin, "In 1666 there will be no king here or pretending to the Crown of England. . . . So Merlin's the ancient prophecy saith, that his seed shall become fatherless in a strange land for evermore" (p. 4). Charles II, therefore, could not be the Chicken of the Eagle. When Merlin said the Chicken of the Eagle "'shall build his nest in the chiefest rock of all Britain,' it imports no more but that, like a fowl, or as a man chased from one place to another, so shall his worldly condition be in this world" (p. 2).

This pamphlet also introduced the *Prophecy of the Scottish Sybill.* Through a series of calculations, Sybill predicted that 1649 would be the last year of the monarchy in England. Similarly, the *Prophecy of David Upan* indicated that "the son of Ann crowned, ends our prophecies" and noted, "King Charles his mother was Ann, sister to the King of Denmark, late deceased" (p. 3). It also cited Nostradamus: "The Senate or Parliament of London shall put to death their king," and "When one named Charles shall be king of the English, he shall be the last King of the Britains" (p. 3).[16] The compiler of these ancient prophecies concluded in a manner that seemed wise in light of the day's politics: "We have examined the prophecies of both the Scottish, Welsh and English prophets and from their writings have discovered that there are no more kings to be expected to reign in England" (p. 9). For the moment, it seemed impossible to consider any member of the Stuart family able to sustain the weight of ancient prophecy. Prophecy was, after all, a sign of God's love of the present order, and certainly Cromwell, and not Charles II, was the man of the hour.

Despite Cromwell's inability to create a stable system of governance, prophecies continued to envision him as the Chicken of the Eagle who saved England from the White King and the Dreadful Deadman. Anna Trapnel's highly spiritual visions, for instance, provided comfort to the Lord Protector during bad times. In her *Newes from Whitehall* (1654) Trapnel wrote of herself in the third person as having a "vision she had two nights before the Lord Protector was proclaimed at which time she saw a glorious Throne with winged angles flying before the throne and crying 'Holy, Holy, Holy Unto the Lord. The great one is coming down with terror to his enemies'" (p. 5).

As late as 1657, the consensus within the community of prophetic interpreters was that astrology and the course of the conflict against the Stuarts were related and that the revolution had been a divine event. In that year Thomas Pugh, Gentleman, did yeoman's work for the commonwealth and the scholar alike. His mammoth compilation of prophecies, *British and Outlandish Prophecies,* is almost 200 pages long and includes virtually every prophecy that had been cited during the interregnum. Indeed, the table of contents at the end of the volume covers nine pages. At the outset of the volume Pugh presented a question-and-answer synopsis of all the prophecies for the reader's convenience. Some of the prophetic truths Pugh advance were: the executed king would be the last king in England; his son will not rule in England; the church will be brought back to its primitive purity; and the Roman Church will fall to the ground through the efforts of the Great Turk.

At the very end of the volume, in a section entitled "Furtherance to the Scope of Prophecies," Pugh summed up the essence of the prophetic tradition created by Lilly. "You make take notice of two wonderful observations," he began. "First, that all the kings and kingdoms of the world are terribly threatened and fore-warned . . . [are] wholly to be subdued and conquered" (p. 180). This was standard Lilly. Second, all these prophecies, with unanimous voice and harmonious consent cry out a Conqueror or Reformer . . . to be the Instrument or instrumental cause of subduing and conquering of most of the kingdoms of the world" (p. 182). In short, the revolution would spread its wings, and because God was on the side of change, "the plots combinations and confederacies shall not prevail against the decree and ordinance of heaven."

However these ancient writings might be interpreted by Lilly and others to demonstrate that God stood behind the revolution, Parliament, and the Lord Protector, other heavenly manifestations all pointed toward less sanguine conclusions. The prophetic voice of the past not withstanding, celestial apparitions, prodigious prodigies, monstrous births, and yet other miracles all indicated that God was very angry with England. These could not be dismissed easily when it was Lilly's own *Supernatural Sights and Apparitions Seen in London June 3 1644* (1644) that persuasively argued that celestial occurrences and other prodigies were indications of God's will. Then, too, there were also royalist prophecies during the interregnum, which will be treated in chapter 11. Though the king had been beaten and beaten yet again, it was difficult but not impossible to argue that God remained on Charles's side or, after his execution, on the side of Charles II, perhaps the true Chicken of the Eagle. Indeed, despite the poverty of Stuart fortunes, this assessment made a great deal of sense for many people who believed they were witnessing the general deterioration of society. "By their fruits shall you know them," Scripture states, and Parliament's rule was a disaster. How else could one explain such new problems as rampant sectarianism, the appearance of religious charlatans, and, of course, the sudden emergence of witches, not to speak of prostitutes and highwaymen? There was no explanation for these problems, unless God had loved Charles all along, always opposed Parliament, and now hated England.

In the end, Englishmen would be hard-pressed to determine which set of heavenly activities, prodigies, and apparitions or astrology and prophecies best represented God's assessment of the revolution. In the meantime, the civil wars dragged on and everything was getting worse.

Part II
Religion in Fallen England

Bloody Newes from Dover.

BEING
A True
RELATION
OF

The great and bloudy Murder, committed by *Mary Cham-pion* (an Anabaptift) who cut off her Childs head, being 7. weekes old, and held it to her husband to baptize. Alfo a-nother great murder committed in the North, by a Scot-tifh Commander, for which Fact he was executed.

Printed in the Yeare of Difcovery, *Feb,* 13. 1647: *1646*

◆ ◆ ◆

5

The Sectarian Cancer

"Rattle-Heads, a company of shallow-pated hair-brained
shittle-witted coxcombes [*sic*] that neither regard law nor religion.
They regard nothing but to make mischief, build castles in the air,
hatch stratagems, invent projects and do mischief with dexterity."

—*Religion's Lottery, or, The Church's Amazement (1642)*

The execution of the king was the most dramatic event of the English
Revolution, but the dismantling of the Church of England was almost
as important in the life of the average Englishman. Both events had
unfortunate consequences. Charles was executed to end tyranny,
but his death introduced more than a decade of hapless and ineffective
politics. Similarly, the dismantling of Anglicanism introduced a period of
religious anarchy characterized by the growth of sectarianism. Scripture
warned that false prophets would proliferate before the end of days, and
many of these sects actually claimed to be heralds of the apocalypse.
Sectarianism, then, like the obvious political anarchy, seemed just one
more sign that God was angry with England.

Students of the English civil war are well aware of the mushroomlike
proliferation of religious sects during the interregnum.[1] Indeed, from the
Anglican perspective, other than the execution of the king and his high
church leadership, nothing was more shocking, outrageous, or frightening than the fragmentation of organized religion. Presbyterians, in large
part responsible for initially dismantling the Church of England, also
soon came to fear the sectarian monster let loose upon the land. Ephraim
Paggitt's flabbergasted prose against England's teeming heresies and
Thomas Edwards, whose rambling compendium of sectarian evil bore
the colorful title *Gangreana,* both reflected the common view that the
cancerous growth of the sects was largely the devil's doing.[2]

A list of these sects would include, among others, Baptists, Brownists and Barrowists, Grindletonians and Socinians, Seekers and Squatters, Diggers and Behmenists, Ranters and Muggletonians, Independents, Familists and Quakers, Antinomians, Anabaptists, Levellers, the Fifth Monarchists, and, of course, the Blackloists. One might also include the Arminians, Apostles, and Adamites, and still wonder whether the Proud Quakers merited a separate category. One should not exclude the Shakers, though they might be included as part of the Ranters, and there were several different types of Sabbatarians. These best known groups had still other rivals, many of whose histories have been largely lost. In fact, a complete roster of mid-seventeenth-century sectarian groups would list hundreds of names. Even this would not do justice to the plethora of sectarian expression; local congregational churches constituted yet another entire universe of separatist religious organization. Scholars have studied their religious treatises, tracts, and polemics, tracing the intellectual origins and conceptual progress and change within the Baptists, Quakers, Ranters, Muggletonians, Fifth Monarchists, and many others. The purpose of this chapter, however, is to discover how ordinary, confused Englishmen understood this unprecedented social development. Hence, rather than describing sects from an ecclesiastical viewpoint, or by analyzing their various tenets and beliefs, I will look instead at this phenomena as many contemporaries did, from the same mental perspective that postulated the importance of prodigies, monsters, apparitions, and other portents heralding God's anger.

There is no doubt that the majority of seventeenth-century Englishmen were shocked by the seemingly sudden growth of sectarianism. Sophisticated urban observers may have appreciated that many scandalous accounts of strange sects were written tongue-in-cheek. Rural townsfolk, however, must have been astonished to read about the number and diversity of churches and sects in London. The pamphlet *The Mathematical Divine* (1642) expressed the mood of consternation. It asked, "Who can number . . . the numerous kinds of most pestilent Anabaptists, Brownists and Barrowists . . . and other sects of innovators and nugators [*sic*]?" (p. 4). Wherever one turned one found more religious sects. There were, according to *The Mathematical Divine,* "more sects by one and a half be risen these last years than in the whole Christian world from the time of the apostles for sixteen hundred years." Even worse, "I hear they increase daily into so great a number," and our author worried about "many thousands of schismatics and heretics, perhaps more tomorrow" (p. 4).

Whatever their number, these sects were an insult to God. *The Mathematical Divine* claimed "that honor of the clergy and sacred order is decayed. The preachers of the holy Gospel . . . are by everyone vilified and made a scorn while mechanics thundering and lightening from the holy tribunal of religion (the pulpit) are worshiped of blocking people" (p. 3). Even worse, these "armies of unbridled heretics persecute our native Protestants . . . under the feigned veil of devotion, with a most hostile heart, are more and more multiplied" (p. 3). Even a decade later, in 1653, this same sense of shock was still evident among those devoted to the old church. For instance, a five-page poem entitled *A New Proclamation* (1653) warned:

> O Land! How doth thy Church to ruin run,
> By schisms broken and sects undone!
> O how they swarm! No age could ever tell
> A brood too monstrous for their parallel. (p. 3)

And the poem continued: "O Woeful England! Whoever thought to see/ Such wretches born and monsters bred in thee!" Rather than conceiving of free religious expression as a positive development on the path to religious toleration, the author believed this "monstrous" condition must inevitably result in England's downfall.

Conservative Englishmen believed that the Church of England embodied the essence of the ancient Christian religious tradition and served as a civilizing influence. From this perspective, "mechanic preachers" and "enthusiasm" were the hallmarks of all that was wrong with Puritanism and the revolution. This was the mood of John Taylor's twenty-two page poem, *A Swarm of Sectaries and Schismatiques* (1641), which expressed his dismay at what he perceived as a Puritan rejection of the civilizing influence of orthodox Christian tradition. In one verse he described the Puritans as "mongrel whelps of hell's infernal litter" (p. 7) who

> . . . join together to consume and burn
> And with confusion waste and overturn
> All ancient order, rule and decency
> And doctrine from the prime antiquity. (p. 18)

According to Taylor, Puritans mocked as carnal, worldly, or devilish any idea they themselves did not accept. Yet in constructing their own religious systems, they turned Scripture into "a nose of wax." "All human knowledge therefore they detest," Taylor wrote. "The unlearned (they say) do know the Scriptures best" (p. 18).

Taylor also believed that Puritans were equally opportunistic in the area of personal morality, and he shared the common view that they hid lecherous behavior beneath a pious exterior of spiritual enthusiasm. He told about

> One Sidrach Cave made baskets late in Elie,
> A constant brother, [he] raised up his maid's belly;
> ... And Cave's wife took the wrong most patiently
> For which the Brethren praised her sanctity.
> ... He said it was not he that did that vile deed,
> But sin that dwelt in him that fault did breed. (p. 5)

When Puritans did not indulge in spiritual hypocrisy, they indulged in outright moral turpitude. He wrote about a group that

> At the Nag's Head, near to Coleman Street
> A most pure crew of Brethren did meet,
> Where their devotion was so strong and ample,
> To turn a sinful tavern into a temple. (p. 8)

Degradation was the sum total of Puritan piety. Taylor's last couplet concluded, "'Tis madness that a crew of brainless blocks/ Dares teach the learned what is orthodox."

Neither Taylor nor other Anglican pamphleteers differentiated between the varieties of Puritan sectarianism; all of them were equally devilish. Hence on the title page, the author of the newsbook *A Discovery of Twenty Nine Sects Here in London* (1641) condemned all sects outright as "most devilish and damnable" and wrote in the opening letter to his readers, "This I have undertaken that the good might see and hate the wicked" (p. 2). The sensational title probably attracted the attention of conservative Londoners, who, no doubt, were shocked and alarmed by the appearance of so many different sects, the descriptions of which can inadvertently leave the modern reader giggling. He noted that "the Persian Sect [evidently Zoroastrians] hath as much religion as a beast and no more for they bow in adoration to the rising sun and I have read as much that elephants adore the moon" (p. 6). Antinomians were "law breakers, men that will live after their own laws. Nay, they will not [even] yield that any one of their own sect shall command another" (p. 6).

A common accusation against sects concerned their alleged illicit sexual activity. The Adamites were "a shameless sect, they ground their religion from our father Adam (and yet they go naked when they hear prayers or prophesying) when he hid himself from the presence of God because he was naked" (p. 4). The Familists were also loose-livers: "Here's a loving sect presented to you. They think that a man may gain salvation by showing himself loving, especially to his neighbor's wife. By their law it is allowed for one man to lie with another man's wife while he sleepeth" (p. 4). Then there were the equally detestable "Assyrians," about whom our author confided, "Syrus [sic] of Syria in Chalcides was the first that ever brought up this sect. He, being in love with a maid, knew not how to enjoy her company without the invention of the conventicle, where there is no talk but must savor of love" (p. 6).

More familiar sects were described no more accurately. Socinians, we are told, follow "Socinus, the wrangling disputant, [who] was the father of this sect. They hold no true point at all with the Protestant but wrangle in every article" (p. 5). Even orthodox non-Anglican Christianity came in for heavy criticism. Indeed, Anglican observers found established non-Anglican churches as troubling as the promiscuous sectarians. The Catholic "is ashamed to pray to God himself because his prayers are so full of idolatry but he must have saints to intercede for him" (p. 3). Luther was a semipapist, "a great recusant till it pleased God to enlighten his eyes and [he] fled hither into England for religion's sake" (p. 3). Calvin was not a papist, but his "opinion was as far distant one way as the papist in the other" (p. 3). And, most obnoxious of all, the Puritan, we are told, "is one which is fluttered from the cage of Amsterdam, striving to poison, as near as he can, the truth with his true-lies [sic]" (p. 2). Taken together, the sects "are as whoring rogues as ever breathed" (p. 8).

The vitriol of these pamphlets indicate that popular fear of sectarianism was undiminished over the years. Despite the prevalence of orthodox Puritan congregationalism, "outrageous sectarianism" remained the butt of pamphlet humor and horror. Yet the members of this category changed as one group after another gained some measure of respectability and wished to disassociate themselves from the remainder of the sectarian rabble. Upstanding Presbyterians might have vehemently opposed the Church of England, but they would certainly have taken offense at being considered radical troublemakers or Adamite libertines. Similarly, Independents to the left of Presbyterians opposed "Presbyterian tyranny" but found their own identification with more extreme Baptists and Anabaptists very distasteful. One defensive Independent chapbook, for instance, noted that an Anglican minister was instantly killed by God because he confused congregationalists with Baptists. In turn, Baptists were horrified at being lumped with Familists and Quakers, who were equally shocked at being confused with Ranters. Hence, as the variety of sects found printers willing to publish their radical religious and political ideas, the press also published scandalous accounts describing each sect's views of all the others even more radical than it. The result was a cacophonous circus of charge and countercharge, of polemic and counterpolemic in which each sect described its more radical opponents as truly dangerous and absurd and their more conservative foes as papists and toadies but defended their own purity and integrity.

Studying the writings of this disharmonious orchestra is something of a problem. The literature is plentiful and squabbling, but, like subsequent socialist sectarian disputes, the writings often expressed intense sectarian internecine warfare. *A Strange Apparition in an Ale-house* (1641) described a heated debate between two Puritans. One defended certain Puritan leaders while the other believed that they should have their ears cropped, "whereupon in an instant he began to sweat and to be faint and taking out his handkerchief to wipe his face and his head, a strange judgment fell upon him. His ears fell a-bleeding and thereby his handkerchief was all bloody." The moral of the story was obvious: "Let everyone beware how they curse God's people . . . and his distressed saints" (p. 3).

Because Presbyterians had been the butt of Anglican anger and the first to organize against the Church of England, they were the first to gain full respectability and to take offense at being considered radical hooligans. Indeed, political power enabled them to replace Anglicans as the defenders of conservative tradition against a continuing tide of revolutionary radicalism.

Yesterday's Presbyterian malcontents were now members of a respectable religion. A good example of this changed Puritan attitude appeared in *Religion's Lottery, or, The Church's Amazement* (1642). The author of this Presbyterian pamphlet explained why his type of Puritan was no ragtag hooligan, like Baptists and all the others. In fact, "The Puritan is the most commendable of all the rest for he would have a religion for which he hath a precedent, to wit, the Kirk of Scotland. To which opinion . . . in the fundamentals we do perfectly agree" (p. A4b). In short, Presbyterians were no Adamite sectarians opposed to the tithe and hellbent upon the destruction of the realm, as every Anglican pamphleteer had incorrectly observed, but fine establishment-types seeking to clone the legitimate Church of Scotland in England. Indeed, the purpose of this chapbook was to attack every other more radical sect and "declare how many sorts of religions there is crept into the very bowels of this kingdom, striving to shake the whole foundation and destroy both church and kingdom" (title page). More radical groups were a thorn in the Presbyterian side, much as the latter had previously been a thorn in the side of the yet more conservative Church of England. Independents, on the other hand, were of particular concern and were all "Round Heads" and "the chief ring leaders to all tumultuous disorders . . . and they will allow no doctrine for good nor no minister a quiet audience" (p. A4b). Allied to the above were the Rattle-Heads, "a company of shallow-pated hair-brained shittle-witted coxcombes [sic] that neither regard law nor religion. They regard nothing but to make mischief, build castles in the air, hatch stratagems, invent projects and do mischief with dexterity."

Religion's Lottery also attacked Papists, Atheists, Arians, and Arminians, as might any supporter of undiluted orthodox, Council of Dort, double-supralapsarian, predestinarian, Calvinist Presbyterianism.[3] All Christian truth, including lists of those going to heaven and to hell, had been determined by God before creation. Proof of God's eternal love of Presbyterianism lay in the incontrovertible fact that the revolution succeeded in removing the bishops and other papist trappings and left Presbyterianism in power. As such, they were God's own chosen spokesmen for all that was right and good. Opposition to them was in and of itself proof of blasphemy.

From the perspective of Religion's Lottery, all dissenters more radical than Presbyterianism were as immoral as they were blasphemous. Without supervision, they "would be mere libertines and live as they list . . . they are so overcome with the flesh that they can not pray" (p. A2b). They "would have no bishop nor governors in the church." Even worse, they would have "all things in common, as wife, children, goods etc." (p. A3a). Clearly, the lot of the besieged Presbyterian was difficult since even within his own kirk there were dangerous tendencies that gave cause for alarm. There were Novolists, or "those that change their opinions oftener than the fashion . . . they are never constant in one thing but always wavering like a reed shaken with the wind" (p. A3b). No better were the Time-Servers, who "are always of the strongest side . . . they are like Virgin's wax, capable of any impression . . . they are of all religions or, as I may justly say, of no religion."

Anabaptists were a good example of the dangers inherent in sects. According to pamphleteers, Anabaptist mothers caused their children to be born without heads. Moreover, as Bloody News From Dover (1646) added, they murdered as well as blasphemed. It seems that in the city of Dover John Champion and his wife had a new baby that Mr. Champion wished to have baptized "according to the ancient custom of the kingdom." Unfortunately, Mrs. Champion "would by no means condescend to it" (p. 2). This conflict could only have a bad end, for "where division and controversy doth arise, sad effects suddenly follow" (p. 4). In this specific case, "on a day when her husband was abroad, [she] took a great knife and cut off the child's head" (p. 3). When Champion came home, his wife said, "Behold husband, thy sweet babe without a head. Now go baptize it."

Anabaptism was apparently so pernicious that it could even drive otherwise normal males to commit murder. As an example, the reader might consider the news story entitled *The Arraignment, Trial, Conviction and Confession of Francis Deane* (1643). Francis Deane and Mr. Daniel had been drinking together in Elbow Lane for most of a day when Mr. Daniel confessed that "he had many feelings out about this Deane's sister who was a rich widow whom the said Daniel bare affection unto." Deane was evidently very annoyed by something Daniel said about his sister because "this Deane, upon his confession, did give the said Daniel a fierce blow on the head with a pole-axe that he instantly died in the place" (p. 1).

The reader with no additional information might assume that Mr. Daniel was another casualty of alcohol, that he may have said something salacious about Deane's sister, or that Deane was just overly protective of her. Surely murders have been committed for all these reasons. But when Deane was about to be executed on April 17 at Tyburn "and having the rope tied about his neck and the hangman beginning to fasten it to the tree, Deane, standing up in the cart said: 'Gentleman, here I come to lose my life and now let me give you some satisfaction to quiet and satisfy my own mind, it being the last time that ever I shall speak in this world'" (p. 2). It is not surprising that with the rope above and hell below, Deane desired to acknowledge the true cause of his drinking buddy's death. "I confess I was baptized (anew) a month before the act was acted, and after and for which I was grieved in mind and much troubled about it," he explained. "I do heartily pray all here present may take this warning by my death and that they suffer no final sins to enter for they will beget bigger [sins] as this in me hath done" (p. 2). Considering how easily one might descend from Anabaptism to murder, Deane's sincerity and concern for the living were very touching, especially his admonition that "these and such like heretical actions might be a great means to move the honorable House of Parliament to proceed in a parliamentary way for the putting down of all sectaries whatsoever." This, of course, was precisely what many Presbyterians had in mind. Still, the lot of the Presbyterian was difficult. What with blaspheming radicals in public houses and in the army and malignant papist abominations in Parliament and hiding in manor houses and with the fickle of spirit within and those with noses for power everywhere, it was fortunate that God had already predestined him, and his friends, to authority and prosperity. Surely otherwise all would be lost.

It must have been bitter indeed for those who had rebelled against the Church of England to find themselves now with as few resources in their own battle against more radical sects as the old church had had against them. But given the balance of power between the army and Parliament and growing popular resistance to Presbyterian rigidity, there was little the Presbyterians could do but to pass ordinances and try to arouse the ire of the population against sectarianism much as the good Anglican John Taylor and others had tried to oppose Presbyterianism just a few years earlier. The single-sheet broadside *A Catalogue of the Several Sects and Opinions* (1647) notes that "many strange sects and opinions are held amongst us so that it is to be feared that what rule so ever our wise and honorable Parliament shall establish, it will not content the unquiet spirits of a lawless generation which would have no rule." The very worst sectarians were the Antinomians, who "out of conscience . . . are ruled by the spirit and despise all . . . ministry, all written prayer, all helps of study." Antinomians also dared their followers to "sin, if thou can, meaning, that regenerate men can not sin." Sects with social programs were the most troubling for they "look for a temporal kingdom of Christ that shall last a thousand years. This opinion is most dangerous for all states for they teach that all the ungodly must be killed and that the wicked have no propriety in their estates." In short, it was believed that the radical sects would overturn the government and take all property in the name of God (which is, in fact, what the Presbyterian Parliament had done to the Church of England and the monarchy). Hence, it seemed reasonable to wonder "should these absurd and gross opinions take place, what division and confusion would they work among us?" Action must be taken and "such is the wisdom and care of our worthy and pious Parliament to provide an ordinance for preventing of the growing and spreading of heresy."

Parliamentary action was the theme of *Hell Broke Loose,* published on March 9, 1647, to commemorate the special parliamentary antisectarian holiday set for the next day. The pamphlet records that on February 4 of that year, Parliament had declared, "We the Lords and Commons do order and ordain that Wednesday being the 10th day of March next be set apart for a day of public humiliation for the growth and spreading of errors, heresies and blasphemies . . . and to seek God for his direction and assistance for the suppression and preventing of the same" (p. 1). The newsbook did not identify individual separatist groups but instead described their despicable ideas, including that the Bible "is but human and not able to discover a divine God" and is no "better terms of assurance than the testimony, common report or authority of men" (pp. 3, 4). Worse yet, they believed that religious institutions were unimportant since "all ordinances as ministry, baptism, etc., that have an end, are carnal ordinances and from the devil" (p. 7). Even worse, neither sin nor punishment was important because "God hath a hand in and is the author of sinfulness of his people" (p. 3). To top everything else, there was no hope for resurrection for "the soul of man is mortal, as is the soul of a beast, and dies with the body" (p. 4).

Of greater immediate concern were sectarian social views. After all, in the end, God would punish blasphemers but in the meantime, righteous Englishman could lose their God-ordained power and property. The conservative Erastian heart was chilled by the radical belief that "the civil magistrate hath no power at all to meddle in matters of religion" (p. 6) and was shocked by the assertion that "[free] worship be granted to all men in all nations and countries" (p. 3). But if toleration and free religion were distasteful and frightening, democracy was even more so, and the author was alarmed that Lawrence Clarkson, here identified as "leader of the Rant,"[4] believed that "trustees, representatives, chosen ones . . . may go no further in anything, nor sit no longer, nor dispose of anything but according to their commission and power received from the represented" (p. 7). Even worse, "the king, Parliament, etc., are their own mere creatures to be accountable to them and disposed of and by them at their pleasure. The people may recall and reassume their power, question them, and set others in their place" (p. 7). The title page summed it up best when the author called March 10 "day of trouble, and of rebuke and of blasphemy."

Radicalism among the urban poor was intolerable, but extremism in the army was frightening both to erstwhile royalists as well as to parliamentary conservatives. Worse yet, the army leadership in the late 1640s was increasingly independent of conservative parliamentary authority. Indeed, junior-level army officers debated Scripturally-based radical political programs for the governance of the new commonwealth. As a result, Presbyterian fears of religious dissension in the army, upon which they were still so dependent, grew. In 1647 a shocked Presbyterian pamphleteer reported that "a company of soldiers in derision of baptism, baptized a horse, [and] having pissed in the font, sprinkled it on the horse and crossed him on the forehead and named him Ball-Esau because he was hairy." His broadside, *A Discovery of the Most Dangerous and Damnable Tenets That Have Been Spread Within This Few Years* (1647), listed forty-nine heretical and blasphemous beliefs found among army sects that, the subtitle tells us, had been spread "by many erroneous, heretical and mechanic spirits." Among the horrible ideas advanced by these radicals were that Scripture is a human document with little spiritual content (items 5-8); that adultery and drunkenness were permissible (item 9); religious toleration (item 19); that God was the author of sin and that believers were incapable of sin (item 21); there was no physical resurrection (item 23); that heaven and hell were states of mind (item 28); and that prayer, ritual and church institutions were evil and of the devil (items 45-47). Many items described what the pamphlet press would come to identify as typical Ranter positions.

To stop the increasingly radical drift in the army a very unhappy Presbyterian wrote *Take Warning Before It Be Too Late ... to Take Heed of Sectaries* in 1648. On the very first page he warned, "I would advise you to disarm all those sectaries amongst you . . . for if you do not, you shall find them ready to cut all your throats." The alarmed author asked, "Have you not a sense already of it? Did you not see yourselves in danger every day to be hanged at your own door? Were you not threatened by officers in the army and members in the Houses?" (p. 7). Should the Parliament take no action, "you [will be] hanged at your doors, your wife's belly ripped up, your children's brains dashed against the wall." To avoid this terrible fate, the author prescribed the following actions: "First, that you put out of office all sectaries . . . Second, that you disarm them." His third point indicated his level of fear of army radicalism. "Next," the author advises, "fetch home the king, treat with him yourselves for your privileges and rights and get . . . religion settled" (pp. 6-7). But if Parliament brought Charles home, the Church of England would not have been far behind.

Despite Presbyterian discomfort and Parliament's displeasure, sects continued to grow in the civilian population as well as in the army. Indeed, by 1648, the sectarian thicket was far denser than even five years earlier. The frightening connection between religious and political ideas was also increasingly evident. Both Presbyterianism and radical sectarians used the Bible very selectively to justify their goals and the means to get there while attacking all other views on the same passages. But authors and readers alike may have become either more sophisticated or more curious about the diversity within sectarian ranks, because later antisectarian pamphlets were more comprehensive. An example of this newer literature, which attempted to explain what radicals actually believed, is *A True and Perfect Picture of Our Present Reformation* (1648). This pamphlet attempted to present the general penny-book reader with "the Christian's perspective, to take a short view of the New Lights that have broke forth since the Bishops went down" (title page). Despite its short length (only eighteen pages), the author itemized over 200 articles of radical belief spanning 17 categories such as scripture, God, free will, sacraments, prayer, marriage, and the like. While many of these ideas were also cited in earlier chapbooks, such as item 6, which noted that "the writings of Moses, Prophets, Christ, Apostles . . . are allegories"(p. 1) or, "that it is as lawful to baptize a cat, dog, chicken, as an infant" (p. 12), the author also included ideas from traditional and therefore more legitimate radical orientations. The section on antitrinitarian views, items 31 through 37 (p. 3), presented the ideas of the early-sixteenth-century radical Michael Servetus.[5] Other ideas concerned sabbatarianism (p. 14), polygamy and sectarian willingness to accept woman preachers (p. 16). All told, this pamphlet provided the most comprehensive short guide published during these years. It was a sign of the times that Independent churches were no longer included among the heretics.

Pamphlets not only reflected the growing popular awareness of sectarian diversity, but they also accorded increasing recognition to the importance of Antinomianism as the spiritual engine of truly radical sectarianism. In fact, Ranters, Quakers, Muggletonians, and Seekers all had strong Antinomian Familist origins.[6] Also, Antinomians were surely the most vulnerable to popular mythology. Those who would scrap Scripture and conventional moral guidelines in favor of the vagaries of the ethereal spirit have always been condemned by orthodox institutional religion. Indeed, the seventeenth-century crusade against Antinomianism was but the latest effort in a timeless campaign against religious enthusiasm. Montanus and other spiritualists in the ancient church were castigated for making the holy spirit a dynamic and living element within the believer rather than a static personality within the Godhead.[7] After the Albigensian-Cathari schism in southern France, Dominicans and other professional heresy hunters continually paraded before the public mind the image of the licentious Adamite or the Brethren of the Free Spirit as the incarnation of the "dangerous libertine" unrestrained by law or God.[8] Though some Adamite-like groups existed during the fifteenth-century Taborite rebellion, and some illusive Free Spirit voices attracted sporadic attention as well, the Adamite myth was largely the product of a morbid medieval Inquisitorial mentality that distrusted religious individualism and believed seditious spiritualists were lurking in every Franciscan house. Alumbrados were another matter, and fifteenth- and sixteenth-century Spain seemed awash with strange *dejamiento* illuminist fanatics.[9]

During the early years of the Reformation, Catholic polemicists condemned orthodox Protestantism for opening the doorway to libertinism. The latter then accused other radicals of being morally depraved spiritualists.[10] Hence, by the seventeenth century the composite Adamite-Familist-Spiritualist-Libertine stereotype was well established in the public mind. Taken together, the pamphlets published during these years attempted to tar all sects with the image of the dangerous libertine. As an example, *A Nest Of Serpents Discovered . . . Called Adamites* (1641) noted in alarm that this sect "of late sprung up in this Nation to the wonderment of all that hear of it" (p. 2). There was some confusion in the author's mind about the sect's history, and he is not sure who "Adam" actually was. On page 2 he noted that there was "one called Adam the Patriarch," but on the next page he observed that "by the subtlety of the devil it was again set up by one called Adam Pastor . . . from whom they that were his disciples were called Adamites" (p. 3). More recently, "they had their main champion in one Pickardus" (p. 4), and before infecting England, Adamites were in Holland, the fount of all heresy. "In the year 1535, there was a knot of them gathered at Amsterdam . . . They climbed naked to the tops of trees and there would sit naked expecting bread from heaven" (p. 5). In fact, Adam Pastor was a sixteenth-century antitrinitarian with no Adamite sympathies at all.[11] Pickardus was not a person but a reference to Picardy, the alleged center of earlier Bogomil dualism and Free Spirit activity.[12] Indeed, "Pickard" may have been the origin of the more familiar Free Spirit appellation "beghard."

Other than waiting for manna in trees, Adamites were alleged to be involved in other forms of nude activity. "They hear their lectures naked, pray naked, receive the sacrament naked" (p. 5), and even more, "they had wont usually to meet in hot houses or stoves or in such places where they might have the convenience of artificial heat to set their natural heat on fire. They put off their clothes at their entrance . . . sit all naked, mixed as they entered, men and women" (p. 4). Consequently, it surprised no one that they "allowed promiscuous copulation, any man with any woman whom he liked best" (p. 4). When the author concluded that "at their discovery more shall be written" and that "they will be caught in the midst of their lewd and abominable exercise which is so scandalous, blasphemous and abominable" (p. 6), it is clear that none had been apprehended and that the author's fund of information was more folklore than fact or that the author was engaged in propaganda.

Unlike the mythical Adamites, Familists did exist but pamphlet descriptions relied more heavily on imagination than fact in viewing them as evil libertines. Indeed, there is no evidence to suggest that Henry Niclaes or his followers were anything but the most ascetic—and dull—of spiritualists. One newsbook of 1641, entitled *The Plot Discovered and Counter Plotted,* was typical in its perception of the libertine threat to the commonwealth: "The libertines, such as I understand, to be the swearer, drunkard, whore-master, profaner of the Sabbath, scorner and despiser of others, following no calling but their sinful lusts, harsh and cruel in their dealings as though God had granted them a charter to do what they list" (p. 10). Neither the plot nor the counterplot referred to in the title were ever clarified, yet it was a standard of orthodox myth that radicals always sought the overthrow of civil society. In short, the seventeenth-century Familist was a composite of all morally offensive human qualities. *A Description of a Sect Called Family of Love* (1641) linked Familism with personal and social disorder. It purported to present an unbiased account of Mistress Susan Snow of Surry, "who was vainly led away for a time through their [i. e. Familists] base allurements and at length fell mad till by a great miracle shown from God, she was delivered."

A gentleman named Snow had a wonderful and dutiful daughter named Susan in whom the devil sought to "subvert and eradicate this well planted virtue" (p. 1). One day, as Susan conversed with her father's workmen about the profusion of sects then appearing, a gardener mentioned a large meeting of Familists in a forest not six miles away. Excited and unable to sleep that night, Susan rose early the next morning, saddled a horse, and "vowing not to return till she had seen some of their behavior" (p. 2), set out to find some Familists. When she arrived at Bagshot, Susan found the Familists congregating in Birchwood Forest, where their spiritual leader first recited sexual poetry by Ovid and Virgil and then presided over a dinner of "exceeding delicacies" (p. 3). He next succeeded in seducing Susan, who stayed in the forest for one week.

Susan eventually found her way home and lied to her father concerning her whereabouts of the previous week. It was soon obvious to all, however, that Susan was a very changed person. She became increasingly melancholy and would stay by herself sulking for days at a time. Susan also became so unruly that "she would break glasses and earthenware and throw anything at the heads of the servants, and was incontinent till she fell stark mad" (p. 4). Seeing his daughter in so poor a state, Mr. Snow called for Master Yoder, "a very honest man and a most reverend divine living in Oxford" (p. 4). When Master Yoder came to interview

Susan she screamed, "'The Devil, the Devil, I am damned, I am damned, I am damned,' with many such like horrible exclamations" (p. 5). After further discussion Master Yoder called for wine, but Susan, still under the influence of the devil, threw the glass at the minister and cried out that she was not a simple material object that she might be so easily fixed. Miraculously, the pieces of the glass came flying back together, and Susan was so overwhelmed by this sign from God that she became sane and was again an obedient daughter to her father and, presumably, no longer smashed her father's property (p. 6).

This account of adolescent moodiness, sexual awakening, and disregard for authority served several functions. The reader was assured that unruly behavior of women came from the devil and that the Familists were the cause of social evil in the world. They were structurally integrated into contemporary life to account for the unfortunate behavior of an otherwise virtuous (that is, prosperous) young lady. In short, the Familist was for this time what the libertine has always been: the source of easy blame for much social discontent.

By the mid-1650s the image of the "Roaring Ranter" replaced that of the Familist as the purveyor of social distress.[13] Indeed, the anti-Ranter press was more extensive than the literature against other sects and may have served as a conservative commonplace by which to condemn the entire revolution. There can be no doubt that the Ranters were the most radical and the most peculiar sect of the Cromwellian interregnum. Coming into prominence in about 1649, the Ranters captivated the English imagination already shocked by libertine sectarianism. The Ranter message was varied, but some general ideas were held by all: Jesus was born a man, suffered the anguish of human life in this material world, and died a saint. His lifetime and death were testimony that every other mortal could overcome the same bounds of physical existence and thereby liberate the entrapped spirit within. Hell was that state of mind when one still lives in the flesh, while terms such as heaven, the New Jerusalem, and the resurrection all described the spiritualized new saint who, like Jesus, suffers in this world and overcomes his physical existence. The saint enjoyed a godlike status of open-ended spirituality and semidivinity and was consequently no longer constrained by moral convention. For the saint, there were neither licit nor illicit forms of behavior, only deeds. Religious institutions were a sham and the only God was only within the self. All governance and property were theft, corruption, and extortion. All social institutions emanated from and fostered class dominance. The Ranters appealed to the lowest strata of English society: the urban poor, the landless rural population, street people, criminals, and prostitutes. In short, where Familists actually were very moral, Ranters actually were not.

Englishmen were of one mind in condemning the Ranters as dangerous libertines, and even Gerrard Winstanley, the leader of the equally maligned and feared Diggers, considered the Ranters an abomination. George Fox fumed about the immorality of those Ranters he met in prison. He observed how they drank, smoked, derided common concepts of God, and, worst of all, "they sang, whistled, and danced."[14] Subsequent authorities have been no more friendly. The 1911 edition of the *Encyclopaedia Britannica* wrote that the Ranters were the dregs of the Seeker movement.[15] Rufus Jones, the otherwise tolerant historian of mystical sectarianism, concluded, "The Ranters got a bad name from everybody who came into contact with them, and there is no question that it was a degenerate movement."[16]

Ranters featured prominently in general catalogues describing radical sects as early as 1648, when *A True and Perfect Picture of Our Present Reformation* was published. This pamphlet described seventeen areas of heresy, but the most striking opinions in each section were those originating from Ranter sources. These included: that God was responsible for sin (p. 2); that God and the devil were one (p. 3); and that hell was a state of mind (p. 10). Most striking of all was the alleged Ranter idea that "if a man be strongly moved to kill, commit adultery etc., and upon praying against it again and again it continue, he should then do it" (p. 18). And furthermore, "that it is lawful to commit adultery or murder as to baptize an infant."

Other pamphlets were even more hostile. *The Ranter's Bible* (1650) divided Ranters into various sects, including Clements, Athians, and Seleutian Donatists, and compared them to proliferating insects (pp. 3-4), which must have raised the specter of unseen Ranters infecting all of England with their pernicious error.

Another pamphleteer J. F., in *A New Proclamation* (1653) observed about the Ranter:

> He's one that would all civil right destroy
> and turn all to a strange community.
> With each man's interest he'll have to do,
> his goods, wife, his maid and daughter too! (p. 5)

In short, "No God, no good, no sin, no hell, no bliss / O Tremble heaven and hell and earth at this!" (p. 7).

Samuel Tilbury's *Bloody News From the North* (1650) included a poem that argued for the continuity between Adamites and Ranters:

> A sect of Ranters of late revived
> Who seem more innocent than ever Adam lived,
> Such as will naked go and think it a sin,
> To wear a garment, they're so hot within,
> With lust, that they all clothing do disdain
> . . . .
> Thus marching naked sisters with a brother
> For want of clothes they cover one another
> In some dark grove thus meet they, where tis fit
> That they the deeds of darkness should commit.
> . . . All must go naked, 'cause they say,
> Truth itself naked goes and so should they. (p. 6)

Ranters were also the worst blasphemers. The pamphlet *Strange News From Newgate and the Old Bailey* (1650) reported the statements of two Ranters, I. Collins and T. Reeve, before court at the Old Bailey on January 20, 1650. We are told that "this Collins, Reeve and others were sitting at table eating a piece of beef, one of them took it in his hand, tearing it asunder, said to the other, 'This is the flesh of Christ, take and eat it.' The other took a cup of ale and threw it into the chimney corner saying, 'This is the blood of Christ' . . . and blowing through two pieces of tobacco pipes, he said that was the breath of God" (pp. 2-3). Subsequent chapbooks repeated these same words and stories, sometimes alleging they were spoken or acted by other Ranter leaders at other times.

The author of *The Ranter's Recantation* (1650) tells us of one Arthingworth who preached to his Ranter flock, "I will do and require you to subscribe unto these ensuing commandments in manner and form as foloweth: (1) That you shall not acknowledge nor yield obedience to any other gods but me. (2) That it is lawful to drink, swear, revel and lay with any woman whatsoever. (3) That there is no sabbath, no heaven, no hell, no resurrection and that soul and body die together" (p. 2). In fact, no Ranter leader was named Arthingworth, although an Elizabethan radical named Arthington had been condemned years earlier.[17] But then this may have demonstrated another well-known truth: that radicals of all ages were part of a continuous Satanic chain of conspiracy stretching over the decades and centuries. Hence, today's Ranter was actually only the latest manifestation of the devil's neverending campaign to pervert Christian society.

The Black and Terrible Warning Piece (1653) also pointed out many dangerous ideas espoused by Ranters "who hold themselves to be above ordinances and that they have walked through all dispensations, denying the sacred Scriptures, the Resurrection of the saints, and like the sons of perdition condemn all gospel promises and Christian privileges, saying there is no God, no devil, no heaven, no hell, and that the soul is mortal" (p. 1). Similarly, *Hell Broke Loose* (1646) condemned views clearly associated with the Ranters: that Scripture "is but human and not able to discover a divine God" (p. 3); that "the called of God have no sin in their consciences" (p. 4); the permissibility, indeed, desirability of adultery (p. 5); and "that all ordinances as ministry, baptism etc., that have a given end are carnal ordinances and from the devil" (p. 7).

No less outrageous were alleged Ranter practices. *The Routing of the Ranters* (1650), for instance, claimed to be "a full relation of their uncivil carriages and blasphemous words and actions at their made meetings" (title page) and charged that Ranters "delight not only in gluttony and drunkenness, chambering and wantonness and the like, but deride the Holy Scriptures, deny Christ, and blaspheming, and, as it were, spit in the face of God himself" (p. 2). The very worst offender was the London Ranter Abiezer Coppe,[18] "being lately brought before a committee to be examined, feigned himself mad, used strange kinds of uncouth behavior, throwing nutshells and other things about the room and talked to himself when questions were put to him" (p. 2). When asked "what he thought of the devil, he [Coppe] answered that it was an old woman stuffed with parsley" (p. 2).

Ranters were also very sexually promiscuous. The author of *The Routing of the Ranters* remembered how "a competent number of them were gotten together, they began to sing filthy bawdy songs to the tune of David's Psalms, after which they drank a health ... this being over, one of them lets fall his breeches and turning his shirt aside another of the company runs and kisses, saying they must all do the like" (p. 4). In another instance, "the meeting began about four of the clock in the afternoon and was continued by some until nine or ten of the clock of the next day, which time was spent in drunkenness, uncleanness, blasphemous words, filthy songs and mixed dances of men and women stark naked" (p. 2).

The Ranter's Religion (1650) informed readers that Ranters "affirm that God is so far away from being offended at the crying sins of drunkenness, swearing, blasphemy, adultery etc., that he is well pleased therewith and that (O Strange and Horrid Impiety!) it is the only way to serve him aright" (p. 4). The Ranter sexual ethic was "that all women ought to be in common and when they are assembled together (this is a known truth!) they first entertain one another, the men those of their own sex and the woman their fellow females, with horrid oaths and execrations, then they fall to boozing and drink deep healths . . . then being full heated with liquor . . . they fall to their lascivious embraces with a joint motion" (p. 5).

One striking feature of many stories about Ranter sexuality was the promiscuous role played by women. This was a major theme of *The Ranter's Last Sermon* (1654) "written by JM (a deluded Brother) lately escaped out of their snare" (title page). By way of introduction, JM tells us that Ranters "taught that they could neither see EVIL, know EVIL, nor act EVIL and that whatever they did was good and EVIL, there being no such thing as sin in the world" (p. 3). As an example, he told of Mistress E. B., who "coming to one of the men, she offers to unbutton his cod-piece, who, demanding of her what she sought for, she answered FOR SIN, whereupon he blows out her candle and leads her to the bed where in the sight of all the rest they commit fornication" (p. 4). JM also related how "the sister who can make 'the beast with two backs' the most strenuously, viz., entertain the most men longest and oftenest, hath a sufficient canonization for a saint triumphant" (p. 6). Ranters themselves allegedly used immorality as a standard of religiosity, and "the man who tipples deepest, swears the frequentest, commits adultery, incest or buggery the oftenest, blasphemes the impudentest, and perpetrates the most notorious crimes with the highest hand and rigidest resolution, is the dearest darling to heaven" (p. 5).

Pamphlet authors often copied each other, and it is sometimes difficult to determine the origins of specific stories. *The Ranter's Religion,* for instance, repeated the story about Collins tearing apart cooked meat and saying "this is my body" (p. 8). The same publication also presented another story found in several other pamphlets. It would appear that many pamphlet authors attest to having been present when "a she Ranter said openly in the hearing of many (a friend of mine accidentally one of them) that she should think herself a happy woman and should esteem herself a superlative servant of God if any would accompany her carnally in the open market place" (p. 8). This and the preceding story can also be found in slightly modified form in the 1650 publication *The Arraignment and Trial of the Ranters, with a Declaration* (p. 3). Some stories were clearly apocryphal. One pamphlet, for instance, claimed that "one of these roisters sitting over his cups (with the rest of his companions) *evacuating wind backwards* used this blasphemous expression, 'Let everything that hath breath praise the Lord'" (*The Ranter's Religion*, p. 8). Another pamphlet described a farting Ranter exclaiming that this was the Holy Spirit leaving God.

Almost all chapbooks presented an account of a Ranter meeting where hundreds upon hundreds of Ranters engaged in immoral behavior, "accounting it no sin for hundreds of men and women (savage like) to lay with each other, publicly all together, either in houses, fields or streets" (*The Ranters' Bible*, p. 5). One Ranter, after indulging in public sex, set his woman "on her head to go about the room on her hands with her coats about her ears . . . and in the presence of about sixty persons entered into venial exercises" (*Ranters' Recantation*, p. 2).

If anonymous accounts of sexual and moral perversity lacked credibility, one could read Gilbert Roulston's "I was there" account of his life as a Ranter. He described himself as "a late fellow Ranter," and his *Ranter's Bible* (1650) recounted that "on the 16th of November, 1650, a great company of this new generation of vipers called Ranters gathered together near Soho in Westminster where they exercised themselves in many riotous and uncivil actions. And after some actions spent in feasting and the like, they stripped themselves quite naked and dancing the *Adamites' Curranto,* which was, that after two or three familist gigs, hand in hand, each man should embrace his fellow female in the flesh for the acting of that inhumane theater of carnal copulation." Other authors tell us of additional Ranter sports, including a seventeenth-century version of sadomasochism. "After the satisfying of their carnal and beastly lust," one author wrote, "some have a sport that they call whipping the whore" (*Strange News*, p. 4). No illustrations were included, and none were really needed.

John Reading also signed his name to his pamphlet *The Ranter's Ranting* (1650). He reported that his friend's friend, "a gentleman of quality (as I am credibly informed)" (p. 5), met a female Ranter in an alehouse and "after a little familiar discourse, he told her he was in indifferent well health but wanted a stomach [that is, he was 'hungry'], whereupon she replied that if he pleased to come to her lodging the next day she doubted not but she should find something to which he had an appetite." The next day this gentleman visited the lady at her lodgings "and appearing in nothing but her smock, [she] asked him how he liked her and whether his stomach would not come to him . . . and immediately presented herself to him naked, saying, 'Fellow Creature, what sayest thou to a plump leg of mutton (striking her hand upon her thigh) with the eats that are now in view'" (p. 5). Our gentleman of quality was so shocked that he ran out of her lodgings and only later did he "discover her to be a proselyte of Coppe and Clarkson and the rest of their infernal gang which have been dispersers of a diabolical opinion that there is neither heaven nor hell, for otherwise she could not be so audacious" (p. 5). One must wonder what brought this gentleman of quality into the alehouse in the first instance or why he thought the young woman making her casual offer other than a working girl. In any event, Reading's message is very clear indeed.

Reading also included a song that he insisted was of Ranter authorship and was sung "to the tune of David's Psalms" (pp. 3-4). The poem was clearly humorous. Its most interesting verses included:

> If Adam was deceived by Eve
> It was because he knew
> Not how to exercise the gifts
> Which Nature did imbue.
>
> The Fellow Creature which sits next
> Is more delight to me,
> Than any that I else can find
> For that she's always free.
>
> Yet whilst I speak of loving one
> Let no mistaking come.
> For we that know our liberty
> In loving all love none.
>
> Then let us rant it to the fill
> And let our love too range
> For it hath wings and they are free'st
> That in their loves do change.

All anti-Ranter authors expressed shock at outrageous Ranter political thought, especially their alleged disregard for existing political authority. The author of *Hell Broke Loose* was horrified that Ranters taught "that the civil magistrate hath no power at all to meddle in matters of religion" (p. 6). Such views may have seemed scandalous in 1646 but other Ranter opinions would have disturbed Englishmen at any time. For example, that government representatives "may go no further in anything, nor sit no longer, nor dispose of anything but according to their commission and power received from the represented" (p. 7). Even worse were Ranter views of popular sovereignty. "The body of the common people is the earthly sovereign," Ranters believed, "and the king, parliament, etc., are their own mere creatures to be accountable to them and disposed of by them at their pleasure; the people may recall and reassume their power, question them and set others in their place" (p. 7).

In 1650 M. Stubbs wrote about the shockingly radical nature of Ranter social thought in his pamphlet *The Ranter's Declaration*. Like Roulston, Stubbs claimed to be "a late fellow Ranter" and reported that at one meeting, many Ranters complained about the hard financial times. "Desiring to know how they should be maintained," Stubbs reported, "answer was made that they should borrow money and never pay it again and that they should not only make use of a man's wife but of his estates, goods, chattels also for all things were in common" (p. 6).

When Ranters were not drinking, swearing, whoring, stealing people's property or overthrowing the government, John Reading's *Ranters' Ranting* alleged that they attempted to murder their adversaries. He wrote of one Ranter named Evan Bevan, "born of good parentage near Bishop's Castle in the county of Salop, [who] was for many years a constant hearer of the Word, yet afterward fell into strange opinions and would admit no sacrament, no baptism, no duty, no obedience, no devil, no hell etc. In a short time after his fall into these grand errors (the devil growing short within him) that for no other cause but that they were conscientious and finding an opportunity, he cut off the heads of his mother and brother for which he was hanged in chains in Shrewsbury" (p. 6).

Samuel Tilbury also told of murderous Ranter doings. The cover of *Bloody News From the North* described "a bloody plot discovered concerning their resolution to murder all those that will not turn Ranter." This keen social observer claimed to be present at a large meeting "at the sign of the star in Stonegate." After much discussion, "at last they came to their diabolical resolution. That each man's wife or woman's husband that denied their just and lawful principles of Ranting for the holding of all things in common, should be massacred" (p. 1). By way of substantiation, Tilbury offered how "one Mr. Smart, living at Fowforth, a mile from the city, repairing home to his house did come to his wife and asked her whether she would turn Ranter. She replied no . . . whereupon he immediately stabbed her to the heart with his knife and presently fled" (p. 1). Tilbury also told of "another of these bloody villains coming from one of their infernal meetings hath also killed his wife and wee children at Pontefract" (p. 1).

The year 1650 saw the high-water mark in the campaign against Ranters when the Blasphemy Act of that year was enacted.[19] On June 14, 1650, the Rump appointed a committee "to consider of a way for suppression of the obscene, licentious and impious practices used by persons under the pretense of Liberty, Religious or otherwise." The committee drew up a report on "several abominable practices of a sect called Ranters" and was then instructed by Parliament to create legislation "suppressing and punishing these abominable opinions and practices." After considerable debate on June 14, July 5, 12, and 19, and August 9, Parliament adopted an act entitled "Punishment of Atheistical, Blasphemous and Execrable Opinions," or the Blasphemy Act.

The main provisions of the act are easily enumerated. Declaring one's self to be God or denying that God exists was condemned as were advocating drunkenness, adultery, or swearing or declaring there to be no difference between moral and immoral behavior, the denial of heaven and hell, salvation, and damnation or teaching there was no difference between them. The Blasphemy Act did recognize the difference between professing the above in private conversation and in public speeches or writings. Only the latter was punishable, however regrettable the former. Any individual found guilty of these charges was to be jailed for six months for the first offense. For the second offense, the individual was to be banished on pain of death should he return to England. The preamble to the act clearly explained that such punishment was necessary because Ranters maintained "monstrous opinions, even such as tend to the dissolution of human society." The stipulations of the bill were to apply to both male and female in England, excluding only "persons distempered in their brains."

Ranters were as disliked by other radical churches from the Quakers to the Diggers as much as they were by the most proper Presbyterian. We have already noted that George Fox disliked the Ranters he met in prison because "they sang, whistled, and danced." Another author reflecting Quaker dislike of his Ranter kin was Richard Farnsworth, whose *The Ranter's Principle and Deceits Discovered* (1655) warned, "Woe unto thee Ranters, this book is as a testimony against you from us whom the world called Quakers, and you and your wicked principles we deny and hold them and you accursed" (p. 19). The first page of Farnsworth's treatise observed that "you have turned the grace of God into wantonness," and on the last page Farnsworth wrote, "You Ranters stink." He concluded his tirade with the statement "The serpent thou art, and you Ranters, scorpions, serpents, you shall not escape the damnation of hell" (p. 20).

The specific object of Farnsworth's anger was a Ranter named Robert Wilkinson, from Coates in Leicestershire. Local Quakers considered

Wilkinson a horrible monster because "he said he was born of God and can not commit sin and said he was both God and the devil, and he said there was no God but him nor no devil but him, and he said whom he blessed was blessed and whom he cursed was cursed . . . he said the apostles were lying deceivers . . . and he said the Bible was a pack of lies and there was neither heaven nor hell but here, and yet he was in both heaven and in hell" (p. 19). In a word, Wilkinson said many things to upset Farnsworth. More disturbing yet were Wilkinson's moral views. Farnsworth concluded, "Thou art a whore-master, as thou saidest, and art in the mystery of Babylon, committing fornication and art full of the filthiness thereof" (p. 20).

Richard Hickock's pamphlet *A Testimony Against the People Called Ranters* (1659) further expressed Quaker horror about Rantism. Ranters were "swearers, cursers, liars, drunkards, adulterous, proud, covetous and all manner of evil workers [who] are in darkness, degeneration, alienation and transgression" (p. 2). Ranters were also "children of darkness . . . whose seed, birth and state is accursed" (p. 2). Even worse, Ranters practiced their filth and then "lay it upon the Lord as him to be the mover and leader thereunto" (p. 2). Such practices could not have come to a good end for "you are turned into that way that leads to hell and destruction" (p. 1). Worst of all, "you are become like a sow that was washed, which is again wallowing in the mire, and to the dog which is swallowing down his vomit which he once had vomited up" (p. 1). Hickock was not favorably disposed to Rantism, but then few Englishman appreciated how important the Friends were. It has long been a staple of Quaker historiography that "except for the Quakers, the Ranters would have over run the nation."

Gerrard Winstanley, the leader of the equally maligned but far more boring Diggers, had only contempt for Ranters.[20] Like the Quakers, he too feared being mistakenly identified as part of that group, a charge that could have, conceivably, dangerously tarnished the good name of his squatters. In his eight-page pamphlet entitled *A Vindication of Those . . . Called Diggers* (1649) Winstanley explained, "This I was moved to write as a vindication of the Diggers who are slandered with the Ranting action" (p. 7, pages unnumbered). The Ranting power was so dangerous that Winstanley warned even "all you that are merely civil, you are the people that are like to be tempted and set upon and torn into pieces by this devouring Beast; the Ranting power" (p. 7).

Winstanley explained that "the Ranting power" expressed itself "in the abundant eating and drinking and actual community with a variety of women . . . is the life of the Beast or living flesh" (p. 2). This sensualism was morally and religiously repugnant, but Winstanley also wished the world to appreciate the dire medical implications of this lifestyle as well. Sensualism "brings vexation to the mind, or man within, when you want your delight in the excessive copulation with women" (p. 3). The physical result of such behavior is that "anger, rage and variety of vexations possesses [*sic*] the mind and inflames [*sic*] their hearts to quarrelling, killing, burning houses or corn or to such like destructiveness" (p. 3). Moreover, sexuality "brings diseases, infirmness, weakness and rottenness upon the body . . . [and] diseases of the body causes [*sic*] sorrow of mind" (p. 2).

Winstanley also believed it a poor idea for males to spend too much time in the company of women. For one thing, "this excess of feminine society hinders the pure and natural generation of man and spills the seed in vain and instead of a healthful growth of mankind, it produces weakness and much infirmness through immoderate heat" (p. 4). This in turn affects not merely the male but the female as well, for in seed-spilling, "the mother hath much more pain in child bearing" or "it [the child] proves a burden to the mother or nurse" (p. 4). Worse yet, the child of seed-spilling parents "proves either not long lived or a fool or else a sickly weakly thing that is a burden to himself" (p. 4). The logic may be illusive, but Winstanley's followers most likely understood him.

Immoderate heat also brought about social problems such as unemployment: "the Ranting practice is the support of idleness . . . [for Ranters] neither can nor will work but live idle lives like wandering busybodies" (p. 4). The social result was "that by seeking their own freedom, they enbondage others" (p. 4). In short, the Ranting power was guilty of "bringing forth nothing but misery to the inhabitants thereof" (p. 2). Should the Ranting power be permitted to flourish, the social results would be disastrous for England, for "the whole body, whole families, nay, whole nations are thus distempered" (p. 2). Winstanley only wanted what was best for England, and whatever his differences with the rest of English society, all could join hands against the Ranter. He explained that "my end is only to advance the Kingdom of Peace in and among mankind, which is and will be torn to pieces by the Ranting power if reason do not kill this . . . beast" (p. 7). Alas, no man is prophet in his own land.

By 1651 the anti-Ranter campaign had begun to run its course. Samuel Sheppard's five-act play entitled *The Jovial Crew, or, The Devil Turned Ranter* (1651) used slapstick humor to describe alleged Ranter antics. Despite some limitations, which included difficulties with plot development, characterization, dramatic action, and language, this play poked good fun at the Ranters and, by inference, mocked their fear-filled alarmist detractors. The title page promised that the play would contain the "cursed conversations, prodigious pranks, monstrous meetings, private performances, rude revellings, garrulous greetings, impious and incorrigible deportments" of the Ranters. The dramatic action of the play made Ranters funny, not fearful.

Like other examples of humorous anti-Ranter literature, the play placed little emphasis on conceptual matters such as the religious or political ideas of the Ranters. Rather, it focused on Ranters themselves, especially female Ranters, as wanton sexual libertines. Women characters got the most lascivious lines. As Mrs. Minks, Wriggle, Fulsome, Crave-Drink, Dissimulatio, All-Prate, and Incorrigible dance, they sing the following song:

> Come my boys, receive your joys
> And take your fill of pleasure.
> Shoot for shoot, away let's do it
> But we must have our measure.
>
> All lie down as in a swoon
> To have a pleasing vision
> And then rise with bared thighs
> Who'd fear such sweet incision?
>
> No hell we dread when we are dead
> No gorgon nor no fury,
> And while we live, we'll drink and ———
> In spite of judge or jury.

Between each of the stanzas, all sing the chorus of

> Come away, make no delay,
> Of mirth we are no scanters.
> Dance and sing all in a ring,
> For we are the Jovial Ranters. (p. 3)

In a later act Mrs. Wiggle and Mrs. Crave-Drink sing the following:

> Come some man or other
> And make me a mother,
> Let no man fear for to board me.
> Come as many as will

I will give 'em their fill
And thank 'em for what they afford me.

. . . .

Come any strong rogue
That would fain disimbogue
Let's mingle and try who's the strongest
I fain would comply.
With him that dare vie
To stand to his tackling the longest. (p. 7)

Act 3 introduced Spanish tobacco, or marijuana, which is passed about the group, with Mrs. Pigwidgen saying, "Let the stream of the strong Indian weed involve us as we sit in the clouds" (p. 10). When all the Ranters feel the effects of wine and smoke, they gather in a circle and sing:

By goats' desires and monkeys' heat
Spanish flies and stirring meat,
By the vigor of a horse
By all things of strength and force

We adopt this happy pair
Of our liberties to share
Arise, arise, blessed souls and know
Now you may rant, *cum priviligio.* (p. 10)

A similar piece was entitled *A Total Rout, or a Brave Discovery of a Pack of Knaves and Drabs* (1653). As in many other poems, the author was half-serious and half-humorous when he asked the Ranters to buck up and walk right, but the images he used make clear that it could as easily have been written about other mythical social groups representing these same immoral values. Though quite long, the following few stanzas well express the author's irreverent mood.

Come leave your "God-Dammees" and hearken to me,
O 'tis pity that fuel for Hell you should be.
Your spirits heroic will quickly be quelled,
When once the General Sessions are held.

Chorus: But hark my poor Ranter, I'll tell thee a tale
    Thy cursings and bannings will buy thee no ale.

You stole 'way their smocks and petticoats all,
Besides did not pay 'um for what you did call.

Fie, Fie, my base Ranter, this is but poor,
A shabby come off to plunder a whore.

Chorus: But hang't my poor Ranter, thou can'st not devise,
     To daube up the constables mouth with thy lies.

Now off goes the silver lace from the coat,
The buttons, so needless, and the points too to boot.
Two shirts are too many and rather than fail
One must be changed for tobacco and ale.

Chorus: Then hang't call a Broker, and let him brink chink,
     We'll sell him our hats, yea, our heads, for good drink.

But oh my poor Ranter, thus tattered and torn,
And almost as naked as 'ere you were born.
What means't thou to live so damnably base,
And die in a jail 'tis a desperate case.
Damnation and hell comes posting together,
And without repentance thou shalt suffer either,
Thy cursed "God-Dammees" and damnable cheats,
Ungodly endeavors and horrible feats,
Are all cable ropes to draw thee to hell,
But yet, prithee, Ranter Serpent, so farewell! (p. 5)

While neither the poem nor the play were world-class literature, the jokes, puns, songs, sexual innuendo, outraged husbands, devils, and drugs all indicated that Ranters were no longer taken seriously. Nevertheless, for Royalists they became an emblem of the immoral excesses of the revolution as a whole. Indeed, some pamphlets counted upon this identification to demonstrate that the revolution itself was tainted with evil. The pamphlet *Hell Broke Loose* described itself as "a catalogue of the many spreading errors, heresies and blasphemies of these times" but used its dislike of Rantism to condemn the revolution as a whole. Similarly, *The Black and Terrible Warning Piece* (1653) was concerned about "the dangerous proceedings of the Ranters and the holdings of no resurrection by the Shakers in Yorkshire and elsewhere" (p. 1). The pamphlet's subtitle, "A scourge to England's rebellion," expressed disgust with Parliament, Cromwell, and everything revolutionary.

On the other hand, Samuel Tilbury's pamphlet *Bloody News from the North* observed that "Ranters seem to be for monarchy and declared that they held themselves bound to yield all due obedience and loyalty to

Charles II." Tilbury's credibility must be questioned, however, for he also reported that Ranters "say there is no God but Pluto."

The most peculiar linking of Ranters with a hated group, however, was the attempt to associate them with Jesuits and the papacy. For instance, in his diatribe against the Ranters, *The Serpent's Subtlety Discovered* (1656), Walter Rosewell, a Presbyterian, personally attacked the mild-mannered Richard Coppin as a secret Jesuit.[21] Richard Coppin was alleged to be "a Jesuited Familist, tutored by Jesuits, prompted by the Devil, he and his older brother Joseph Salmon should be sent for a present to their Holy Father, the Pope of Rome" (p. 16).[22] Both Salmon and Coppin were guilty of "undermining the very foundation of the Protestant religion and persuading Protestants to believe that there is no Anti-Christ in the world but what is to be found in the most zealous Protestant ministers nor any other whore of Babylon but the Reformed and Reforming Protestant Churches of England. Consequently, the Pope of Rome is not the Anti-Christ" (p. 16). They had been "sent forth *tanquam legatos a latere* [that is, like Papal messengers or agents] to propagate the faith of Rome whose faith is faction, whose religion is rebellion" (p. 16).

Despite Ranter outrages against God, against the king, against Parliament, the true church, morality, human decency, and almost everything else, only one pamphlet described how God miraculously intervened against them. This is surprising, since seventeenth-century Englishmen easily saw God in the clouds, in apparitions, in the existence of monsters, and in anything more disturbing than spring rain. Yet only *The Ranter's Recantation* (1650) tells of fifty-nine souls won back to Christ when a Ranter leader "went to the chamber door and called for a Turk's Head, that is, a piss-pot, and in an instant, upon a great flash of fire, vanished and never was seen more to the great admiration of the spectators" (p. 5).

Early in the civil war, Thomas Edwards, Ephraim Pagitt, and many other well-known orthodox sect-hunters expressed the alarmist view that sectarianism reflected the devil's influence just as Matthew Hopkins discovered that witches were involved in the same satanic enterprise. They shared this view with their Anglican opponents, and once Charles II returned to London in 1660, many Anglicans anticipated the repression of sectarianism. Quakers did not fare well during the restoration. Unfortunately for them, there were no longer any more radical sects that they might attack. They did the next best thing and tried to gain respectability by joining the anti-Ranter crusade.

Despite the devil's best efforts to overturn Christianity in England, he failed. Neither the Anabaptists, the Quakers, nor even the Ranters proved a dangerous threat to church or monarchy. But then, the devil had other agents with whom he might torment the English, including religious charlatans, Roman Catholics, Turks, and Jews, who were, as everyone knew, even worse than Ranters.

The Ranters Ranting :

WITH

The apprehending, examinations, and confession of *John Collins,*
I. Shakespear, Tho. Wiberton, and five more which are to answer
the next Sessions. And severall songs, or catches, which were sung
at their meetings. Also their several kinds of mirth, and dancing.
Their blasphemous opinions. Their belief concerning heaven and
hell. And the reason why one of the same opinion cut off the
heads of his own mother and brother. Set forth for the further
discovery of this ungodly crew.

Decemb: 2   LONDON
Printed by B. Alsop, 1650

◆ ◆ ◆

6

Religious Imposters and Charlatans

"THERE IS NO SIN BUT AS MAN ESTEEMED IT SIN. THEREFORE NONE CAN BE FREED
FROM SIN TILL IN PURITY IT BE ACTED AS NO SIN . . . TILL YOU LIE WITH ALL WOMEN AS ONE
WOMAN AND NOT JUDGE IT SIN, YOU CAN DO NOTHING BUT SIN."
—*Lawrence Clarkson, The Lost Sheep Found(1660)*

f Englishmen were shocked by the proliferation of religious sects and
self-ordained mechanic preachers, they were outraged by the appearance of religious charlatans.[1] The charlatan had no calling other than
his own needs, no method other than the exploitation of human ignorance and gullibility, and no defenders. Even sectarian leaders hoping for
greater religious freedom of conscience understood that the charlatan
was no less a thief of spirit than a pickpocket was a thief of one's wallet.
Yet despite universal condemnation, charlatans abounded in the religiously permissive atmosphere of the interregnum.

The sources for studying charlatanism are various. Unlike reports of
sects, which were often fictitious or gross elaborations upon the smallest
kernel of truth, the deeds of charlatans, their successes, and their failures
were recorded in court records, newsbooks and spiritual biographies.
Eventually, the Blasphemy Act was as useful against the charlatan as it
was against extreme Antinomians.

The charlatan or religious imposter was not unknown to English readers.
In earlier decades John Moore, Elizeus Hall, John White, Edward
Wightman, and several others claimed to be one divine personality or
another.[2] Each was tried for blasphemy and sentenced to jail or executed
if they did not recant when offered the option. Most were probably harmless and possibly more than a little troubled. William Hacket was doubly
dotty. In 1591 he claimed to be a divine being and then multiplied his

trouble when he foolishly challenged the authority of Queen Elizabeth and became enmeshed in the power struggle between Puritans and the crown.[3]

The imposter's effect upon society had traditionally been limited by ecclesiastical courts and other powerful church institutions of social control. Additionally, efficacious controls over the press under the Tudors and Stuarts kept public information to a minimum—to those things the government wished the few literate people to know. During the civil war years, however, all this changed. The absence of ecclesiastical courts made it difficult to stop the charlatan, and less effective censorship meant more about religious charlatans was published.

All of the individuals discussed below might have been more successful charlatans had large numbers of followers taken them seriously. Few did because contemporaries knew they were probably insane. Bacon, Hobbes, Casaubon, and many others had already drawn close connections between claims to divinity and physical illness, and even during the Puritan decades, when there was less tolerance for this sort of thing, authorities understood that those claiming to be the incarnation of a Scriptural personality were probably deluded and mad.[4] It was for this reason that the Blasphemy Act of 1650 clearly excluded from consideration those "not sane in their heads."

Among those claiming to be some biblical person was Roland Bateman. According to the newsbook *Beware of False Prophets* (1644) Bateman determined that he was Able the Righteous and would be resurrected after his death. Insanity was definitely the case with Evan Price, described in *Strange News From Newgate, or, A True Relation of the False Prophet,* published in January 1647. According to the text, on January 10, "at Butolph's church near Bishop's Gate, in sermon time, there arose a great disturbance by one Evan Price, a tailor, who in the midst of the sermon stood up and declared himself to be Christ" (p. 3). Price was hurried off to prison but remained resolute in his conviction "that he was Christ and none but he could free them from their sins" (p. 4). He was tried on a charge of blasphemy on January 15, but, probably because he was insane, no sentence was passed. No additional reports were written about Price, and it is likely that he was told to go home and behave himself. In any event, he had no followers and posed no threat to society.

The same was true of Thomas Tany, surely one of the most creative madmen of any age.[5] Tany, or Theauraujohn His Aurora, as he preferred to be called, claimed to be the High Priest Aaron, the King of France, and the Ruler of Rome and Reme, among other similarly curious titles.

In several unusual treatises, which seem quite normal at first cursory reading, Tany created his own alphabet, grammar, and Scriptural sources, all of which incontrovertibly proved why and how his religious views were correct. Indeed, his treatises are actually quite entertaining once his method and purpose are apparent.

Other than the obviously deluded, several other borderline charlatans attracted considerable public attention. While neither John Pordage nor Thomas Webb was a total fraud, both were considered outrageous and were disciplined by the Parliamentary Committee for the Ejecting of Scandalous Ministers. John Pordage, the rector of Bradfield in Berkshire, had visions, made combat with spiritual dragons, and conversed with angels.[6] *Truth Appearing Through the Clouds of Undeserved Scandall* (1654) and *Innocency Appearing Through the Mists of Pretended Guilt* (1655) both reveal that he was called before the Berkshire County Commissioners to account for his views and finally dismissed from his position in 1654 by the Parliamentary Committee for the Ejecting of Scandalous Ministers. Yet despite his mystical ideas and considerable personal peculiarities, Pordage did not attempt to abuse his parishioners for personal gain. He neither practiced faith healing nor financially exploited his devotees. He was morally ascetic and advised his followers to avoid all sexual activity, within marriage or without. In the end, the court's incredulity regarding his beliefs not withstanding, Pordage was finally expelled from his position more for poor management of church property than for violations of personal ethics.

Thomas Webb was another dubious character. This sexually promiscuous minister of Langley Buriel had sexual relations with the men and women of his parish and also was ejected from his post. Edward Stokes's well-written account of this truly outrageous man, *The Wiltshire Rant* (1652), was severe in its judgment, but despite Webb's personal excesses, his abuse of the parish funds, and his assault on parish morals, Webb never claimed to be the reincarnation of some biblical personage though he did use his religious position to foster his promiscuous life-style. Webb's problem was that he liked the ladies who, in turn, seemed to like him. Indeed, Webb was something of a wit, and parishioners claimed that he once preached "there is no heaven but women and no hell save marriage" (p. 4).

Then there was James Naylor.[7] In 1656 Naylor rode into Bristol on a donkey while his female followers shouted hosannas and threw flowers in his path. While not necessarily a charlatan, Naylor was certainly an egotist of the first order. In any event, as soon as Naylor attracted some few followers, Parliament was on his tail as well.

Unlike the above, others were clearly impostors and frauds and exploited their followers.[8] Some, such as John and Mary Robins, were moderately persuasive. A few, such as the infamous couple William Franklin and Mary Gadbury, experienced incredible success. Others, such as Richard Farnham, John Bull, John Mowlin, and Thomas Lipeat, practiced garden-variety lechery and used religion as the wedge into someone's bed. Lawrence Clarkson's spiritual autobiography may require more than a grain of salt, yet there is nothing in his confessions that is really hard to believe or that we do not know to be true about individuals much like himself. He carefully described his lustful motives, the novel ideas he developed to seduce female devotees, the names and places of many of his conquests, how many times he was in trouble with authorities, and why, and, finally, how he came to lose faith in religion and substituted fortune-telling and magic as instruments of personal influence.

The most transparent charlatans were Richard Farnham and John Bull. According to the newsbook *False Prophets Discovered* (1642), as early as 1636 these two weavers from Colchester "held themselves to be prophets not ordinary but the two great prophets that should come at the end of the world" (p. A2a). Indeed, they claimed to be the two witnesses mentioned in chapter 11 of Revelation. They convinced their small band of followers that "England is full of abominations, idolatries and whoredoms" (p. A2b). Nothing could rectify this grave situation because "Christ's death was not for mankind but for some certain persons." But when the end of time arrived, only their followers would be saved because "they have the power to shut heaven . . . and power over water to turn them to blood and to smite the earth with all plagues" (p. A2a).

In the meantime, Farnham also participated in less apocalyptic activities. It seems that Farnham had a strong yen for a Mrs. Haddington, one of his female devotees, "a woman of fine parts." Mrs. Haddington was married to a sailor and became involved with Farnham while her husband was at sea in the Far East. Always resourceful, Farnham conceived of an interesting way to justify their adultery. He claimed, "God hath moved Richard Farnham the weaver as he did Hosea the prophet, to take himself another man's wife, viz., a wife of whoredoms" (p. A2b). According to Scripture, Hosea was to degrade himself by marrying a whore, and Mrs. Haddington of the fine parts was completely convinced that Farnham was Hosea and that she was his whore. According to the transcript, "he deluded and persuaded her that he was a prophet [and] she, in obedience to him as a prophet (so she sayeth) was married to him not withstanding her husband was alive at sea" (p. A2b). Local authorities were less convinced that Farnham was a new Hosea, although they agreed that Mrs. Haddington was a whore, and arrested them both. At about this time, Mr. Haddington returned home only to find his wife was in jail. The text explained that "shortly after coming home," he went to see her there, and "he laid his wife in Newgate, where she was arraigned and condemned for having two husbands" (p. A2b). The authorities were in a quandary but decided that if the seaman still claimed Mrs. Haddington as his wife, despite her questionable actions, "that the seaman should have his wife again, who, accordingly, took her and lay with her in prison." Mrs. Haddington was released from prison into her husband's custody.

Matters became more complicated when Mr. Haddington went back to sea. Mrs. Haddington "returned to Farnham in Newbrideswell, where he was a prisoner" (p. A3a). Despite the fact that Mrs. Haddington's behavior placed her in legal jeopardy, for she evidently had sex with Farnham in jail, the transcript stated that "she was content to lose the glory of being esteemed an honest woman and to be accounted a wife of whoredoms that she might occasion, as she did conceive, the fulfilling of the prophecy" (p. A4a). Matters became less complicated when Farnham and Bull, who had also been imprisoned, contracted the plague and were released from prison as they neared death. When both died shortly thereafter the problems associated with the Farnham/Bull sect seemed to have resolved themselves . . . almost.

Farnham's handful of followers did not believe their prophets were dead. Indeed, they were convinced that Farnham had already died once earlier, "which accordingly he did upon January 8, 1641" (p. A3a). Like Christ, Farnham and Bull would also rise after three days, and their followers "drank to these dead friends Farnham and Bull, saying that they be certain they are alive and shall return to rule this kingdom with a rod of iron (p. A3b). When they did not rise on the third day and return to the sect, the best opinion was "that Farnham and Bull are gone to covert the ten tribes." When they eventually returned from their world mission, which would be quite soon, "Richard Farnham should be king upon David's throne and John Bull should be priest in Aaron's seat and they should reign forever" (p. A2a). At that time, "then Scripture was fulfilled and not before."

The court wondered how Farnham was able to inspire such loyalty among his followers. According to the transcript none of his devotees was strange or peculiar, indeed, "setting their delusion aside, [they] are esteemed by understanding men to be women of good parts, honest conversation and very ready in Scripture" (p. A4a). The court could only note in passing "how fearfully these poor souls are deluded" (p. A3b).

What happened to Farnham's followers is unknown, but it is likely that they eventually followed other charismatic leaders such as John Mowlin and Thomas Lipeat. The small pamphlet *The Devil in Kent or His Strange Delusions at Sandwitch* [*sic*] (1647) presented the testimony of these messianic pretenders before justices Henry Foster, William Wilson, and Andrew Goffrich meeting in sessions at Sandwich on May 13.

According to Mowlin, one day, while he toiled at his tailor's table, "there appeared a vision before him," and tears soon gushed from his eyes. Soon a strange power came upon him, and he was cast into a great depression. In this terrible state "he saw a being in the shape of a man in a sad colored coat without a seam, with a powerful voice, [who] said, 'I am he that have holes in my hands and feet'" (p. 1). This Christ-like apparition told Mowlin not to be depressed, for his "joy shall be such as no man shall take from thee." Mowlin's commission was "to declare to those baptised persons with whom he was a member" all the truths he would be given (p. 2). Soon thereafter he met with sixteen members of his small church at Goody Foreman's house "and in the presence of all the parties aforesaid he did declare what he had expressed" and made converts, who were then baptized anew at Brewer's Bridge.

Mowlin's missionary activities consisted primarily of faith healing and some fooling around with the ladies. Indeed, his extraordinary healing power was only effective with his female devotees; Mowlin seemed unable to effect miraculous cures for his male followers. In one instance he was told by God to restore sight to a blind man, and "this informant laid his thumbs on his closed eyes and said, 'Henry, open thine eyes and receive thy sight'" (p. 3). Unfortunately, blind Henry remained sightless. The text tells us no more about Mowlin directly, but additional information is available in the second part of the chapbook, which was concerned with Mowlin's associate, Thomas Lipeat.

Evidently, all was not well within this community of saints. According to Lipeat, he, too, was the recipient of a divine calling. He said that "between three and four of the clock in the morning there was a light [which] did shine in my chamber . . . and casting my eye aside, I saw a round ball of fire and from thence did stream forth great streams of light . . . and in the light there did speak a voice to me and said that I should have a message to declare to the sons of men" (p. 4). Lipeat later received another vision that "said to me that I must go to John Mowlin and he should breath on me and I should be filled with the Holy Spirit"

(p. 5). Thereafter, spiritual voices spoke to Lipeat every day, and he now possessed greater spiritual powers. Moreover, he now believed that Mowlin had been led astray by a demon "in the form of a gentleman." As evidence, he noted that one night, "I had something revealed to me from the Lord in a dream that in the morning I should see him that had deceived John Mowlin in the shape of a man and said . . . 'he shall entice thee with money, but take it not'" (p. 5). Sure enough, Lipeat claimed that "in the morning it appeared to me in the likeness of a gentleman very complete in his habit with a fair continence, who said to me, 'Why dost thou not go to John Mowlin?'. . . and he did then offer me gold and silver . . . and he said 'Why dost thou not believe my sayings? There be six with John Mowlin that do believe my sayings,' and so he went away" (p. 6). Despite the verbal haze, it would seem that the devil in the form of a wealthy stranger had Mowlin's confidence and attempted to bribe Lipeat, who, in turn, was attempting to establish his own position as leader of the church by freeing it from Mowlin and the devil. Unfortunately, once again we do not know what happened to either imposter. Possibly, both faded away after receiving the six-month jail sentence usually accorded religious troublemakers. Fortunately, much more is known about other more successful religious charlatans.

The divine duos John and Mary Robins and William Franklin and Mary Gadbury received more publicity than other charlatans because they were clearly fraudulent. The newsbook bearing the simple title *Justices of the Peace of Westminister* (1651) discussed some of John Robins's followers, who were tried for blasphemy before Lawrence Whitaker of the court of Assize in Westminster. The defendants listed in this account include Thomas Tydford, Elizabeth Sorrell the Elder and Elizabeth Sorrell the Younger, Margaret Dunlape, Anne Burley, Frances Bedwell, and Thomas Kearby. Thomas Tydford spoke for the group as whole and swore that John Robins "is the God the Father of our Lord and Savior Jesus Christ, and saith that the wife of the said Robins, alias Roberts, shall bring forth a man child that shall be the savior of all that shall be saved in this world. He affirmeth further that Cain, who slew his brother Abel, is the third person of the trinity and that those that deny it deny their own salvation. He saith further that the said John Robins, alias Roberts, hath power to raise the dead" (p. 3). Frances Bedwell added to this that she had actually witnessed Robins "striking a woman dead and raising her again" (p. 4). Tydford and the others put their fingerprints to this confession, and having made their statement, "they were all committed to prison without bail and mainprize until the next general session"

(p. 4).[9] This group of Robins's followers did not all remain in jail. With the exception of Thomas Kearby, all promptly submitted petitions abjuring their beliefs, which the court accepted, and "upon this they were ordered to send for good bail to appear at the next sessions and to be of good behavior in the meantime, and so putting in bail and paying their fees, were dismissed" (p. 7).

Thomas Kearby, however, continued to maintain his faith in Robins. He alone returned to court to be tried before justices Thomas Latham and John Hooker. After he reiterated his views about Robins's divinity, they found Kearby guilty of blasphemy and demanded that he "be removed from hence to the Gatehouse prison from whence he was brought and shall be immediately removed from thence to the house of correction for the said city and Liberty, there to remain for the space of six months without bail or mainprize, according to the direction of the said late [Blasphemy] Act" (pp. 8-9).

Kearby's punishment resulted more from his unwillingness to recant his views than from originally maintaining them. Not only were the others released as soon as they recanted, but the court, in this newsbook account, did not take Kearby's views themselves very seriously. When Kearby asserted that Robins could raise the dead, the court noted in droll fashion, "If he have power to raise the dead, there is work enough not far off to try his skill. Here are good store of churches and churchyards about the city and upon which he may make experiment" (p. 12). Elsewhere the same humor is evident. One justice observed, "I have heard also the said disciple [i.e., Kearby] give out that Robins either hath or shall have the power to divide the sea as Moses, and pass over dry land. The Thames is near, he may do well to try experiments there first" (p. 14). When Kearby remained steadfast in his faith, "the keeper of the said house of correction was hereby strictly required to set the said Thomas Kearby to hard labor and to give him corporal punishment as occasion requireth."

Kearby's faith in Robins was put to the test again a few months later when the divine Robins was himself hauled into court along with a second group of followers. Robins's legal difficulties were described by GH, an "ear witness," in a small newsbook entitled *The Declaration of John Robins* (1651). GH attended the several trials involving Robins's followers and later interviewed them in Clerkenwell Prison. Although he never explained his own interest in these matters, GH does not appear to be of malicious spirit.

According to GH, this second group of Robins's followers remained convinced that their leader was God. In an interview with Mr. John King on Saturday, May 24, 1651, GH asked if "the report was true, that they acknowledge John Robins to be their God and (his wife) Mary Robins the Virgin Mary, and the child conceived by her (for indeed she is very big) to be Christ" (p. 3). John King answered, "Yes, all this I verily believe for this man whom you call John Robins is God, he is both King, Priest, and Prophet, he is that Malchisedek [sic] formerly spoken of and is now come to redeem the world to its former condition as it was before the fall of the first Adam" (p. 3).

GH was also able to interview John Robins himself. He asked, "How have you the power to cast down and raise up unless it be by some satanical art and abominable witchcraft?" Robins answered, "All arts come from the Devil but mine proceeds from the inspiration of the Holy Ghost." When asked by GH, "Why do your followers term you a third Adam?" John Robins explained, "So I am for these reasons. The first Adam was made a living soul, the second a quickening spirit . . . the first, the servant of death appointed, the second the Son of Life thereunto foreordained. And I am the third Adam and must gain that which the first lost."

Whether he was God or the third Adam, Christ, Melchizedek, or the Spirit, once in court Robins abjured all claims to divinity and made an orthodox statement of faith. When asked by a judge, "I pray Sir, what belief are you on?" Robins prudently signed a recantation, swearing, "Whereas I John Robins do at this very instant lie under the censure of the people to be the God of the Shakers and their only Lord in whom they put their trust. I do here declare . . . that I am free from assuming any such power or title to myself." It is probable that this statement was intended to avoid being charged under the terms of the Blasphemy Act. Nonetheless, Robins told the court that he had "received the inspiration of the Holy Ghost and have had great things revealed to me and am now sent to call the Jews to conversion, which will be accomplished this present year, 1651." This was probably of little concern to the court since Jews were only to be readmitted to England in 1656. Robins would have had to go to Holland to find any.

Curiously, despite his recantation, Robins continued to hold the faith of his followers. One of these, Joshua Garment, went to jail. From his cell in Clerkenwell New Prison he wrote the pamphlet *The Hebrews' Deliverance At Hand,* published on August 23, 1651. Garment explained, "In the year 1650 I saw the man called John Robins riding up on the wings of the wind in great glory. Then the word of the Lord came unto me saying, *this* is thy Lord, Israel's King, Judge and Law giver, thou must proclaim his day . . . so that he may enter in" (p. 4). Employing language identical to that used by Tydford, King, and other Robins disciples, Garment explained, "This is the Melchizedek that Abraham met in the way, even the Abraham that was the first created who is restored, set and sent by God his creator with the name of God his creator, God Almighty, written on him" (p. 4). A page later he wrote again of the discredited Robins, "I tell you in the name of God that John Robins is the man ordained by the creator of heaven and earth to lead the Hebrews, dividing the sea in the power of God his creator" (p. 5). Like the Moses of old, Robins would bring about the redemption of God's children and "twenty days before next Michaelmas day the sea shall be divided and many Jews that are here in England shall go through on dry foot towards Judea and the Lord said, I will gather all Jews in the world in one place and with signs and wonders in great power bring them through all countries" (p. 5). The unredeemed would suffer, and Garment warned "I know he will destroy thee and that suddenly, even before next March 1652" (p. 7).

Nothing additional is known about either John Robins or Joshua Garment. The former wrote no treatises at all, and the *Hebrews' Deliverance* would seem to be Garment's only work. It is likely that Robins's other followers merged into the large and often undifferentiated sectarian mass or attached themselves to some other charismatic personality. There was no lack of such personalities available to consumers of extreme enthusiasm, although few were as enticing as Mary Gadbury or as successful as William Franklin, surely the most accomplished confidence operators of the interregnum.

The best source for the fantastic activities of Franklin and Gadbury is the long pamphlet *Pseudo-Christus* (1651) by Humphrey Ellis, a local Southampton minister who attended their trial and interviewed the defendants and their followers. Ellis was a fair and objective man who permitted the court records to tell an incredible story. He was more than a good observer, however. Because he knew many of the townspeople who believed in Gadbury and Franklin, he scrupulously traced the defendants' individual histories. Ellis was as curious about these two people as he assumed his readers might be, and, like them, he wished to understand how this strange series of events could have come about.

William Franklin was thirty-six years old, married, and had three children. He originally came from Overton in Southampton but more recently resided in Stepney Parish and made his living as an apprentice ropemaker in London (p. 6). All who had known him in Overton thought well of him. Neighbors considered him "a civil man, diligent in his calling, honest in his dealings, careful to provide for his family" (p. 6). Local religious authorities also thought well of Franklin, calling him "very zealous in the duties of religion and very constant in the practice and observance of the ordinances of the gospel" (p. 6).

Praise of Franklin was universal until 1646, when he became seriously ill. According to his physician, Dr. Charles Stamford, Franklin had suffered from frequent fits of some sort and had remained distracted since that time. When he began to proclaim "that he was God, that he was Christ" (p. 7), his neighbors suspected that Franklin was a seriously changed man. When Franklin denied the truth of Scripture and church ordinances, spoke in tongues, and uttered strange prophecies, his sectarian communion knew William Franklin was "acting after a strange fashion" and expelled him from their fellowship. The next four years of Franklin's life would prove to be very exciting.

Mary Gadbury was an equally interesting person. She was about thirty years old and sold lace, pins, and other small wares for a meager living in Watling Street, where she lived in London. Her neighbors thought well of her, considering her "to have been of honest conversation and to have lived in good repute and religiously amongst them" (p. 8). Still, Gadbury was unhappy and had lived alone since her husband had deserted her and run off to Holland with their housemaid.

According to Gadbury's confession, a neighbor introduced her to Franklin, and from their first glance each had a peculiar effect upon the other. Each time they met Franklin spoke in tongues, Gadbury had fits, and they each had visions. In one instance Gadbury "suffered terrible shaking and trembling fits and then a voice sounded to her, declaring, 'It is the Lord, it is the Lord'" (p. 10). At other times she saw bright lights and heard trumpets, and on one occasion she experienced a very severe convulsion and afterwards proceeded to tell Franklin many intimate details of his earlier life previously known only to him.

Franklin was convinced of the spiritual significance of their extraordinary relationship. He explained to Gadbury that his past life, including his wife and children, no longer applied to his spiritual self but to the old William Franklin born of the flesh. Franklin also explained that God had sent Gadbury to him and set her apart for his use (p. 11). Gadbury continued to have visions; Franklin continued to speak in tongues; they continued to see each other as often as possible.

At some point the two began experiencing identical visions. They must have been experiencing other things, too, because Gadbury became pregnant and since Franklin was still married, they decided to pull up stakes and leave London. A vision told Gadbury to sell all her goods and depart for the land of Ham, which she understood to be the county of Hampshire (p. 14). Since Franklin had experienced the same vision, they considered this to be their long-anticipated divine commission. Then Gadbury had an additional vision in which she was told, "I have made an end to sin and transgression for me and my people" (p. 15). Finally, "he [Franklin] was proclaimed by her to be the Christ, so she declared herself and was acknowledged by their seduced followers to be the Spouse of Christ . . . to apply to herself the Scripture of the *Lamb's marriage being come and his bride to have made herself ready* . . . Thus is Franklin now in the room of Christ to her . . . and she putting herself in the room of the Church, Christ's mystical body, to be the *Spouse of Christ, the Bride, the Lamb's Wife*" (p. 16). In short, Franklin and Gadbury were about to reenact in the land of Ham the sexually promiscuous lives of the ancient fanatics Simon Magus and Helen, where the divine Mary was not Christ's mother but his enticing spouse and lover.[10]

Mary Gadbury appears to have been the brains of the operation, and according to her confession they devised an interesting strategy to make converts to their cause. While Franklin returned to London for two weeks to borrow money from friends, Gadbury took lodging at the Inn of the Star in Andover where she proceeded to "tell abroad that she had seen Christ in the person of a man, not declaring him to be the person at present whom she did thereby intend, that by the time he should return it would somewhat appear how their design would take and what might be the effect of it" (p. 17).

Accounts of Gadbury's strange visions soon spread throughout the town. According to Ellis, Gadbury developed a very large following of troubled people who believed in her prophecies that Christ, in the form of William Franklin, would appear in two weeks. Moreover, she directed her pregnancy toward each individual who came to see her. She told each that her labor pains were for him or her and "she would pretend her travail to be for such a one" (pp. 21-22) about to be "reborn in Mary." In every instance the person, "being at length wholly wrought upon and seduced by her," became an ardent enthusiast for Franklin as Christ. Within a short two weeks Mary Gadbury succeeded in building so large a following of Franklin's supporters that when he finally arrived from London they were forced to give up their residence at the Inn of the Star because their followers caused constant disruptions. Those with the spirit never want, however, and the divine duo soon moved into better uptown quarters.

According to Ellis, the majority of Franklin's followers consisted of "credulous persons, wavering and uncertain in matters of religion, having itching ears after some new things, were soon drawn away and seduced by them" (p. 31). Even so, he admitted that Franklin possessed a charismatic personality and that Mary Gadbury was able to deliver powerful sermons in a slow, austere, and eerie voice. Yet, like Robins, Gadbury enjoyed a following among intellectually and socially sophisticated individuals, including Edward Spradbury, Mrs. Woodward, and later, Mr. Woodward, the local minister. Indeed, when the celestial set left their lodgings at the Inn of the Star, they were invited by the Woodwards to live with them and to use their large house as their special quarters (p. 25). This move provided excellent opportunities: the house promised spacious quarters befitting God's elect, and the Woodwards' endorsement conferred local legitimacy upon Franklin and Gadbury. Ellis sadly reported that "multitudes of persons now resort to Mrs. Woodwards, to see, hear, and speak with them" (p. 31).

Gadbury was so enticing and Franklin so persuasive as Christ that it soon became impossible for them to meet the needs of their growing community by themselves, and they were forced to appoint "very active persons to be the preachers, spreaders and publishers of it abroad to the people" (p. 31). Each new member of the church hierarchy was given a special title. John Noyce was made John the Baptist and Henry Dixon and William Holmes were appointed as the destroying angels mentioned in Revelation. Edward Spradbury was to be a witness mentioned in Revelation and also a healing angel. Despite the silly titles, these second-tier ministers were effective missionaries. Ellis reported unhappily, "This infection dispersed abroad by such active publishers of it, began to spread exceedingly that too many now began to be taken with it" (p. 33). The new church grew so rapidly throughout the region that ministers from other churches became increasingly upset as their members deserted them. Ellis wrote how "such notice and great offense is a justly taken threat by diverse godly and well affected ministers and others." The local justices of the peace were finally brought into the picture in order "to stop the further spreading of this so great an evil" (p. 33).

In January 1650 arrest warrants were issued for William Franklin and Mary Gadbury, Mr. and Mrs. Woodward, Henry Dixon, Edward Spradbury, and Goody Waterman. Noyce and Holmes could not be located (p. 34). The trial was held at the January quarter session in Southampton before Justices Thomas Bettesworth and Richard Cobbe. From the very outset the trial was a veritable circus, with the court in an uproar every time one of the defendants rose to speak. Witnesses for the prosecution testified that Franklin had presented himself as God, and Fortunatus of Woodhay swore that he had heard Franklin affirm he was "Christ, the Son of the living God, the Messiah that sits at the right hand of God . . . that his spirit was abroad gathering souls and that he now came in the fullness of time to save the very Elect." Others testified that Franklin called himself by the sometimes Ranter names for God, "I AM" and "the very King of Heaven" (p. 36). When questioned, Franklin's followers indicated that they had indeed preached as charged and continued to maintain these opinions. Franklin's missionary disciples indicated that Franklin was the risen Christ, indeed, that he was God himself. Margaret Woodward declared to the court that Franklin "is her Lord and her King, and that she is saved by his death and passion" (p. 39). They all testified that they had been spiritually reborn through the efforts of Mary Gadbury, "the Queen of Heaven" (p. 39). It was also established that Franklin and Gadbury "did call themselves man and wife and that they lay together in one bed in his [Woodward's] house" (p. 39).

Franklin's personal testimony confirmed the case made by the state. After presenting his background and history, "he claimed to be the Son of God," and he noted "that it was revealed to him in a vision that she [Mary Gadbury] should be set aside for his use" (p. 41). In her statement, Mary Gadbury also affirmed the testimony of prosecution witnesses and declared that it had been revealed to her in a vision that Franklin was Christ. Perhaps because she understood their legal vulnerability to charges of cohabitation, adultery, and even bigamy, Gadbury strenuously denied ever having had sexual intercourse with Franklin (p. 41).

Before throwing the whole lot into jail under the terms of the Blasphemy Act, the justices urged Franklin to recant. If indeed the two had hundreds of followers, finding them guilty as charged would have created martyrs in whom their followers would continue to believe. A recantation, on the other hand, would prove more useful. When the justices met with Franklin in private chambers, they evidently scared him sufficiently regarding the charges against him. Both he and Gadbury could be prosecuted for adultery as well as blasphemy; the former offense could lead to their executions.[11] After his conversation with the justices, Franklin immediately entered the court and made a full recantation that he was neither Jesus Christ nor God after all (pp. 42-43). His followers, shocked and dismayed, began jumping and shouting. Edward Spradbury shouted, "Thou villain, how hast thou deceived us by thy lies?" (p. 43). Gadbury cried out, "Hast thou done this? Is this by thy hand?" Franklin's sole response was to turn to Mary, shrug and declare, "You see what the times are."

The results of this turnabout were as follows: Dixon, Spradbury, the Woodwards, Gadbury, and Franklin were turned over to the next Assize for trial according to the terms of the Blasphemy Act. Additionally, Mary Gadbury and William Franklin were found guilty of adultery and bigamy but were sent to Bridewell and the common jail, respectively, to await further trial at the next Assize. Later, at Franklin's request, Gadbury was transferred to the common jail so that they might be together (pp. 44-45). Ellis did not explain why the justices of the peace would have honored Franklin's request, but it is possible it could have been part of the deal cut in the judges' chambers.

Franklin's recantation should have discredited him with his followers, but such was not the case. According to Ellis, Franklin "rather labored to put it off, to deny it, to make it to be the mistakes of others . . . [and] no particular acknowledgement of anything could be got from him" (p. 47). Mary Gadbury seemed confused. She continued to affirm the truth of her visions and the content of her spiritual message, but at other times "she would say she was deceived, even undone by him and lay all blame upon him" (p. 48).

Rather than inhibiting the growth of the sect, Franklin's recantation and subsequent imprisonment had the opposite effect. Crowds of people came to see Franklin and Gadbury in jail, and their fame continued to spread through the area. Many people wrote letters to prison officials protesting the imprisonment and declaring Franklin and Gadbury miracle workers and "how they never miss to make trumpets sound in the very bellies of their converts and great ships appear to the view of all people near them" (p. 46). Ellis was amazed by this loyalty and concluded, "Let them discourse with whom they will, priests or else, they are all converted, leave all and follow them" (p. 46). Ellis admitted that since going to jail, "for the most part it is thought they have converted to them five or six hundred" (p. 47).

In March 1650, Franklin and his followers came before Lord Chief Justice Rolls of the court of Assize. Franklin and Gadbury both issued recantations of their views, and Gadbury denied ever having had sexual intercourse with Franklin. Sentencing was routine for cases of this type. William Franklin, the Woodwards, Spradbury, and Dixon were sentenced to the common jail, there to remain until they "put in good security for their good behavior." All the women, however, were sentenced to stay in Bridewell for six months until the next Assize. Because she was pregnant,

Mary Gadbury petitioned for her freedom and was released on April 22, 1650, at which time she returned to London. Charges of adultery were probably dropped in exchange for full recantations. Nothing more is recorded about either personality. The short but brilliant careers of William Franklin and Mary Gadbury had finally come to an end.

Not every imposter claimed to be God. A different type of charlatan assumed the more plausible role of an inspired teacher or spiritual adviser who preached his way into his devotee's beds. This form of fraud is so classic in all ages and stations of life that one is surprised, and in a perverse sense charmed, by the admissions of Lawrence Clarkson in this regard.[12]

Lawrence Clarkson, or Claxton, as he also called himself, was certainly the most intelligent, candid, and literate of all interregnum religious confidence operators. Indeed, he must rank as one of the most outstanding and colorful personalities of the revolutionary decades. He combined a flamboyant life-style and a charismatic preaching ability with a clear literary style, and he soon emerged as "Captain of the Rant." In itself, Rantism was a legitimate, if unusual, expression of spiritual anarchism that emphasized the importance of perfecting the inner spirit and discouraged the practice of external religious rituals. In Clarkson's hands these same ideas provided a religious foundation for sexual promiscuity. Unlike other charlatans, Clarkson provided posterity with abundant information about his deeds and misdeeds. His humorous spiritual autobiography, *The Lost Sheep Found* (1660), was written when Clarkson no longer considered himself a charlatan and sheds light on his personal and intellectual development as well as the whys and wherefores of religious chicanery rarely available from other sources. Although detail cannot be accepted at face value, the run of events he described was certainly not unusual for confidence operators.

Clarkson indicated that he had experienced a very confusing adolescence during which time he traveled from one sect to another but still could find no religious peace. Along the way, however, he discovered that he "had a small gift of preaching and so by degrees increased [it] into a method" (p. 10). Seekers in Norwich, Yarmouth, Pulom, and Russel paid Clarkson to preach, and he was finally offered a permanent position in Pulham Market in Norfolk, where "for a time I was settled for 20 shillings a week and very gallantly provided for, so that I thought I was in heaven" (p. 11). Yet, "notwithstanding I had great power in the things of God," he explained, "I found that my heart was not right to what I pretended, but was full of lust . . . [and] I was subject to that sin" (p. 20). As a result,

Clarkson was involved in one scandal after another, and "I concluded that there was none that could live without sin in this world" (p. 20). Clarkson soon found himself in trouble with the authorities. On one occasion, two constables, several soldiers, and an officer from Parliament came to arrest Clarkson, and he was detained at Bury St. Edmunds Prison. Captain Blayes of Woodbridge served as chairman of an investigating committee that questioned Clarkson about his baptizing people in the nude. The court complained, "We are informed you dip both men and women naked" (p. 15), and more serious yet, "We are informed you dipped six sisters one night naked . . . nay further, it reported that which of them you liked best, you lay with her in the water" (p. 15). In this first of many challenges to Clarkson's sexual integrity, he was sentenced to sit in jail for an unspecified period of time.

Eventually released, Clarkson continued to make a meager living as an itinerant Antinomian preacher, gaining freedom if not financial reward. But there was a small but significant change in his thinking. "Now observe," he noted, "at this time my judgment was this, that there was no man that could be freed from sin till he had acted that so called sin as no sin" (p. 25). Seeking followers with whom he might share his faith, he followed his calling. "I set my cane upright upon the ground and which way it fell, that way would I go," he wrote (p. 21). He also enjoyed a very fine social life with the ladies. In Canterbury there "was a maid of pretty knowledge who with my doctrine was affected and I affected to lie with her . . . and satisfied my lust, afterwards the maid was highly in love with me." There was also deceit involved here, for "not knowing I had a wife she was in hopes to marry me . . . and would travel with me" (p. 22). Clarkson promised his new friend that he would return quickly but avoided the city thereafter. In those instances when Clarkson did return to a town in which he had preached, loved, and lied, he "found none of the people so zealous as formerly" (p 22). Clarkson lamented, "I was very often turned out of employment" (p. 23).

Clarkson gradually made his way back to London, where his views became even more exploitative. He taught that "there was no sin but as man esteemed it sin, and therefore none can be freed from sin till in purity it be acted as no sin . . . for to be pure all things, yea, all acts were pure" (p. 25). He recounted how influential these ideas could be: "Making the Scripture a writing of wax, I pleaded the words of Paul, That I know I am persuaded by the Lord Jesus Christ that *there was nothing unclean but as men esteemed it*" (p. 25). Once again, his thinking took another turn toward even greater promiscuity. He now argued, "*Till you lie with all*

women as one woman and not judge it sin, you can do nothing but sin . . .
so that I understood no man could attain perfection but this way." Sin
may have created the need for redemption, but voluntary and active participation in sin was the only pathway to perfection, or, in other words,
redemption through evil.[13]

There is little reason to doubt Clarkson when he reports that he was a
very fine preacher and that his sermons were unusually effective with the
ladies. At one meeting, "Sarah Kueling, being then present, did invite me
to make trial of what I had expressed . . . she invited me to Mr. Wat's [res-
idence] in Road Lane where was one or two more like her and I lay with
her that night" (p. 26). His spiritual communion with Sarah Kueling and
her friends was apparently so satisfying that Clarkson took up permanent
residence with them to better perfect his religious calling. He was evidently quite successful with other seekers of the internal spirit, noting, "I
had clients many that I was not able to answer all desires, yet none knew
our actions but ourselves" (p. 26). Indeed, "being, as they said, Captain of
the Rant, I had most of the principal women come to my lodging for
knowledge" (p. 26). In time, his service to women became tedious, and
"at last it became a trade so common that all the froth and scum broke
forth . . . that I broke up my quarters and went to the country, to my wife,
where I had by the way disciples plenty" (p. 26).

There were other reasons to leave London at that time. Though he
"was careful with whom I had to do, this lustful principle increased so
much that the Lord Mayor with his officers came at midnight to take me"
(p. 26). And so, if only to permit the London atmosphere to become a little less charged, Clarkson returned to house, home, and heart and his
wife. Indeed, he saw no contradiction between his promiscuous social life
and his fidelity to his legal spouse. Over and again he informs the reader,
"I was made still careful [*sic*] for moneys for my wife, only my body was
given to other women" (p. 26). But then, how else could he spread his
doctrine of redemption?

Eventually Clarkson grew tired of life with his wife and returned to his
old ways. "Mary Middleton of Chelmsford and Mrs. Star was [*sic*] deeply
in love with me, so having parted with Mrs. Middleton, Mrs. Star and I
went up and down the countries as man and wife spending our time in
feasting and drinking" (p. 28). Returning to London, Clarkson officiated
over a full Ranter community. "Taverns I called the house of God, and
the Drawers [of wine] Messengers; and sack, Divinity; reading in
Solomon's writings it must be so in that it made glad the heart of God"
(p. 28). These meetings had a profound religious effect on participants

and "improved their liberty, as where Doctor Pagit's maid stripped herself naked and skipped among them" (p. 28). Clarkson would not describe the apostolic nature of their communal commitment, but he did note, "Being in a cook's shop, there was no hunger" (p. 28).

Clarkson was able for a while to avoid capture, but Parliament eventually considered him a danger to the community. It issued a warrant for his arrest and set a £100 bounty for his capture. A bounty hunter named Jones eventually apprehended him. On September 27, 1650, the Committee for Suppressing Licentious and Impious Practices labeled Clarkson's very radical religious tract *The Single Eye* an "impious and blasphemous book." Further, it was "resolved by the Parliament that the book called *The Single Eye* and all printed copies thereof, be forthwith seized and burned by the hand of the common hangman . . . that all and every person and persons whatsoever who have in their hands or custody any of the books entitled *The Single Eye,* or printed copies thereof, be, and are required and enjoined forthwith to deliver the same to the next Justice of the Peace . . . to be publicly burned." Clarkson was then called upon to answer for his sexual conduct while in residence at Road Lane. When asked about his promiscuity, he responded, "I never lay with any but my own wife" (p. 30). Parliament knew otherwise and resolved "that the said Lawrence Clarkson be forthwith sent to the House of Corrections, there to be kept at labor for one month and from that time to be banished out of this Commonwealth and the territories thereof, and not to return upon pain of death."

Despite the fuss and official promulgations, the sentence was never put into effect. For the next few years, Clarkson's life was even more riotous and his preaching even more effective. In addition to the gospel of redemption through sin and sexual libertinism, "I attempted the art of astrology and physic which in a short time I gained . . . improving my skill to the utmost that I had clients many, yet could not be therewith contented but aspired to the art of magic" (p. 32). Clarkson was soon performing all sorts of miraculous deeds: "I improved my genius to fetch goods back that were stolen, yea, to raise spirits and fetch treasure out of the earth" (p. 32). In performing these feats, "a woman of Sudbury assisted me pretending she could do by witchcraft whatever she pleased" (p. 32).

Despite his own admission that he was involved in a confidence game, Clarkson did believe that he had some sort of power. While he admitted "something was done but nothing to what I pretended," he also noted, "I have cured many desperate diseases," and in one instance he was able to cure a bewitched young lady. He also reported that "several times [I] attempted to raise the devil that so I might see what he was, but all in vain so that I judged it was all a lie and that there was no devil at all, nor indeed no God" (p. 32). Clarkson continued telling fortunes because the adoration of the crowds pleased him and "it puffed up my spirit and made many fools believe in me" (p. 32). In any event, these activities were lucrative, and "monies I gained and was up and down looked upon as a dangerous man" (p. 32).

Eventually Clarkson resumed his religious odyssey. He found the Quakers morally stifling because "they had a righteousness of the Law which I had not, which righteousness I then judged was to be destroyed" (p. 33). In 1657 Clarkson fell under the influence of John Reeves, who, with his cousin Ludwig Muggleton, created a sect predicated upon their being the two witnesses mentioned in Revelation. Reeves, the brains of the operation, had been a follower of John Robins some time earlier. When Reeves died, Clarkson wrestled with Muggleton for control of the sect but was beaten in this battle for power in large part because the latter had been able to forge the sect around himself as a tight cult of personality. Clarkson was permitted to remain within the fold but only if he agreed never to write again and conceded that Ludwig Muggleton alone enjoyed the status of divine prophet. After all was said and done, Clarkson had spent too many days and nights with women while Ludwig Muggleton had labored to build a church around himself that combined his egotism with his religious fanaticism. Like the Quakers who disowned Naylor after the infamous events of 1656, Muggleton understood that the charismatic moment may have passed and that the future would belong to those with a sense of organization.[14]

And yet, Clarkson deserves more than easy dismissal. Despite the fact that he was an irresponsible, self-admitted lecherous fraud, it is unlikely that he forced himself upon any woman against her will. Like Mrs. Haddington, who knew her needs and returned to her savior/lover in jail at the earliest opportunity, it is likely that Clarkson appealed only to those wishing the particular form of consolation that he offered. Moreover, his writings are among the most interesting and original of the age. Clarkson expressed himself in a clear writing style, knew Scripture well, and possessed a sophisticated sense of religious argument and mystical theory. He was also part of a select group of theologians truly able to navigate in the dangerous but invigorating swift waters of the doctrine of redemption through evil. Perhaps that was also part of the threat he posed; most lechery is premised on far less noble grounds than religion if only because few possess the skills for so heady a mixture.

Englishmen may have been frightened by the proliferation of sects and shocked by the claims of religious impostors and charlatans, but the anarchy of the times remained ripe for still more dangerous religious developments. Even worse than subversive sectarianism or the personal religion of the charlatan were Roman Catholics, Jews, Turks, and, of course, witches. Equally unfortunate were the bandits, whores, rogues, and drugs that also infected the bloodstream of English society at this time. Any one of these powerful enemies of all that was good, clean, and English could pose a threat to society. Coming together as they did during the interregnum, supposedly because God wished to punish England, made them particularly frightening.

A TRUE AND

wonderfull Relation of a *Whale*, purſued
in the Sea, and incounterd by multitudes of other Fiſhes, as it
was certiſied by divers Mariners of *Weymouth*, who comming
from *France*, in the good Ship called the *Bonſventure*, did ſhoote
the ſaid *VVhale*, which making to Land did ſtrike upon the
Shore, within three miles of *VVeymouth*, where being
opened there was found in the belly of it a Romiſh
Prieſt, with Pardons for divers Papiſts in *England* and in *Ireland*, whoſe names are
here inſerted.

Nom: 7ber   Printed according to Order by I. H.   1645 .

♦ ♦ ♦

7

Catholics, Turks, and Jews

"IF THE TARES OF BLIND SUPERSTITION AND IDOLATRY WERE ROOTED OUT . . .
THEN SHOULD WE KNOW HOW TO PRAISE THE LORD AND REJOICE IN HIS HOLY NAME."

—*Ireland's Amazement, or, The Heaven's Armada (1641)*

f sects were up to no good and religious charlatans were profane and
blasphemous, Roman Catholics, Turks, and Jews were willfully evil and
sources of general misfortune. The Spanish, French, and Irish, for instance, all traditional enemies of God's island, were Roman Catholics,
and a week's worth of debate might be required to determine which was
more detestable. But at least Roman Catholics were Christian. Turks com-
pounded a peculiar foreign religion with an alien culture and an inde-
cipherable language, and Jews were perverse in almost every sense
possible. Even worse, all three impinged upon the English sense of place
and peace in the world, posing a great threat to England during the years
of revolution.

In popular views, Roman Catholicism was bad for England. The Spanish Armada, the Gunpowder Plot, Jesuits, Mary, Queen of Scots' conspiracies, and everything concerning Ireland were all examples of the
worldwide Catholic conspiracy to undo England. Indeed, the English
blamed Catholics for almost everything. They caused the civil war by
infiltrating into Parliament's army. They caused Charles's execution and
were in league with radicals of all sorts, especially Ranters. They caused
fires, floods, and plague. They even maliciously killed cattle.[1]

Despite the fact that some English Catholics sided with Parliament,
from early in the revolution, pamphlet attacks upon Catholics were common. One publication after another blamed Catholicism for England's
poor state. In fact, some pamphlets, such as *Camilton's Discovery of the*

Devilish Designs . . . of the Society of Jesus (1641), compared events in Germany before the Thirty Years' War to conditions in revolutionary England. The pamphlet described what "these incendiaries of Christendom have brought upon the German nation, to the astonishment of all the world," and even more, "that the same wheel of mischief that wrought all the woes of Germany since the year 1618 hath some years past hath been set also at work in England, Scotland, and Ireland" (p. A3a). The evidence was overwhelming. "Witness all the factions in church and state, the disturbances and discontents between the court and the city, between King and His Commons . . . all of which have received their birth and breeding from the devilish designs of those sons of division, the Society of Jesuits." W. Cranshaw's *The Bespotted Jesuit Whose Gospel is Full of Blasphemy* (1641) observed that "all the world can witness they are not purged from their ambitions, covetousness, treacheries, blood, cruelty, deceitfulness and all carnalities but have grown more ripe in rottenness" (p. 10, pages unnumbered). *Rome's ABC, The Pope's Benediction, Newes From Rome, The Pope's Proclamation, The Jesuit's Creed, The Discovery of the Jesuit's Trumpery,* and *The Lineage of Lucusts, or, the Pope's Pedigree* all made the same point. The Pope wished to overturn Anglicanism, and the civil war was therefore essentially a popish invention to accomplish that end. In *The Papist's Petition in England* (1642) we read about "the Devil's Counsel to the Pope," which consisted of the advice "to cut them off by some damnable plot, by your adherents among them confiscate their pernicious Parliament, destroy and put to the sword the principle men thereof, confound them in their devices by civil mutiny" (p. 7).

The same argument was advanced in *Seven Arguments Plainly Proving That Papists Are Traitorous Subjects* (1641), which argued that even the glut of cheap publications expressing unhappiness with contemporary events were all Catholic-inspired: "Many wicked and traitorous pamphlets have been scattered in this realm," the author explained, "to darken the glory of the Lord's Anointed, to weaken the good wills of his highnesses loving subjects, to win worthless malcontented malicious wretches treacherously to conspire with our sworn enemies" (p. 5).

Later pamphlets blamed the civil war on Jesuits. As early as 1641 *The Black Box of Rome Opened* noted that "all plots against the prince or the state were contrived and determined to bed, executed by the papist . . . with many others and by whom else of these last days I can tell what their intentions may be . . . are so replenished with priests and their people" (p. 18). *A Wonderful Plot, or, A Mystery Of State Discovered* (1647) alleged that even Presbyterian Independents were in league with the Jesuits. This pamphlet took the form of a dialogue between one member of each faith. In its opening lines the Jesuit salutes the Independent: "Welcome dear brother, or rather, son of our dearest affections, from whence comest thou?" The Independent answers, "Well met Holy Father Jesuit, ingenious and profound inventor, contriver and very atlas of the rule of Independency, I come from the army." After several pages of discussion of how they will overthrow the realm, they agree that "we shall never meet with another nation so easy, so flexible, so wavering, so apt to be taken with new impressions, new light of doctrines, as the English." In that same year *Look About You, or . . . Take Heed of the Jesuits* asked "hath not the Jesuit a chief hand in making our seething nation burn and boil! over into the fire of his own kindling? . . . who dresseth all or most actors in this bloody, popish, hellish, Jesuitical tragedy?" (p. 2). *The Jesuit's Character* (1642), *The Impudence of the Romish Whore* (1644), *Babylon's Beauty* (1644), and *Speculum Impietis* (1644) were other pamphlets attacking Jesuits. By 1650, *Mutatis Polemo, The Horrible Stratagems of the Jesuits* was able to declare how "Presbyter, Cavalier, yea and Catholic too, have joined interests" (p. 7). *Mutatus Polemo Revisited* (1650) added even more revolutionaries to the list of Catholics. As we have already seen, at one point even Ranters would make the list of Jesuit enemies of England.

By 1652, popery and Catholicism often became code names for anyone simply holding views more conservative than one's own, as well as for England's foreign enemies. In that year, *A Beacon Set on Fire . . . Concerning the Vigilance of the Jesuits, A Second Beacon Fired,* and *The Beacon Quenched* all attempted to demonstrate how the revolution had created conditions that were ripe for a Catholic conquest of England. As the first of these asked, "If the approvers of Popery should grow most numerous, how then can we have other than a Popish Parliament and a Popish army?" (p. 4). Others might see different dangers facing England, but this author wrote how "the old vanquished Popish Party, Jesuits and Papists are with indefatigable pains endeavoring all along to entice the people of this commonwealth unto the Popish religion" (p. 5). *The Plots of Jesuits* (1653) claimed to be a translation of Jesuit writings indicating their plans to pervert England.

While the Catholic menace to England was universal in scope, Ireland was England's particular Catholic cross to bear. Here again, problems between Ireland and England lay at the feet of the Papacy, Jesuits, or Catholicism in general; indeed, England was actually Ireland's victim. In 1641 an anonymous pamphlet entitled *Ireland's Amazement, or, The*

Heaven's Armada explained poor England's subjugation by evil Catholic Ireland. The title page was subtitled, "Being a true relation of two strange and prodigious wonders or apparitions which was seen over the city of Dublin, the one December 24 and the other December 30, 1641." The author described how two armed troops fighting with horse and canon appeared in the sky. There were also terrible noises and flashes of lightning, all of which, we are told, "struck the beholders with great astonishment and admiration" (p. A2b). Heavenly visages of conflicting armies were not unusual in 1641, but *Ireland's Amazement* asserted that "these prodigious apparitions in the heavens do show and forewarn us from . . . the hand of those merciless and irreligious caitiffs of the blood sucking rebels of Ireland, under whose tyranny our Protestants lie groaning." The only righteous course of action lay in undoing this Irish repression, for "if the tares of blind superstition and idolatry were rooted out and cleansed from the good seed of the gospel, then should we know how to praise the Lord and rejoice in his holy name" (p. A3a).

Odious Catholic behavior was the topic of several pamphlets and newsbooks. From the Puritan perspective, Roman Catholics were capable of any inhuman activity. It made good sense, for instance, that they would murder their own children. In the newsbook *The Lord Osmond's Overthrow, Which was the Chief Commander of the Rebels* (1642) we are informed that Lord Osmond, the leader of the Irish rebels against England, "was distracted and in this distraction killed his one and only son upon which his lady poisoned her self and three of her own daughters" (p. 3). Their servants were frightened "and fled to the Protestant party unto whom they revealed the intentions of their lord and his confederates which hath stood the Protestants in very great stead insomuch as by them they know their going out and coming in" (pp. 3-4). From this one incident, the author drew what he thought to be reasonable conclusions. "How merciless were those female furies who came over from Ireland," the author intoned, " . . . their knives were more bloody than were the swords of their companions" (p. 10). It is not clear which female furies these were, but one thing was certain: they were Roman Catholic. In *The Impudence of the Romish Whore* (1644) the entire Irish rebellion against England was dismissed as nothing more than Roman Catholicism run amok. Despite reasonable Irish grievances, the author wrote, "I perceived the motives to be so false and the propositions so absurd that me thought I saw in them and through them the very quintessence of that Brutish Malignancy which might be extracted out of Popery and barbarism united" (p. A2).

Since nothing touched by Catholicism could flourish, it was Rome's hope to pervert single individuals as well as whole societies. *The Pope's Benediction* (1641) explained that Catholics did not fear sin since everything might be absolved through paying for absolution. Adultery was nine shillings; beating a pregnant woman was seven shillings, six pence; killing a mother, father, wife, sister, or all of them, would be five to seven shillings per person. Indeed, Catholicism tried to influence its followers to sin so that they might become indebted to the church and, even more, indebted to their patron, the devil. *The Apprentice's Warning Piece, Being a Confession of Peter Moore* (1641) reported that young Peter came from a good home, whose parents were "a very sufficient couple whose chief delight was in him, their son Peter Moore" (p. A2a). After a fine education, young Peter was bound as an apprentice to Master Humphrey Bidgood, an apothecary in Exeter, "with whom for a certain space he lived very well and was willing to obey their commands in everything." Yet Peter fell under the influence of a Mr. White, "a papist, who did often times seduce me to abuse God's ministers and to spend my time in that diabolical study of reading magic, in which I took too much delight" (p. A4a). As a result of this influence, "the devil by his allurements and wicked enticing made me partaker of each damned vice" (p. A3a). Peter became so corrupted that "you could scarce name a sin wherein I had not become an actor." It was while Peter lived a loose moral life under the spell of this Catholic, magic-practicing devil that he did a very foolish thing. "Seeing a mess of potage about dinner time provided for my master," Peter confessed, "I, most unnatural servant, put powdered white mercury into it, so privately that no man could perceive me, which so soon as the good man had tasted, presently began to swell and after awhile he died" (p. A3b).

After committing terrible crimes, those awaiting punishment in prison often found their repentance thwarted by swarms of Catholic locusts wishing to prey upon those with guilty consciences. When Nathaniel Butler killed his homosexual lover in 1657, newsbooks told and retold the story several times from every imaginable perspective. The last of these pamphlets, however, pointed out what others had missed. *The Penitent Murderer* (1657), published "by Randolph Yearwood, Chaplain to the Right Honorable, the Lord Mayor of the City of London," promised to be the most authoritative account of all. The Lord Mayor himself wrote the opening letter to what was a collection of statements by the fifteen ministers officially sent to convert Butler before his execution. Their collective point was that everything had a very happy ending because Butler, previously a homosexual and a thieving murderer, became a penitent convert.

But there was an additional point on the ministers' agenda. In the opening "Epistle to the Reader," Yearwood begged the reader, "Grant me one request, not to look upon the following discourses as a bare story or a piece of news and so having read and seen it, there is an end." And in the "Serious Advice to the Citizens of London" attached to the end of the work we are informed that "'tis not enough for you to punish sin where tis before you, but you are to endeavor the preventing of it" (p. 8, pages unnumbered).

Curiously, the sin to be prevented was neither murder nor theft, neither homosexuality nor gambling, to all of which pursuits young Butler was given, but Catholicism. One minister wrote that "he would humbly desire the magistrate of London to look after the suppression of popish priests and Jesuits for some of the popish party had been with him [i.e., Butler] in prison, persuading him (but in vain) to lie in the Roman Catholic religion" (p. 34). Thomas Case, another attending minister, wrote that Butler "was very firm and fixed in the principles of the Protestant religion . . . insomuch that being several times encountered in prison by some priests and other papists that came to seduce this poor dying wretch . . . [he] sent them away with a great deal of contempt and indignation. [Indeed,] he wished the civil magistrate would be watchful and restrain their liberty" (pp. B3a-B3b). Even worse, there were Jesuits loose in the city. The "Serious Advice to the Citizens of London" tells the Lord Mayor, "We hear and fear 'tis too true that priests and Jesuits (those Romish Locusts) do swarm amongst us in the city and suburbs. We beseech you . . . to put forth your power to the utmost for the discovering and suppressing of them" (p. 9). All of this demonstrates how God moves in mysterious ways—the good ministers were able to turn a homosexual love affair gone bad into a blast against Roman Catholicism.

Most publications expressed a hidden fear that England was too weak to stand firm against nefarious Rome and thus demanded death for seditious Catholics, especially those in league with Jesuits. *The Black Box of Rome* (1641) cried, "It is a great weakness in us either to suffer their insolence or not secure ourselves against their hatred and tyranny" (p. 19). Part of the problem lay in the Catholic persistence toward evil. *The Confession of a Papist Priest* (1641) described the alleged admissions of a captured priest who had been banished three or four times, but "still he returned to gather souls for Rome." Only the most painful death could guarantee that he would not return again: "He was hanged half a quarter of an hour and then taken down and ripped up and his members and bowels burned in the fire, then his body quartered and put in a basket and brought to Newgate to be parboiled" (p. 4).

A True and Wonderful Relation of a Whale (1645) argued that Rome actually polluted nature. On October 19, 1645, the ship *Bonaventure of Weymouth* was en route to England from France with a full cargo of goods. The sea seemed unusually calm, when all of a sudden the sailors suddenly observed "a mighty rowing and working upon the water" (p. 3). Making this disturbance was a great whale "to transcend all other whales in length and compass." There was, however, something peculiar about this whale. According to the sailors, it was being chased by a great army of angry fish, and "in most violent manner they did beat against the whale, making a most hideous and fearful noise and falling upon her . . . did use whatsoever weapons of offense that nature had afforded them to assault the whale" (p. 4). The sailors were amazed, noting that "it being common and ordinary for the whale to pursue other fish to devour them and not see a multitude of other fishes . . . to pursue a whale and to do the utmost of their endeavor to destroy it " (p. 5). The whale desperately sought relief from the host of attacking fish and "making a most terrible cry, did what she could to come near the ship" (p. 4). Yet, despite its great size and strength, the whale was mortally wounded and began to die. According to the author, "she made haste to the next shore to die on for the whale (although when she is living will be covered with the sea) yet when she feeleth Death coming on, she doth renounce to that watery element and will admit to no other coverture than the wide vault of heaven" (p. 6). In this manner did the whale expire.

The explanation for these peculiar events became obvious once the beached whale was cut open and "there was discovered in the bowels of it a man . . . his head shaven, he was surely some priest." In his hand he held a case, and "in this box was found diverse pardons from the pope for diverse papists now in England and Ireland as for John Flower in England and for one Humphrey Vaux, of kin it is believed to that Guido Vaux who would have blown up the Parliament House in 1605. There was after this found diverse pardons for diverse papists in Ireland who would have labored to the utmost of their endeavors to blow it up again . . . with the assurance of the benediction of the Holiness of Rome" (pp. 7-8).

This tale, essentially a reworking of the story of Jonah, accommodated English dislike of the Irish and affirmed the subversive role of Catholicism in the world. "The reason why the fish . . . did persecute this whale was by reason of the person it interred . . . in the belly of the whale. You may see by this how strong and how deep a dye is the tincture of guilt . . . [that] the fishes would not endure their own element until they had expiated the waves by their destruction of the whale that did receive him and inter him . . . and would punish with death amongst the greatest of their own inhabitants" (p. 8). This odor of guilt affected not only the other fish of the sea but even the poor sailors cutting open the whale. So badly did the whale reek of Catholicism that "it may be a question whither their noses can ever have the capacity of scenting anything that is sweet again" (p. 6). Clearly, Catholicism was unnatural and putrid in itself but was also corrupting of nature in its influence. This story, like those about other monsters and prodigies, was yet another indication of how the mysterious and the mundane, in this case a Jesuit in the whale, were interwoven and how God's judgments were reflected in nature. It must have been a comfort for Englishmen to know that even the fish of the sea were good allies in the battle against smelly Roman Catholicism.

Turks were even more peculiar than Roman Catholics.[2] "Turks," the general term used to designate all followers of Islam, were something of a cosmic enigma. Catholics were strange and curious, by definition, but at least they were Christian and believed in the rudiments of true faith (which, of course, they grossly perverted). Arab heathens, however, were incomprehensible. That people so wrong-headed could build a wealthy and powerful civilization that controlled much of the Mediterranean Sea was terribly perplexing, and therefore it was assumed that they had to be in league with the devil. Fortunately, Turks were far away, and it was because of this safe distance that English pamphlets about Turks were less malicious but more fantastic than those discussing Catholics. Stories of Catholicism inevitably discussed Irish perfidy; those about Turks wove edifying tales of Christian mythology.

New News and Strange News from Babylon (1641) presents the problems that the popular English mind encountered when dealing with an alien culture in general and Islam in particular. Babylon, the location of this story, was an ideal site because it had been the seat of a fabulous ancient civilization mentioned in Scripture and because it was far enough east to be identified with everything strange, peculiar, and bizarre. The fact that the city no longer existed was not very important. Indeed, the authenticity of this story was beyond dispute since it purported to be "a copy of a letter which was sent from the 'Master of Malta' to a gentleman and kinsman of his resident [representative] here in England."

According to this letter, an important Islamic leader lived somewhere near Babylon: "He calleth himself the Great Prophet," and he had cat's teeth and a beast's claws on his fingers and toes, and "his eyes sparked like gold." Like witches and deranged hermits, "he loveth to walk solitarily in the fields and he eateth very little and that which he doth eat is very coarse" (p. 1). Despite his austerity, "he much delighteth in and loveth images and pictures and very devoutly will pray seven or eight times each day." Indeed, whenever he entered his temple, he was "conveyed with such a sweet harmony of music that hath not been heard on earth before and at his coming out thereof there was such a clang of drums, guns, and trumpets in the air which made the whole country amazed" (p. 2).

The Great Prophet's views were what Englishmen expected to hear from the mouth of a heathen: "He will not abide to hear of the Scriptures for he saith there was no such thing as is there specified but they are all most strange lies and not to be believed by man" (p. 2). Also, he preached ill will against Christendom and warned that "at his death there should be wars and rumors of wars in so much that all the western countries shall be laid desolate but this country shall flourish." Nothing more substantial about the Great Prophet's teachings was presented, but this may indicate the author's ignorance of exactly what an eastern prophet of Islam might actually believe, other than malevolence toward Christians truly possessing God's truth. Despite the fact that "many poor silly people do believe this man to be the savior which was promised and now is come" (pp. 2-3), this pamphlet concluded that "this is rather the Antichrist than any true prophet" (pp. 2-3).

Considering the millenarian ferment in England at this time, it seemed reasonable to identify Turkey (as well as Rome) as the home of the Antichrist. It was also logical to assume that once deluded Turks learned the truth, they would immediately convert to Protestantism. Unfortunately, their evil leaders kept them in spiritual darkness. This was the essence of the pamphlet *Extraordinary News From Constantinople* (1641). On August 12 very severe winds whipped through Constantinople, and "all this was made the more fearful and destroyable [*sic*] by the aspect of two comets or blazing stars with double tails or forked posteriors" (p. 2). This ominous apparition frightened the population, and even the sultan, or the "Great Turk," as he is called, had terrible dreams in which he combatted centaurs, griffins, and eagles and was eventually devoured by lions. When the anxious sultan consulted his astrologers and advisers, they agreed that these dreams were portents of the demise of the Turkish empire at the hands of Christian forces (p. 3). Unwilling to accept his inevitable fate, the Great Turk threw his advisors into jail and set them afire, "who, not withstanding, were not hurt at all, no, not so much as blackened or singed." As a result "the inhabitants of Constantinople they were greatly astonished at this miracle insomuch that some of them procured themselves to be baptized" (p. 6). This very edifying apparition, so similar to the story of Daniel, underscored the veracity of the Christian religion and the inevitable destruction of Turkish blasphemy. Of course, it stood to reason that were Mohammedans to hear the Christian message, they would embrace it immediately despite the efforts of their evil leaders to destroy God's truth.

The eventual conquest of Islam by Christianity was also the message of *Strange and Miraculous News From Turkie, Sent to our English Ambassador Resident at Constantinople* (1642). According to the text, a terrifying apparition appeared at Mohammed's grave in Arabia. After severe storms, the following words appeared written in the firmament: "Oh why will you believe in lies." Moreover, "there was seen a woman in white . . . having in her hand a book." Across the nighttime sky and opposed to this representation of Mary holding a Bible "were the armies of the Turks, Persians, and Arabians and other Mohammedans, ranged in order of battle and ready to charge her, but she kept her standing and only opened the book at the sight whereof the armies fled and presently all the lamps about Mohammed's tomb went out." The meaning of this apparition was obvious.

The text then explained that "one of the dervishes, which is a strict religious order among the Turks like unto the Capuchins amongst the Papists, and live in contemplation, stepped up very boldly and made a speech unto the company" (p. 2). The content of the dervish's speech was that Islam was a false religion and that Christianity was true. The heathen multitudes would have converted on the spot but, fearing this mass baptism, Moslem leaders "immediately put [the dervish] to death." Indeed, much as the Great Turk had his astrologers thrown into a fiery den for disclosing a Christian message, here, too, the leaders' recognition of Christian truth led them to torture the poor body of this witness to Christianity. "As their rage against him was violent, so their execution was extraordinary for they neither cut off his head nor strangled him as they usually do but they tortured him by degrees. Stripping him naked they gave him a hundred blows on the soles of his feet with a flat cudgel . . . and after which they took a bull's pizzell and beat all his body until the sinews cracked. In the end they laid him upon the wheel and with an Indian sword, they broke his bones to pieces, the poor man crying to the last gasp, 'O thou woman with the book save me' and so he died at which time there was a fearful tempest" (p. 5). Unlike the astrologers who emerged unscathed from the Great Turk's fire, this speaker of truth was the hapless victim of the Turk's cruel and unnatural forces.

While Roman Catholicism perverted all nature, Islam attempted to smother Christian truth at every opportunity. The English were fortunate that the Irish were under control and the Turks were very far away. Even so, much as Roman Catholicism worked ceaselessly to undo Protestant truth, the Turk was similarly tireless in his quest to conquer Christendom. *Newes From the Great Turke* (1645) warned Englishmen of "a blasphemous manifestation of the Grand Seignior of Constantinople against the Christians, of his entrance into Christendom" (title page). The publisher of this pamphlet claimed it to be an internal message secreted out of the Great Turk's bureaucracy and sent to an Italian merchant, who in turn informed a great London merchant. In this document the Great Turk wrote, "Our will is that this our army shall be the terror not only of Christendom but to the whole world, that by the multitude of our gallies and ships the sun, moon and stars administration thereof shall be changed, the fishes shall hide themselves in the deepest bottom of the sea . . . the beasts of the forests shall be afraid and the very tress rooted out and beaten down. And all Christendom shall by this our great might feel our anger and wrath" (pp. 2-3). Even worse, "by letter from Venice it is certified that their ships have met with some part of the Turkish fleet" (p. 4).

No less significant was the danger to Christendom posed by Islamic armies. *The Great Turke's Letter Sent unto the Prince of Transylvania* (1645) warned of an impending Turkish land attack on three fronts. According to this alleged translation of a secret directive, the Great Turk wrote to the Prince of Transylvania, "Thou and thy people ought to fear and must expect nothing else but death . . . for I will destroy thee with thine own people without hindrance. I will plunder thee and leave thee a memory of my bloody sword after me. . . . I will moreover plant my own religion effectively therein and destroy for ever thy crucified God whose wrath I fear not" (p. 3). As if blaspheming the Lord were not sufficient, the Great Turk went on, "I will besides this couple thy sacred priests to plows and make dogs and wild beasts to suck the breasts of women . . . I will have you all burnt" (p. 5).

After pointing out that "the Goliath is already at the gates of Transylvania to pass from there to Hungary" (p. 4), the supposed translator of the letter asked, "Shall we not take pity on our brethren who are Christians? Shall we be so base as to let that Infidel invade the empire of the west as he hath done to that of the east? Shall our hearts be so frozen as not to be kindled with the zeal of avenging the injury done to the divine majesty of God?" (p. 5). And all the while, England lay helplessly paralyzed by rebellion in Catholic Ireland and at home.

Jews were every bit as unnatural as Roman Catholics, as peculiar as Turks, as opposed to true Christianity as either of them, and the greatest enemy to humanity for the longest number of centuries. They combined the worst features of all other seditious heathens while adding a few touches all their own. Like Catholics, Jews were unnatural, strange, devious, and evil, and practiced an immoral religion. Like Turks, they were the ruthless opponents of the Christian truth, which in their secret (and black) hearts they knew to be true. Whereas Roman Catholicism existed in a geographic dimension with a world center in faraway Rome or in Ireland, which could be smashed and defeated, and the Turks were even further away than that, Jews were eternally, if not literally, present in England. Jews were the function of evil in time: They had rejected Christ in the past, continued to do so in the present, and perpetrated all that was wrong in the world. They poisoned wells, caused plague, cheated at commerce, and smelled bad. Yet some Englishmen seriously urged the readmission of Jews, who had been expelled in the thirteenth century, to England.[3] Indeed, the second decade of the interregnum witnessed a very lively debate in which some argued that welcoming Jews to England would prove economically beneficial and would even stand England in good stead with God. For others, however, inviting Jews to England was like internalizing a cancerous infection. In either event, the great Jewish debate of the 1650s promised to affect every Englishman's life directly.

The problem was simple; the presence of Jews might be good for business, but England had to consider its long history of anti-Semitism.[4] Throughout Europe, medieval society had been able to exorcise its own fears of the world by heaping responsibility upon "devilish" Jews for any and every unfortunate natural occurrence such as plague, drought and other natural disasters. But England had been more innovative than other countries. In 1144 it was the first country to try a Jew for the alleged ritual murder of a young Christian child in order to obtain blood for making Jewish Passover bread. Then in 1215 and in 1290 England was the first country to expel an entire Jewish community. Since then the only Jews with whom Englishmen had had to cope were the stereotypical images in Marlowe's *The Jew of Malta* or Shakespeare's *The Merchant of Venice,* both of which affirmed English dislike of Jews. The locale for both of these stories was, of course, in Catholic lands.

On the other hand, the new mercantile economy of the seventeenth century placed Jews in a more favorable light. Some Englishmen noted that local economies flourished wherever Jews and New Christians (that is, those Spanish and Portuguese Jews who converted to Christianity) were permitted residence and cited the prosperity of Antwerp, Amsterdam, Hamburg, Venice, Bordeaux, Marseille and other important centers of international trade.[5] The English, like others, commonly believed that Jews and New Christians controlled large segments of trade with the Indies, the Orient, and South America. Few considered the possibility that good trade laws and open government were good for trade and, incidentally, initiated tolerance of Jewish residence as well. In short, the pamphlets had it upside down. While some Jews were involved in trade, as were the Dutch and the English, linking Jews to the control of international trade was largely a fable, much as the Jewish control of plagues had been a popular belief in earlier centuries. The stereotype of the Jew in international trade, however, was of special value to the Englishman during the interregnum. To put this into a clearer English perspective, those countries giving Jews and New Christians residence and a free hand economically, most notably Holland and northern Germany, were able to despoil Spain of her trade routes. And after England's own trade wars with Holland in the early 1650s, some Englishmen wished to make economic allies of the Jews against the Dutch. Hence, despoiling Spain of its trade routes and weakening Dutch economic power could be brought about by inviting Jews back to England.

The traumas of revolution, regicide, trade wars, inflation, and starvation further raised the specter of Armageddon, the battle of Gog and Magog, and the appearance of the anti-Christ. The Fifth Monarchists were most notable for maintaining these views, but apocalyptic expectation was widespread during the revolution as it had been during the Reformation and other significant periods of change.[6] Large numbers of Englishmen joyfully anticipated Jesus' imminent return in 1656 and on the continent, too, serious scholars believed that 1656 would usher in a new age. It had long been thought that the conversion of the Jews would herald the millennium, but this latest twist in apocalyptic logic also postulated that Jesus could return only after Jews were spread throughout the world. Since no Jews lived in the British Isles, Jesus could not return until they were readmitted into England.[7] Indeed, some authors believed that Jewish conversion would be almost a certainty should England invite Jews to God's island. *The Resurrection of Dead Bones, or, The Conversion of the Jews* (1655) reported fictitious meetings of Jews who earnestly wished to convert. Samuel Brett's *A Narrative of the Proceedings of a Great Council of Jews Assembled in the Plains of Ageda in Hungaria, to Examine the Scriptures Concerning Christ* (1655) described an alleged eight-day conference in which 300 Jewish leaders on the verge of conversion debated Christ's virtues. In the midst of the debate emissaries from Rome appeared and made the case for a Roman Catholic interpretation of Scripture and Christianity (p. 11) . The Jews were so horrified that the good news of the Gospel might be understood in this fashion that "they were exceedingly troubled thereafter and fell into high clamor against them [i.e., Roman Catholics] and their religion, crying out 'No Christ.' . . . They rent their clothes and cast dust upon their heads and cried out aloud, 'blasphemy, blasphemy,' and upon this the council broke up" (p. 11). Brett was truly disturbed by these events, although they never really occurred. In point of fact, Brett created the whole story top to bottom, although it certainly expressed current English attitudes. He noted, for instance, that had it not been for the Roman Catholic delegation, "I do believe that there were many Jews there that would have been persuaded to own the Lord Jesus." Indeed, because Rome also recognized that most Jews would convert to Protestantism, some Jewish leaders were convinced that Rome would "cause an unhappy period to their council" to do all it could to discourage Jews from converting at another council meeting. This rabbi "professed to me that he much desired the presence of some Protestant Divines and especially of our English Divines of whom he had a better opinion . . . for he did believe that we have a great love to their nation . . . and understood that they did ordinarily pray for the conversion of their nation which he did acknowledge to be a great token of our love towards them. And especially he commended the ministers of London for excellent preachers and for their charity towards their nation" (p. 12). Clearly, "it appeareth that Rome is the greatest enemy to the Jews' conversion."

The debate about Jews raged. W. Tomlinson's *A Bosom Opened to the Jews* (1656) met its response in Thomas Collier's *A Brief Answer . . . Against the Coming of the Jews* (1656). William Prynn wrote a two-volume work entitled *A Short Demurrer to the Jews Remitter into England* (1656) and was answered by D. L.'s shorter but more passionate *Israel's Condition and Cause Pleaded* (1656). Even Jewish leaders aided in this process. Mennasseh ben Israel, an important leader of the Jewish community in Holland, wrote to Cromwell about Jewish residence in England, believing that Jews should return to England for messianic reasons. Hence we find such pamphlets as Moses Wall's *The Hope of Israel by Menasseh ben Israel, Whereunto are Added Some Discourses Upon the Point of The Conversion of the Jews* (1651).

If one grew bored with the debate concerning the readmission of Jews into England, one could speculate whether Native Americans were, in fact, Jews.[8] Thomas Thorowgood's *Jews in America, or, Probabilities that the Americans Are of That Race* (1650) was just one of many works that

argued that Native American rites and language were directly related to
ancient Jews and Hebrew. Like all other participants in this debate,
Thorowgood was unfamiliar with the languages and customs of either
group. Nevertheless, he assured his readers that the Jews believed the
connection existed. He wrote, "I was told of a Jew who came from America to Amsterdam and brought to the Jews residing there news concerning the ten tribes, that he had been with them upon the border of their
land and had conversed with some of them for a short space and seen and
heard remarkable things while he stayed with them" (p. E1b). Thorowgood was not alone in his convictions. He cited a work by Antione Mon-
terinos, who wrote, "The first inhabitants of America were of the Ten
tribes, moreover, that they are scattered also in other countries which he
names [that is, China, India, and points east] and that they keep their true
religion, hoping to return again into the Holy Land in due time" (p. E2).

Not everyone was convinced, however. Hamon L'Estrange, in his *Americans No Jews, or, Improbabilities That the Americans Are of That Race*
(1651), argued that Native Americans were only innocent pagans whereas the Jews were completely evil because they had rejected Jesus. In the
end, the latter view prevailed, a point of real importance to the Puritan
who in 1648 had written *An Endeavor After the Reconcilement of That
Difference Between Presbyterians and Independents About Church Government in a Discourse Touching the Jews Synogogue.* Had Thorowgood's views rather than those of L'Estrange prevailed, and had it been
determined that Native Americans were really Jews, ecumenical Puritans
attempting to prove Christian legitimacy on the basis of ancient Jewish
ritual would have been hard-pressed to reconcile their differences with
Native American lore as well, which, to say the least, was not quite Presbyterian.

As if this were not peculiar enough, there was an outbreak of philo-
Semitism during the revolution. Some Puritans believed themselves to be
yet a newer version of "true Israel," that perennial self-proclaimed man-
tle of sainthood continually adopted by Christendom's most recent elite
of truth.[9] Some even came to believe that the English were in fact descen-
dants of the ten lost tribes of Israel. This ideological philo-Semitism even
reached the shores of the New World, where some Pilgrims envisioned
themselves as the new Children of Israel making their way out of
Europe's Egypt. Some even wished to make Hebrew the official language of the New Canaan, despite the fact that none knew the language
and others wished to reinstitute the provisions of the old covenant.[10]
More extravagant still: Ranters, for whom everything was inside out,

believed that the English Revolution was but the first stage in a world-wide cataclysm that would turn the entire world's social system upside down. In order to end up on top, they thought it best to be on the bottom of things before the great cataclysm took place. With no one lower than a Jew, John Robins, Thomas Tany, George Foster, and other Ranters, using convoluted logic, identified themselves as Jews. Tany claimed to be the high priest Aaron, John Robins stated that he had been commissioned to redeem the Jews, and George Foster changed his name to Israel Foster after wrestling with English poverty just as Jacob the Patriarch changed his name to Israel after wrestling with the angel.[11]

Not everyone was in favor of encouraging Jewish residence in England. If some theological pamphlets expressed the positive side of Jewish residence in England, other publications attempted to reinforce the medieval stereotype of the foreign, strange, and dangerous Jew. *The Wandering Jew,* published at the height of the public controversy in 1656, retold the classic medieval story of the mythological Jew rejecting Jesus. According to the story, when Jesus labored as he carried the cross, he requested a cup of water from a Jewish bystander. When the Jew would not give Jesus even this small solace, he was cursed to wander the earth for all time until the second coming.[12] This apocryphal and very stereotypical representation of Jews emphasized the need for Christian societies to follow Jesus' example and reject the Jews. In short, there was no place for Jews in revolutionary England until after Jesus returned.

Several years earlier, in 1647, another version of this classic tale had been published under the title *News From Holland.* It was reprinted in 1655 with the added subtitle "A short relation of two witnesses now living, of the suffering and passion of our savior Jesus Christ, the one being a Gentile, the other a Jew, which sufferings they beheld as eye-witnesses when our Lord was crucified." (However, the Gentile was unimportant to the story.) The main character, here given the name Ahasuaros (the name of the King of Persia in the Book of Esther), was another traditional wandering Jew. In this account, however, he stridently criticized fellow Jews. Apparently, the author thought that if you could not believe a Jew's negative assessment of other Jews, who could you believe? Ranters?

Another pamphlet also advanced the cause of Jewish exclusion by connecting traditional dislike of Jews with hatred of other enemies. *A False Jew, or, a Wonderful Discovery of a Scot, Baptized at London for a Christian, Circumcised at Rome to Act a Jew but Rebaptized at Hexham for a Believer but Found out At Newcastle to be a Cheat* (1654) tied together three of England's foes: Scots, Catholics, and Jews. The title page of this curious pamphlet informs us that Thomas Ramsey, "born of Scotch parents at London, sent lately from Rome by a special unction and benediction of the pope, landed at Newcastle under the name of Thomas Horsley but immediately gave himself out for a Jew by the name of Rabbi Joseph ben Israel, Mant. Hebr. soon after baptized at Hexham by Mr. Tillam and by a special providence of God found out by the magistrates and Ministers of Newcastle upon Tine to be an imposter and emissary of Rome and since sent up to the General and Council of State to be further inquired into" (title page). Throughout the pamphlet, the text continually referred to Ramsey the Catholic Scot as a Jew although his only identification with Jews was that he lied about being Jewish. Still, the pamphlet drew the conclusion that the infection of Jewish residence, once let loose upon God's island, would have dire consequences. "Dear brethren," the author intoned, "keep the door strictly closed, let none come over the wall nor do not you brake [sic] it down to let such in." Clearly, Scots, Papists, and Jews were all out to hurt England.

It was a measure of English confusion that even negative stories presented Jews as experts on world affairs, faraway places, and distant events. At times, the wandering Jew even possessed miraculous prophetic abilities. In 1660, one way to demonstrate that Charles II's return was in keeping with God's wishes, and not the result of political necessity, was to have the eternal wandering Jew appear as an extraordinary witness to Charles's coronation. *England's Warning Piece* (1660) indicated that the pamphlet contained the "most strange and wonderful predictions of Cleombrotus, a heathen Jew, prophesied in the year 1272, upon the reigns of 29 kings of England, from Edward I to Charles V, 1799." The Jewish prophet in this chapbook was a reworking of the wandering Jew theme, but in this version the Jew was employed to express the view that Parliament will be disbanded and the monarchy restored in 1660 and will thrive thereafter until 1799.

Despite the hysteria, the readmission of Jews to England was resolved in 1656 with much less drama than the partisans of either side would have liked. After hearing all sides argue their cases, Cromwell could not decide which course of action to take, and in 1656, a committee created to judge this matter finally determined that Jews had never been truly expelled from England in the first place and could therefore settle in England should they wish. Thereafter some Jews did return to England, but they were most likely New Christians. Hence, neither fears nor hopes were fulfilled. The readmission of Jews brought about neither an increase in poisoned wells nor vast new wealth. And if Jesus did not return as hoped, at least Charles II did.

Part III
Sin and Society in Fallen England

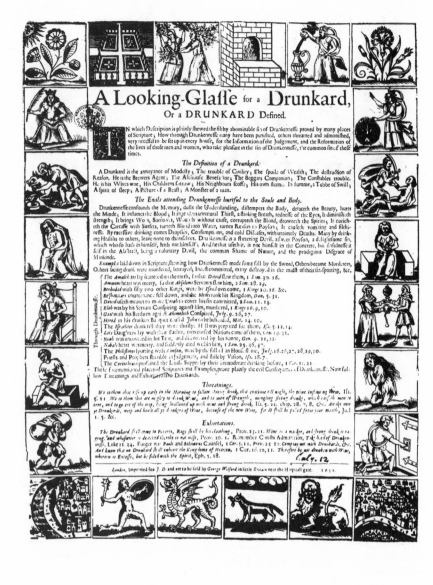

A Looking-Glasse for a Drunkard,
Or a DRUNKARD Defined.

IN which Description is plainly shewed the filthy abominable sin of Drunkennesse proved by many places of Scripture; How through Drunkennesse many have been punished, others threatned and admonished, very needfull to be set up in every house, for the Information of the Judgement, and the Reformation of the lives of those men and women, who take pleasure in the sin of Drunkennesse, the common sin of these times.

The Definition of a Drunkard:

A Drunkard is the annoyance of Modesty; The trouble of Civility; The spoile of Wealth; The destruction of Reason. He is the Brewers Agent; The Alehouse Benefactor; The Beggars Companion; The Constables trouble. He is his Wives woe, His Childrens Sorrow; His Neighbours scoffe; His own shame. In summe, a Tubbe of Swill; A spirit of sleep; A Picture of a Beast; A Monster of a man.

The Evils attending Drunkennesse hurtfull to the Soule and Body.

Drunkennesse confounds the Memory, dulls the Understanding, distempers the Body, detaceth the Beauty, hurts the Minde, It inflames the Blood; It ingenders unnatural Thirst, a stinking Breath, rednesse of the Eyes, It diminisheth strength, It brings Woes, Sorrows, Wounds without cause, corrupteth the Blood, drowneth the Spirits, It enricheth the Carcasse with Sorrows, turneth Bloud into Water, turnes Reason to Poyson; It causeth vomiting and filthinesse. By excessive drinking comes Dropsies, Consumptions, and cold Diseases, with untimely Deaths. Many by drinking Healths to others, leave none to themselves. Drunkennesse is a flattering Devill, a sweet Poyson, a delightsome sin, which who so hath in himself, hath not himself; And he that useth it, is not himself in the Concrete, but sinfulnesse it self in the Abstract, being a voluntary Devil, the common Shame of Nature, and the prodigious Disgrace of Mankinde.

Examples laid down in Scripture, shewing how Drunkennesse made some fall by the Sword, Others became Murderers, Others being drunk were murdered, betrayed, Incest committed, many destroyed in the midst of their sinsporting, &c.

Through Drunkennesse.
- The Amaleckites lay scattered on the earth, that David slew them, 1 Sam. 30. 16.
- Ammons heart was merry, so that Absalom Servants slew him, 2 Sam. 28. 29.
- Benhadad with fifty two other Kings, were by Israel overcome, 1 Kings 10. 16. &c.
- Belshazzars countenance fell down, and the Medes took his Kingdom, Dan. 5. 31.
- David useth meanes to make Uriah to cover his sin committed, 2 Sam. 11. 13.
- Elah was by his Servant Conspiring against him, murthered, 1 Kings 16. 9, 10.
- Gaal with his Brethren against Abimelech Conspired, Judg. 9. 26, 27.
- Herod in his drunken Banquet caused John to be beheaded, Mat. 14. 10.
- The Israelites drank till they were thirsty. Hell was prepared for them, Isa. 5. 13, 14.
- Lots Daughters lay with their Father, two cursed Nations came of them, Gen. 19. 31.
- Noah was uncovered in his Tent, and discovered by his Sonne, Gen. 9. 21, 22.
- Nabals heart was merry, and suddenly died within him, 1 Sam. 25. 36, 37.
- The Philistines sporting with Samson, were by the fall of an House slain, Judg. 16. 25, 27, 28, 29, 30.
- Priests and Prophets stumble in judgement, and faile by Vision, Isa. 28. 7.
- The Corinthians profaned the Lords Supper by their immoderate drinking before, 1 Cor. 11. 21.

These forementioned places of Scriptures and Examples, prove plainly the evil Consequences of Drunkennesse. Now follow Threatnings and Exhortations to Drunkards.

Threatnings.

Wo to them that rise up early in the Morning to follow strong drink, that continue till night, the wine inflaming them. Isa. 5. 11. Wo to them that are mighty to drink Wine, and to men of strength, mingling strong drinks, which causeth men to erre, and to go out of the way, being swallowed up with wine and strong drink. Isa. 5. 22. chap. 28. 7, 8, &c. Awake now ye Drunkards, weep and howle all ye Drinkers of Wine, because of the new Wine, for it shall be pulled from your mouth, Joel 1. 5. &c.

Exhortations.

The Drunkard shall come to Poverty, Rags shall be his clothing, Prov. 23. 21. Wine is a mocker, and strong drink is raging, and whosoever is deceived thereby is not wise, Prov. 20. 1. Remember Christs Admonition, Take heed of Drunkennesse, Luke 21. 34. Forget not Pauls and Solomons Counsel, 1 Cor. 5. 11. Prov. 23. 20. Company not with Drunkards, &c. And know that no Drunkard shall inherit the Kingdome of Heaven, 1 Cor. 16. 10, 11. Therefore be not drunk with Wine, wherein is Excesse, but be filled with the Spirit, Eph. 5. 18.

Gal. 5. 12.

London, Imprinted for J. D. and are to be sold by George Wolford in little Britain neer the Hospitall gate. 1652.

♦ ♦ ♦

8

Signs of Sin Everywhere: Alehouses, Alchohol, Drugs, and More.

"ALE WILL MAKE A MAN A LINGUISHT [SIC]; IT WILL TEACH HIM GREEK IN TWO HOURS."

—*John Taylor, Ale Ale-vated into the Ale-titude (1653)*

No one was happy about the apparent social anarchy evident in London and elsewhere. Many Englishmen believed the collapse of traditional institutions to be divine punishment for Charles's death. Advocates of political change, of course, viewed the current social unrest as God's punishment for England's toleration of popery and Catholicism. But even supporters of the revolution feared that the fragmenting of organized religion constituted a dangerous slide into anarchy. The seemingly sudden appearance of sects and religious charlatans provided yet another sign that society was unable to control its dangerous fringe elements and would soon prove impotent to impose even the simplest standards of law and order. The increasing religious and political radicalization of officers in the army was nothing short of alarming, especially since the government depended upon the army for its own stability. Many people also believed that there was a decline in social ethics and that personal morality was going unchecked. There was an increase in crime, or so people believed; there was in increase in prostitution, or so people believed; there was an increase in alcoholism, or so people believed. There were vagrants and masterless men and women everywhere and no signs that society could heal itself anywhere. In short, the process of disintegration, which had already affected the dismantling of state and church, was now visible in society at large. There were, in other words, signs of sin everywhere. Only a further revolution in morality, or, alternately, a return to monarchy, could rectify England's woes.

The word "Puritanism" still evokes associations with sexual prudery. In fact, the years of the English Revolution did witness governmental attempts to reform personal and public morals.[1] Yet despite a large volume of Puritan treatises and polemics excoriating Londoners for their immoral ways and the on-again, off-again parliamentary intention to remedy this dreadful situation, the campaign probably influenced the average seventeenth-century Englishman only marginally. Like Prohibition in the twentieth century, it provided more steam than whistle. Indeed, it is even possible that the Puritan decades actually witnessed an increase in the English sensual appetite as opium, marijuana, tobacco, and coffee took their places alongside long-loved ale.

Even before the two decades of the Puritan revolution initiated legislative attempts to reform personal and public morals, many Englishmen had come to believe that society was succumbing to the sewer of immorality. Indeed, a leading Puritan accusation against the bishops was that Anglican ecclesiastical courts were soft on sexual offenders and that the entire system of clerical regulation was more interested in maintaining empty ritual and priestly garb than in advancing meaningful Christian morality. In his address before Parliament in February 1641, Nathanael Fiennes, a leading Presbyterian personality and spokesman, demanded that ecclesiastical courts be stripped of their authority in the areas of personal and social morality.[2] In that same year the Long Parliament created the Commons' Committee for Religion to investigate the continuing viability of these courts and dutifully followed the committee's recommendations for their disbanding. Puritans hoped to enforce standards of personal behavior through government regulation instead of ecclesiastical offices. But while Parliament disbanded the clerical courts, it was unable to create either new legislation or effective governmental supervisory agencies. Instead, it created even greater chaos.[3]

Between 1640 and 1641 rhetoric rang in Parliament demanding greater government power to punish incest, adultery, prostitution, drunkenness, swearing, blasphemy, and other vices. Yet despite considerable parliamentary discussion, it enacted only simplistic programs of moral reform: it closed the legitimate theater and imposed Sunday blue laws. However, it created neither new legislation nor agencies of social control to replace traditional ecclesiastical authority.

Parliament took up the task of reforming the public's personal, social and religious behavior again in earnest six years later in 1647. A new law that combined the current penalties against drunkenness and swearing was just the beginning.[4] Two years later, in 1649, Parliament placed restrictions on the right of publication, and legislation to curtail blasphemy in 1650 limited public speeches, sermons, or writings expressing extreme religious views. Committees for the Ejecting of Scandalous Ministers attempted to cleanse the countryside of infamous ministers and prosecuted, jailed, or removed from their positions some of the most notorious. Despite these new laws, the complete control of blasphemy still proved elusive because the government could not control and censor the increasing number of small hand presses in London.

In 1650, the true cornerstone of the Puritan campaign for Christian decency—legislation against prostitution, adultery, and fornication—finally appeared. The Commonwealth's Act of May 10, 1650, "for suppressing the detestable sins of incest, adultery and fornication," attempted to place the full weight and authority of the revolutionary government behind the enforcement of a standard of sexual morality.[5] Incest and adultery became felonies carrying a death sentence. Fornication merited three months in jail. Brothelkeepers were to be whipped, pilloried, branded, and jailed for three years for the first offense and executed for the second offense. Through these various laws the government hoped to curtail the most violent antigovernment opinion from reaching a potential audience, the most outrageous blasphemy from being preached and published, drunkenness curtailed, and deviation from a steadfastly monogamous sexual norm discouraged. Like many other programs of moral and social purification undertaken by revolutionary governments in other centuries, implementation fell short of the goal.

Assessing the actual effect of this new panoply of restrictive legislation is difficult. Despite controls on the press, for instance, large numbers of scandalous newspapers, some even quite pornographic, appeared. The proliferation of blasphemous "mechanic preachers" was a social commonplace. Radical political and religious publications found hospitable presses and an avid readership. It is likely that the residents of a city as large and unruly as revolutionary London easily ignored the new morality laws. In fact, the campaign for moral reform met with stiff resistance all over England, but, even worse from a Puritan perspective, much "immorality" had already been integrated into the institutional framework of English life.

If one institution epitomized the world of immoral behavior it was the alehouse.[6] Other types of drinking establishments such as inns and taverns served the established classes, but the alehouse was in a league of its own. According to one report, London suburbs teemed with alehouses that also served as brothels, where "many immodest, lascivious and shameless women generally reputed for notorious common and professed whores, who are entertained into victualizing or other houses . . . for base and filthy lucre, sitting at their doors, exposing and offering themselves to passers by."[7] Similarly, alehouses were allegedly centers of crime. One alehouse proprietor near Billingsgate supposedly "procured all the cutpurses [i.e., pickpockets] about this city to repair to his house [where] there was a school-house set up to learn young boys to cut purses."[8]

Alehouses were also the center of radical political activity for Ranters, Levellers, and many other despised groups. Most offensive of all to the Puritans, the alehouse was a place of fun. People drank, sang, danced, cursed, laughed, and gambled there. The alehouse epitomized the "life in the creature" that so many abstemious Puritans found deplorable. As one sour and dour moralistic Puritan pamphlet explained, "It is better to go to the house of mourning than to the house of feasting. And sorrow is better than laughter for by the sadness of the continence, the heart is made better. The heart of the wise is a heart of mourning but the heart of fools is a heart of mirth."[9]

Aside from its after-hours reputation, other factors contributed to the popularity of the alehouse. It was one of the few places, perhaps the only place, where the poor served the poor in a relaxed and easygoing atmosphere. Unlike taverns and inns, the alehouse was an informal affair, often consisting of no more than a few benches in a back room of someone's house. Alehouse drink, too, was informal. Unlike wines, aqua vitae, beer, or other beverages served to a wealthier clientele in better surroundings, ale was easy and cheap to brew. Since it did not keep well and had to be sold quickly, ale encouraged heavy consumption, which, in turn, may explain why the alehouse was the scene of so much singing, dancing, and sex.

The alehouse also met definite social and economic needs. With rising unemployment and wartime social and demographic dislocation, increasing numbers of rural peasants came to London in search of employment. Many set up informal, often temporary, alehouses to supplement their incomes. Moreover, in an age when families were disrupted by war and employment, significant numbers of widows or older single women found themselves alone and without financial or family support. The alehouse was one of few business possibilities open to women. Then too, the alehouse drinking ethic also made for greater gender equality. One pamphlet made a point of describing "jolly sisters [who] pledged and did agree it was no sin to be as drunk as he."[10] And an alehouse with prostitution as a sideline, as was common, would do even better if managed by women. Many alehouses, if not most, were unregistered and remained so for the remainder of the century. For all these reasons, alehouses proliferated, and there may have been as many as 35,000 alehouses in England by mid-century.[11] Hence, the Puritan effort to eliminate alehouses was as much an attack upon class as it was a condemnation of a specific way of life. "In sum," one scholar has recently concluded, "there was a broad consensus of opinion among the middling and the upper ranks of society in Tudor and early Stuart England that alehouses were a new and increasingly dangerous force in popular society . . . victualizing and harboring the destitute and vagrant, breeding crime, disorder and drunkenness, fostering promiscuity and other breeches of orthodox morality; and that they served as the stronghold of popular opposition to the established religious and political order. In other words, the alehouses was perceived as the command post of men who sought to turn the traditional world upside down."[12]

From the Puritan perspective, whores, street rogues, alehouses, crime, blasphemy, alcoholism, and even "mechanic preachers" were all tied together in a devilish Gordian knot, and there could be no reforming society without the elimination of them all. Indeed, at least one publication linked all these Puritan enemies in one united, alcoholic front. The pamphlet *A Brown Dozen of Drunkards, alias, Drink-Hards* (1648) attacked those who had become anti-Presbyterian, all of whom it identified as base drunks. In addition to a classical harangue against drinkers and drinking, it asserted "no disease [was] more spread over millions of microcosm like a canker, more domineering, more incapable of cure than this swelling gangrene or a swilling drinking dropsie except a tympany of more than antichristian, even Luciferian, pride in many sectaries" (p. 4). The anti-Puritan drunkard "is so intoxicated in his giddy brain . . . that he staggers in his motions like our old and new Enthusiasts, Familists, Anabablers [*sic*] once in Germany and now in England with our new Seekers" (p. 1). In other words, the real problem was the disease "called Liberty of Conscience, to plant every nation and nature with more immunity and more impunity than in Poland and Holland [with] his own brain-bred religion, through a blasphemous Alchoran or Talmud or Valentinus his renewed fond aeons, or the reawakened dreams of Montanus and Priscilla or the deluding dotages of the Fratricellians and Beghardines [*sic*] and filthy Familists and Adamites which fired Italy and Germany" (p. 7). Other separatists also could not maintain sobriety; the author condemned "another strange bachanalia . . . that poor, silly, simple, vulgar Mechanic idiot drunk with blind and bewitching zeal and self conceit for his suppositions and imaginary gifts, [who] should conceit himself to be as legal as able as gifted as called a preacher as any other Sons of the Prophets . . . on whom the Church hath called to the function of a Pastor" (p. 17).

Identifying alcoholism with radical sectarianism may have seemed reasonable to some abstemious Puritans, but it incurred the risk of turning drinkers against the revolution and providing monarchists with a popular hammer to use against the cause of religious reform. This indeed proved to be the case, and some of the most effective, humorous, and sophisticated antirevolutionary literature concerned the issue of ale. Whatever else Englishmen thought of religious reform, many fondly remembered that the old church supported May games and feasts at which much drinking took place or that Archbishop Laud supported Church-Ale parish celebrations in Somerset in 1633.[13] Presbyterians especially frowned upon the general popularity of the *Book of Sports,* first published under James I in 1618 and reprinted in 1633. It not only condoned drinking, but the holding of May games, Whitsun Ales, morris dances, and maypoles after Sunday service. While Puritans often emphasized their frustration with the drinking of "healths" (or toasts) rather than opposing ale itself, their pamphlets indicated that it was the sinner and not the sin that was hated. Ale was a religious issue, and those who drank were, quite simply, immoral. Insofar as these various patterns of degenerate behavior were also identified with the poor, who constituted the overwhelming percentage of the population, Puritan reformers had their work cut out for them. Additionally, as more of the common poor could read, the shabby logic of those calling for moral reform became increasingly obvious.

The surest arrow in the Puritan quiver of moral reform was to attack the drinking of "healths" as particularly onerous and thereby discredit alcohol consumption and alehouse culture in general. A case in point was *A Divine Potion to Preserve Spiritual Health* (1648) by John Geree, pastor of St. Faith's church in London. The pamphlet took aim at the drinking of "personalized healths," a customary drinking practice whereby friends would sit in a circle and toast the health of an absent friend by emptying their cups in a single swallow, which led to rapid drunkenness. Additionally, *A Divine Potion* argued that drinking to someone's health opposed the truth of predestination, in which God made these decisions and not man. Indeed, the drinking of healths was even attacked as an infringement upon the privacy of the absent friend. Geree called the practice "both uncivil and unlawful . . . when all must be compelled or engaged upon pain of censure and scorn at least to drink to such a measure with such a ceremony. Therefore, health drinking is unlawful" (p. 3). It is unlikely that anyone took Geree very seriously. Certainly those voluntarily entering taverns and saluting their absent friends would pay little attention to his pamphlet. In any event, Geree had little personal reason to fear that alehouse denizens would drink to his health and thereby insult either him or God.

Another pamphlet took this same argument one step further and tried to enlist the king in the effort against alcohol. *Mr. Prynne's Letter and Proposals to King Charles* (1637), originally dedicated to Charles I, was republished in 1660 and rededicated to Charles II. The chapbook argued that drinking to the king's health was an insult to the king's honor; Prynne's tone, however, demonstrated how Puritans hated the drinker more than the drink. Prynne asked, "Is not this a great affront, indignity and dishonor to your Majesty that your sacred health, your name and Royal Crown should be thus profaned and banded up and down in every drunkard's mouth, in every cup and can, in every tavern, taphouse, hall or cellar, that every dangerous, infamous and stigmatical Belialist, every debased and brutish pot-companion should so far debase and undervalue them as to prostitute them to their swinish sins and lusts?" (p. 3). It is possible that this logic was more obvious to nondrinkers than to those saluting their king. In any event, it is doubtful whether Charles II was influenced by this Puritan logic. He may well have remembered that it was not the drinker to his father's health who rebelled against the king and cut off his head.

Some publications associated the evils of alcohol with other sins. The author of *Wine and Women* (1646) claimed to be a reformed courtesan who "spent the time past of my life walking in wantonness, riot, surfeiting and drunkenness." The pamphlet consisted of prohibitionist verse alternating with passages from Scripture against the twin evils of substance abuse and sexual immorality. Line after line informed the reader that "he that loves women, doubtless favors wine" (p. 7), or that "'tis hard to find a drunkard that is chaste." The identification of immorality with the lower classes was also apparent when the author wrote, "Take heed of being private with a woman/ But chief if her looks proclaim her common" (p. 8); or, "It would be strange to see one fair and poor/ That were not envious, proud nor yet a whore" (p. 12). Hence, if Puritans often hated the sinner more than the sin, poor sinners, especially females, were most hateful of all. After thirty pages of such wisdom the pamphlet concluded, "By following harlots no man can do well/ Because she leads to death and hell" (p. 27). It is doubtful whether rhyming couplets had a profound effect on the targeted reader.

The broadside *The Great Sins of Drunkenness and Gluttony Set Forth in the Proper Colors* (1656) vilified the two sins of its title and added, "Why wilt thou swear, curse, lust and lie?" To this perplexing question the author gave the depressing answer: "Think'st thou on this, that all must die." On the happier side, the broadside presented interesting pictures of a glutton and a drunkard on its masthead. Four years earlier another broadside, entitled *A Looking Glass for a Drunkard, or, A Drunkard Defined,* had published no less than thirty-three small humorous pictures of diverse drunken activities around its border. This author conceived of the novel contention that drunkenness was actually divine punishment for an individual's prior committed personal sins, something like a soteriological hangover. Hence, immorality, like poverty, was a deserved sign of God's displeasure, along with monsters, apparitions, and prodigies. Since reforming the drunk was impossible, it was thought that slandering his character might diminish his thirst, and so the drunkard was condemned as "a tub of swill." It is unlikely that readers were offended, however, because they had probably read these very same ideas in an identical single sheet entitled *The Drunkard's Character,* published six years earlier in 1646, without the funny little pictures around its border.

If the large number of sermons excoriating Englishmen for loose morality indicate the intensity of Puritan desire for reform, the far larger number of pamphlets mocking this campaign must attest to a more powerful contrary attitude prevalent in the population at large. Moreover, compared with the rather boring publications championing Puritan temperance, those opposing the campaign were far more amusing and varied. There were also commercial interests opposed to the harsh laws against drinking, especially against the campaign against Sunday drinking. It was a common practice for laborers and apprentices to spend much of Sunday drinking in alehouses, finally staggering to church in the afternoon. Many more refined churchgoers found this offensive, especially when fistfights, or worse, disturbed their meditations. John Addy cited one instance where "Edmund Saurer was drunk at morning upon a Sabbath day and that he did vomit upon the communion table."[14] To curb this distressing condition, new Sunday blue laws passed in 1641 prohibited the sale of liquor, tobacco, and even cooked meats on the Lord's day. Reasonably, this legislation elicited an immediate response; one example was the pamphlet *The Lamentable Complaints of Nick Froth the Tapster and Rulerost the Cook Concerning the Restraint Lately Set Forth Against Drinking, Potting and Piping on the Sabbath Day* (1641). The sentiments placed in the mouths of two merchants unhappy with these new developments probably expressed the views of many operators of small commercial establishments and their clients. In this conversation, Rulerost, the cook, asked Nick, the tapster, "Have you not heard of the restraint lately come out against us from the higher powers whereby we are commanded not to sell meat nor draw drink upon Sundays as we will answer to the contrary at our peril?" (p. 4).

Like his friend, Nick was discouraged by these new laws and demanded "why my trade should be put down, it being so necessary in a commonwealth" (p. 5) and further observed "all my profit doth arise only on Sundays . . . [and] I got more by uttering half a barrel in time of divine service than I could by a whole barrel at any other time." In any event, he concluded, drinking was harmless: "It is the soul of good fellowship . . . and it makes a man as valiant as Hercules, though he were as cowardly as a Frenchman." Rulerost agreed, adding, "I used to make eighteen pence of that which cost me but a groat provided that I sold it in service time . . . and my smoke which I sold dearer than any apothecary" (p. 6). Both merchants lamented "those happy days, now past," and both were cynical about the motives of the governing agencies. The official rationale for the new legislation was that "they should be at some church" (p. 6), and Rulerost noted, "I fear the Church wardens, Side-men and Constables will so look to our red lattices that we shall not dare to put our heads out of doors on a Sunday hereafter. . . . We must shut up our doors and hang padlocks on them and never as much as take leave of our landlords" (p. 4).

Similarly, when legislation attempted to proscribe the production of powerful ale in favor of low potency "Parliament ale," the Company of Brewers was quick to respond with the publication of *A Vindication of Strong Beer and Ale* (1647), written for "the distressed Company of Brewers, whose sad condition groans for speedy relief." The brewers and alehouse operators were frustrated by Parliament's zeal, and they hoped that this publication would drum up popular support for their cause. The opening letter noted that brewing "is very needful and also profitable to this city and suburbs, yet looked upon with an unkind aspect." Moreover, there was no justification for the consumption laws, which were "occasioned by those who may be well affected but being mistaken in their judgment."

The brewers' arguments were twofold. First, strong beer and ale had the value of good nourishment "most cherishing to poor laboring people without which they can not well subsist, their food being for the most part of such things as afford little or bad nourishment" (p. 3). Second, strong ale "was not only a sustenance against hunger but a preservative against sickness." Indeed, ale was "more powerful to expel poisonous infections than are well publicly known or taken notice of." In a tone of desperate sincerity, with hand on heart, the brewers wondered, "Should the Almighty (being provoked by our sins) afflict these parts with the infection of the plague, in what deplorable condition would the poor of the city and suburbs be if they should be deprived of the comfortable fruition of strong beer and ale?" (p. 3).

In common with many pamphleteers, the brewers believed that the Sunday blue laws and the prohibitionist campaign against potent ale stemmed from hatred of the poor. They condemned those in Parliament "whose better fare maketh them so unsensible of poor men's wants, and deny them that good beer which is so needful to their meaner food" (p. 4). The brewers were also critical of the Puritan revolutionaries, "that sort of people who . . . with an austere continence and supercilious eye and speeches agreeable thereunto, slight and despise the creature and those that deal therein. . . . The creature is made the patient of evil, groaning as it were to be delivered therefrom and yet burdened with hard censure" (p. 4). They reminded Puritans that "zeal without discretion is like heat without moisture—every way destructive," and they intoned that "God is a severe judge against those who [while] passing themselves presume to censure others, which is one of those crying sins for which the land now mourns" (p. 5).

Alehouse tapmen, roast meat vendors, and smoke shop proprietors certainly opposed the new morality for reasons of self-interest, but other pamphlets defending strong beer and ale and everything else "of the creature" also found an attentive audience. Indeed, as Puritan prohibitionists fussed and fumed about the evils of drinking, humorous publications in favor of drinking, possibly some written by royalist propagandists, became increasingly common and increasingly anti-Puritan. In fact, some of the most witty pamphlets written during the interregnum were those defending every Englishman's right to his pint of strong bitter. Judging from the large number of such publications, even assuming that many were written in jest or were sarcastic comments upon abstinence, many Englishmen disregarded Puritan admonitions.

A Health to All Vintners, Beer-Brewers and Ale Tonners (1642) sent best wishes to all "Tapsters, Bezlors, Carrowsers and Wine-Bibbers, Bench-Whistlers, Lick-Wimbles, Down Right Drunkards, Petty Drunkards, Bacchus Boys, Roaring Boys, Bachanalians, Tavern Ancients, Captain Swaggerers, Fox-Catchers, Pot and Half-Pot Men, Quart, Pint and Half Pint Men, Short Winded Glass Men, and in general, to all and every privie drunkard, Half pot companion etc. And to other Good Fellows of this Our Fraternitie whom the presents may concern, GREETINGS!" The above was signed by, among others, "Simon Sacke, Martin Muskadine, Clement Claret, William Whitewine, Benjamin Beer-Barrell and Abraham Ale-Barrell," none of whom, one suspects, were Puritans.

Even more amusing and contemptuous of temperance was an eleven-page poem published in that same year entitled *The Ex-ale-tation of Ale, the Ancient Liquor of This Realm.* In a series of verses, the anonymous author made clear that he thought the world of ale but did not think much of Puritans. Ale was good for clerks, philosophers, scholars, laborers, widows, prisoners, and beggars because it made everyone more amorous. In short, ale was good for everyone except rebels. The poem hinted of the growing political alienation resulting from consumption laws. One verse in particular expressed discontent with Puritan-sponsored, lower-alcohol "Parliament beer," which was becoming increasingly identified with the worst of Holland's Puritans:

> But now as they say, beer bears all away
> The more is the pity if right might prevail;
> For with this same beer came up heresies here
> The old Catholic drink is a bottle of ale. (p. 6)

Indeed, had the rebels loosened up a bit and relaxed in their holy battle against the bottle, they would not have made such a bloody mess of England:

> They that sit by it are good men and quiet
> No dangerous plotters in the common-weal
> Of treason or murder, for they never go further
> Than to call for and pay for a bottle of ale. (p. 9)

Another publication making many similar points was the five-page poem *A Preparative to Study, or, The Virtue of Sack* (1641), which enumerated the many virtues of sack. One four-line section praises alcohol in this way:

> Thou makest us Lords of Regions large and fair
> Whilst our conceits build castles in the air
> Since fire, earth and air thus thy inferiors be
> Henceforth I'll know no element but thee. (p. 2)

Most of all, sack made one feel young again; indeed, "Inestimable Sack! Thou makest us rich, wise and amorous, anything, I have an itch!!" (pp. 3-4).

John Taylor's witty chapbook *Ale Ale-vated into the Ale-titude* (1653) began congenially: "Ale! Beloved Brethren! I am come this day to make an oration in a tub, having drank all the ale the barrel is turned into a tub and the tub transformed into a suitable pulpit. My hope is I shall please you better than with a tale of a tub." The last sentence was a play upon the anti-Puritan proverb, "Empty tubs make the loudest noise."

In order to prove that drink stood at the very foundation of Western culture, Taylor first described the significance of the word *ale*: The Hebrews developed the first writing with the letter *ale*ph, while the Greeks turned this into the *ale*-phabet. In turn, Greek culture was spread to the rest of the world by *Ale*xander the Great, who is so called because his knowledge of drinking was collected and deposited in the great library in *Ale*xandria (p. 6). Subsequent scholars of Greek culture learned that "ale will *ale*-vate and lift the spirits with *ale*-acrity, *ale*ias mirth, *ale*ias courage, *ale*ias exhilaration and jocundity" (p. 9). And ancient wisdom was converted into medieval lore, which in turn led to the development of the mystical art of *ale*-chemy, which taught mankind a great lesson about the magical qualities of ale:

> It will turn your gold to silver wan
> And your silver into brass.
> A taylor it will make a man
> And a man it will make an ass. (p. 9)

The remainder of Taylor's learned oration attempted to describe the intellectual benefits accrued from drinking. Alcohol lead to "*ale*-loquence," and "a constant ale drinker, he will speak *ale*-gories" (pp. 11-12). More than that, "ale will make a man a linguisht [*sic*], it will teach him Greek in two hours" (p. 17). But ale had more general intellectual applications. The drinker "is mounted and *ale*-vated to an *ale*-titude . . . that he will talk of religion beyond belief, interpret the Scriptures beyond all sense and show you points of law above all reason that can be *ale*ged" (p. 12). In short, "ale is an enemy to idleness, it will work and be working in the brain as well as in the barrel" (p. 15). The oration ended with a complete recitation of the poem cited earlier, "The Ex-ale-tation of Ale, the Ancient Liquor of This Realm."

Even more humorous and more disdainful of the campaign for moral reform, *The Eighth Liberal Science, or, the New Found Art and Order of Drinking* (1650) joked about drinking from a "scholarly" vantage point. The chapbook opened with a short history of ale and beer, noting that

Noah was the first serious drinker and that from his time the noble practice has spread over the whole world. It then discussed the great variety of different national drinking habits. The nastiest drinkers were, of course, the French: "The French are our neighbors. I will spare to speak much of them but it seems they love the best of their own grapes so well that they keep the choice and chief wines to themselves and send the smallest refuse into England and other countries" (p. A4a).

The English, of course, were by far the most skilled drinkers and possessed many endearing names to refer to inebriated brothers, including, "A True Trojan, a Stiff Blade, one whose nose is dirty, one that drinks up-se freeze, and He is True Blue" (p. A5a). The English were so serious about drinking that they made a scholarly study of it. A person with a B.A. degree was "a lean drinker." An M. A. was "a fat corpulent fellow." The highest and most venerable degree was the Ph.D., which indicated "he that hath a red nose" (pp. A5b-A6a). It was also believed, within the university, that members of each discipline drank differently, and depending upon one's personal characteristics while drunk, it was possible to identify one's academic discipline. The following chart helped novices:

- He that builds castles in the air: Metaphysics
- He that sings in his drink: Music
- He that brags about his travels: Cosmography
- He that rhymes *ex tempore*: Poetry
- He that calls his fellow a drunkard: Logic
- He that brawls and wrangles in his cups: Barrister (p. A6b)

Drinking was equally popular outside the university, and the author presented equivalent descriptions of drinkers in military service and in the navy. In each case, the higher the rank, the greater the drunk's privileges regarding how, when, and where he might be sick. An admiral, for example, was entitled to vomit on your shoes, while a vice-admiral could vomit only on his own shoes, although he was permitted to urinate under the table. An intelligence officer was defined as "he that swears and lies in his drink," while an old soldier was "he that drinks three days together without respite" (p. B1b). Still other equally thoughtful descriptions of officers of the court and members of the civil service were listed. The last part of the pamphlet presented stories about the many endearing things drunkards do when they have had too much to drink. Each story has the drunkard in question urinating on himself, urinating on someone else or vomiting over himself, over someone else, or anywhere else he might be at the time.

Many Englishmen were either oblivious or indifferent to the campaign against ale and alehouses. Because the Sunday blue laws generally went unheeded, in 1646 the mayor of London published a single broadsheet entitled *A Whip for a Drunkard and a Curb for Prophaness*. He complained that many people continued to come to church red in the nose and disrupted the service. Even worse, when hauled into court, those charged with transgression of the new laws were often successful in pleading ignorance. The document therefore listed the many provisions restricting consumption of ale and strong beer in favor of lower-powered "Parliament beer." All church wardens had to distribute the mayor's broadside by "setting up a table in their respective churches" for the education of their inebriated churchgoing brothers. It is more than likely that given a choice between church and ale, a good many Englishmen opted for the latter. No one, even in jest, wrote about the need to keep people from going to church. After all, an abundance of drinking was the initial occasion for all this legislation to begin with and the probable cause of its failure as well. Drinkers, whatever their number, were learning about the benefits of revolution.

By 1649 the identification of the revolution with abstemious behavior and unpopular antialcohol legislation increasingly provided a basis for condemning the revolution as a whole. *A Curse Against Parliament Ale,* "with a blessing to the Juncto," was at first a condemnation of Parliament low-potency brew but soon became an undisguised attack upon the authority of the revolution: "The ancient drink of England to forbid/ The [most] cursed act the Juncto ever did" (p. 3). As for the rebels themselves: "Base miscreants, Rebels, could ye not invent/ Some other plague in your damned Parliament." By way of thanks to Puritans for all their efforts: "May all counties rise and pay no excise/ Till King Charles be set on his throne." And in the meantime: "May your wives all turn jades and live on their trades and their children be marked like Cain" (p. 6). The pamphlet concluded with the question "We desire to know from whence you derive your power?" (p. 7). It may seem strange that prohibitionist legislation would lead people to question authority, but it is likely that many, if not most, Englishmen were already predisposed toward this attitude. Puritan chapbooks had already questioned the moral sincerity of those who drank, but in 1649 the Puritan campaign was just building steam. The following year would see laws against free publication, blasphemers, fornication, and adultery, followed by the execution of Charles I. If Puritans had not turned most Englishmen against them with prohibitionist legislation, other aspects of the Puritan campaign would shortly accomplish that end.

While it is undoubtedly true that ale was the single most popular intoxicant, and was singularly condemned by Puritans, other mind-altering substances were becoming available that pamphlets described in glowing terms. Least obnoxious of these from a Puritan point of view was chocolate. Seventeenth-century chocolate enthusiasts did not realize that it contained phenylethylamine (PEA), the same chemical that is released in the brain when people fall in love or experience sexual excitement. Nonetheless, they appreciated it for its effects. James Wadsworth's *Chocolate, or, an Indian Drink* (1651) indicated that "it vehemently incites to Venus and causeth conception in women and hastens and facilitates their delivery." Indeed, "it is an excellent help to digestion, it cures consumption and the cough of the lungs, the New Disease, or the plague of the Guts and other fluxes, the Green Sickness, jaundice . . . it cleaneth the teeth and sweeteneth the breath, provokes urine, cures the stone and stangury, expels poison and preserves from all infectious disease" (p. A4a).

Another substance finding its way into the English heart and brain at the time was tobacco, consumed as snuff or smoked in pipes. Imported from the New World and from the Orient via Spain, tobacco became an increasingly important item of trade. The English smoked 140,000 pounds of it in 1621 and 11,300,000 pounds by 1700.[15] Fine quality unblended tobacco was a mild stimulant, but, when perfumed, it could have a powerful sedative effect. Englishmen smoked "Spanish tobacco," or marijuana, and opium as well.

Almost every pamphlet about tobacco treated it with awe but none more than the poem *Hymnus Tobaci, A Poem in Honor of Tobacco* (1651), a hymn to the effects of Spanish tobacco. The author wrote:

Fill me a pipe (boy) of that lusty smoke
That I may drink the God into my brain. (p. 13)

Nor let us be ashamed now to call
Tobacco our *Health*, our *Spirit*, our *Life*, our *All.* (p. 18)

Because many conceived of smoking to be a form of air-drinking, it was generally believed that Bacchus first discovered tobacco as well as wine. The poem had this divine Greek noting, "I do acknowledge thee a gift divine, And of near kindred to that Tree of mine" (p. 16). Indeed, wine and tobacco went together "like a pair of friends all ages wonder/ They taste far nobler joined then when assunder" (p. 55). Like wine, tobacco also had a liberating effect and dampened inhibitions. "All things are filled with smoke, songs, dances and cries," the author explained, "till mid-night pours sweet sleep into their eyes" (p. 21).

Many believed tobacco, like wine, to have medicinal value. "Mouth but the smoke awhile and thou shalt see," the author observed. "Both pain and swelling banished will be" (p. 47). Even more, it was a tonic for the healthy.

> Most blessed drug, hads't thou no other power? . . .
> Thou do chase dull drowsiness from them, now again they rise
> Their feet are firm, lightning comes from their eyes. (p. 17)

While it is possible that the author was writing about regular tobacco, it is far more likely that he was describing marijuana. The author was also familiar with opium, and he correctly distinguished between the different effects of the two upon the body:

> Tis not like the drowsiness gotten by
> The deadly poppy which the mind does tie
> In iron chains. . . .
>
> But whom tobacco's clearer spirit shall bind
> In silken ties shall in the morning find
> Both mind and body strong and with delight
> Shall tell how quietly he passed the night. (p. 64)

"Tobacco, King of Plants I may well call," he wrote about either tobacco or marijuana. "Others have single virtues, this hath all" (p. 4).

The connection between tobacco or marijuana and good sex was also understood. *Wit's Interpreter* (1656) reported:

> You that in love do mean to sport,
> Tobacco, Tobacco.
> Take a wench of the meaner sort,
> Tobacco, Tobacco . . .
> Then take occasion, time and place
> To give her some tobacco.
>
> She will be ready at your call
> To take tobacco, pipe and all
> So ready she will be to fall
> To taste your good tobacco. (pp. 124-125)

A certain Dr. Everard was so ecstatic about Spanish tobacco that he titled his chapbook *Panacea, or, The Universal Medicine, being a*

Discovery of the Wonderful Virtues of Tobacco (1659). Everard's description of the effects of smoking by Native Americans would definitely seem to indicate something more unusual than ordinary tobacco. He tells of a Native American who "drew the smoke into his mouth by a cane or a tunnel as nowadays our countrymen do too much (the more the pity) being made so drunk with the smoke until he fell asleep being deprived of all his senses and being rapt into a certain ecstasy, he fell down upon the ground where he lay most part of the day or night, not able to move" (p. 40). Even more telling, "when his drunkenness was over he told them he had conferred with the devil and as he thought, so he delivered his mind" (p. 1). Other "Indian physicians, made drunk with this smoke and having lost their senses, would relate a thousand things concerning the counsel of the Gods" (p. 41). These descriptions remain accurate portrayals of Native American ritual use of peyote and marijuana in the American Northwest and Canada.

The central part of the pamphlet enumerated "tobacco's" many positive medical uses, which included cures for lesions, warts, and ulcers of various types. It was useful in treating "the breaking of wind," venomous snake bites, vaginal disorders, and baldness. In order to extract its most beneficial medicinal benefits, the "tobacco" should be smoked, boiled, or chewed, or the oils extracted and mixed with other elements, in one case, two ounces of goat's suet. These concoctions are curious in that tobacco oils in this concentration can be toxic, and eating even small amounts of the weed itself will cause severe gastric distress and can prove fatal if ingested in adequate concentration. Marijuana, however, can be eaten, and does in fact possess medicinal value for those suffering from cancer, glaucoma, and gastric distress, especially serious nausea.

Everard claimed that all who used tobacco appreciated it. Seamen and soldiers received regular allotments, and much like the use of coca leaves in Latin America, "farmers, plough-men, porters and almost all laboring men plead for it, saying they find great refreshment by it and very many would as soon part with their necessary food as they would be totally deprived of the use of tobacco." The upper classes were affected by its use as well: "The nobility and gentry who find no fault with it but that it is too common amongst the vulgar, do ordinarily make it the complement of all their entertainment." Indeed, Everard lamented that "oft-times all their entertainment besides it is but a complement." Residents of London had the most experience with these drugs, and Everard spoke of those "keeping tobacco shops as also others keep wine taverns, tap-houses and the like, [who] do in the meantime increase their estates by keeping whores and bawds which they live by" (p. 65).

Everard was concerned about those individuals "who by their daily miscarriage abuse themselves and spend good time in tobacco shops and make their brains . . . a chimney and a common shore and disgrace a medicament that is otherwise very good" (p. 43). The young, in particular, must be protected from the drug. Everard cautioned that much as "wine must not be given to young men because it makes then prone to anger and to lust . . . doth not the smoke of tobacco do this far more?" (p. 48). Everard warned all those abusing the substance, "Take heed, you that love tobacco that you do not exceed in using too much of it and enslave yourselves to this fulgenous smoke by hunting after it and making a God of it" (p. 54). Despite Everard's fears of marijuana abuse, he could indicate that "there is no one kind of foreign commodity that yields greater advantage to the public and there is scarce any to be compared with it." "In a word," the author concluded, "it hath prevailed so far that there is no living without it."

Another pamphlet extolling "the virtues of tobacco and coffee" was William Rumsey's *Organon Salutis: An Instrument to Cleanse the Stomach* (1657). The introductory letter by Henry Blount noted that "the Turks and Persians and most the Eastern world have hourly use of tobacco and coffee, but especially coffee." James Howell's introductory letter indicated that "formerly apprentices and clerks with others used to take their morning draught in ale, beer or wine, which by the dizziness they cause in the brain make many unfit for business, they use [coffee] now to play the goodfellow in this wakeful and civil drink."

The remainder of the pamphlet described the physical ailments that might be cured by the use of these substances and the preparation of the drugs for medicinal use. Coffee was to be prepared in the following manner: Equal parts of butter and "sallet-oil" should be mixed with three times the volume in honey and then heated. Enough coffee should then be added to make the composite into "a thick electuary" (p. 5). If you could manage to get it down and keep it down, the elixir was bound to have some effect.

Tobacco presented other possibilities. Readers could add one-quarter of a pound of tobacco to a quart of ale, white wine, or cider, mix in three or four spoons of honey and twopenny worth of mace and then "infuse these by a soft fire in a closed earthen pot . . . and then strain and keep it in a closed bottle" (p. 6). They might alternatively add one-quarter of a pound of tobacco to a pint of "sallet-oil" or fresh sweet butter, then strain and pound the tobacco with nutmeg and cloves. "Later one may add Burgundy-pitch or frankincense." The concentrations of actual tobacco in either formula could prove harmful if ingested, while the same proportions of marijuana could be used safely and would in fact help alleviate gastric difficulties, especially if made into suppositories, using the second formula. Perhaps one chose recipes depending upon which end of the digestive system required help. Indeed, the narrator of Samuel Rowland's *The Melancholy Knight* (1615) wrote of tobacco: "This is brave physic for brave Cavaliers/ This at both ends, upwards and downwards clears." Once being so clarified, the individual became a "trumpeter," or one who could, as the *Wits Interpreter* indicated, "belcheth either backward or forward" (line 329).

Not everyone was ecstatic about tobacco. In 1604 James I had written his anonymously published *Counterblaste to Tobacco,* which characterized the drug as "loathsome to the eye, hateful to the nose, harmful to the brain and dangerous to the lungs." Others also thought tobacco highly overrated. The Gloucestershire hangman's pamphlet "to the smokers or tobacconists in London" entitled *Harry Hangman's Honor* (1655) indicated that those suffering from many maladies allegedly cured by tobacco could find better remedies elsewhere and offered the following bit of curious information: "Take a fresh stoole from a sweet proper beautiful lady or gentlewoman, aged forty years, being wrapped up in a sweet clean linen handkerchief and applied to the nose, it is an excellent antidote against the plague" (p. 8). Moreover, "the juice thereof being strained into a dish, dipping a licorice stick into the same and anointing the lips and teeth therewith and chewing the same, cures tooth-ache, kills the cankers and is good for the caught of the lungs." The modern reader may find this peculiar, but human, horse, and even pig feces were considered to be valuable medicine. Indeed, W. Parks's *The Curtain-Drawer of the World* (1612) listed the dung of humans, hens, wolves, and doves as well as the vomit of dogs as medicinally valuable (p. 6).[16]

So, too, was urine. One contemporary method of medical diagnosis involved carefully observing the sick person's urine; practitioners of this art form were called "piss-pot prophets." John Collop's *Poesis Rediviva* (1655) has a physician-prophet observe, "Hence, looking glasses, Chamber pots we call/ 'Cause in your piss we can discover all" (p. 50). Similarly, dog urine, especially night water, was considered beneficial to the skin. Laurence Price's *Here's Jack in the Box* (1656) advised the reader, "Every morning when you rise you must wash your face in Puppy dog water, and then lay on the painting [i.e., cosmetics]" (p. 11). Dog urine must have been a fairly common foundation for cosmetics—even the cosmetic-hating, normally reasonable, and always entertaining Samuel Pepys bought puppy's night urine for his wife.[17]

These several prescriptions, crude and useless to modern eyes, were significant. Had these several authors been attempting humor, their recipes would indicate the level of humor of seventeenth-century journalism, but they were quite serious. Their remedies must indicate that English sensualism was far more complex than usually believed. Indeed, the legitimate bounds of an enchanted world included objects as shamanistic health amulets and cures now considered revolting. Consequently, to judge the total cultural accomplishment of the age, they must be included, along with poetry, theological discourse, astute political observations, or Newtonian physics. More to the point, however, assessments of the Puritan campaign for moral reform, as well as the campaign that opposed it, must consider that English tastes were far more diverse than a campaign against ale might indicate.

Other than condemning the alehouse (the house of sin) and alcohol and tobacco (the substances of sin) several publications described other manifestations of sinfulness, including the people of sin (whores and witches), the medium of sin (prostitution and pornography), the wages of sin (venereal disease), and, finally, the cause of sin (women), to which we turn in the next chapter.

The Sisters of the Scabards
HOLIDAY:

OR,

A Dialogue between two reverent and very
vertuous Matrons, Mrs. *Bloomesbury*, and Mrs.
Long-Acre her neare Neighbour.

Wherein is Discoursed how terrible, and costly the *Civill Law*
was to their Profession; and how they congatulate
the welcome Alteration.

PRINTED, 1641.

◆ ◆ ◆

9

Naughty Women and Worse

"HUNGRY DOGS LOVE THEIR DIRTY PUDDING."
—*Mysteries of Love and Eloquence(1658)*

At one time it was fashionable to speak of a new, more romantic seventeenth-century attitude toward women.[1] Another fiction explained that the outbreak of witchcraft in the seventeenth century was a particularly Catholic phenomena since Protestant emphasis upon predestination and denial of all ritual precluded the essence of magic.[2] Both arguments, while interesting in some theoretical sense, are wrong. Witchcraft trials occurred in Catholic France, in Protestant Germany, during the height of the Puritan revolution, and in Salem, Massachusetts, where there was hardly a hint of Catholicism.

The concept of Puritan romanticism is no less a fiction. Some Puritan theologians may have found women potentially capable of some measure of redemption by their fathers or husbands. But this missionary impulse does not constitute a romantic view of women. Rather, it revealed a profound hope that women might be changed into something they were not. In point of fact, the reform programs of the English Revolution certainly witnessed, and perhaps initiated, a war against women. Women stood damned as the general source of evil in society and the particular source of three specific sins: sectarian sexuality, prostitution, and witchcraft. Unlike the stories of later ages, which often pictured women in passive roles—and hence unable to assume social responsibility— the pamphlet literature from the interregnum condemned females for their active participation in spreading evil.

Discovering writings that blame women for the sins of society and the degradation of contemporary affairs is only a little more difficult than finding shells at the seashore. In fact, the seventeenth century teemed with pamphlets intent upon "discovering the true nature of females." What the scholar discovers, however, is an often negative contemporary male consensus about female wickedness that was endemic only in these pamphlets and not in the nature of women.

The pamphlet *A Brief Anatomy of Women* (1653) defined gender relations very succinctly. "If we but seriously consider the nature and qualities of the generality of that sex, even in all ages from the fall of man unto this present," the author explained, "we may well perceive that they have not been only extremely evil in themselves but have also been in the main instruments and immediate causes of murder, idolatry and a multitude of other heinous sins" (p. 1). Even more, women "express the true performance of their duty to their great Lord and master, Lucifer ... that they may more really appear to be his" (p. 2). As a result, there are hardly any good females, other than Mary, Elizabeth, and other saintly women, and "in this age there are very few of those and they are hard to be found out."

Equivalent to but opposing feminine evil was male innocence. Indeed, human history was but the story of mankind attempting to free itself from womankind. "We must consider," the author explained, "how man's fall from that estate of grace and innocence wherein he was first placed, was acted and brought to pass by women" (p. 4). And since Eden, males have continued to be the victims of women."It is most apparent," the author wrote, "that they only are the greatest and most powerful temptations to evil of all, the very gulf where man's reason, governance and discretion is often swallowed up." Even worse has been their influence "in this present and that of late years by men of no mean degree and quality that have deeply suffered by those causes."

Male animus towards women was more than a simple theoretical construct predicated upon Eve's responsibility for original sin. Most pamphlets also emphasized how women were responsible for a large variety of contemporary conditions in which males felt victimized. Consider the innocent soldier returning home from the civil wars only to find his sweetheart married to another. This was the case in *Strange News From Warwick* (1642). A young man from Coventry named Richard Boad went off to fight in the wars. Before leaving, Boad and his sweetheart, Anne Kirke, swore everlasting love and agreed to marry upon his return. To guarantee her fidelity, "she on her knees did swear in private to him ... that if ever she made a promise to any other in his absence or thought of marriage unless with him, that the same day she was married, the devil might fetch her and have no pity nor compassion but take her away when she proved false in thought or deed" (p. 7).

When Boad returned home hoping to marry Anne, he found his erst-while fiance about to wed another. The young man went to the wedding party and reminded Anne of her vow, and "she then replied that a rash vow is either broken or kept" (p. 8). It was not the young lady's rash vow that lay at the foundation of this injustice, however, but the essentially evil character of the female. In a word, women were incapable of dealing fairly with men.

Young Boad may have been more fortunate than he realized, for married women were believed to be deceitful predators, preying upon their spouses. Indeed, they often murdered their devoted husbands for no apparent reason at all. The pamphlet *Murder, Murder, or, A Bloody Relation of How Anne Hamton . . . Murdered Her Dear Husband* (1641) presented a standard account of a woman unjustly killing her husband. The newsbook opened with the admonition, "Hearken to me you that be wives and give attendance you which as yet are unmarried . . . every wife should love her own husband and . . .not be high-minded toward him but humble, not to be self-willed but diligent, not to be like a strange woman which wandereth abroad in the twilight to get a prey, but to be constant and loving to him" (p. 1). More to the point, killing a husband was un-natural. "Let all the forests wherein fierce lions are contained be joined in one," the author intoned, "and privy search made to know if ever female did the male destroy. OH NO!" (p. 2). Having set the proper moral tone for discussion and the a priori social principles governing gender relations, the author could finally turn to the facts of the situation.

In St. Margaret's Parish in Westminster, Anne Hamton was married to a very loving man who "delighteth in nothing more but to see his wife pleasant." Anne, however, was "a light housewife, [who,] when he was working, would be gossiping with one young fellow or other or else with such women as were like herself" (p. 3). While Mr. Hamton thought only of his wife's happiness, "never was she more joyful than when she was out of her good husband's company" (p. 3). When he tried to explain to Anne her obligation to love him and work for him and be satisfied with that, "she, forsooth, took it in distaste and giving him a scalding reply, she left the room" (p. 4).

One evil woman to a story should have been sufficient, but this one had two. Anne told her landlady, Margaret Harwood, that her husband had cruelly abused her, "in which she lied for he always spoke in a very loving manner unto her, except she overmuch provoked him" (p. 4).

Harwood, also an evil woman, "cried out it was her own fault for letting such an abject villain to live; hang him, cut his throat or poison him, for he is unfit to live upon the earth amongst good fellows!" (p. 4). Following the advice of her evil neighbor, Anne purchased five drams of poison, which she fed to her loving husband so that "his visage was so much defaced by the quick operation of the scalding poison" (p. 5) . The loving Mr. Hamton proceeded to blow up like a balloon, "his hands did seem only like two great boils, his belly seemed as if hot irons had been thrust into it."[3]

The surgeon consulted by the authorities was able to determine that Mr. Hamton had been poisoned, and Anne Hamton and Margaret Harwood were carted off to jail to await trial. Unusual for this sort of literature was the paucity of hard information about when and where the murder took place and where the trial was to be conducted. The pamphlet did make its point about women, however. Even its title indicated the importance of gender.

If women were faithless spouses, they also killed as a result of moral decay. The pamphlet *The Witch of Wapping* (1652) described why Prudence Lee was burned in Smithfield for murdering her husband, Philip Lee. The explanation for this dastardly deed lay in Mrs. Lee's character; she confessed that "she had been a lewd liver and much given to cursing and swearing" (p. 7). Only at the end of the account are we informed, as an afterthought, that Mr. Lee "was a very wicked liver and kept the company of strange women" (p. 8). Indeed, it was her husband's constant philandering that finally got to Mrs. Lee, for "when she committed this abominable murder, she found him in company with another woman at the sign of the Last, an alehouse in Rotten Row in Old Street, which occasioned very evil language to pass between them upon which she drew her knife and stabbed him" (p. 8). Like other women who had killed their husbands, Mrs. Lee was not merely hung; "the executioner set her in a pitch barrel, bound her to the stakes and placed straw and faggots about her . . . and [when] the executioner put fire to the straw, she cried out 'Lord Jesus! Have mercy on my soul,' and after the fire was kindled she was heard to shriek out terribly some five or six times" (p. 8). Had Mrs. Lee been a reasonable woman she would have accepted her husband's personal needs in stride. But then, had Prudence Lee been capable of reasonable behavior, she would have looked after her husband more adequately. Once again, the pamphlet's title was indicative of its author's agenda.

The unreasonable and malicious nature of female violence was also the point of *The Devil's Reign Upon Earth* (1655). This short but intriguing compendium of horrible familial violence was an essay in domestic disgust. Mistress Grace Griffin, a silk-thrower's wife in the Borough of Southmark, "did live in good repute and fashion" (p. 8). But when her husband suffered from a terrible head cold and asked her to fetch him some honey to soothe his throat, "she did but put poison therein and so poisoned him." Like Mrs. Lee, "she was burned to death according to the law at Kingston upon Thames, August 6, 1655" (p. 8). To answer why a seemingly sane women would do such a terrible deed, *The Devil's Reign* told another story to demonstrate the unpredictable and unstable nature of the female character. At the same time that Grace Griffin was put to death, another woman was executed as well. This second murderer had gotten into a heated discussion with her friend and "quarrelling with another woman, [she] violently thrust a napkin down her throat and choked her" (p. 8).

The same (particularly female) emotional deficiency that resulted in poisoned husbands also led women to kill their children. Stories of infanticide committed by women were popular during the German Reformation and again during the Thirty Years' War, when each side in these conflicts envisioned mothers of the wrong religion murdering their babies. The civil wars provided fertile ground for similar stories.[4] *Bloody News From Dover* (1646) confirmed the worst English fears about female Anabaptist murderers. It seems that in the city of Dover John Champion and his wife had a new baby that Mr. Champion wished to have baptized "according to the ancient custom of the kingdom." Unfortunately, Mrs. Champion "would by no means condescend to it" (p. 2). This conflict could only have a bad end, for "where division and controversy doth arise, sad effects suddenly follow" (p. 4). In this specific case, "on a day when her husband was abroad, [she] took a great knife and cut off the child's head" (p. 3). When Champion came home, his wife said, "Behold husband, thy sweet babe without a head. Now go baptize it." Similarly, *The Devil's Reign Upon Earth* (1655) described several cases of infanticide. On August 6, 1655, a woman was executed "for beating out the brains of her own child with a hammer" (p. 8). A week earlier in Lidford in Somersetshire, a carpenter had gone off to work, as he did every day, "but at his return home, he found all his four children murdered and put into a chest. It is supposed that his wife did this bloody act by reason she is not to be found" (p. 8).

When women were unable to murder their own children, they killed the children of other families. The author of *A True Relation of the Most Horrid and Barbarous Murders, Committed by Abigail Hill* (1658), for instance, wrote that the essence of the female disposition was deceit itself, and "had not the complexions of some women been so tempting and their inclinations so tender by nature, it is likely they had never been such devils as they are" (p. 10). A story was presented as a case in point. Abigail Hill from Southwark "was supposed to be a good nurse into whose charge and care the nursing up of young children should be committed" (p. 11). Over the years, the community came to respect Hill, and she "was looked upon by all her neighbors for a woman inclined to much compassion. She seemed to pity young children that were in distress and, according to her power, relieve them." Even more, "at any time [that] any child [was] forsaken by the wicked mother and left upon the parish, she would be ready to receive [it] and undertake to bring it up" (p. 11).

The community should have realized that something was amiss when more children entered the Hill household than left it, but "for seven years she lived, and no notice was taken of what became of her children if any were missing, it being believed that they died by sickness" (p. 11). Eventually, some neighbors did become suspicious when one or another of the children seen about the village would suddenly disappear, but others said that nothing was wrong, that "having so many of them lying on her hands, she had delivered the charge of them to some other poor woman to be careful of them" (p. 11).

In the end, truth must out, and "this wicked woman and her husband did fall out where, in the heat of his passion, he did upbraid her with the children she had made away" (p. 12). Abigail Hill was then brought before the local justice of the peace, and an investigation indicated that several children had mysteriously and unaccountably disappeared from the Hill home. Hill was also charged with having made a fraudulent trade of the children in her care. It seems that "on Quarters Day she would borrow children of her mere acquaintance and bring them to the masters of the parish, as if they were those she had taken into her custody to nurse, and having received her pay for them she would return them again unto those of whom she had borrowed them" (p. 13). At her trial in the Old Bailey on December 15, 1658, Hill was charged with the murder of four children, although it was believed that she had murdered many more. When asked why she had killed them, Hill denied that she had done them any harm, although she did admit that some "children being sick and but little hope of life, she did wring it up by the neck and killed it to put it out of its pain" (p. 13). On December 22, at Cheapside, Abigail Hill was hung by the neck. Why did Abigail Hill and these other women kill innocent and helpless children? The author postulated that "it is an ancient proverb in this nation that seldom [is] any notorious murder committed but a woman hath a hand in it" (p. 9).

When murder was impossible, a mother might instead drive her child to commit suicide. This was the case in Thomas Mince's suicide, described in the pamphlet *The Troubled Spirited Man's Departing* (1653). All who knew Thomas Mince liked him. He was a good shoemaker and a good soldier in Colonel Whaley's regiment, where for seven years he had served with honor. He taught himself to read and write and was considered a man with a fine future. Yet Mince grew depressed, and soon "he was a melancholy man, troubled in spirit" (p. 4). His depression, which no one could understand, grew more severe, and he lost his faith in religion, declaring, "he had prayed long and did not find any good thereby for God had forsaken him" (p. 6). Yet it was neither depression nor his loss of faith that led to Mince's death but his mother's greed. It seems she owed him some money but refused to make good her obligation. Unable to convince his mother of his own financial need, "he uttered these words, 'My heart is broke,' and forthwith pistoled himself and fell down dead" (p. 4). Mince's early death was tragic; that it was his own mother's greed that had provoked this sad suicide was wretched. Indeed, Mince's death was but one instance of the cruelty females routinely wreaked upon their male victims.

Sexual deceit was even more central to a woman's character than the murder of children, spouses, or peers. Indeed, wanton lewdness was so endemic to the very definition of the gender that all other evil activities could be defined in terms of dirty female sexuality. Consider, for instance, the lascivious nature of female sectaries.[5] In the minds of contemporaries all radical sectaries were evil. Male radicals blasphemed and were promiscuous, but female radicals were especially given to sexual license. In the pamphlet *A Strange Wonder, or, A Wonder in a Woman* (1642), which is subtitled "wherein is plainly expressed the true nature of women," the author explained that all women were essentially whores, "especially of some eminent women in this city" (title page). Of the various types of whores the author described, the religious whore was the worst. "But yet of all whores," the author carefully explained, "there is no whore to a Holy Whore, which when she turns up the white of her eye and the black of her tail, when she falls flat on her back, according as the spirit moves her, the fire of her zeal kindles such a flame that the devil can not withstand her . . . she can cover her lust with religion" (p. 4).

Sexual license by women in the name of religion was the major theme of *The Ranter's Last Sermon* (1654), "written by JM (a deluded Brother) lately escaped out of their snare" (title page). He told of Mistress E. B., who "coming to one of the men, she offers to unbutton his cod-piece, who, demanding of her what she sought for, she answered FOR SIN, where-upon he blows out her candle and leads her to the bed where in the sight of all the rest they commit fornication" (p. 4). JM also related how "the sister who can make 'the beast with two backs' the most strenuously, viz., entertain the most men longest and oftenest, hath a sufficient canoniza-tion for a saint triumphant" (p. 6).

JM also included a hymn sung at all Ranter gatherings that described the active sexual role played by Ranter women:

> Oh hug them hard and suck them in
> Until they even burst your skin,
> Spread forth the crannies of those rocks
> That lie beneath your Holland smocks.
> Stretch out your limbs, sigh, heave and strain,
> Till you have opened every vein.
> That so, love's gentle juice that flows
> Like divine nectar out of those
> That press you down may run a tilt
> Into your womb and not be spilt. (p. 5)

The Ranter's Religion (1650) presented a story also found in several other pamphlets. Its anonymous author, like many others, alleged being present when "a she Ranter said openly in the hearing of many (a friend of mine accidentally one of them) that she should think herself a happy woman and should esteem herself a superlative servant of God if any would accompany her carnally in the open market place" (p. 8). *The Ranters' Recantation* described to us a Ranter couple fornicating in public "after which he was to set her on her head to go about the room on her hands with her coats about her ears . . . and in the presence of about sixty persons entered into venial exercises" (p. 2).

Many pamphlet authors could not differentiate between female sec-taries and whores. This was the conclusion of John Reading's pamphlet *The Ranter's Ranting* (1650). He reported that his friend's friend, "a gen-tleman of quality (as I am credibly informed)" (p. 5) met a female Ranter in an alehouse and "after a little familiar discourse, he told her he was in indifferent well health but wanted a stomach [that is, that he was "hun-gry"], whereupon she replied that if he pleased to come to her lodging the next day she doubted not but she should find something to which he had an appetite." The next day this gentleman visited the lady at her lodgings "and appearing in nothing but her smock, [she] asked him how he liked her and whether his stomach would not come to him . . . and immediately presented herself to him naked, saying, 'Fellow Creature, what sayeth thou to a plump leg of mutton (striking her hand upon her thigh) with the eats that are now in view'" (p. 5). Our gentleman of quality was so shocked that he ran out of her lodgings and only later did he "discover her to be a proselyte of [Abiezer] Coppe and [Lawrence] Clarkson and the rest of their infernal gang which have been dispersers of a diabolical opinion that there is neither heaven nor hell, for otherwise she could not be so audacious" (p. 5).

Radical females were sexually perverse, but even worse, they wished to dominate males. *Newes From the New Exchange, or, The Commonwealth of Ladies* (1649) opened with the statement, "There was once a time in England when men wore the britches" and *The Parliament of Women,* published first in 1646 and again in 1656, described what would happen if women ran Parliament. This idea was not so strange in 1656 since by that time almost everyone else had tried to do so. However, the pamphlet had women pass one major piece of legislation in favor of polyandry. Over and again, women in this pamphlet expressed the view that they could not be satisfied by one man, "that it was not only fitting but necessary that every woman should have two husbands, for saith she . . . have not most great houses two doors? Likewise, have not most taverns a fore-door and a back-door, with two signs and two bushes?" (p. A4b). And if women owned men, they should also own their property. "If the husband be ours," one women asked, "then be their goods ours, their lands ours, their cash and coin ours, and al their moveables . . . and at our command?" (p. A7b). Even more, should women come to own most property, they would also wish to sit in Parliament and govern men, which is what this pamphlet was all about.

All of these pamphlets reveal a curiosity. In each instance, men created stories about female evil with which to frighten themselves, succeeded in doing so, and then blamed women for not knowing their place. Even more curious, there was no true limit in these pamphlets to the things for which females might be held responsible. Indeed, it was even possible to blame the worst of the Irish problem on women. In the newsbook *The Lord Osmond's Overthrow, Which Was the Chief Commander of the Rebels* (1642) we are informed that Irish women were worse than Irish men. "How merciless were those female furies who came over from Ireland," the author intoned, "their knives were more bloody than were the swords of their companions" (p. 10).

It is a very small jump from picturing a woman as powerful, lurid, and lewd to imagining that woman as provocative, alluring, and desirable. Indeed, the image of the sexually dominating female has been a major theme in conventional pornography for centuries. Hence, the same decades that created the Puritan sexual ethic and gloried in the image of the dirty female also produced the first English pornography.[6] As the author of *Mysteries of Love and Eloquence* (1658) wrote, "Hungry dogs love dirty puddings. There's many a man hath lost his nose [i.e., through syphilis] by verifying this proverb" (p. 12).

There was no doubt that all women were "dirty puddings." The author of *A Brief Anatomy of Women* (1653) explained that "their body itself is a magazine of corrupt and ill humors, which hath continual recourse to all the rest of the members . . . so that from the crown of their head to the sole of the foot, there is not a good member, no not one" (p. 3). He wrote further that "their rolling eyes like the shining pearl, seem to be the baits that ensnare men in their love, whose fruit is destruction. . . . Their lips are like posterns from whence issueth lying, deceit, and all manner of dissimulation." As for female erotic zones, "Their neck and breasts are left bare unto the open view . . . to signify that nature hath fairly acted her part without, although there remain no grace within." In short, the female may have appeared attractive, but in reality they are "like those Indian apples, which are seemingly fair without, but poison within" (p. 3).

Even pornographic pamphlets blamed on women male fascination with the female body. *The Horn Exalted, or, Room for Cuckolds, with An Appendix Concerning Women and Jealousy* (1660) explained that "there's a natural lasciviency [*sic*] in them which if day by day it be not cut, like a luxuriant plant, there sprouts out some scurvy matter" (p. 73). Women were incapable of true morality, and "though you guard them with a hundred eyes they will deceive and hoodwink them all and blindfold you so that had you [John] Dee's show-stone . . . you should never detect them" (p. 73).

Pornography may be of poor quality, but it gives us great insight into the male psyche because it was the function of the fictitious prostitute to say all the things that men wanted to hear from women and do all the things men wanted women to do but were afraid or ashamed to request. Indeed, one universal component of pornography has been an attachment to that which is forbidden. The dirtier the woman was, the more exciting she could be. Moreover, these words and deeds had to be those the reader could not anticipate from the women he knew, for why else go to all the trouble of creating this fiction if it was available in reality?

The Practical Part of Love (1660) presented a series of short, mostly unrelated, pornographic stories about three exciting courtesans. Though written by a man, the language was attributed to the female narrators of each tale. The stories told about using dildos, the savoring of female urine, and male servitude to female-oriented oral sex, in all of which the male was a victim of the whore. The male reader may not have known a single woman capable of the actions described, but it was still possible to make the whore the emblem of all women. The author explained: "If we [i.e., women] are not most of us common whores, yea, more of us are private ones" (p. 21); "One man is not able to satisfy us, [though] he may tire us for the present" (p. 21); "Variety delights women which occasions so many cuckolds everywhere" (p. 21); "She that will be a whore before marriage, though upon never so good a score, will be sure to be so after marriage upon any" (p. 73). Women were so entirely sexual that without frequent sexual activity they went insane. "Widows by retention of their seed become melancholy and afterwards mad" (p. 14), the prostitute explained. Men also appreciated sex, a male character noted, but "women love that which we so eagerly sue for more than we can ourselves because they enjoy ten times the pleasure that we do" (p. A5a).

Seventeenth-century moral critics believed pornography was another product of female wickedness since it was the woman's body that was either pictured or discussed. Indeed, unable to help themselves, males were victims of pornography. Thus, for instance, in *The Life and Death of John Atherton* (1641), the Lord Bishop of Waterford and Lysmore in Ireland explained at his trial that he was led to committing adultery, buggering his man John Childe, and raping his sister because of dirty pictures of women. This made a lot of sense to other members of the Irish church, and in *The Penitent Death of a Woeful Sinner* (1641), by Nicholas Bernard, Dean of Ardegh in Ireland, the bishop's many terrible deeds were again explained as the result of "his reading of naughty books . . . viewing of immodest pictures, frequenting of plays" (p. 14).

If most females were whores, women were certainly responsible for prostitution.[7] While prostitution, fornication, and adultery all entailed the cooperation of both genders, the female, rather than the male, was usually held responsible. As a result, compromised males, whether guilty of soliciting or rape suffered less than their partners. The surest remedy for prostitution always has been public humiliation of male customers rather than the arrest of the prostitutes themselves. Yet seventeenth-century authorities took the very opposite tack. Rather than arresting clients, they closed down whorehouses and threw the prostitutes in jail. Hence, the morality laws of this age of reform fell essentially upon female shoulders. According to the Commonwealth's Act of May 10, 1650 ("for suppressing the detestable sins of incest, adultery and fornication"), incest and adultery became felonies carrying a death sentence. Fornication merited three months in jail. Brothelkeepers were to be whipped, pilloried, branded, and jailed for three years for the first offense and executed for the second offense. Keeping male customers off the streets and at home with their wives produced no revenues, yet the authorities continued to harass prostitutes and close brothels, citing the sanctity of marriage as their reason for doing so. The law claimed that "the principle of monogamy is the most salutary institution for the joint welfare of men and women and ought to be strictly enforced by law."[8] Popular pamphlets believed bribery was a better explanation for their actions since public officials could always use a little pocket money as a reward for looking the other way.

As early as 1641 there were serious attempts to close down whorehouses and rid the streets of "night-walkers" and others providing illicit nocturnal entertainment. Several pamphlets indicated that the campaign was less a matter of morality than finances. In 1641 a pamphlet entitled *The Sisters of the Scabard's Holiday* presented a cynical view of this Puritan zealotry. The subtitle indicated that this was "a dialogue between two reverend and very virtuous Matrons, Mrs. Bloomsbury and Mrs. Longacre, her near neighbor, wherein is discussed how terrible and costly the civil law was to their profession" (title page). (The names of both madams were taken from infamous London red-light districts.) Essentially, the new morality consisted of street sweeps. Working girls were picked up, processed, fined, jailed, and eventually let out on the street again. Government officials collected their fees and declared victory in the battle against immoral female behavior. Mrs. Longacre described how a public official "would warn both me and my whole harmless household to appear in [St.] Paul's the next court day to answer for keeping a common bawdy house, ready furnished with mercenary whores who daily commit the carnal act of incontinency and for many other misdemeanors" (p. 3). The female entrepreneur explained that working girls preferred a shakedown to a closedown, and to avoid subsequent trouble would bribe those declaring victory in the battle with sin. "First, I must pay the Apparator [*sic*] his whole fees . . . then I must repair to these Gentlemen. . . and make my composition with them and give them larger fees . . . or else leave off the trade and be utterly undone" (pp. 3-4). Despite recent payments, however, the women were still rousted, and

Longacre angrily concluded, "I intend to pay no more quarterage to these skruing [sic] Gentlemen."

Mrs. Bloomsbury reported having similar experiences and declared, "I paid them constantly ten pounds a year and still was in fear of them for all that and was sure to ride once a year in a single coach with two wheels up Cheapside where I make no question but you know how I was used" (p. 4). In the end Bloomsbury concluded, "Though the civil law be likely to have a fall and the greatest part of our enemies break, yet I believe our profession (though never so necessary) will have new enemies, our prosperity will be envied. We shall stand in awe to one or other by whom we shall be corrected in case we transgress" (p. 5) .The pamphlet concluded with the couplet, "Let our foes do what they may/ we Sisters of the Scabard will keep holiday." In fact, the sisters had an easier time than they realized. The civil war and its many problems did not permit the passage of meaningful legislation in 1641, and although street rousts may have been annoying, business continued.

The new law of 1650 against fornication complicated soliciting in the streets. In *A Dialogue Between Mistris Macquerella, A Suburban Bawd, Ms. Scolopendra, a Noted Courtezan and Mr. Pimpinello, an Usher* (1650), the three discussed the recent act against fornication. One said "I have not had a cullee [i.e., a client] worth half a crown to me this half a score days" (p. 1). Her friend had also experienced recent hard times and added, "Ah wicked world, that I should live to see this day. A fine age of faith when procreation must do penance in a halter." They agreed that "the act, the late act against fornication and other venial sins, 'tis that hath done us all" (p. 2). Still, in the end, the laws would prove meaningless. One of the three said, "A fig for all the law in the world . . . what is intended for our detriment and obloquy shall prove to our profit and glory." And alluding to the censorship laws as an example of their own plight, one of these madams quipped, "If the old maxim be true that the worst books of sale, when once called in sell the best, this edict will enhance our prizes" (p. 6). Another agreed and reminded her colleague about the crackdown on working girls of the previous decade, when "my own salary trebled to my former rates and this mutation we may well justify alleging the hazard we run and the inevitable danger of our persons in case of discovery" (p. 6). In short, they believed, or the author did, that nothing much would change one way or the other.

The last years of the interregnum did actually witness the flowering of prostitution. The "ladies trade" profession was described in a series of publications, including *A Strange and True Conference Between Two*

Notorious Bawds, Damrose Page and Pris Fotheringham (1660) and the several issues of *The Wandering Whore* (1660) usually attributed to John Garfield. Of the two, the latter collection was far more important. Like the famous pamphlet *The Whore's Rhetoric* (1681) of later decades, these pamphlets were an alleged exposé of London's red-light district. They were also quasi-pornographic and included the names and neighborhoods of different types of whores available for the Londoner's rental. Each pamphlet consisted of conversations between "Magdalena, a Crafty Whore, Julietta, an Exquisite Whore, Francion, a Lascivious Gallant, and Gusman, a Pimping Hector," in which the profession was allegedly described from the point of view of the trade. The front page of the first issue informed the reader that the purpose of these publications was "to destroy those poisonous vermin which live upon the ruin and destruction of many families, by a late convert amongst them." All subsequent numbers also included an opening letter to the reader wherein the publisher again explained that the names and places of prostitutes were provided so that everyone, except the law, might avoid them.

It is difficult to assess the author's real motives. The discussion in each pamphlet varied but generally described some of the practices, perversions, and preferences of these lusty women who "kiss with their mouths open and put their tongues in his mouth and suck it. Their left hand is in his cod-piece, their right in his pocket. They commend his trap-stick and pluck their coats above their thighs, their smocks above their knees, bidding him to thrust his hand into the best cunt in Christendom." (#2, p. 12). Throughout, males were presented as the victims of female guile.

At no point were the whores' discussions far from the subject of money, and many stories described prostitutes robbing their clients. Stories in each issue also emphasized the money prostitutes earn. In truth, most lived in poverty, and white slavery was a standard method of brothel recruiting.[9] Despite their own vulnerability, prostitutes seemed to have understood what the authorities did not: clients feared public disclosure. In one instance, a whore would bring her client to her room, and while they had sex, "up comes two slippery ruffians (finding him upon her) with drawn swords, pistols cocked, as if they intended to have pistoled him or cut in pieces . . . swearing "thou villain, what hast thou done to my wife? Thou rogue, how hast thou abused my sister?" (#4, p. 7). The client would be so frightened that he would agree to pay the robbers whatever they demanded.

Another trick for a prostitute to fool a rich client was to "pretend herself to be with child" (#4, p. 7). This was a common ploy once the customer became used to a particular whore and came to believe that his sexual fantasies, as well as his public identity, were safe with her. Indeed, even though Julietta was well treated by her loyal client Francion, she still robbed him by claiming to be pregnant by him. Rather than face public disgrace, Francion agreed to settle a small annuity upon Julietta. Was it difficult reconciling fraud with conscience? Gusman said, "Should we once leave our old custom of cheating our best (as well as our worst) cullies, we must leave off to live. . . . Dishonest actions are proper . . . and for our profit, dishonesty with riches is honesty, honesty with poverty is dishonesty" (#2, p. 11).

The prostitute was more than able to exact revenge for her honor from an abusive client. In one instance, Gusman described, "a wandering whore, watching her opportunity . . . drew him [i.e., an abusive client] into a dark passage where he fell to feeling her with freedom after which she felt him likewise . . . whereupon she drew out a sharpened knife for that purpose and holding his prick close by the root, she cut it clear and sheer off, leaving him, his member and knife together where he continued dancing and roaring" (#4, p. 6). The cully had no recourse against the whore for she was protected by the authorities. Julietta says of Venice that "for paying an annual tribute to the senate we have as secure protection as any people in the dukedom of Venice" (#2, p. 13). This was true of London as well, although it was more prudent to write about Venice.[10]

Perversions included classic abuses of women and self-abuse of men.[11] One of the discussants told of a young woman "as she was showing tricks upon her head with naked buttocks and spread legs . . . sack was poured in on one side . . . and sucked out the other, which is a new fashioned cup for roaring boys to drink in" (#1, p. 7). In another instance, a whore "stood naked upon her head with naked breach and belly whilst four cullyrumpers chucked in sixteen half crowns into her commodity" (#2, p. 8). Men enjoyed other games. One young man "will not be contented with doing the business but will have half a dozen girls stand stark naked round a table whilst he lies snarling underneath as if he would bit off their whib-bobs and eat them for his pains." Another "had rods in his pockets for that purpose will needs be whipped to raise lechery and cause a standing prick." Another still "would fain be buggering some of our wenches" (#3, p. 9) or, alternately, "will needs shit in one of our wench's mouth."

To provide stimulation, brothels often featured paintings of whores on their walls: "one holding a chamber pot betwixt her legs, another striving might and main to enlarge the orifice of her Mysterium Magnum . . . [another] pointing at one that hath lost the hair of her Whib-bob" (#2, pp.

13-14). Love potions also played their part. One made from certain dried flowers was popular. Another required taking "the largest and fondest nutmeg tied in a string and thrust up to be soundly soaked and pickled in [a whore's] Whib-bob for three or four nights together, which being grated into a cup of ale with a toast" (#1, p. 8).

Prostitution inevitably involved venereal disease, which, contemporaries believed, was widespread.[12] A London associate of Pepys indicated to him that "the pox is as common there, and so I hear of all hands, that it is as common as eating and swearing."[13] Another contemporary noted that fear of the disease was so widespread that as soon as someone showed any "pox" marks on their faces, "no man dares to lies in their bed, or to wear their clothes or to drink in their cup or to sit in their chairs."[14] Almost every pamphlet concerning women and sex mentioned the pox again and again. Like sex itself, or pregnancy, disease was a woman's fault. *The Practical Part of Love* (1660) explained that the pox resulted from women not giving men enough sex, that "men [who] abound with so much blood and seed that the spermatical vessels are over filled and oppressed so that being over much extended, a gonorrhea ensues, if not prevented by feminine congress . . . [which] cureth the *iskurie* [sic] or difficult making of water" (pp. 13-14). Even worse, a retention of sperm in males could actually lead to insanity, as could a retention of water in females.[15]

Most authorities considered venereal disease to be the product of the naturally dirty and infected female. Dr. John Wynell's *Lues Venerea, or, A Perfect Cure of the French Pox* (1660) explained that "the spirits [of the pox] have their chief residence in those parts, the genitals and seminary vessels for generation" (p. 13). Indeed, it was even possible that venereal disease was a natural product of the female organ, and consequently, a "long stay in carnal coitus makes much to infection . . . but they that soon withdraw and are less inflamed are not easily stung" (p. 38). Because women were the point of origin of the disease, they transmitted it to others in a variety of ways. It was generally believed, for instance, that virtually all midwives and wet nurses were infected and that breast milk was a vehicle by which the disease was passed to male victims. This explanation, however, had its limitations.

Wynell did not believe that males could infect females and noted that "reason and experience both will discharge the [male] genitals from being the subject of this disease" (p. 15). How then did the doctor explain that males often contracted the disease, if they did not do so from prostitutes? For one thing, one could contract the disease from toilet seats, from sharing an infected person's cup, or through other perfectly normal forms of human interaction. Men bringing the pox to their wives after visiting prostitutes probably found this very reassuring. And why were male sex organs often the first organ diseased if indeed they were not the most immediate area of contact with the disease? "No greater reason can be given than the tenderness of those parts, their impotence to resist such an enemy and their exquisite sense" (p. 13).

The most important means of male infection, however, was from the female. She was the "enemy" and had the pox in her dirty "commodity." He might get "stung" by her even without having had sex with her because his private parts were so "exquisitely delicate," but the poor male was "impotent" to resist her infection. In *The Devil Incarnate* (1660) the author described the sexual act as a battle with the devil, where "she fights like a bear lying on her back, and if any man comes at her with a single rapier, she draws him in presently. Thus she thinks to frighten men by giving them the forked end" (p. 6).

There were a variety of methods for dealing with the pox. In *The Wandering Whore* Julietta observed that "I know of no better way or remedy more safe than pissing presently to prevent the French Pox, Gonorrhea, the perilous infirmity of burning" (#1, pp. 12-13). Once contracted, the disease could be cured through the use of tobacco smoke, which was also effective for curing crabs and lice. According to Julietta, the female would be turned upside down with her legs spread, "and lighting a pipe of tobacco, gave those many footed vermin such a rout at her Cinque Ports by thrusting in the small end of the pipe into one hole and then the other, blowing the smoke at the other end of the pipe" (#1, p. 7). This cure may seem curious, but the use of tobacco was considered an improvement over previous treatment. Half a century earlier William Clowes, the great authority on sexually transmitted diseases, described the use of wood or charcoal smoke for "fuming" a patient suffering from venereal disease in his monumental *A Profitable and Necessary Booke of Observations and a Brief and Necessary Treatise Touching the Cure of the Disease Now Usually Called Lues Venera* (1596). He explained how the patient should be placed in a tent of sorts "in the midst thereof shall be placed a stool with a hole in the middle, like a close stool of easement, whereupon the patient shall sit naked to receive the fume . . . and let there be put under the aforesaid stool a chafing dish of coals" (pp. 192-194).

Because prostitution was expensive, involved potential public humiliation, and always presented the risk of disease with its accompanying fearsome treatment, some pamphlets attempted to wrestle with the problem of how an honest man could cope. *The Ladies Champion, Confounding the Author of the Wandering Whore* (1660) found prostitution a necessary evil. "But Sirah," the author, Eugenius Theodidactus, asked, "would not a whore be a necessary evil (as is usually said of all womankind) if thou hadst not the gift of continence?" The author went on to ask, "What cause or remedy shall a man take and use who . . . may neither lie with his own pregnant wife, nor his maid, his nurse nor with a whore?" (p. 6). Did this imply that women were truly nothing but commodities? The author concluded, "Were woman not brought into the world with such instruments for no purpose of profit?" (p. 5). Rather than encouraging prostitution, however, "I judge and conceive and conclude to be polygamy . . . as the best expedient . . . way to have few or no whores at all" (p. 6).

In another pamphlet, *A Remedy for Uncleanness* (1658), an unnamed "Person of Quality" also advised the adoption of polygamy. The logic of this upright Englishman was simple: it was both cheaper and morally more acceptable to own than to rent. "He that takes another man's ox or ass is doubtless a transgressor. But he that puts himself out of the occasion of that temptation by keeping of his own, seems to be a right, honest and well meaning man" (p. 6). Hence, polygamy enabled men to avoid the snares of sin simply by owning more sources of sin and thereby, without giving up a thing, be judged virtuous. In short, male sexuality was fine as long as female "commodities" were owned. The author then asked his reader "whether it [i.e., polygamy] be not the fairest accord and correspondency therewith" (p. 6).

Whether she was a whore, a deceitful Eve, or merely a commodity bought to be used, a woman was always a "dirty pudding." And if she was a witch, she was also extremely dangerous. The phenomenon of witchcraft is complex and largely extraneous to the themes in this volume. However, the witch craze occurred during the height of the revolution and at the same time that these other pamphlets were published. The disrupted economic and political stability of the period, the prevalence of poor female beggars, as well as the introduction of continental concepts of witchcraft have all been cited as causes of the phenomenon, but the element of gender cannot be overemphasized. Because 80 to 90 percent of those tried for this crime were women, there can be no doubt that this was another instance in which society held females responsible for its ills. As if this gender base alone was insufficient, witchcraft was also highly sexual in nature although few scholars stress the sexual nature of evidence raised in courts of law. Indeed, the witch's confession of having had sex with the devil was a prominent feature of witchcraft trials and prosecution. These confessions were considered truthful and were accepted at face value for they were little more than what most males already expected of women.

In *A True and Exact Relation of the Several . . . Late Witches . . . at Chelmesford* (1645), Elizabeth Clark "confessed that she had had carnal copulation with the Devil six or seven years and that he would appear to her three or four times in a week at her bed side and go to bed to her and lie with her half a night together in the shape of a proper gentleman" (p. 2). Far more perverse was Clark's sexual relationship with her imps or familiars, the animal agencies through whom a witch acted out her devilish desires. Familiars often took the form of household pets. According to her own testimony, the imps told Clark that "they would do her no hurt but would help her to a husband who should maintain her ever after. And that these two things came into this examinant's bed every night or every other night and sucked upon the lower parts of her body" (p. 6). Another condemned witch, Anne Leech, testified about her imps "that when they were employed she was healthful and well and that these imps did naturally suck those teats which were found about the private parts of her body" (p. 9). Similarly, Anne Cooper also testified "that she had three black imps suckled on the lower parts of her body" (p. 8), and Margaret Landishe also admitted that "something came up to her body and sucked on her private parts" (p. 32).

The year 1645 was a good year for newsbooks describing the sucking of private parts. In *The Examination, Confession, Trial and Execution of Joan Williford, Joan Cariden and Jane Holt,* Joan Williford conceded that the devil often sucked her: "She likewise sayeth that the devil sucked her twice since she came into prison" (p. 2). Joan Cariden admitted that "the devil sucked this examinant and hath diverse times since sucked her and that it was no pain to her" (p. 3). Jane Holt noted that in her case the devil "came to her once or twice in the month and sucked her" (p. 4).

In 1646 yet another series of witches' confessions appeared under the title *The Witches of Huntingdon.* This newsbook claimed to be a truthful description of fourteen separate cases of witchcraft presented before the local court. Elizabeth Weed, for instance, admitted that the devil came to her "in the shape of a young man [and] did speak to her asking her if she would renounce God and Christ. She answered she would. And the Devil then . . . said she must convenant with him [and] that he must have her soul at the end of one and twenty years, which she granted" (p. 1). When she was asked why she willingly submitted to the devil and was unable to refuse Satan's advances, she indicated that "he came to bed with her and had carnal knowledge of her and did so diverse other times . . . and the office of the man-spirit was to lie with her carnally and as often as she desired and that he did lie with her in *that* manner [i.e., being sucked] very often" (p. 2). Another accused witch, Elizabeth Chandler, also admitted that the devil appeared to her "upon Saturday night last, in a pushing and roaring manner. And she saith that she found her body sore about the bottom of her belly after he was gone from her" (pp. 7-8). Ellen William admitted that her imps "sucked her upon and about the hips and they have used very often to come to her since" (p. 10). Joan Wallis also testified that "the Blackman [i.e., the devil] had the use of her body once, twice and sometimes thrice in a week" (p. 13).

Another sign that a person was a witch was the discovery of witches' teats. Because the process of discovery involved strip searches, the public found the topic of witches' teats very exciting. The newsbook *A True and Exact Relation of the Several . . . Late Witches . . . at Chelmesford* was a gold mine of information about this dimension of witchcraft. This pamphlet consisted of fifty-two edited statements submitted by individuals charged with witchcraft or by those giving testimony against the accused before the court of Assize at Chelmsford. It mentioned the usual hexings of cows and children but focused on identifying "witch's teats" as a prime subject of controversy. Some earlier pamphlets had indicated that these marks might appear on many different parts of the body, but the witches at Chelmsford seemed to have had them only on their sexual organs: "they were not like piles, for this informant [i.e., a witch searcher] knows very well what they are, having been troubled with them herself" (p. 24). Establishing the credentials of the witch searchers and the veracity of the method of investigation for determining witchcraft was extremely important since there was often no other evidence against the accused.

The witch searchers Elizabeth Hunt and Priscilla Brigs, for instance, were very highly esteemed. Indeed, the court record indicated that "these informants have been formerly employed to search other women suspected of witchcraft who have had the like bigges [*sic*] and have afterwards confessed themselves to be witches" (p. 16). They reported finding the telltale marks on Mary Greenleife, that "the said Mary had bigges [*sic*] or teats in her secret parts . . . and that they verily believed these teats are sucked by her imps." When the court asked Mary Greenleife "how she came by those teats which were discovered in her secret parts, she saith she knows not unless she were born with them but she never knew she had any such until this time . . . and she does deny that she ever had any imp suck on these teats" (p. 17). Because the expertise of these two searchers was above criticism, the court knew Greenleife was lying, and she was executed.

Other witch searchers were also well respected for their skills. Francis Milles, another court appointed witch searcher, reported that when she searched Margaret Moone, "she found three long teats or bigges [sic] in her secret parts, which seemed to have been lately sucked" (p. 24). Hence, the court ordered Margaret Moone's daughters, who had given no indications of witchcraft, to undergo a similar search. The result was that "upon the searching of her daughters, this informant found that two of them had bigges [sic] in their private parts as the said Margaret their mother had" (p. 24).

Searching for witches' teats demanded considerable expertise. The problem had been concisely stated in *The Witches of Huntingdon*, which noted that simple strip searches for teats were not always effective because witches knew how to circumvent the searcher's efforts. It reported that one accused witch admitted that her marks would not be found because "I cut mine off three days before I was searched" (p. 15). Fortunately, Matthew Hopkins, the redoubtable witch finder extraordinaire, published the short pamphlet *The Discover of Witches* (1647), in which he provided the lay public, in easy question-and-answer form, with an experienced and authoritative opinion on the subject of witches' teats.

Hopkins argues that experienced searchers "can justify their skill to any" critic; indeed, these skills were fundamental to the discovery of witches. True experts would not be confused by bogus witches' teats and would be able to "show good reasons why inch marks are not natural, neither that they can happen by any such natural cause" (p. 3). Moreover, only the truly expert witch searcher could distinguish between "variations and mutations of these marks into several forms" (p. 4).

Despite considerable expertise on the part of a trained searcher, the witch was sometimes able to deceive even the most experienced eye. Hopkins explained that "if a witch hear a month or two before that the witch-finder (as they call him) is coming, they will, and have, put out their imps to others to suckle them . . . [and] these upon search are found to have dried skins and films only and be close to the flesh" (p. 4). In such an event, Hopkins advised to "keep her twenty four hours with a diligent eye that none of her spirits come in any visible shape to suck her." He recalled one instance when this was done, and "the women [searchers] have seen the day after [that] *her teats are extended out to their former filling length, full of corruption, ready to burst.*" The final proof came when "leaving her alone one quarter of an hour and let the women [searchers] go up again, she will have drawn her imps close again" (p. 4).

Disbelievers who rejected the existence of witches, witches' marks, the need for witch searchers and witch finders were inevitable proven wrong. Hopkins told of an accused witch "who was apprehended and searched by women who had for many years known the devil's marks, and found to have three teats about her, which honest women have not" (p. 2). Following his advice, and "upon command from the justice, they were to keep her from sleep two or three nights, expecting in that time to see her familiars." In fact, Hopkins was correct. On "the fourth night she called [them] in by their several names and told them what shapes [to assume] a quarter of an hour before they came in, [with] there being ten of us in the room" (p. 2). Dissolute intellectuals might scoff, but it was difficult to argue with the careful empirical observations of ten trained observers.

It was no accident that images of lascivious female sectaries, lewd whores, and lurid witches were so common. The press could have discovered in women any quality it wished, but dirty sex was what it published. It was easy to create sexual fantasies about the female as a witch, as a radical sectary, or as a dirty whore because in all three instances the status of outsider made her foreign to all that was good and decent. By placing herself outside normative moral controls, the female outsider was able to indulge herself sexually. Puritan society pilloried the whore, jailed the sectarian, executed the witch, and thereby demonstrated its piety. Women could save themselves only by catering to their husbands. These appraisals and remedies, however, indicated more about the society making such judgments than about the unfortunate individuals subject to the majority's lurid fantasies. Certainly, repressed sexuality offered that women were primarily whores and temptresses and responsible for the sexual victimization of men. Even more perverted sexuality surely motivated those delighting in accounts of strip-searched women to determine when their teats had been sucked last.

Fortunately for all concerned, neither Ranters nor witchcraft trials made it past the interregnum. Charles II permitted the 1650 laws against adultery and fornication to lapse. It is doubtful if men thought any the better of women after the restoration, but at least they no longer blamed them for every social evil. That women are generally responsible for mankind's ills, unfortunately, remains a commonplace.

THE
BROTHERS

of the BLADE:

Anſwerable to

The Siſters of the *Scaberd.*

OR,

A Dialogue betweene two Hot-ſpurres of the Times, *Serjeant*
SLICE-MAN, *alias* SMELL-SMOCK of *Coney-Court* in *Chick-lane*, and
Corporall DAM-MEE of *Bell-alley* neere *Pick-hatch.*

At their firſt meeting in the walkes in *Mocrefields*, upon the Re-
turne of the one from the Leaguer in the *Low-Countries*, and the late
comming to *London* of the other from the Campe in the *North*,
at the disbanding of the Army.

Printed for *Thomas Bankes* and *Iohn Thomas,* 1641.

◆ ◆ ◆

10

Bawdy Men and Better

*"Captain Hind is as swift as a hind, as rapacious as an eagle . . .
and to palliate all these he is a fine companion, facetious and witty."*
—*A Second Discovery of Hind's Exploits (1651)*

The English revolution stimulated an extensive volume of pamphlet literature extolling the popular Robin Hood-like virtues of royalist antirevolutionary heroes.[1] Indeed, it is possible that the popular hero as a man of the people truly came into his own during these complex times when identification with the dead Charles I or the future Charles II was impossible. For one thing, these publications appeared only after Charles I was executed. Also, they rejected the possibility of using Oliver Cromwell as a popular hero in place of the king. Despite his authority and military ability, Cromwell did not capture the attention of the pamphlet press. Perhaps he was too much identified with Charles I's execution or with the subsequent failure of his governmental experiments or was too embroiled in the mire of day-to-day governance involving policies ordinary Englishmen disliked. James Hind, on the other hand, was another story altogether.

Captain James Hind was significant: the first popular bandit-hero actually created and made famous by the popular press of his day, he was the subject of at least seventeen pamphlets.[2] Their appearance must be considered an historical accident of the civil war. During more stable times, the government would not have permitted pamphlets extolling the public virtues of a common thief to have been published. But then, during more stable times the government would have executed Hind as a traitor too quickly for a myth to take hold in the popular mind. As we shall see, the government did not make this same mistake a second time. Just a few years later when Richard Hannam, another royalist-cum-criminal was caught, he was quickly tried and executed.

Social banditry is a complex phenomena. It is a historical common-place that in the aftermath of civil war, when the new regime proves unpopular or unjust, bandits are sometimes transformed into "popular heroes": men who break unjust laws. This is especially the case if the decades during and after the fighting also witness many of the poor dispossessed of their traditional living and forced into a more competitive and harsh social world. After the American Civil War, for instance, the James brothers, former Confederate soldiers with no place in post-war Missouri, turned to robbing the new railroads then making their way across the continent. In the minds of many of their contemporaries, Jesse and Frank James actually upheld the true moral law of the range. Poor farmers had lived on land that the railroads acquired virtually for free when corrupt politicians passed laws of eminent domain. In robbing the new railroads of their gold and silver, the James brothers simply returned wealth to its original source. Similar accusations were heard during the French Revolution, the Russian Revolution, and the nationalist revolutions in China, Iran, Egypt, and elsewhere. During the English conflict, charges of war profiteering and parliamentary cronyism led many Englishmen to suspect the worst about those who materially benefited from Parliament's battle against royalist tyranny.

The new press also played a role in the popularity of the antisocial hero. J. A. Sharp has noted that "ever since the popular press had been established in England, much of its output had been devoted to crime, its major concern being the sensational and newsworthy cases."[3] Upright moralists may have clucked their tongues, pulled their beards, and wagged their heads, but innovative criminals often found more popularity than did those hunting them down. Indeed, the civil wars only heightened an already strong popular interest in highwaymen and other daring crooks.[4] Many soldiers had been recruited from jail, as was the normal practice of the age.[5] When the soldiers were released, they returned to their previous pursuits as petty criminals. Curiously, however, when women broke the law, they were an example of all that was morally decrepit about their sex. When men broke the law, often as common thieves or as pimps to prostitutes, they became a symbol of the independence to which many men aspired.

The Brothers of the Blade, described in the pamphlet *The Brothers of the Blade, Answerable to The Sisters of the Scabard* (1641), were a male underclass equivalent to prostitutes, or Sisters of the Scabbard. The "Brothers of the Blade" lived by their wits when possible, committed petty crimes and went to jail when things went poorly, and only joined the army when they could do nothing else. In turn, release from the service inevitably resulted in more unemployment followed by yet another stint in jail. Indeed, Sliceman, one of the characters in this pamphlet, reported to his friend Smellsmock that he had already served a second time in jail even though he had been very recently released from the army.

The names of the characters, Sliceman and Smellsmock, were hardly accidental. A sliceman was a petty thief, and a smellsmock was a male who served as a "hector," "pimp," "usher," or general all-around gopher to a "smock," or a whore, so named after the garment she wore, which was slit up the front and rear for appropriate access. These had been their trades before the revolution. After the army, both now hoped to return to their former occupations. Sliceman reasoned, "If all strings sail in the bow of my expectation, I'll fall to my old trade, turn high-way lawyer [i.e., a bandit] or padman [i.e., a petty thief]." Smellsmock considered these activities too dangerous and said, "If at any time they get a booty and are taken in the act, then their long durance and captivity in the jail in a short time exhausts them of all" (p. 3). Rather, hoping for something a little softer, "I would I were in service (as I have been before I went into the northern parts) with some courtesan . . . I could serve her turn well for a gentleman usher, or at a shift upon occasion to be a pimp for her ladyship" (p. 7). The two soldiers grew nostalgic for the good times before the revolution, and one recalled how "those were my golden days for in those term times I could with dexterity in a crowd dive into a pocket and fetch up with the slight and activity of my hand twenty or thirty pieces at a time." The other agreed, recalling when, "according to the saying, *lightly come, lightly go,* so it fared with me. What I picked resolutely on a Monday morning from country clients was spent dissolutely before Sunday evening among the Sisters of the Scabard" (p. 3).

The Brothers of the Blade were no less cynical about the course of reform than were the Sisters of the Scabard. Morality laws simply meant more officials to bribe. Like working girls, street rogues experienced periodic shakedowns. The two former soldiers recalled how only bribery kept then from being "noosed" by Judge Richardson, who "would have jeered thee to the gallows." Fortunately, the golden door was always open, and "having sent to him the night before 'a good angel' [i.e., a bribe delivered by a jail guard who was himself also bribed], by the means whereof and favor of him, I had the law in my own hand" (p. 2). Now, unfortunately, everything would be different. Smellsmock regretted, "I must confess, thou and I have been in times past as errant rogues as ever Newgate harbored" (p. 3), and Sliceman agreed, saying, "I make no question but if thou had'st thy desert, thou had'st been noosed many years ago" (p. 2). Sliceman feared that "the hangman hath long since marked us for sheep for his own slaughter" (p. 2).

As their conversation turned to their reduced condition, the two former soldiers retired to an unregistered alehouse operated by Mrs. Snip, a part-time whore. Sliceman says to his friend, "As I understand, Snip's wife has two or three tubs of ale continually in her house which she draws in black rammalian pots for her friends and acquaintances that visit her" (p. 8). Smellsmock tells Sliceman, "They say she's as blyth and buxom, as witty and wanton and as plump and impudent as ever she was. Fame is false if you have not been very inward with her." Sliceman admitted, "The time was when I struck fire in her tinder-box, and it has took . . . and once a whore, always the same." Unfortunately, he said, "She'll take us for a couple of poor rogues to come to her house without a sliver in our pockets." This, of course, raised yet again the whole question of gainful employ-ment. In the meantime, "Let not that trouble thee for I doubt not but before we come to Redcross Street we shall meet with some or other . . . Brother of the Blade or Sister of the Scabard and take occasion to bor-row a shilling or 6 d. till Doomes-day" (p. 8).

Sliceman and Smellsmock may have been permanent fixtures of the London underclass, but they had fought the wars and then returned to a disapproving society intent upon reforming them out of existence. Perhaps it is no coincidence that for as long as Parliament required the military services of rogues and the unemployed, no reform laws were put into effect. Rather, these laws followed the disbanding of the army with-out pay. Sliceman and Smellsmock's sentiments were no less true in 1651 than in 1641.

Under the right circumstances, the criminal could be converted into a socially acceptable bandit. Even more, in times of social unrest, when those in power lack charismatic leadership and possess little more right to power than force, the criminal-cum-bandit may even take on heroic char-acteristics. The bandit can be transformed into the image of everything the government is not, and the bandit's every action can become the example of resistance to the government that most poor and common people cannot themselves act out but wished they could.

The bandit's disavowal of social mores and established law stood as proof of his masculinity and independence in the face of intolerable injus-tice. By supporting the hero, the community shared his virtues. In the face of general unhappiness with the regime, the hero's deeds against the government vicariously redeemed the community. Bandit-heroes who "robbed from the rich and gave to the poor," such as Robin Hood, Cola di Rienzi, and Jacque Cade had already appeared in earlier centuries. Revolutionary England produced its own popular heroes in the persons of Captain James Hind and Richard Hannam. One particularly important element of the popularity of both men was that they were strong royalists, with Hind in particular coming to represent in the popular mind all the heartfelt virtues one would like to find in a king.

Unlike other public representatives of royalism, Hind was of common stock.[6] He was the son of a saddler from Chipping Norton in Oxford who was unwilling to learn his father's profession and was thus apprenticed to a butcher. Even more unhappy with his new prospects, young James ran off to London and joined a fraternity of thieves led by the infamous "Bishop" Allen who disguised themselves as ecclesiastics to gain the confidence of those they robbed along the highways. The civil war provided many young men with opportunities for personal adventure and social advancement. Hind spent the years from 1646 to 1648 as a highwayman pretending to be a royalist officer selling protection to merchants. In 1648 his disguise ceased to be a fiction when he received a captain's commission from Sir William Compton in the king's cause against Parliament. When Fairfax captured Colchester in August of 1648, Hind escaped from that military debacle disguised in women's apparel, a fact that colored many subsequent stories describing his imagination and valor. When Parliament asserted its political control, Hind avoided capture by continually moving about the countryside as a highwayman and by travelling abroad to the Hague, Ireland, Sicily, and the Isle of Man, where he lived a life of crime. By the beginning of 1651 Hind's public image as a daring rogue was becoming well established to London readers. In November of that year, in ill health, Hind was apprehended in London, where he was living at a barber's house under the assumed name of James Brown.

Hind was considered a dangerous criminal, and his apprehension was a major coup. According to *The True and Perfect Relation of the Taking of Captain James Hind* (1651), published by George Horton immediately upon Hind's capture on November 9, London police authorities "with great privacy and care, so ordered the business that there was not the least notice or suspicion until such time that they came to his chamber door, forced the same open and immediately entered with their pistols cocked" (p. 1). Taking no chances, Hind's captors attached iron chains with heavy bolts to his legs and put their prisoner under a guard consisting of "four files of musketeers." Despite his criminal image and reputation, Hind was not to be tried as a highwayman. Rather, he was told

"Captain, you are not brought hither for robbing but for treason" (p. 6), and he was questioned "in relation to his late engagement with Charles Stuart and whether he was the man that accompanied the Scots king for the furtherance of his escape" (p. 2), after the battle of Worcester on September 3, 1651. From Parliament's perspective, the man that had facilitated Charles II's miraculous and embarrassing escape would finally be brought to justice.

Despite the government's suspicions of Hind's war-related crimes and his continuing overt loyalty to the dead king, there was no hard evidence against him. According to the chapbook *The Trial of Captain James Hind* (1651), "he stands indicted upon high treason by the Council of State and thereupon the court made no further progress against him by reason that no bill of Indictment was brought in so that he was ordered to be remanded back to the place whence he was brought" (pp. 4-5). The government, however, would not release him, and on December 13, Hind's trial was "adjourned from the Old Bailey to the city of Oxford . . . that he may receive punishment in the same county where first he committed his fact and crimes" (p. 8). In other words, Hind would be shipped out of London, where the crowds loved him, to Oxford where, it was hoped, it would be possible to indict him for some crime.

Moving Hind to Oxford, however, was foolish. It was not only the highwayman's hometown but a royalist stronghold. In any event, Hind was confident that little could be done against him, and "when he stood at the Bar, he deported himself with undaunted courage yet with a civil behavior and smiling countenance" (p. 5). At one point he turned to his followers and said, "'These are filthy gingling spurs,' (meaning the irons about his legs) 'but I hope to have them exchanged 'ere long' which expression caused much laughter" (p. 5). In fact, Hind was correct about the charges, if not about the leg irons, and "as for bills of indictment or witnesses to prove the allegations, nothing can be made apparent, neither are any come in" (p. 8). With the case against Hind in Oxford no more successful than the one in London, he was sent to Reading on March 1, where he was tried on a charge of manslaughter for killing an associate several years earlier. Hind was found guilty but, inexplicably, was exonerated from this criminal charge under the Law of Oblivion, even though that legislation normally forgave only war-related political activities and not capital offenses. Despite his exoneration, Hind was not released from prison.

The government's position was awkward. It was running out of charges at the same time that many adoring chapbooks about Hind began to appear in London. These pamphlets seemed to take great pleasure in the government's discomfort and freely exaggerated Hind's exploits. *A Second Discovery of Hind's Exploits* (1651), printed by William Ley, was typical: "For slights and stratagems none can parallel him, and he may be called a Master in the Art of Thievery, the cunningest and wisest of the company for difficult and dangerous thefts" (p. A3b). Hind, we are informed, "is as swift as a hind, as rapacious as an eagle . . . and to palliate all these he is a fine companion, facetious and witty." Yet another chapbook, *The English Gusman, or, The History of That Unparalleled Thief, James Hind* (1652), by G[eorge] F[idge], consisted of twenty-seven stories of Hind's daring deeds and attempted to provide a complete history of this infamous highwayman for a more common and poorly educated readership. A preface cautioned educated readers that "thou wilt not find this ensuing history set out and garnished with a fine style and studied phrase but (which is best of all) an orderly expression, a natural story and a pure jest. That so the meanest may understand what they read and not be perplexed with difficult words." In short, style would suffer to accommodate the expanding vulgar market.

As the case against Hind ground to a near halt, the government was increasingly afraid that Hind, a recognized quick-change artist, would break out of jail. His association with "Bishop" Allen led to exaggerated stories about his ability to disguise himself, and the pamphlet *Hind's Ramble* (1651), printed by George Latham, kept this prospect before the public eye. We are informed, for instance, that Hind hardly ever dressed in normal fashion, and "sometimes he went in the habit of a gentleman of great fortune, sometimes in poor habit and sometimes in a serving man's habit" (p. 20). In one story Hind took a page out of "Bishop" Allen's book and avoided capture when "he turned up his horse to grass, pulled off his own coat and turned it—which was black within—and with a priest's girdle he had in his pocket girt it to him and taking a little book out of his pocket, walked under a hedge as if he had been in study for a sermon" (p. 37). Similarly, Hind's now legendary escape from the Battle of Colchester dressed as a woman provided pamphlet authors with a good foundation for their own story.[7] According to Robert Wood, printer of *A Pill to Purge Melancholy, or, Merry News from Newgate* (1652), Hind was once in the company of some whores "at a private vaulting school in Chancery Lane," where he was becoming very drunk and very playful. At one point one of the whores said to him, "Prithee, go into my chamber and put on my gown and petticoat that lies on the table and go down and see if my landlady will know thee" (p. 4). Hind emerged from the whore's quarters to the tavern below as a totally convincing female. One customer in particular "was so sweet upon him that he [Hind] could not be rid of him" (p. 5). The girls thought this was immensely funny and "one of the ladies desired Hind to walk forth and take up a cully [i.e., client]" (p. 5). In fact, Hind does turn a trick, in this case, a fat parliamentary lawyer, and if the story seemed too contrived, the author wrote, "Let them say what they will . . . I care not if they count it false or true" (p. 3).

In the end, Hind could not escape from his captors, and his execution in September 1652 put an end to the developing myth about his exploits. But during the ten months from his capture to his execution, chapbook authors succeeded in creating a hero first loved as a man of the people, then respected and honored as a representative of divine order, and finally conceived of as a surrogate for the missing king. What is surprising is the degree to which these authors were able to build this myth on the meager materials provided by the life of a highwayman. How this transformation came about in the space of just a few months must be considered as profound as the transformation itself and attests to the new influential power of published media even in this very early age of sensational journalism.

Pamphlet authors seem to have hit every right button in building Hind into a popular hero. The best popular heroes came from common stock to ensure popular identification, but their intentions had to be noble. Pamphlet authors expunged Hind's record of any truly antisocial crimes, ignoring, for instance, several charges of murder. The author of *The True and Perfect Relation of the Taking of Captain James Hind* even had him denying any serious wrongdoing. "I owe a debt to God," he intoned. "Blessed be his name that hath kept me from shedding blood unjustly, which is now a comfort to me. Neither did I ever wrong any poor man of the worth of a penny" (p. 5). Later newsbooks even deleted Hind's earliest criminal history, while others romanticized this period of Hind's training in crime with "Bishop" Allen's gang. Not a single pamphlet, however, accepted the reality of Hind's criminal life. According to *Hind's Ramble,* for instance, Allen's crew was not a gang of true cutthroat felons but a mutually supportive fraternity of good friends. At one point the older rogue told Hind, "I would have you be my companion and friend and not a servant . . . You shall eat and drink as I do and if I have any money, you shall have part and want none. And if I want [for money], you must help to get some as well as you can" (p. 4).

When Allen was eventually hanged at Tiburn, Hind assumed leadership of the "fraternity of mutually caring males." Once again, Hind's activities were converted from acts of crime to "devilishly delightful deeds." At this time Hind began disguising himself as the king's officer and sold protection in the king's name around Banbury. He was successful, for "no carrier could pass his roads without paying tribute to his company or losing the best of their goods." As a result, many local merchants "promised him and his company a certain stipend a week to let them pass" (pp. 14-15). When his followers took to calling him "Captain," much as they called Allen "Bishop," Hind modestly chided them, "Gentlemen, you call me captain but I will desire you to call me so no more till I am one or may deserve it" (p. 24). Unfortunately, the royalists lost Banbury and Hind lost his cover and employment. It was at this point that Hind first officially joined the royalists, possibly with the hope of continuing to sell protection.

To maintain the myth of Hind as a respectable hero, many publications used his royalism as a cover to justify his other activities. J. S.'s five-act play, *An Excellent Comedy Called, The Prince of Priggs Revels* (1651), structured each act around an incident in which Hind and his crew of Turbo, Latro, and Spolario robbed yet another socially unpopular type, including businessmen, high-born ladies and an alderman of the city of York. Yet despite this levity, the fifth act presents us with a more serious side of Hind's behavior. The captain, on bended knee, says to Charles:

Make me your guide (Sir) and never doubt your safety,
For though to others I have been untrue,
Let me be hanged if I prove false to you. (p. 14)

Hind's chroniclers continually claimed that he was a political prisoner, not a thief, and even the highwayman's "road-side manner" had been misunderstood; Hind was actually a respectable citizen. George Horton's *The Declaration of Captain James Hind* (1651) reported Hind saying, "At what time so ever I met with any such person [i.e., on the highway] it was my constant custom to ask who was he for. If he replied 'for the king' I gave him twenty shillings. But if he answered, 'for the Parliament,' I left him as I found him" (p. 2). And if by chance someone was actually separated from his purse, it was only the fat, the rich, and others, who deserved everything they got. *The True and Perfect Relation* told how Hind "made bold with a rich bumpkin of a lying lawyer whose full fed-fees from the rich farmer doth too much impoverish the poor cottage-keeper" (p. 5). But "neither did I ever take the worth of a penny from a poor man." In one story in *Hind's Ramble,* an early chapbook that set the tone for subsequent publications, Hind was the friend of the poor and protector of the common man. He "borrowed money of a poor man and paid him double at a time and place appointed" (p. 21), cozened a usurer and thereby saved an innkeeper's indebted business (pp. 16-17), and robbed only committee-men (p. 18), fat parsons (p. 28), and other social types easily made the butt of slapstick humor.

Chapbook authors also portrayed Hind as a friend of the working classes. As a man of humble origins, Hind may have served as a role model for others of his social background who lacked the courage to run away from nasty masters. According to Fidge's *The English Gusman* Hind once robbed a master of thirty pieces of gold and later explained to the master's servant, "I seldom take anything from the master but I give the servant something. Here is something for thee to drink to my health . . . My name is Hind" (p. 18). Hind justified this less than legal transfer of wealth with the classic argument advanced by members of his profession: "To deceive the deceiver," he said, "is no deceit" (p. 25).

His class solidarity notwithstanding, Hind also possessed personal integrity that transcended class lines. According to Latham's *Hind's Ramble,* he once escaped his pursuers by ducking into the house of a local gentleman. This gentleman, ignorant of his guest's true identity, offered him the hospitality of his home and fed him and put him up for the night. The following morning, the gentleman offered Hind £50 for his fine horse. The captain took the money and then rode away, leaving his surprised host all the poorer. But Hind had second thoughts about his ungentlemanly behavior. He returned later that day to say, "Sir, you have entertained me civilly, and therefore I were unworthy if I should have carried your money with me" (p. 26). He returned the gentleman's money, and, additionally, he "gave the gentleman a word to pass all highway men of his gang and then bid him farewell."

Two groups unpopular in English society, doctors and lawyers, often served as the objects of Hind's pranks. *Hind's Ramble* recalled a story about a doctor from Hind's stay in Holland. It seems there was a famous but obnoxious physician known more for boasting about his wealth than his diagnostic skills. One day, Hind pursued the physician in the street and said to him, "Sir, I have heard much of your renown for cures . . . and if you would please to go along with me to my house, I have a wife much troubled with a flux in her belly for these fourteen days" (p. 22). The physician followed Hind, and once inside his residence, Hind "takes in one hand a pistol and in the other a great empty purse . . . and he said, 'Sir, here is my wife (meaning the empty purse). She hath been a long time troubled with a flux in her belly and you are the only man that can only remedy and find out a means to cure this disease'" (p. 23).

Lawyers were held up to even greater contempt. Remember that it was a drunken and corrupt lawyer who had been enchanted with Hind when he dressed as a woman in *A Pill to Purge Melancholy, or, Merry News from Newgate.* The remainder of this story indicated common attitudes toward officers of the court. "This lump of corruption," as the lawyer was called, was totally smitten with Hind and said to him, "Lady, I am confident I have been formerly acquainted with you . . . let us drink half a pint together at the Devil's Tavern." Hind agreed, "and so they went hand in hand to the Devil—as all lawyers and thieves will." Eventually the two agreed on the price of Hind's attention, and the lawyer took his new friend into his chambers. Once they were alone the lawyer turned to Hind and "desired him to sit upon the bed by him, which he did, and then the lawyer began to put his hand under the petticoat but . . . Hind, putting his hand into his pocket, pulled out his pistol immediately" (p. 6). To make a long story short, Hind "gagged him and bound him and cased his pockets of his gold and in that manner left him, returning to his company and giving them a relation of his adventures at which the wenches laughed heartily" (p. 6). So much for lawyers, or at least this one.

Government bureaucrats were lawyers once removed and no less offensive. I. H.'s *The Last Will and Testament of James Hind, Highway Lawyer,* written at the end of 1651 while Hind sat in jail, was not meant to be taken literally but still expressed popular contempt for government officials. This "last will and testament of a 'highway lawyer'" made clear that Hind was only a vehicle for common popular opinion. Hind, for instance, "bequeaths all my fallacies, frauds, vagaries, slights, stratagems, circumventions, assassinations, dissimulations and ambages to the present gown-men who fight at barriers, at the upper bench, chancery and where ever else . . . that they may be more renowned for their evasions, inhibitions, remoras, collusions etc., and generally for all their egregious procrastination, gulleries and knaveries practiced upon their poor deluded clients" (pp. 1-2). Hind may well have been an a thief and an outlaw, and he may have dressed as a woman, but the objects of his art represented unpopular social types against whom Hind could do little wrong. Thus, if Parliament's stealing from the poor and the helpless was immoral, not stealing from lawyers and their ilk was downright sinful. Indeed, Captain James Hind emerged in the chapbooks as a social reformer.

The difference between James Hind the bandit and Captain James Hind the royalist celebrity and social reformer reached a high point with the publication of George Horton's *We Have Brought Our Hoggs to a Fair Market, or Strange News From Newgate* (1652). The cover of this oddly titled piece pictured Hind in gallant royal form astride a horse rearing up in the air. The caption read "Unparalleled Hind," and the author made every effort to turn Hind into a more than human character. In one story Horton reported that after a great robbery in Leicestershire, Hind was apprehended at a nearby inn. He turned to his captors and said, "Gentlemen, I am a man sent to do wonders and many visions have appeared and sundry voices have I heard saying, 'O thou great and mighty lion, thou art decreed to range the countries to work and manifest to the people strange wonders.' At which instant a rampant lion appeared visible but immediately vanished, to the great admiration of the spectators who peaceably departed to their several habitations to tell the strangeness of this wonder" (p. 7). Needless to say, those who left in amazement were Hind's pursuers, who, like Paul on the road to Damascus, realized Hind's virtue and their own error.

Not only was this contribution to the Hind myth more miraculous than earlier stories, but it attempted to portray Hind as a socially responsible personality who greatly valued the sanctity of property rather than as a crook on the take. Fidge's *English Guzman* epitomized Hind's attitude toward property with the dictum "to deceive the deceiver is no deceit." That same attitude was expressed in *Hind's Ramble* when Hind preached to his colleagues, "Remember what I say unto you . . . Disgrace not your selves with small sums but aim high and for great ones, for the least [too] will bring you to the gallows" (p. 15). But in *We Have Brought Our Hoggs to a Fair Market, or Strange News From Newgate,* Hind reportedly said just the opposite. He now allegedly preached, "I, James Hind do here strictly charge and require all and every one . . . that they do not recede or flinch from their principles, nor to betray each other for lucre . . . I do likewise conjure you to keep your hands from picking and stealing and to be in charity with all men . . . And that you keep your hands from the shedding of innocent blood, that you relieve the poor, help the needy, clothe the naked" (p. 1). Of course, as a popular hero Hind could not include all social types under this umbrella of genial morality, at least not "the caterpillars of the times, viz., Long-gown men, Committee-men, Excise-men, Sequestrators and other sacrilegious persons" (p. 1).

These romantic portrayals of Hind's activities hardly squared with the facts. All pamphlet authors, especially George Horton, conceded that Hind was a highwayman but maintained that he never robbed from the poor or from the weak, was a true friend of servants, was honorable to all who knew him, and was always very witty and up to some good-natured mad prank. If Hind did find himself in possession of other people's goods, it was only from need, only after the defeat of the royalist cause, and then only from fat bumpkins, dishonest lawyers, and other groups eliciting little sympathy among London's urban dwellers. There is adequate reason, however, to discredit most of the apocryphal stories about this good-natured, morally justified theft. For one thing, Hind became a criminal long before joining the king's cause and effortlessly resumed that same life thereafter. Indeed, despite his claim that he was a political prisoner, Hind's much-heralded royalist commission may have resulted more from the high quality of his criminal skills and royalist desperation for new talent to aid their ailing cause than because of his deep and abiding faith in God's chosen ruler of England.

Having been transformed from a butcher's apprentice into a social redeemer and from a thief to a miraculous personage and lawgiver, Hind's execution brought an abrupt end to the myth. When the manslaughter charge against Hind proved insufficient to bring him to the gallows, and the government's fear of his flight was very great in September 1652, Hind was spirited off to Worcester, where he was tried and condemned on the charge of high treason. On September 24, 1652, far away from the public's view, Captain James Hind was hanged, drawn, and quartered.

Hind's death caused problems for pamphlet authors, who now had to invent another hero. John Clowes prepared for Hind's eventual execution with *Hind's Elder Brother, or, The Master Thief Discovered* (1652), whose hero was Major Thomas Knowls, another royalist officer who turned freebooter when the fighting ceased. Knowls's early life was a parallel to Hind's. Like Hind, he was an officer in the king's army and, again like Hind, able to elude Parliament's grasp (p. 9). In an attempt to merge the two images of Hind and Knowls, the cover illustration presented a picture of two horsemen attacking each other, one labeled Hind and the other Knowls, and the chapbook includes a story of Hind and Knowls meeting each other with the latter besting the former for "mad pranks."

Captain Knowls was a devious man. Like Captain Hind, he came to London at the age of fourteen and became apprenticed to a master thief, in Knowls' case, "Punteus the Mountebank" (p. 2). Much as Allen was a master thief who dressed like a bishop, "Dr." Punteus, "who then was recently come into England," was a Frenchman skilled in the purveying of snake oil and other folk remedies and practiced medicine and dentistry as a sideline. Knowls was quick to learn, and "he added much to the sale of his master's antidotes by his witty jests, buffoonish behavior and nimble vaultings so that he became chief man to Punteus." Much as Hind was a master of disguise, various stories find "Knowls and his comrade fitting themselves with false beards and antic apparel" (p. 2). When a usurer with a toothache and a reputation for never paying his bills sought medical attention and relief, "Knowls cries out to his comrade, 'a prize! . . . Give me my master's gown, fasten me on that black beard, stand bear, and . . . call up that usurer'" (p. 3). The pained man enters, and "Knowls, out supposed Punteus, says he will apply his best skill for God's sake . . . and while Knowls pulled out the tooth, he pulled out of his pocket a cat's skin purse with twenty nine pounds, two rings and a watch" (p. 3). The usurer did not realize that his pocket had been picked, but when Knowls demanded payment, the patient feigned poverty and claimed that he had no money and could not pay. "Says Knowls, 'since you swear before witnesses I am content, God speed you well.'" Only later did the usurer realize that he had been robbed of his purse, but there was little he could do. The narrator tells us that "Knowls thought this robbery was but just, to rob the man that nobody would trust," which was reminiscent of Hind's axiom that to rob the rich was no crime. Hence, much like Hind, Knowls was not a true thief but a confidence man able to con usurers and other socially unpopular types. Indeed, Knowls was really an expression of social conscience rather than a disturber of the social contract, and other stories thus presented him as a great patriot as well. In one instance, Major Knowls duped a committee of Scottish commissioners, and another time, dressed in "black, very neat, and more like a Scotch Laird," he was able to steal much silver plate from these enemies of England. Indeed, the narrator told us "Thus witty Knowls did borrow plate of those which cozened King and State" (p. 5).

As with Hind, Knowls' larceny was also a scourge for greater dishonesty. In one story he avoided incarceration through subterfuge and bribery. The end of the complicated account finds Knowls a free man while the two soldiers he bribed were cashiered from the army. The author's conclusion was to blame the soldiers for taking a bribe rather than Knowls for offering it. "Let Knowls his slippery example be," he wrote, "to all those guards which love a fee" (p. 10).

Because only one chapbook about Knowls was published, either readers did not warm to this substitute for Hind or the author was distracted by other subjects. Readers were not left in the lurch, however. Shortly thereafter another major criminal would appear on the scene in the person of Richard Hannam.[8] When Hannam was captured in 1656, several chapbooks converted him, too, into a popular hero.

All four pamphlets describing Hannam's career were dated June 17, the day Hannam was executed. It is clear from the information each provided that only one of these, *The Speech and Confession and Richard Hannam,* which presented Hannam's speech before leaping from the gallows to his death, actually appeared that day. The two newsbooks *Hannam's Last Farewell to the World and The English Villain, or, The Grand Thief* also present his gallows speech and include small amounts of anecdotal information about his various daring escapes from prison. The best and most complete of the four is the unusually long, fifty-five page *The Witty Rogue Arraigned, Condemned and Executed, or, The History of that Incomparable Thief, Richard Hannam,* printed by E. S. Taken together, these four publications tells us a great deal about Richard Hannam.

As was the case with Captain Hind, a chasm separated myth from reality in Richard Hannam's life. E. S., for instance, claimed that Hannam came from an old and reputable family, that he was well educated, knew Latin and several other languages, spoke well, and was witty in his conversation. Actually, he was the ill-educated son of a shoemaker from Shaftesbury, Dorsetshire. Apprenticed to a silk weaver, Hannam believed his talents could be put to better profit elsewhere. He therefore came to London as a young man, where he supposedly met both Allen and Hind. Like Hind, Hannam became involved in robbery and in confidence tricks and, to avoid capture, also traveled abroad to Denmark, Sweden, and Holland for short periods of time. Like Hind, Hannam escaped from jail several times through the use of some very ingenious ploys and mechanical devices. Additionally, Hannam was also a royalist. He was arrested for the last time, tried for his deeds on June 14, 1656, and hanged at Smithfield three days later.

According to the pamphlets, Hannam was not a highwayman but a slick, big-time confidence operator and skilled black bagger. These skills enabled him to rob some of Europe's most prominent personalities, including the King of France, the Earl of Pembroke, the Duke of Normandy, several ambassadors, and a great many wealthy gentlemen and merchants. Many stories emphasized Hannam's organizational abilities. For example, when Hannam decided to rob the Earl of Pembroke (pp. 4-6), he first became acquainted with Mr. Herbert, a servant in the earl's household, from whom he learned the household's daily routine. Hannam then acquired a uniform and was able to circulate in the house during dinner service, when he waylaid much of the earl's silver plate as it was being returned from the table to the kitchen. As a result, neither the kitchen nor the table staff was truly aware of what had been taken until much later, when neither set of servants could explain how the items disappeared.

In another story Hannam gained entry to a rich Dutch merchant's house by declaring his intention to woo the daughter. Hannam, like Hind, had the social skills of a gentleman. When his charm won the merchant's good will, he was invited to stay the night. After the family retired, Hannam emptied the merchant's vaults and, not wishing to overstay his welcome, left before dawn (pp. 6-8). Hannam displayed his social sophistication once again when he introduced his "son" into a prominent merchant's household staff to improve the young man's character. According to the terms of their arrangement, the flattered merchant would pay nothing for the young man's services as a secretary. The young man, like his alleged father, was as smooth as silk, and the merchant was soon induced to show his new secretary his account books and the secret locations of the family gems. This information was then passed on to Hannam, who proceeded to empty the vaults of their contents at the most opportune occasion (p. 9).

Hannam was also an accomplished black-bag operator. He owned a special hat with an inner compartment into which he could slip gems when visiting a jeweler's shop (p. 26). He was also an expert at slight-of-hand, where one item might be replaced by another (p. 18). When these well-honed skills failed him, and he faced exposure, Hannam was thoughtful enough to cover his escape with a series of backup surprises such as a handful of pepper thrown into his pursuers' eyes.

In addition to his many adventures, Hannam's daring escapes from prison captivated the pamphlet-reading audience. "All the care which could be used or thought upon," the author informed us, "nor all the locks and bars which could be made, were strong enough to hold him, so subtle was he in his tricks and slights that he would break the iron chains like thread" (p. 20). These stories had Hannam scampering over walls and climbing through dangerous places, in one case up through a very tall chimney. In another instance he made an impression of the jail key with candle wax from his cell (pp. 19-20) and then tore his cloak into strips to weave into a rope (p. 20). Hannam also possessed a series of mechanical devices that enabled him to better his situation. For instance, he owned "climber's hooks," or "three screws with which he used to ascend a house by thrusting them into any wall of stone or brick . . . One of these screws he takes and winds into a prison wall; then taking another with which he does the same a step above the former, and so a third, and by these screws he got to the top, the undermost of which he pulleth forth and setteth it above the others" (p. 16). Equally useful was the special file he devised for himself. "This file was of such a nature," we are told, "that should you stand in the room where it was filing off a thick iron bar, yet you could not hear the noise" (p. 45).

If Richard Hannam was daring and dashing, sophisticated and skillful, he also embodied a rough-and-ready notion of commonsense decency. In one instance, "he was informed that a certain man at Newington had in his house some monies lately delivered unto him." Hannam broke in to the house and robbed the man and only later realized that his victim was truly poor. As a result "he returns it to him again ... and with these words left him, 'there, honest man, take your monies. I come not to rob the poor'" (p. 23). Like Hind, Hannam possessed a strong sense of fair play that extended past class lines. When he stole from the rich and well placed, he sought only their money and never took personal papers for he believed a gentleman should respect the integrity, if not the property, of another gentleman. As an example, when he robbed the Justice Marsh at Hackney, "he found in silver and gold to the value of four hundred pounds and a small cabinet, wherein were diverse writings, which, when he came to open and after his perusal, he found them to be of some concernment to the Gentleman." Rather than distastefully exploiting the judge's personal affairs, "he fairly parts stakes, keeps the money and by a messenger of trust returns the gentleman his writings" (p. 31). This may have been mythical male concern for other men or perhaps the professional courtesy one confidence operator offered another. On the other hand, showing deference to a judge may also have been an insurance policy for the future.

Hannam also disliked unnecessary violence against important people. Once, some associates robbed the house of Alderman Hancock and "when they returned informed him that they had wounded the alderman." Hannam was so annoyed "he denied to share of their booty, protesting that above all things he abhorred the shedding of blood" (p. 32). Like Hind, Hannam was also an ardent royalist, and at his interrogation he was asked about reports that he had stolen from Charles II. Hannam became indignant, and "he denied that he robbed the King of Scots and said he would rather have parted with a thousand pounds than have been so asperst" (p. 47).

Hannam's end came on June 11, 1656, when he and Mr. Rudd, his father-in-law, and another associate named Mrs. Dales took a room at a small inn at King's Head in St. Swithin's Lane in order to break into a chest just now coming into their possession. The proprietor, Mr. Langhorn, suspected that something was wrong and sent for the authorities. Hannam realized that he had been betrayed and while he was able to escape, both Rudd and Mrs. Dales were taken into custody. When Hannam foolishly returned later that night to stab Langhorn, he was subdued by several young men and was taken into custody. Hannam was hanged three days later (pp. 42-43).

In terms of gross take, Hannam was a more successful thief than Hind, but for a variety of reasons, he did not capture the popular imagination as successfully as his predecessor. The large number of Hind publications would seem to indicate that readers liked James Hind and believed him to be a true hero, whereas Hannam was never presented as possessing Hind's honor. Also, Hannam was incarcerated for only three days, and so pamphlet authors lacked adequate time to develop his character, whereas the government dawdled with Hind in its custody for many months. Whatever their differences, both became in the pamphlets popular heroes with a sense of flair and personal charm more often associated with the colorful Cavalier than the sanctimonious Roundhead. Their daring lifestyles and monarchist politics flew in the face of existing political realities and underscored popular discontent with the king's recent, and unpopular, execution, Cromwell's continuing troubles with Parliament, his subsequent purge of the army, the new troubles with Holland, and the severe economic conditions. The government's continuing inability to deal effectively with many of these problems helped Hind and Hannam, as representatives of the old order, look good by comparison. Hence, it is no surprise that in many pamphlets Hind and Hannam represented almost every virtue readers might find beneficial in a government official or even a king. Many Englishmen may have hoped to discover in these daring fellows the virtues and values they found lacking in a revolutionary government peopled by lawyers, committee men, and other bureaucratic creatures of public scorn.

Despite their eventual capture and execution, Hind, Knowls, and Hannam were the incarnation of every poor apprentice's dream of running away from his cruel master, acquiring polished social skills, cultivating a fine wit, and succeeding in a hard world. If "Bishop" Allen and others were idealized, it may well have been the poor boy's enjoyment in seeing the rich, the educated, and the powerful bilked and made fun of when reality more often presented the opposite situation.

The carefully manufactured myths that converted these bandits into popular heroes may seem fragile and naive. There is, however, reason to believe that the revolutionary government was more than mildly disturbed by them. Although Hind was incarcerated for eleven months, from November 1651 through his execution in September of 1652, all seventeen publications about him were published in the three-month period between his capture in November and the following January. There are no indications as to why the publications about Hind should have come to an abrupt end during the eight months from February to September of 1652 when the previous three-month period witnessed more than one new chapbook a week. While it is possible that the reading public grew tired of him, it is also possible that government pressure was brought to play.

When monarchy returned to power in 1660, it quickly looked to exploit the power of popular imagery and myth for its own purposes. Part of the coronation celebration in Nottingham consisted of a play in which Robin Hood's loyalty to King Richard was emphasized and exaggerated while his independence from legal society was diminished.[9] In *Robin Hood and His Crew of Soldiers, A Comedy Acted at Nottingham on the Day of His Sacred Majesties' Coronation* (1661), a messenger from the king told Robin, "I am come to require and command your armes and a cheerful and ready submission to his majesties' laws, with a promise of future obedience" (p. 2). In return for Robin's submission, he and his band would be pardoned of all previous crimes. Little John, however, did not wish them to lay down their arms, "to be caressed by their slavery and doat [*sic*] upon their hateful bondage" (p. 6). The king's messenger explained that times had changed, that England was no longer ruled by [Cromwell's] tyranny and "by the laws which careful princes make, we are commanded to do well and live virtuously, free both from giving and receiving injuries, which is not slavery but priviledge" (p. 7). Robin was entirely won over by these ideas and found himself a changed man. His last speech had him say, "I am quite another man, thawed into conscience of my crime and duty, melted into loyalty and respect to virtue. What a harsh beast I was before, not differing from the fiery lion or the cruel bear . . . Let us all then join in the present sence of our duty, accept the proffered pardon and with one voice sing with hearty wishes, health to our King!!" (p. 9). But then, Robin, like Hind, only broke the corrupt law of the land to uphold a higher law. Hind did not thwart the efforts of legitimate government but, like Robin, opposed those who usurped royal authority. Eventually, the monarchy found it more convenient to place tight controls over the press rather than to continue to appeal to popular mentality through creative publications supporting its image. This may have been a mistake, but then the later Stuarts had more than one public relations problem with the English public.

The Hind pamphlets, like those about witches and whores, demonstrated the creative power of the press to express and forge public sentiment by exploiting gender relations. Men breaking the law were honored as heroes while their female counterparts were spouse murderers, witches, and whores. Men were permitted to uphold a higher moral law, but women were not capable of true inner morality and required a strong husband's direction. Curiously, even after the passage of several centuries, the same double standard remains true today.

Part IV
England Redeemed

The VVonder of our times:

BEING

A true and exact Relation of the Body of a mighty Giant dig'd up at *Brockford* Bridge neer *Ipswich* in *Suffolk*, this present *November* 1651. his height 10.foot, his Head as big as half a bushell; with a description of the severall parts of his body, and manner of his interring.

Certified in a Letter from a Gentleman in the Country, to his Brother (a merchant) in *London*.

Newcut. 18.

London : Printed by *R. Austin*, for *W. Ley*, at PAUL's Chain. 1651.

◆ ◆ ◆

11

More Ancient Prophecies

"CHARLES WILL SHINE IN THE SUN OVER ALL THE EARTH, TO ANSWER THE EXPECTATION
OF ALL THE NATIONS AND FULFILL THE PROMISE OF OUR LORD, JESUS."
—*The Mystery of Prophecies Revealed (1660)*

For more than a decade William Lilly, the parliamentary astrologer and interpreter of ancient prophecies, persuaded Englishmen that God smiled upon their revolution despite the evidence of apparitions, portents, and prodigies to the contrary. Charles I was the evil White King, and everything would work out for the best when the Chicken of the Eagle put things right. As late as 1657, Thomas Pugh's mammoth collection of ancient prophecies continued to underscore the fact that the ancient texts supported the revolution.

How confusing the events of 1660 must have seemed. Could it be that God initially overturned Charles I and the Church of England to later overturn the Presbyterians, Parliament, and Lord Protector Cromwell and thereafter restore Charles II and reestablish the Church of England? By 1659 a new set of prophecies had been discovered that indeed predicted that Charles II would be restored to authority in 1660 as if there had never been any doubt about this all along. Once again, ancient prophecy affirmed the developments of the present in the name of an all-seeing past. Previously, the flow of political events permitted William Lilly to give the White King a prophetic funeral. Now, however, Stuart loyalists took heart when it was Charles II who eventually emerged as the Chicken of the Eagle.

The prophetic break with the revolution and Cromwell was not as abrupt as the restoration in 1660 might suggest. There had been isolated monarchist prophetic voices raised even during Charles I's darkest hours. The astrologer George Wharton, for instance, was an early supporter of Charles I and wrote a large number of pamphlets favoring the king.[1] For instance, his *Astrological Judgment Upon His Majesties Present March* (1645) tried to put a good face upon a deteriorating military situation and to bolster faith in Charles I. Although Wharton conceded that "His Majesty can not be expected to be secured from every trivial disaster that may befall his army," he remained steadfast in affirming an eventual Stuart victory, explaining that "the heavens do generally render His Majesty and his whole army unexpectedly victorious and successful in all his designs."[2] Despite his optimistic and cheerful message, two things limited Wharton's influence compared with that of Lilly: He did not lend his hand to the more popular genre of ancient prophecies, and, perhaps more important, his forecasts were totally wrong.

Another individual taking upon himself the difficult burden of interpreting ancient prophetical writings in favor of monarchy was Christopher Syms. Very little is known about Syms, although in one pamphlet he referred to himself as "your Majesties faithful subject and late servant in your army in Ireland in the year 1640, being then paymaster of the train of artillery there."[3] Syms's several works also demonstrated the difficulties facing the unfortunate publicist defending the losing side.

Since he could not very well claim that Charles was actually victorious, Syms believed his best strategy lay in convincing readers that Lilly was wrong. In a series of pamphlets, Syms argued (a) that the White Knight and the Dreadful Deadman were not the same; (b) that they were not Charles I in the sense that Lilly claimed; and (c) that the Chicken of the Eagle was neither Cromwell nor any other personality on Parliament's side. Syms, however, was more pedant than publicist. In *The Sword's Apology* (1644) he denied that Charles was the White King through a series of complex and technical, grammatical arguments based on ambiguities within the medieval Latin text. After demonstrating how difficult Latin grammar might be, Syms concluded that the Latin text "is just too confusing to permit naming specific individuals because these particles of time (*then* or *after*) in the beginning of every clause" (pp. 13-14). Considering that Lilly had expressed no displeasure with the Latin but used the more convenient English text for the basis of his interpretation, the average reader, knowing little or no Latin, may not have appreciated Syms's logic. In any event, this propaganda technique did not permit Syms to create a set of images to rival those Lilly reinterpreted from Merlin and Mother Shipton.

If proving Lilly wrong was unsuccessful, trying to reinterpret the king's poor condition as great luck was even more so. At the very outset of *The*

White King Raised and the Dreadful Deadman Revived (1647) Syms noted that "the late occurrences, issues and successes in England since the year 1644 accomplished have been so strange and admirable, that every man imbued with common sense may perspicuously [*sic*] discern divine providence and the powerful hand of the Lord of Hosts working in all" (p. 3). Syms would have been better advised to downplay contemporary events since it was probably far more obvious to London readers that developments had not worked out for Charles at all.

Syms's attempts to elevate the image of the White King from a tragic persona to a victorious one also rang hollow. Syms asked, "Who can be so blind as not to take notice of these words in the White King Prophecy, viz., He shall raise his head again, have it for his own, betaken him to be king, [with] many things to be done?" (p. 3). This interpretation may have been textually accurate, but it was not easy to identify Charles's heroic deeds and too easy to remember Lilly's image of the White King who used foreign troops against England.

Syms's reading of the prophecy of the Dreadful Deadman led him to conclude that "it is palpably evident and without controversy that the Dreadful Deadman shall set England on the right way and putout all heresies" (p. 5). Syms was even able to see bright light ahead and concluded with an admonition to the faithful to keep the faith. "In the meantime," Syms wrote, "let all men who shall hereafter behold an emblem of the Lion and Eagle give it a favorable countenance and not disdain and condemn it because already in the mount is the Lord seen." Indeed, Syms hinted that Charles was even more than he seemed. "It can not be hidden from your profound judgement," he wrote to Charles, "that you are the annointed of the Lord of Hosts, designed for the last wonders of the world, for the destruction of the enemies of God, of truth and peace, first Magog, then Gog, and for the spreading of God's name from east to west and for the building up of God's new Jerusalem, the holy Zion, and city of God, that is, His true worship whereof your two Parliaments with Great Britain have laid the foundation. And it will be perspicuous unto you that your Majesty is according to the predictions of God's holy prophets chosen and fore-appointed to finish the building" (pp. 7-8). In a word, Charles would first defeat his adversaries and then initiate the second coming.

Had Charles carried off a last-minute victory, Syms would have been hailed a far-sighted seer. It must have been frustrating when a year later conditions were such that Syms himself thought it best to modify his earlier prophecy. Even he eventually realized that the times had not been kind to Charles I, and in *The Prophecy of the White King Explained* (1648) he explained that it was not *Charles I* who would be the glorious Chicken of the Eagle, but *his son.* Concerning Charles I, Syms wrote, "this time is near at hand but not to be fulfilled in his life. It shall not be accomplished in his time but when he is dead . . . The king that succeeds him shall be such a one as must be king of all Britain, both England and Scotland, as the king his predecessor was" (p. 1). Having attempted a messianic bait and switch, Syms would continue to interpret ancient prophecies in light of the Stuarts but in 1650 Charles II's chances for a glorious future were about the same as his father's.

Edward Calvers and William Sedgwick were also royalist prophets.[4] The former wrote *Calvers' Royall Vision* (1648) and predicted Charles I's peaceful restoration. Sedgwick's *The Spiritual Madman* (1648) also predicted the return of Charles I. Neither pamphlet was impressive because neither could create a set of images to rival Lilly's White King. It did not help the professional reputation of either that they were proven so decisively wrong so very soon.

Despite the royalist inability to produce a set of images rivaling those created by Lilly, for a brief moment in 1650 the king's cause seemed to have found a prophetic foundation in the writings of Paul Grebner.[5] Grebner was a German theologian who had visited England in 1588 and had presented to Queen Elizabeth a prophecy with the catchy title *A Brief Description of the Future History of Europe From anno 1650 to 1710.* Not temperamentally given to this sort of speculation, Queen Elizabeth deposited the manuscript in the library of Trinity College at Cambridge University. During the civil wars the prophecy was rediscovered and made the rounds in manuscript form. An altered text was finally published under its full title in November 1650.

The prophecy predicted the effects of the Protestant Reformation and presented "King Charles" in a very favorable light. According to the text, Charles would vanquish all of his many European enemies, such as the French, the Spanish, and the Dutch, "and afterwards most happily governs his kingdom and be greater than Charles the Great" (p. A4r-v). Applying Grebner's prophecy to Charles II gave royalists heart, but Lilly, for one, pricked this balloon in his *Monarchy No Monarchy in England* (1651). Lilly correctly noted that parts of the original text had been deleted from the 1650 publication, such as the small detail that the prophecy's Charles was Swedish and not English. Since neither Charles I nor his son could pass for Swedish, this prophetic possibility quickly fizzled.

These failures demonstrated the problem facing all royalist prophetic interpreters/publicists: It was hard to put a good face on rotten developments. Indeed, things looked so unpromising that only miraculous stories offered any prospects of moral support. *Vox Infantis, or, The Prophetical Child* (1649) claimed to be "a true relation of an infant that was found in a field near Lempster in Herefordshire, July 16, 1649" (title page). The essence of the child's conversation indicated that God was angry with those who were putting Charles to death, "who, for acting such a bloody tragedy shall come to untimely ends [and] not any of them shall die in their beds." Even more prophetic, "his son [shall] be restored to the crown of England . . . and shall destroy his and his father's enemies and be a great and powerful prince" (p. 4). After finishing his prophecy, the child requested that he be returned to where he was found. He then wished his listeners well and vanished from sight. The local people were amazed, and though they could reach no agreement about the child's identity, "some of the inhabitants do believe it to be an angel sent from heaven . . . unto whom God gave power and strength to reveal his will." Whatever momentary solace this pamphlet might have offered the faithful, the promise of an eventual revenge in the distant future offered only cold comfort. Who then but a wild-eyed fanatic would take up the Stuart cause after 1651? Arise Evans established a reputation as a stalwart prophet of Charles II in the teeth of Cromwell's power.

Arise Evans was a very complex man.[6] Born in 1607, Evans was disinherited by his family and made a meager living as a tailor. The civil wars found him a stalwart Anglican and royalist although there was some confusion about this. Thomas Edwards thought Evans was an Independent, while the Independents knew Evans was actually an Anglican spy and therefore tried to avoid him.[7] Evans succeeded in confusing other authorities as well. He fought with virtually every religious organization and sect at one time or another, and in 1647 he was thrown into jail at Newgate on grounds of religious irregularity for declaring himself to be God.

Evans possessed all the charm and amiability of an ego-driven fanatic. He was long-winded, intellectually vague, politically inconsistent, and evidently personally disliked by all. Even royalists considered him a crank, and he did not endear himself to Charles II either. According to Aubrey, "Arise Evans had a fungus nose and said it was revealed to him that the king's hand would cure him and so at the first coming of King Charles II into St. James Park, he kissed the king's hand and rubbed his nose with it, which disturbed the king, but cured him."[8]

Evans was bitter and believed that success had unfairly eluded him. He had taught Lilly astrology and was jealous of his student's success. After a decade of competition with him, Evans grumbled that Lilly "knows nothing, nor ever did know anything but as the Parliament directed him to write."[9] This curt dismissal was beside the point; the student understood what the teacher was never able to learn. Both public authority and public opinion were hungry for precise and lucid astrological prognostication that guaranteed England a happy ending. But Evans's works were anything but precise or lucid. Rather than consistently basing his predictions on astrology, Evans wrote prophecies that were strange, first-person, spiritual meanderings. They recounted the divine agencies that appeared to Evans, but the resulting prophecies were shapeless. Rather than supporting one side or the other, his words supported both at once. In short, where Lilly based his predictions upon the seemingly scientific method of astrology and seemingly authentic writings of Merlin and Mother Shipton, Evans gave his readers vague predictions based upon the good faith and credibility of his own dreamlike trances.

Evans's writings from 1653 to 1654 are a case in point. In May 1653, when the army expelled Parliament, and Cromwell faced yet another crisis of confidence, Evans used the occasion to send Cromwell a petition, *To The Lord General Cromwell and His Council,* demanding that Charles II be called back to England and settled upon the throne. Yet in that same year, Evans's *Declaration of Arise Evans* advised readers, "Therefore I say unto you, bend your prayers for the present power, submit unto Oliver your Supreme Governor and Lord Protector" (p. 4). In *King Charles, His Star* (1654), which concerned the comet seen in December 1652, Evans wrote, "I do plainly declare that his said mighty Majesty King Charles shall come victoriously to his crown, and maugre all the opposition man can make against him" (p. 43). Three pages later he concluded, "I do declare this truth from a sincere heart. That King Charles shall victoriously overcome all his enemies" (p. 46). Yet in *The Great and Bloody Vision* (also dated 1654) the title page reads: "Foretelling the Establishing of a Glorious Government under His Highness the Protector, likewise the Restoring of the Churches." Later in this same pamphlet, Evans again wrote "a new government is to be established in Britain, that is, the commonwealth of England, Scotland and Ireland, more glorious than ever was upon the earth" (p. 8). And a few lines later, Evans described the Protector as "his Highness who in due time will shine in the sun over all the earth, to answer the expectation of all the nations and fulfill the promise of our Lord, Jesus." In short, Arise Evans predicted both the restoration of monarchy under Charles II as well as the creation of a glorious Cromwellian protectorate, depending upon the publication. But then in 1654, who could successfully predict what would come? And who but Arise Evans tried? And this, no doubt, accounts for why his works were read.

Just when royalist prognostication had seemed to run out of steam and England's revolutionary accomplishments seemed more characterized by the chicken than the eagle, events reversed themselves and brought Charles II back to England, to the consternation of prophetic interpreters. It was increasingly obvious that Lilly and others had been terribly incorrect. However, Stuart loyalists had been proven wrong so consistently that they had not established a foundation for the return of Charles II either. How then did ancient prophecy explain Charles II's historical buoyancy? With enough scratching and patching some older prophecies *could* be reinterpreted to indicate that Charles II was Mother Shipton's mariner from abroad who returned to mourn London, and Merlin's Chicken might mean nothing more than that Charles II was his father's—the Eagle's—chick. But Merlin and Shipton were too closely associated with Charles as the White King and the Dreadful Deadman to bear last-minute reediting. And though it strained the imagination to believe that a second set of prophecies had been miraculously retrieved from dusty libraries, this time monarchist in tone, this is precisely what occurred. Completely new and untainted sources of prophetic authority were needed to herald this new and unprecedented recall of a king, and once again, Londoners did not have long to wait for precisely such publications to appear.

The Strange and Wonderfull Prophecy of David Cardinal of France (1660) was allegedly written by a Frenchman during the time of Richard the Lion-Hearted. Cardinal's prophecy, hitherto lost, described England during the mid-seventeenth century. According to this ancient text:

> Charles Mighty Monarch shall the "C" Begin,
> After Whose death a tyrant "C" comes in.
> By will and force he shall a while bear sway,
> Nothing but blood will his fury allay.

The publisher of this prophecy pointed out, "This prophecy hath been fulfilled in part in our age . . . as it was King Charles the first of blessed memory, after the cruel murder committed on him, came in that usurping tyrant Cromwell . . . he tyrannized for a time over them that installed him." Fortunately, another part of the prophecy was about to come true. "His sacred Majesty Charles the second, whose royal issue (as is plain by this prophecy) shall govern the Kingdom in peace for three hundred years" (p. 5). This royalist equivalent of Mother Shipton was curious only in that its author was obviously Roman Catholic.

Another hitherto silent source of prophecy was entitled *A Prophecy Lately Found Amongst the Collection of the Famous Mr. John Selden* (1659). The text consisted of a series of statements that could only apply to the events of the civil war years and, finally, to Charles II. Unfortunately, the creator of this prophecy failed to create a prophetic persona, such as David Cardinal or Mother Shipton, and thus there is no indication of who wrote this ancient prophecy or how old it was. The prophetic text itself was printed in Latin in an old-fashioned, very hard-to-read exaggerated gothic style of print. By comparison, the English version was printed in an easy-to-read, very common typeface.

The prophecy described Charles I in the following manner: "The Second Prince from Scotland shall marry a Popish Wife, after which he shall become the most unhappy of Princes" (p. 1). This was certainly a curious interpretation of Charles I's loss of authority, but the compiler noted in the margin, "This needs no comment." Next came a description of the civil wars: "Various troubles shall arise, and the people shall choose to themselves three generals successively, viz., an *earl,* a *knight* and an *obscure* person," an obvious reference to Cromwell, "who with strange arts and pretences religious shall acquire himself the power but not the title of King." The compiler thought this, too, was clear and his marginalia reads, "Neither this."

The obscure person, we are informed, "shall endeavor to set up an oligarchy and Vane Monarchy, as was never to be seen upon the earth. The Enthusiastick [*sic*] and Fanatique [*sic*] Head whereof shall invade the Office of the Preacher" (pp. 2-3). True [i.e., Anglican] religion would suffer, and the "Papists, who under many shapes shall endeavor to establish their religion in England . . . shall be like itself and shall kindle many fires." Despite this ungodly tyranny, "many shall then fall off and the people shall shake off their yoke." Without specifically mentioning Charles II, the text predicts "the younger son may, more happily, tune the harp. It goes well if a Monk [i.e., Monck] dance to his tune" (p. 2). A period of joy would then follow during which Charles II would resume governance, "under whom, the whole body (exhausted with long war) shall flourish and be wonderfully enriched, and shall enjoy a firm and general peace and shall be happy by Sea and land . . . Happy days return." The compiler's marginalia read, "Let all who love their country say Amen."

Lest the reader become complacent with so much good news, the publisher ended the pamphlet with a modest and solemn prayer. "The Lord in mercy look upon us," he wrote, "and deliver us from *the plots of the Jesuit, lurking under the disguise of Quakers, Anabaptists and very many other professions.*"

The return to political and religious orthodoxy in 1660 also occasioned a return to more traditional, Scriptural sources of prophecy. *The Key to Prophecy* (1659) was a demonstration from the book of Revelation "how the little horn and the Beast of the Bottomless Pit, the beast with two horns and Son of perdition do mean the Parliaments of England and Scotland, which killed the two witnesses and a threefold king is proven by demonstration." More to the point, this was a proof of "The Speedy Resurrection of King Charles II, out of banishment into advancement" (title page). The author believed that Cromwell was the Son of Perdition and that Charles II would lead England into its final glory. A similar claim appeared a year later in *The Mystery of Prophecies Revealed* (1660), where the author also interpreted Scripture to prove that Charles II's restoration had been predicted in the Bible. Additionally, he also employed the old medieval millennial formula of time (Fairfax) plus time (Oliver Cromwell) plus one-half time (Richard Cromwell) to account for the total period of the interregnum (p. 4).

For Stuart loyalists long depressed by the sad fate of Charles I, the restoration represented more than the return to legitimate government. Charles II "was a person imbued with an extraordinary gift of curing diseases but by touch only as is manifest to all the world . . . [he is] the David of these days, the man spoken of in the Revelation, riding on the clouds of heaven and ordained to have the Government over Nations." Even more, he had returned to England to serve as a new messiah: "You shall again observe him to be a person of extraordinary suffering . . . to be the Son of an innocent sufferer, which are both of them extraordinary . . . we may conclude him to be the undoubted person and heir marked out for extraordinary glory and greatness . . . that he is the person most dear in God's eye and preserved for some extraordinary advancement . . . as the governing of these three Nations and restoring the ruined Church" (p. 8).

Consistent with the notion that Charles II's return to England also augured well for the whole world, the author of *Joyful Newes for All Christendom, Being a Happy Prophecy* (1661) could report that even the mighty Turk would, finally, suffer defeat at Christian hands. After noting that "I shall not make mention of the prophecies of Merlin, Shipton's Wife or that learned Cardinal David of France, the last of which is fulfilled in the happy Restoration of our Royal Sovereign King Charles II," the author noted how "there is good hope that a happy and perfect peace will soon be settled throughout the dominion of his [Charles's] Royal Majesty" (pp. 2-3) and how "there is a great hope of a happy unanimity between all Princes of Christendom" (p. 6).

In addition to these ancient and contemporary prophecies indicating that Charles would usher in the fulfillment of time, there were also miraculous prophecies of Charles II's return. *The Age of Wonders, or, Miracles Are Not Ceased* (1660) noted the birth of three prophetic infants, all of whom indicated Charles's imminent return. The first was an eleven-week-old boy in Sudbury who "was plainly heard, as well by his parents as others, to speak before his Majesty's march to Worcester and say 'a king' which he often repeated, a truth generally known to the inhabitants of those parts" (p. 4). The second instance involved a child who "from his birth spoke and ever in his speech named 'a king' which to this day he not only continues with other expressions but if anyone in his presence do but name the word 'king,' the boy seems overjoyed" (p. 4).

Even more amazing was an infant female who "was heard plainly to say 'a king' which she repeated seven times after each other and did the same three nights together about the same hour in the evening, which child never spoke before nor since." If the reader missed the significance and subtlety of this child's prophecy, the author reminded the reader that the number three was the means "by which God delineated to mankind by Kings who in their government have no less than a Divine Trinity, themselves . . . their divine counselors . . . and their politic Magistracy" (p. 6). Even more, "seven is accounted the most excellent of numbers and hath been the conduit to convey diverse of God's great blessings to us" (p. 6). Clearly, the simple message spoken by these children, too young to be coached and too innocent to be corrupted, was that God approved of England's return to normalcy.

If Charles II's reputation changed in 1660, so too did that of William Lilly. Events had proven more complex than Lilly could explain. His predictions certainly could not account for a Stuart reversal of fortune. After 1660, Lilly continued to practice astrology, although he did have some difficult moments. He was taken into custody at the restoration and questioned about any role he may have played in the execution of Charles I as well as about some fires he was said to have predicted, but he was eventually released. He was detained again in January 1660 or 1661. On this occasion, Lilly paid a fine of £13, wisely took a personal oath of loyalty to Charles II, and conveniently claimed never to have truly opposed monarchy. This expedient reversal did not go unnoticed by the public. One wag wrote *Lilly Lash't With His Own Rod, or, An Epigram on the Quaint Skill of that Arch Temporizing Astrologer, Mr. William Lilly* (1660), and there were others, too, who were ready to make a name for themselves by riding Lilly's fallen reputation. One of these was Lilly's erstwhile friend, John Gadbury.[10]

In the early years of the revolution, Gadbury had been a true child of the times: first a Presbyterian, then an Independent, and eventually even a follower of London's own Ranter leader, Abiezer Coppe.[11] By 1651 Gadbury was a friend of Lilly's, with whom he first studied astrology, and became a student of Dr. N. Fiske a year later. At the time Gadbury was filled with admiration for Lilly's astrological and prophetic skills. William Lilly was certainly a tower of importance in astrological circles, and when he was attacked in William Bromerton's *Confidence Dismantled* (1651), Gadbury took upon himself the task of defending his friend in his *Philastrogus' Knavery Epitomised with a Vindication of Mr. Culpepper, Mr. Lilly, and the rest of the Students in that Noble Art* (1651). It was signed "written by J. G[adbury], a lover of all ingenious arts and artists." But times and loyalties, like Stuart fortunes, changed.

Prophetic political prognostication, which attempted to put the best face on an often desperate situation (like its more modern cousin, public relations), was a ticklish business; when Charles II returned to the throne, Gadbury believed it best to make new associations. Not only was Lilly now an embarrassment, but Gadbury believed he might even make a name for himself attacking Lilly's skills and integrity, as he did in his *Pseudo-Astrologus, The Spurious Prognosticator Unmasked* (1659). The pamphlet examined Lilly's many statements and writings of the previous decades and pointed to what were, in retrospect, obvious errors. A more caustic pamphlet, not signed by Gadbury but written by him, was *William Lilly, Student in Astrology, His Past and Present Opinion Touching Monarch in These Nations* (1660), a satire on Lilly's recent oath to Charles II. In this publication, all its words from the alleged mouth of William Lilly, the author has the astrologer take credit for predicting the worst abuses of the commonwealth government.

Once again, Gadbury paraded before the reader many of Lilly's more strident statements and noted the many times Lilly wrote that "God Almighty was our Parliament's loving patron and guardian" (p. 2). Similarly, Lilly's professional ethics were condemned. At one point Gadbury has Lilly say, "Could any man be so senseless as to think our predictions should hold true longer than our Almanac should last?" (p. 5). Even Lilly's oath of loyalty to Charles II came in for derision. "You must understand," Gadbury's Lilly observes about his recent reversals of opinion, "we write both ways, that way we may better please all sorts of people" (p. 5).

To further disassociate himself from Lilly, Gadbury denied ever learning astrology from him, although he had been more than willing to claim that pedigree in 1651. In *Britain's Royal Star* (1661), subtitled "an enquiery made into the use and abuse of astrology" (title page), he wrote, "Nay, I protest freely (and this without any boasting or ambitious living up myself) for I know my knowledge . . . and understood more art before I was ever acquainted witah Lilly than he was ever capable of learning in his life. Not withstanding his great fame for (doing nothing else in truth but) deluding the world" (p. 32). Gadbury went on to a fairly prominent life as an astrologer, and, despite some abuse, so did Lilly. After leaving London, Lilly devoted his attention to the study of medicine and was granted a license to practice in 1670, which he did in Hershem until his death in 1681.

Prophecy and prognostication would remain important genres of popular publication for the same reasons that they initially brought Lilly to prominence. Who would not like to know the future? Who dares spurn the sage advice of the past? Charles II's ascension to the throne put a damper on direct political prophecy of the sort published during the interregnum. Honed skills, however, were not forgotten, and 1688 was only a prophet's day away. For the moment, however, there was only joy and harmony.

THE
Lying-VVonders,

OR RATHER THE
Wonderful-Lyes,

WHICH WAS LATELY

Publiſhed to the World, in a Lying-Pamphlet, (called *Strange and True News from Glouceſter*) Containing a Relation of the wonderful power of God, ſhewed for Injuſtice at *Fairford*, by Frogs and Toads; And in the ſudden death of the Clarks Daughter at *Brokington* in *Glouceſterſhire*.

Preſented to the view of the World, with ſome Obſervations in the end on another ſuch like Pamphlet (*The Lords loud Call to England*)

I. That the ſubtilty of *Deluders* may be diſcerned.
II. That the ſimple may from their deluſions be preſerved.
III. That the Lovers of Truth may be ſtrengthned.
IV. That all men about theſe Wonders may be ſatisfied.

By ROBERT CLARK, Miniſter of Gods Word in *Norleach*.

Fidei perfidia Error Veritati cedat.

If any man ſhall ſay unto you, Lo, here is Chriſt, or there; beleeve it not : for there ſhall ariſe falſe Prophets, and ſhall ſhew great ſigns and wonders, Matth. 24. 23, 24.
Their coming is after the working of Satan, with all power, and ſigns, and lying wonders, 2 Theſſ. 2. 9.

London, Printed in the Year, 1660. Sept. 20.

◆ ◆ ◆

12

Events in 1660: The Battle of the Frogs and Fairford's Flies

"TELL HIM OF MAGNA CARTA, HE WOULD LAY HIS HAND ON HIS SWORD
AND CRY MAGNA FARTA."

The English Devil, or Cromwell (1660)

t is in the nature of counterrevolutions that everything is, once again, turned upside down. That which was once true is so no longer, and that which was formerly sedition is now orthodoxy. Most people found such political acrobatics complex and confusing, especially since they believed that governance reflected God's will. God, therefore, seemed as confused as an Englishman.

There had been periods of anxiety in earlier times, but the interregnum had no real precedent. The War of the Roses occasioned decades of disruption, but the Tudors were popular and gained respectability over time. The English Reformation elicited some measure of public cynicism about "official religion" when one after another of Henry VIII's children kept reestablishing the one true church. Once again, time worked toward acceptance of religious change, and England's Catholic enemies abroad certainly helped to tarnish the love of the old faith. But events during the English Revolution were more complex. A king had been executed rather than killed on the field of battle, the constitution had been disrupted, the church had been disenfranchised, and all in the name of a variety of truths that did not gain credibility with the passage of time. The return of the monarchy and the old church meant overturning all the new truths and returning to the old truths, old institutions, and, eventually, old problems.

In the spirit of that great historical maxim "Then was then and now is now," the world of popular publication in 1660 demonstrated how history was a great merry-go-round. In a word, everything previously written about the demise of the late Charles I and the correctness of Puritanism or Parliament was now officially inoperative, at least until further notice. In the meantime, the new (old?) monarchy had to come to terms with the power of the press. Charles II was aware of the important role of the press in molding public opinion. When he came to power in 1660, he appointed Sir John Berkenhead to suppress all existing newsbooks, and in 1663, Sir Roger L'Estrange became Surveyor of the Press. Sir Roger had very definite ideas about his role and the dangers posed by a public possessing information about government policies. He noted, "I think it makes the Multitude too familiar with the actions and counsels of their superiors, too pragmatic and censurious, and gives them not only an itch but a kind of colorable right and license to be meddling with the govern-ment."[1] Even non-newsbook publication was limited according to the stringent terms of the Printing Act of 1662. Printing was restricted to the master printers of the Stationers' Company, the universities at Oxford and Cambridge, the Archbishop of York, and the number of master printers and even their apprentices was rigidly controlled. No new presses would be created until the number of such enterprises had dwindled by reason of death to twenty, the number of publishers that had existed several decades earlier. The official position of Surveyor of the Press, with unre-stricted powers of search and seizure, was created to enforce the act.

Charles did not stifle all publication, however, for there was ample room for pamphlets and newsbooks favoring his cause, as discussed earlier. There was now obvious enthusiasm about Charles II's return. Indeed, the new monarch had become a great hero overnight. The volume of poems, odes, sermons, and general statements wishing Charles II well was enor-mous. Even a small sampling of the titles of pamphlets published in 1660 would require pages. The following typify the mood expressed by most: *England's Genius Pleading for King Charles; Maiestis Irradiant, or, The Splendor Displayed of Our Soveraigne King Charles; The Royal Joy; God Save the King; England's Jubilee, Britania Rediviva;* and perhaps most indicative, *King Charles I. His Imitation of Christ, or, the Parallel Lines of Our Saviour's and Our King's Suffering.* Some prophecies even empha-sized Charles's divinity. It was probably comforting to believe that Charles II was not king by chance but because he "was their king,born so, not made by the people's voice, but a king by providence, not by choice" (p. 4).

Once the monarchy had been restored, apparitions demonstrated how the Stuart cause had been righteous all along. We observed earlier that the short pamphlet *The Just Devil of Woodstock, or, A Narrative of the*

Several Apparitions, the Frights and Punishments Inflicted upon the Rumpish Commissioners (1660) explained that the goodness of Charles's cause had actually been proven as early as 1649. According to that story, ghosts haunted the Rump Parliament's commissioners sent to assess the value of Charles's property near Woodstock on October 16, 1649. We have also observed how popular prophecies were discovered that demonstrated that Charles II was God's favorite after all.

Next to the person of the monarch, the greatest reversal of fortune affected Parliament, the Rump in particular. The Rump came under severe attack, and dozens of pamphlets appeared, the titles of which indicate the tone and mood of the times. Some of these titles include: *Fortunate Uprising, or,The Rump Upward; The Rump Dock't; The Rump Ululant; The Rump Served in With a Grant Sallet; A History of the Second Death of the Rump; Rump Enough; The Rump's Last Will and Testament; The Character of a Rump; Arsy Versy, or, the Second Martyrdom of the Rump; The Rump's Despairing;* and *Mistriss Rump Brought to Bed of a Monster.*

The return to monarchy also encouraged attacks upon the integrity of many leading personalities of the previous regime. There had always been snipes at corrupt government officials, especially at those hiding their own personal immorality behind a posture of public piety and calls for moral reform. As early as 1652 the *Mercurius Democritus* laughed at Puritan pretentions. Two years later the truly smutty *Mercurious Fumigosus, or the Smoking Nocturnal* appeared. During this two-year period at least half a dozen other newspapers devoted to poking fun at revolutionary ideals and pretentions appeared.[2]

Condemning those associated with the previous government became standard fare after 1660. Scores of pamphlets lampooned Hugh Peters, John Lambert, and, of course, Oliver Cromwell. Pamphlets such as *Oliver Cromwell, The Late Great Tirant;* John Gauden's *Cromwell's Bloody Slaughter-House* and *Cromwell's Conspiracy;* and *The English Devil, or Cromwell* presented the former Lord Protector as an evil man. *The English Devil* depicted him as so cruel a tyrant that should you "tell him of magna charta, he would lay his hand on his sword and cry magna farta" (p. 3). A few months after the king's return, the play *Cromwell's Conspiracy* had the former Lord Protector appear in a nightshirt and make a salacious speech after seducing Mrs. Lambert.[3]

As the year passed an increasing number of pamphlets condemned those responsible for Charles I's death. Titles such as *The Great Memorial, or, a List of Those Pretended Judges Who Sentenced Our Late*

King and *A Hue and Cry After the High Court of Injustice . . . Who Condemned the Late King's Majesty to Death, with a Perfect List of All Their Names* suggested that those responsible for Charles's execution be called to account for their actions. Publications later that year such as *England's Black Tribunal, A Looking Glass for Traytors,* and the *Trial of Traytors* were more adamant still and advanced the myth that only a few craven traitors had betrayed the majority of Englishmen and rebelled against Charles. Other pamphlets such as *The Royal Martyrs . . . The State Martyrology* listed all those who had suffered under the previous regime. Some compromised individuals wished to make clear that they had played no role in the late king's execution, and publications such as *A Declaration and Vindication of the Nobility, Gentry and Others of the County of Kent, That They Had No Hand in the Murther of Our King* explained their innocence.

More cynically, "Mercurius Philalethes" published several attacks on public personalities under the title *Select City Quaeries.* Most of the scandalous queries were related to sex. The first edition, or part 1, intended to "discover several cheats, abuses and subtilties of city bawds, whores and trapanners," or, in other words, public personalities. In thirty-five short, numbered paragraphs *Select City Quaeries* "revealed" the private lives of controversial figures. Paragraph 1 asked "whether Ireton, the late Lord Mayor, resembles the Whore of Babylon nearer than the pope; His Holiness being too old for a whore and his Worship's chin too effeminate for a man?" (p. 3). Paragraph 3 demanded "whether the most honest Alderman Atkins (during his Knightship) did ever beshit his spurs or linings?" (p. 3). Others inquired whether a certain city official "licked his fingers so often, may not have many fingers at other men's honeypots" (pp. 3-4), "whether Bunbury dotes most upon a smooth-faced apprentice or his own doxy?" and "whether Henry Marten loves the King's bench better than Aretino's postures?" Indeed, Henry Marten came in for special attack more than others. This rabid republican had the honor of being called a whoremaster by both Charles I and Cromwell. The publication of *Henry Marten's Familiar Letters to his Lady of Delight* (1662), allegedly his love letters to an erstwhile lover, added fuel to the anti-Puritan fire.

In other instances the queries were meant to further embarrass those already making public spectacles of themselves. The author asked "whether Parson Askin, near the artillery, beat his wife" and "whether Starky the Hosier has not spent more money on trappans and with wenches than ever his wife did in suing him for alimony?" (p. 5).

Sometimes the question was outrageous and required proper interpretation. The witty author asked "whether Sir Richard Maleverer did ever lodge in Susan Leming's [a recognized London whore] Back Room and whether (notwithstanding the smallness of her house) there is not yet room enough for him?" (p. 6) and, a page later, "whether Mrs. Huzzy, a late coffee merchant, has not more rooms to let than beds to lie in?" (p. 7).

The second edition wondered about the mistress of a famous nobleman: "Does [she] not carry a fiddle in her ass because of the frequent fingering of her instrument?" (p. 9) and asked "whether the Goldsmith in Lumbard Street might not be compared to an old rat which loves cheese; for rending the Druggist's wife's smock to get at her notch?" (p. 13). Finally, and most outrageously, it guessed "whether Mrs. S———, does not stop the orifice of her cunt with a clout to keep the old man, her husband's rag, out?" (p. 16).

The third edition presented more of the same. Paragraph 3 wondered "whether Lambert, Vane, Disbrow, Hesilrigg, Saloway, Ireton and Titchburn, *cum multis aliiis* of the Rump's Seminary, should complain about the danger of Kings, Bishops, Deans, Chapters and especially sequestered lands, unless they are living in the Phanatiques Land of Forgetfulness." There were also more salacious quips: "Whether Mistress Reading the strongwater and tobacco seller in Whitecross does not muffle her downdiddle with Holland drawers lest the ferrets should mistake it for a Black Cunny" and, "whether the Brocker's wife, her neighbor, hath not her cunnyburrough entered oftener by friends and acquaintances than by Cornucopia her husband?" People currying favor with the new government received no kindness. Did "Betty Lucas (La Puttana Errante) did not spoil an indifferent good face and rump with Monsieur's new come over?" (paragraph 13). Was it true that the wife of a well-known local politician "lay two hours in a trance naked, till she was raised by a fumigation received at her posteriors?" (paragraph 25).

Ecclesiastical matters also rode the new-thinking merry-go-round. At least one pamphlet, *Laudensium Apostasia, or, a Dialogue in which is Shewen . . . the Greatness of the Late Archbishop,* attempted to revive the religious legacy of the formerly hated Archbishop Laud. Even worse, after years of abuse, Roman Catholics used the Restoration to argue that they were loyal subjects of the new king and had been loyalists of the old one as well. *A Vindication of the Roman Catholics of the English Nation* (1660) angrily denied the accusation that Catholics "are generally reputed to be enemies to the king, that they obstruct what in them lay, his return and that they are favorers of the Phanaticks [*sic*]" (p. 4) or that "the cutting off of the late king's head was the plot and work of Papists" (p. 9). Had "not the Catholics ever suffered since the king's death under Cromwell and his pretended Parliaments which made most severe laws gainst them?" (pp. 11-12). Similarly, *A Good Catholick No Bad Subject* (1660) vehemently denied charges that Catholics were poor subjects. Its anonymous author wrote, "I am ready by Oath to confirm to all men in the face of heaven that my loyalty to my Sovereign is an indispensable duty from which no power spiritual or temporal, domestic or foreign, under any pretence of excommunication, deposition, or any other whatsoever, can free me either wholly or in part . . . and I do in the meantime renounce heartily all dispensations, absolutions, and whatsoever to the contrary which may raise jealousy in my Sovereign or dissatisfaction in my fellow subjects" (pp. 5-6). Charles II was not a hard sell when it came to Catholics, and it was believed that his court was riddled with them. This was further corroborated when he married a Catholic and when his brother converted to Catholicism.

The return of the Church of England in 1660 meant that negative opinion came full circle. Presbyterians and Independents were now subject to a barrage of criticism as intense as that previously heaped first upon Anglicans and other "jesuitical papists." One contemporary noted how "every pulpit turned to raillery of the dissenters to the total neglect of the papists."[4] Should an innocent soul still wonder if perhaps some Puritans had been sincere, John Clark's *The Plotters Unmasked: Murderers, No Saints* demonstrated what everyone now thought of those who had held power in the name of religious reform. Francis Kirkman's pamphlet, *The Presbyterian Lash, or, Noctroff's Maid Whipt* (1661) exploited the news that the Presbyterian divine Zachary Crofton ["Noctroff"] had sexually whipped his maid. This little play included graphic descriptions of Crofton's technique. When the young maid squirmed, she allegedly reported that "he put his hand between my thighs to keep me on the form, and he tickled me [with the whip] so that I was almost ravished with it" (scene 5). In the play Crofton simply shrugged away his deeds: "Have I not many years since lived by deceit? Making the pulpit and the Word a cloak to my designs whilst not the advancement of that but myself have been my chiefest aims?" (scene 4). The image of the phony Puritan made for terrific propaganda, and the pamphlet enjoyed several reprintings. Two decades later *The Fifteen Real Comforts of Matrimony* continued to tell about "the Presbyterian Parson who had taken so much pleasure in whipping his maid" as if the good parson, now dead, were still alive.

Those separatists who had previously believed they were creating God's society and who refused to rejoin the organized church were in a far worse situation than the Presbyterians. Hitherto these Puritans had interpreted the revolution as a sign of God's hatred of Anglicanism and as a divine sanction for them to create a more scripturally true society. As was befitting the community of saints, they had created morality laws, controlled blasphemy, and prosecuted Ranters, Familists, and Quakers. Not only was Charles II on the throne and the hated Church of England once again restored, but, adding insult to injury, local authorities hated the Independents and "counted them Anabaptists and Quakers and [the saints] were in fear of being plundered therefore" (*The Lord's Loud Call to England* (1660), p. 21).

How frustrating to realize that from the new orthodox perspective, Independents shared more with the most detestable radicals than with the society of saints they thought God loved. Even worse, they were now pressed to rejoin the very church they had hitherto so abused. The pamphlet *The Lord's Loud Call to England,* by HJ (Henry Jessey) tells of brothers and sisters in Carmethan who were imprisoned "merely because they would not forego their meetings and join with them [i.e., the Church of England] again in their traditional worship, from whom the Lord had separated them" (p. 14). Elsewhere the situation was worse, and the author reported that "we have been much abused as we pass in the streets and as we sit in our houses, being threatened to be hanged if but heard praying to the Lord . . . we have been stoned when going to our meetings . . . and imprisoned when peaceably met together to worship the Most High in the use of his most precious ordinances" (pp. 15-16).

In some places, the counterrevolution was even more violent. In Gloucester, Cavaliers rode "about [the county] armed with swords and pistols . . . to disarm the fanatics and all the pastors of congregational churches and officers that had formerly served the Parliament, especially the Rump, as they call it, together with all church members" (p. 17). In that same city a minister was forcibly thrown "out of his house, his wife and children and goods thrown into the streets by the rude multitudes" (p. 19). The same thing happened to Edward Finch, a Puritan minister in Lenington, who "was hauled out of the parsonage house. He, his wife, and children cast out into the streets where for some nights they lay, no one daring to receive them into their houses" (p. 21). Another Independent preacher, Mr. Edward Fletcher, reported how the local Anglican minister "took hold of the silk scarf that was about my neck and tore it and struck me in the face with his fist and kicked me in the belly with his foot, saying, 'You rogue, you dog, the times are turned and I will have you out' . . . and he took a stick that was in his hand and struck me on the bare head . . . and also abused my maid in the street at the same time, holding up a great stick that he pulled forth out of a hedge, over her, calling her *whore* and commanding her to kneel down and confess where she had been" (pp. 22-23). Even the common man turned against the saints. HJ reported that "not only soldiers but the people who had long obscured their malice to the people of God, are now confident and act barbarously" (p. 18). The story was the same everywhere. One minister concluded that "the wicked spirit amongst men that formerly was curbed and restrained, doth now audaciously and impudently show itself with boasting and glorification" (p. 24).

The Quakers, certainly the most successful of the sectarian churches, received special abuse, even after they purged their Ranter and Proud Quaker elements. *A Wonder in Staffordshire, or, A Staffordshire Wonder* (1660) charged that Quaker sectarianism was the direct product of the devil's influence. A "fanatic" and the devil appeared in this small pamphlet as close allies, the latter assuring the former that he wished "to advance your interests" (p. 4).

Other pamphlets, such as *The Old Anabaptists Grand Plot Discovered* or Richard Blome's *The Fanatick History, or, An Exact Relation of the Old Anabaptists and New Quakers,* reintroduced, almost rediscovered, older sectarian heresies. Indeed, it was once again possible, as it had been in 1640, to tie all dissenters and separatists into one terrible bunch, as the pamphlet entitled *A Brief Description of Character of the Religion and Manners of the Phantastiques in General, Especially Anabaptists, Independents, Brownists, Enthusiasts, Levellers, Quakers, Seekers, Fifth Monarchy Men and Dippers* attempted to do. William Brownsword's *The Quaker-Jesuite, or, Popery in Quakerisme* (1660) gave a point-by-point analysis of both religions. By comparing such items as free will, views of the sacrament, morality, and the like, Brownsword could conclude "that their doctrines . . . are fetched out of the Council of Trent, Bellarmine and others and that their practices are fetched out of the rules and practices of Popish Monks" (title page). In 1660, as in 1640, ascribing the opposition's influence to a pact with the devil, with Jesuits, or with the Pope himself was a legitimate propaganda spoil of victory. Curiously, there were few new descriptions of monsters born to sectarian parents. However, this may indicate the changed perception of monsters rather than of dissenters.

While it is doubtful that the Puritan morality laws had much of an effect during the interregnum, they had rubbed most Englishmen the wrong way.[5] The restored government abrogated many of the laws, causing many pamphlet authors to breath a sigh of relief. The prefatory letter of *The Horn Exalted, or, Room for Cuckolds, with An Appendix Concerning Women and Jealousy* (1660) told how "the world begins to spring and put a new face on . . . The mask of enthusiasm is now out of mode and the stoicism of religiousness is found but a juggle." During the past few terrible years many "have run a roguing after strange Gods and bowed down to a Rump as to their head." Now, however, things were different, "and therefore, upon this their return to their wits, 'tis fit they should partake a while of course commons and feed on horns and husks with the hogs." The happy result was a congenial mood of moral anarchy. England had returned to "the times when men are butting and pushing and goring and horning one another."

The return to a liberal morality started with the court itself.[6] Even before the king's return Richard Baxter had observed that "prophaneness is inseparable from the Royal party, that if you ever bring the King back, the power of Godliness will most certainly depart from the land."[7] The court was back; immorality was back. In *The Lord's Loud Call to England,* HJ wrote that the king's supporters "drink to the King's health stoutly and rage against any that have the face of godliness" (p. 18) and then "compel men violently to drink the King's health" (p. 19). Monarchist Newcastle was "in the reigns of liberty and licentiousness," a place of "may-poles and plays and jugglers and all things else pass current" (p. 24).

Charles's erstwhile enemies were easily defamed, and rather than assuming a self-righteous pose in the face of ignoble defeat, most, like Lilly, found it wise to kiss the frog. Most, but not everyone. If Charles's return to power demonstrated God's unfaltering love of the Stuart monarchy and the Church of England, Puritan polemicists in 1660, as in 1640, wished to inform the public that God still loved them, despite all appearances to the contrary. As an example, HJ reported in *The Lord's Loud Call to England* that in Oxford a group of actors were deriding Puritans in an immoral play. One actor, who played the part of "the old Puritan" and wore a broad hat with a narrow band and had short hair, broke "a vein and vomit[ed] so much blood . . . he now lieth desperately sick" (pp. 1-2). Elsewhere, too, God exacted his vengeance. Mr. O, the local minister in Barwick, hated Independents, and "he called them Anabaptists . . . and even whilst he was preaching in the manner, he fell into a swoon and was speechless, as one dead, for about two hours, and it was feared he would never come out of it" (p. 8). Even the proclamation day that celebrated the king's return provided examples of God's love of Puritans and his hatred of Anglicans. On May 8, 1660, an old lady went to

London to make garlands for the king's parade. When she returned to Wapping, "a cart went over part of her body and bruised her very sore" (p. 29). Similarly, a cooper from London made a great bonfire to celebrate the return of monarchy, and "as the fire burned he took a fagot and said, 'here is a Roundhead,' and cast it in the fire, which burned . . . But the Lord struck him that night so that he never saw the morning, attested by several of the same town" (p. 29). At that same time, a woman requesting that all drink to the king's health said that "she wished that they were struck lame that [would] not drink" (p. 30). God eventually would not permit this punishment, and "she herself was struck lame and her own mouth that so spake was turned awry so ill was she taken . . . and she is not recovered to talk or walk so well as before" (p. 30).

There were even greater signs of God's continuing love of Puritanism. Despite their having lost the revolution and that the old church was back, the true reformed faith was surely vindicated by one of the most neglected conflicts of the civil war period, one that can only be called the Battle of the Frogs.

On August 2, 1660, an angry Puritan minister published the pamphlet *Strange and True News from Gloucester,* in which he described what would happen to those disturbing the apples of God's eye. The author was very defensive about events in 1660, and for good reason. After years of explaining Charles's death and the demise of the Church of England as expressions of God's will, the author had to acknowledge that both were back. Despite the Restoration, or perhaps because of it, he warned that "great and heavy judgments God hath always attended [upon] those who have reviled these his chosen people" (p. 1) . As a case in point, he wished to warn residents of the city of Fairford, where a peaceful meeting of Puritans was disturbed when "a company of rude people" broke up the Puritan assembly. The well-meaning community of innocent saints appealed to the local justice of the peace, who "refused any ways to assist them, but rather spoke harshly unto them by way of threatening, he being encouraged thereto by the Lord of the town, who also had that power to assist these people" (p. 2). The harassment continued, and the next day the Puritans again appealed to the justice of the peace, "which admonition little availed with the Justice, but rather heightened him in rage and fury against them."

God would not tolerate this affront. The following morning the area was awash in frogs and toads "marching in two companies, even as soldiers in a field, and came fast on towards the town . . . and there the one party took their way to the said judge's house and the other into the house of the said Lord of the town" (pp. 2-3). When the justice's house-maid saw all these frogs jumping about, she cried out, "Lo, this is the just judgment of our God upon us for your refusing to help those innocent people according to your power yesterday" (p. 3). Since the justice was not a foolish man he accepted the frogs as God's warning to mend his ways. As soon as he swore to redress the grievances of the community of saints, "the said frogs and toads did perfectly separate themselves in two several bodies and made a perfect lane or passage for the justice." And when the justice of the peace warned the gang of anti-Puritan bullies against future disturbances, "the frogs and toads were departed and vanished so suddenly and wonderfully as no man can tell how, when or where they are gone." The Battle of the Frogs, however, was far from over.

In what at first appears to be an unrelated series of events, *Strange and True Newes* reported that the local clerk in Burton and Stow was an ardent Anglican and a great opponent of the Puritans. For many years he had fought against them and "had opposed and reviled them, uttering hard speeches against them" (p. 5). Indeed, his entire family was well known for its strident opposition to all forms of independence. On one occasion his daughter and mother came to mock a small congregation at their prayer meeting, and during the sermon, "while he [the minister] was preaching upon these words, the hand of the Lord of Hosts went out against that daughter . . . for she gave a sudden shriek and fell down dead before them all" (p. 5). The justice of the peace appeared "and would have taken away prisoners and charged them with the death of the maid," but the preacher said, "Nay, we have not killed her but the Lord hath done it." The clerk recognized God's hand in his daughter's death, and "since that time the clerk spoke well of that people, saying 'these are the people of God'" (p. 5). Curiously, despite these lofty proofs of God's love, local malignants continued to harass the saints. It was particularly curious to HJ, who, twelve days later, wrote *The Lord's Loud Call to England,* in which he retold and underscored the importance of these events to as wide an audience as possible.

A few weeks later, on September 20, Robert Clark, the Anglican minister from Nerleach, a small town only a mile away from Fairford, took pen in hand to respond to HJ's account of the miraculous frogs. The dedicatory epistle of *The Lying Wonders, or Rather, the Wonderful Lies* noted, "I could never have brought my understanding to believe that such groundless lies, as this pamphlet contains (called *Strange and True News from Gloucester*) should have such a vent of belief in the hearts of men as they have." Clark wished to set the record straight regarding how the frogs or a girl's death "may be said to be God's judgments on the revilers of those his chosen people, and it craveth our inquiry" (p. 5). Clark denied the accuracy of both the story about the frogs as well as the one about the death of the young girl and stated, "As for the Army of Frogs and Toads which the informer saith he saw at Fairford and the sudden death of the clerk's daughter when they met at Brokington, how they can be thought to be examples of God's judgment, as those the informer nominateth?" (p. 5).

Although this pamphlet was an ostensible rejection of the earlier story, the author could not deny some details. Clark affirmed "that Sarah, the daughter of Thomas Woodward, clark of Senington, about seventeen years of age, was there with her mother and that the maid did die there suddenly is a truth which can not be denied" (p. 14). However, Clark categorically rejected the idea that God killed the young girl because she was a member of the Church of England. Rather, the minister argued, the girl was killed because she was actually a Puritan. "Both the daughter and the mother," the Anglican asserted, "are great lovers of these persons, great approvers of their meetings and ways. Nay, the parish clerk himself, the maid's father (as I am informed) is one of their followers" (p. 14). Hence, Sarah's death was not proof of God's hatred of Anglicanism but proof of his hatred of Puritanism, and "I think them to be of the safer judgment that conclude her to be an example of God's justice for frequenting the meetings of such impostors" (p. 15).

Whether Sarah Woodward's death was an example of God's love of Anglicans or Puritans was a moot point, but Fairford's frogs remained an intriguing puzzle. Clark considered the story of the frogs absurd and laughed when "the relater faineth an army of frogs which had received a commission from the almighty to plunder the houses of the lord of the town and the said justice, or to bring them away prisoners" (p. 9). Clark might have concluded his discussion by simply denying that frogs ever inundated Fairford, yet he admitted that "there might have been a great number of frogs and toads laying upon the ground" (p. 8). The minister explained that anyone "might see at that time of year frogs and toads enough by reason of so many ponds, ditches and moorish places" (p. 8). Indeed, he affirmed that it was "no wonder to see them . . . fallen from the rain, from the clouds . . . and generated by the heat of the sun" (p. 8). Even more, Clark was willing to state, "I shall without hypocrisy certify to the world that in the town of Fairford . . . some spirits came often there in the likeness of frogs" (p. 9). In short, the fact that thousands of frogs fell from the sky and landed in Fairford was not a miracle. However,

Clark denied that these frogs might be "such well disciplined frogs and toads as can march in rank and file, turn to the right or left hand and keep court of guards" (p. 8). Clark was under no illusions about the motives of those who would compose this silly lie about frogs. The Puritans, he claimed, wished "to cloud the beauty of the church from the eyes of the world by damnable and hellish untruths that thereby he may beguile the simple into the ways of separation from the Church of England that thereby they may be led into error and held therein at his pleasure . . . to allure them to join with them in their private conventicles" (p. 2). In other words, Clark was angered because Puritans claimed to have better miracles than Anglicans.

Puritans argued that a large mass of marching frogs was proof of God's anger while the Anglicans conceded that there had been large numbers of frogs but were unwilling to believe that they could march in columns. The poor London reader was in a quandary. Fortunately HJ offered a solution to this croaker conundrum in his pamphlet *The Lord's Loud Call to England,* in which he hoped to demonstrate once and for all the divine significance of the marching frogs. To prove the Puritan interpretation of Fairford's marching frogs, the author published, for the first time ever, the equally amazing story of Fairford's Flies.

According to the Puritan account, the marching frogs convinced the local justice of the peace to mend his ways. He then warned local roust-abouts against any future disturbances. The local noble lord of the area, however, remained unrepentant in his Anglicanism. As a result, two weeks after the incident of the frogs, "there appeared in the Lord of the manor's orchard a great swarm of flies, about the size of Caddus flies, with long wings. They that saw them said they might have taken up baskets of them. And the same day also, an honest Christian man saw the Lord of the manor's garden covered with these flies, in heaps like unto swarms of bees" (p. 5). Since this was the very same lord who had previously prohibited the justice of the peace from taking action on behalf of God's true saints, this must surely testify to God's judgment. The author was aware that the Anglican Clark and many others as well might doubt the veracity of these stories, but he assured the reader that "some went from London purposely to inquire at Fairford the truth thereof." Their conclusion was obvious: "The truth of the substance of the relation about the toads and those flies is credibly certified by several persons, though some would obscure the works of the Lord." Among those wishing to obscure these great works of God's justice was Robert Clark, whose Anglican pamphlet rejected the idea that frogs could march in columns. But Clark got his comeuppance. Though Clark is not mentioned by name, Nerleach was only a mile from Fairford, and HJ was "credibly informed that a minister of a place within a mile of two of [Fairford] . . . died suddenly after" (p. 5). After all was said and done, it would appear that God was truly angered by Clark's rejection of his divinely inspired frogs, who, it seems, were able to march in columns after all. In short, Puritans not only maintained that they had better miracles than Anglicans, but even more, that those who rejected their claims would die.

With so many signs of God's justice and love, HJ reported that Puritans all over England were convinced that "our Lord and King, whom we serve, hath brought us under his own pavilion and his banner over us hath been and still is Love" (p. 24). As a result, "our societies from whence we were taken are exceeding cheerful and a very lively spirit of faith and prayer is amongst them" (p. 25). Throughout the ups and downs, the great lesson God had taught Puritans was "to love your enemies and pray for such as revile you and abuse you" (p. 31).

But there was more to the story. On the same day that Clark wrote against the mysterious appearance of frogs, Mr. G. Brown added his support to Clark's position in his pamphlet *A Perfect Narrative of the Phantastique Wonders Seen in the West of England.* According to Mr. Brown, he received a letter from friends in Fairford in which they reported that on "June 16 last, it pleased God to send us plenty of rain and thunder showers . . . after which rain my landlord, Esquire Barker, having some old fish ponds in his orchard . . . these ponds being filled afresh with the rain and other supplies there did appear forth of these ponds and ditches a great store of young frogs and water toads which in length were an inch . . . shifting and hopping to and fro, being out of their watery element" (p. 2). The pamphlet went on to say that on no account did these frogs march in columns. In fact, most hardly marched at all, although some of them were reported to have jumped quite a distance. Of course, Brown never denied that they could have marched in columns, had the Lord so wished, and, in any event, believing HJ came down to accepting the word of a Puritan. Whether Brown, like Clark, died mysteriously thereafter is unknown.

And so, despite everything that had occurred, God would once again be pleased with England. At least superficially everything was almost the way it had been before the revolution. Monarchy and the Church of England had returned, as well as all the historical mystique surrounding royalty. One scholar has noted that "the ceremony of 'touching for the King's evil' . . . reached new heights of popularity during this period."[8]

Censorship was in effect again, although restrictive blue laws had disappeared, and strong beer and ale were again available. Nonetheless, clamorous Puritans claimed God loved them, as would soon become painfully obvious to all who opposed them.

The heady times of political change can become an intoxicant, and if Puritanism had suffered political defeat in 1660, the Puritan social ethos lived on and became even more powerful in subsequent decades. After the Glorious Revolution, the Societies for the Reformation of Manners, the charity school movement, and similar organizations maintained the spirit of puritan virtue.[9] Hence, if in 1660 some Englishmen felt more secure in knowing they had a proper government, a proper church, and proper ale, it would take only until 1688 for other Englishmen to long for political, social, and moral change once more.

A MOST
Certain, Strange, and true Difcovery of a

VVITCH.

Being taken by fome of the Parliament Forces, as fhe was
ftanding on a fmall planck board nd fayling on
it over the River of *Newbury*:

Together with the ftrange and true manner of her death, with
the propheticall words and fpeeches fhe vfed at the fame time.

❀❀❀❀❀❀❀❀❀❀❀❀❀❀❀❀❀❀❀❀❀❀❀❀❀❀❀❀❀❀❀❀❀❀❀

Sept. 28

Printed by John Hammond, 1643.

♦ ♦ ♦

13

Conclusion

This examination of over 325 newsbooks and pamphlets published during the two decades of the interregnum indicates that many people were not necessarily concerned about the events of the day for the reasons usually given by historians. Instead, they feared that God was going to punish them for killing Charles I. Parliament had erred in killing Charles. Signs of divine anger about the execution of His anointed were certainly legion: the weather was bad and getting worse (which was always an indication of God's anger); the proliferation of celestial apparitions, monsters, Ranters, strange sects, religious charlatans, witches, seditious Catholics and peculiar Jews, whores and street rogues; alehouses, where crime and revolutionary talk dominated, were found behind every closed door. In short, the fabric of society was clearly dissolving. England's disintegration might have continued indefinitely but for Charles II's return to the throne to set things right. Of course, all this had already been predicted in ancient prophecy.

Could it be that most people in England perceived the English Revolution as a conflict involving rival powers of enchantment and opposing readings of ancient prophecy? The modern pragmatic mind balks at the idea that large numbers of western, English-speaking people might conceive of political conflict in miraculous terms or see every natural occurrence as heavenly vindication or punishment. Such views would put the seventeenth-century English in company with most of the rest of Europe. Carlo Cipolla's fascinating study of seventeenth-century reactions to the plague in Tuscany has clearly demonstrated, most people chose enchantment rather than science as the frame through which to see the disaster, even when pragmatic, demonstrable, scientific answers existed.[1] The people of Monte Lupo faced a choice of authorities: They could follow their health officials, accept a naturalistic explanation for the plague, and deny the contagion the ability to spread by suspending large public gatherings, or they could follow hysterical voices decrying the disease as God's punishment of a wicked minority that must be purged from their midst and chance further spreading the contagion by holding large religious parades so that the statues of saints might be shown throughout the city. The townsfolk chose the latter policy, and, quite predictably, enormous numbers of people died. Eventually reason prevailed but only until the next outbreak of the plague, when residents made the same choice and enacted the same dance of death. Similarly, an unexpected death, especially of some child, in Germany, England, France, or the colonies often led to hysteria and a search for witches. Often, after a supposed witch had been burned, communities looked in horror at what they perceived to be a terribly mistaken action. This realization, however, did not inhibit subsequent outbreaks of witch fever in the same places and for the same reasons. The same communities in Germany and in Eastern Europe tried and convicted Jews for allegedly killing Christian children and draining their blood in order to bake Passover matzoh. In each case, abusive parents eventually confessed to the dead child's disappearance, but this had little effect upon subsequent charges of libel in the same communities.[2]

The ideas presented in English pamphlets would constitute additional curious bits of information about superstition in early modern Europe were it not for the fact that they were not published as a frolic but as serious attempts to explain England's sorry condition. Eminent scholars cite many reasonable political, economic, institutional, religious, regional, and demographic factors to explain what took place between 1640 and 1660, yet rarely mention enchantment as a factor. But then none of these pamphlets ever suggests the many causes scholars find so convincing. Indeed, it is almost as if contemporary pamphleteers and subsequent scholars were describing two different events, and even when the factors now cited by scholars do appear in pamphlets, they emerge transformed. For example, historians have stressed the importance of religion and have described Presbyterian ecclesiastical policy in the most minute detail. Only a relatively few publications of the time argued this terse political issue, and they were the work of tedious polemicists (usually allied to parliamentary factions) writing for other professional theologians. The level of general interest in this interchange of polemical ideas was limited. Modern scholars neglect the far larger volume of pamphlets that cited miracles, apparitions, and monsters or that found great meaning in ancient prophecies proving God favored them over their opponents. However we understand Fairford's Flies and the Battle of the Frogs, the observation that Anabaptist mothers murdered their babies, or the peculiar deaths of actors at Oxford, the pamphlets discussing these manifestations of God's anger all shared one characteristic: none of these pamphlets took up a single "legitimate" religious idea or concept on either side of the Anglican-Puritan religious conflict. For those facing the fact of inexplicable crisis, monsters, myth, and prophecy were more indicative of religious truth than a debate over the virtues of episcopacy.

The same discrepancy between the findings of twentieth-century scholars and the claims of seventeenth-century pamphleteers appears in the area of political thought. Scholars have analyzed Charles I's abuse of power, parliamentary theories of government, and Leveller programs and ideals. But how is it possible to reconcile the historical importance of Parliament's considerable legal claims to authority with the possibility that most people believed this to be largely beside the point? The king was a Christlike figure sent by God whose blood could heal illness. Opposition to him *could, would,* and *did* cause the weather to turn foul and strange things to appear in the clouds.

In the area of social thought, the same discrepancy exists. Scholars have given much life to the image of the reforming Puritan. Books continue to be written about Puritanism and the family; Puritanism and sexual attitudes; and Puritanism and gender roles. All of these studies accept the idea that Puritanism was largely adopted by English culture, but in fact, most English subjects disowned it in every way possible. Puritans loathed the theater and the alehouse, and it is certainly likely that some thought it possible to create the Moral Englishman. After all, they had just won the civil war, dismantled the Church of England, destroyed the monarchy, and executed the Archbishop of Canterbury, all in the name of religious purity. Additional statutes could decapitate English sensualism as easily as the king. But if the pamphlets analyzed here are indicative, few English people seemed to support these programs. The campaign for a saintly society left most people cold, if not actively hostile.

Most pamphlets mocked Puritan morality as a front behind which to hide political maneuvering. Pamphlet authors praised alcohol and the pleasures of the flesh. If alcohol would, as John Taylor observed, "make a man a linguisht [sic] and teach him Greek in two hours," it certainly indicated that the joy of life would not be extinguished by those seeking a godly society. Toasting friends would continue to accompany every important social occasion in the calendar of life. In short, given the opportunity, people would, like Noah of old, drink to celebrate life, good fortune and good friends, and the hope of better things tomorrow. It is beyond doubt that some voices hoped to call down the curses of heaven upon all the free-living libertines poisoning the revolutionary Eden. But it is doubtful that many took them very seriously. As the mayor of London conceded in the broadsheet *A Whip For the Drunkard* (1646), which he wished to circulate in all parish churches, no one much cared about the new laws.

There would seem to be two sorts of revolutionary realities. The first, as recorded by scholars, is the alleged objective reality of revolutionary actors, including all those who fought for, sought, or abused power. These groups and individuals may have argued about church structure, the uses and abuses of power, and the provisions of the law because they had something to gain, lose, or keep. They also left copious records, and as a result over the decades scholars have discovered a *Puritan* revolution, a *whig* revolution, a *democratic* revolution, a *capitalist* revolution and/or a thwarted *socialist* revolution, and so on.[3] It is not difficult to identify contemporary constituencies advocating each of these positions. Yet attempts to expand each of these minority opinions to the revolution as whole, and to the English people in general, have not proven convincing. Each school of thought has devotees but has also spawned endless counterarguments demonstrating the opposite. In a word, scholars have discovered many types of revolutions supported by many different constituencies finding their origins and inspiration in many diverse sets of conditions and ideas. Yet even if all these constituencies together represented 100 percent of all the historical actors involved, something is still missing. In the end, all of the traditional scholarly explanations help to clarify why the revolution initially took place. They certainly do not explain why it failed.

To understand the latter requires investigation into the second of the two revolutionary realities. Recent scholarship has suggested that most English people probably wished a pox on both houses in this conflict.[4] War meant taxes and more taxes; the appropriation of property by both sides; marauding enemy troops; quartering friendly troops (and then the reverse); and violence and danger to all women. There is certainly ample evidence to demonstrate the existence of these attitudes among the English people on a local level. But neutrality, disinterest, or even anger at both sides is not the only picture that emerges from these pamphlets. Rather, they indicate that people did indeed care about the revolution. If standard, objective, historical factors favoring a revolution are absent from these pamphlets, so too are voices of popular impatience and anger with monarchy. Rather, an abundance of monsters, apparitions, witches, ancient prophecies, and reports of bad weather appear regularly. Those favoring the king did so for reasons having little bearing upon the economic, political, or regional factors allegedly motivating Parliament. Those favoring the Puritans found Anglicans monstrous and Cavalliers in league with the gruesome Deadman. In other words, once out of the realm of easily defined objective causes for revolutionary activity on the part of easily identified revolutionary constituencies with something to gain or lose, we enter the more nebulous world of portents, prodigies, and prophecies.

Significantly, almost all reports of prodigies, apparitions, and monsters made a better argument for the king than for Parliament. So too did all the accounts of sectarian activity, of terrible Ranters, Quakers, and Adamite-Familists as well as all the literature about alcohol, morality, and gender stereotypes. All the accounts of these excesses demonstrated God's anger with England for executing Charles, not for England's inability to create a satisfactory revolution. Parliament's best chance had been with William Lilly. Had Lilly not been censured by the very Parliament he hoped to strengthen, he may have continued to exert profound influence upon popular sentiment.

The scholar's problem lies in correlating the enchanted, often superstitious, and always conservative explanations of the time with the rational, objective, institutional, and political factors that now provide reasons for the outbreak of revolution. This is very difficult since little logically connects the two. Moreover, many modern historians experience great difficulty when asked to consider enchanted and superstitious ideas. Some find it preferable to deny the validity of the vulgar and superstitious sentiments and to argue that the true and real political, economic, and theological aspects of the English Revolution were simply beyond the scope of many commoners. If one looks behind events, as historians are trained to do, one can detect their real historical mainspring. This method usually has the historian, as critic, rearrange yesterday's events to suit some set of social ideals from the historian's own intellectual world. Indeed, as with literary deconstructionism, the primary authors, here the actual historical actors, become secondary to the scholar's inventiveness. Since so many historians follow predictable patterns of thought, the writing of history often becomes a reenactment of some small revolutionary clique's self-interested views spread over the entire revolution. Hence, it was only among the poor and ill-educated that the perception of the revolution was more miraculous.

But did these enchanted views really represent the attitudes only of the ill-educated? In pre-Enlightenment England, it is simply not true that only the lower classes were superstitious. University-trained pastors debated the merits of marching frogs. Educated people believed in witches, as the erudite debate about witchcraft that tore through the elite classes must surely indicate. Indeed, the educated clergy was often responsible for witchcraft accusations. Equally well-educated judges sat in judgment of the evidence and decreed death for witches. Had only the poor and the ignorant believed in witches, no one with power would have paid much attention. After all, no one with power paid attention to the poor and ignorant on any other issue.

Legitimate seventeenth-century journalism covered specious news as well as clearly factual stories. The age did not differentiate between the real and the spurious in journalism any more than it made these distinctions anywhere else. Seventeenth-century witchcraft trials were reported right alongside other news of the day such as apparitions, success on the field of battle, monsters, and marching frogs. Nothing has changed: legitimate newspapers still report about UFOs, Eastertime stigmata, and local sightings of images of Jesus and the virgin Mary on water tanks.[5] Indeed, sightings of the virgin Mary have become almost commonplace and are reported in *The New York Times* and other respectable journals, much as was the case in the seventeenth century. Even more, other publications specializing in the astounding enjoy the widest circulation of all newspapers, journals, and magazines published. The *National Enquirer*'s weekly circulation of 4. 3 million copies, for example, dwarfs all major daily newspapers. In the seventeenth century, the increasing numbers of literate Englishmen found published news about apparitions, monsters, and witchcraft important and plausible.

Even in twentieth-century England, such superstitious explanations have remained historically important until recently. Peter Laslett has written that the same shamanistic mentality still characterizes the thought of early twentieth-century rural England.[6] Totemism and animism retain their cultural grip in Africa, Latin America, and in most of Asia. In all these places holistic cultures of enchantment successfully compete with more modern ideas even among members of the educated middle classes.

Even more important, there are modern equivalents for every medieval attitude dealt with in this volume: UFOs have replaced apparitions, AIDS carries the same stigma as medieval monstrosity, and Jesse James was certainly a match for Captain James Hind. The electronic media has certainly produced a rich group of religious charlatans, and sects continue to exist, although now we call them cults. New Age thinking is a modern equivalent to early modern Antinomianism. And what are we to make of the Harmonic Convergence of 1988, when 500,000 New Yorkers descended upon Central Park's Sheep Meadow to hold hands, close their eyes, and hum?

Pornography, gender biases, drugs, and prostitution endure. Anti-Semitism remains, as does hatred of Roman Catholics, if not so openly voiced by polite society. The gullible and the hopeful still buy snake oil, strange medical remedies, and universal cure-alls. Copper bracelets have been replaced by the power of pyramids, but there is no difference between lucky charms, rabbits' feet, quartz crystals, and other objects that people hope will bring good fortune. Similarly, seventeenth-century millennial dreams have their modern equivalents. Utopianism, scientific socialism and psychoanalysis are modern variants of traditional hopes associated with the second coming. Hippies and Bohemians are modern equivalents of revolutionary-age Ranters, the medieval Brethren of the Free Spirit and the Adamites of Christianity's long history.

If the seventeenth-century voice of popular prophecy has ceased to exist, channeling has opened whole new possibilities. Nostradamus remains in print and is still the subject of serious exegesis. Many thoughtful individuals who find the notion of prophecy preposterous gravely ponder the imagery and symbolism of last night's dream, talented athletes wear the same jersey, socks, or shorts for an entire winning season, and children in all cultures try not to step on the cracks. Even the lure of astrology remains: Scholars dismiss William Lilly but remember that Ronald Reagan made foreign policy decisions helped by the advice of a California astrologer, and Linda Goodman's several books on sun signs sell a hundred thousand copies every year to a largely educated and middle-class audience.

Even pure apocalyptic thought is still popular. Sophisticated rationalists may laugh those carrying signs indicating that the world will certainly end next Tuesday, but the myriad of warnings concerning the imminent collapse of a planet a billion years old—that the world will run out of oil and oxygen and that the greenhouse effect will strangle all remaining life—are only more respectable versions of the same fear. The diminishing ozone layer and the warming of the world suggest the specters of melting ice caps. The fear of a great flood is not exactly new. Now, as in the seventeenth century, individuals from all economic classes, educational backgrounds, political views, and walks of life eagerly accept ideas of gloom and doom and the imminent end of the world.

Could it be that humanity possesses a fairly set fund of basic ideas that are continually modified to fit new circumstances? Could it be that humanity is innovative when necessary but conservative by nature and happily irrational throughout? Could cultural change over time be less a transition from the superstitious to the rational than the rejection of older versions for newer renditions of the same irrational/enchanted ideas?

Even more noteworthy is the importance these ideas assume during times of crisis. Whether it be war, revolution, plague, or other natural disasters, otherwise reasonable individuals in every society will turn to ideas of enchantment as acceptable explanations for complex events. Much as the children of both rich and poor, of both the educated and ignorant, are afraid of the dark, their parents turn to adult versions of these ideas predicated on the fear of foreigners, when their world teeters toward the inexplicable. Whatever the legitimate, rational, objective factors involved in demands for change, conservative solutions based on fear and superstition will usually prevail. In other words, rather than disparaging enchanted ideas and superstitious fears as illegitimate historical factors, scholars would do better to embrace these truly classical intellectual underpinnings of all societies as factors that may continually frustrate true change.

Some may object that this analysis is too glib, that it reduces the proud heritage of Enlightenment rationalism to a thin cultural veneer lightly covering a far more primitive cultural personality that emerges in times of danger. Yet one need only consider the amazing durability of prejudices regarding gender, race, religion, and class and the dehumanizing images used during recent revolutions and wars to paint one's opponent. In fact, the English Revolution, in common with other periods of inexplicable disruption, witnessed the interplay of two levels of culture. While scholars use objectively stated, rational factors to explain all the reasons for, and types of, English Revolution that might have taken place, the pamphlet literature indicates why the English people as a whole feared change and why the revolution therefore failed.

The myths, epithets, and invectives each side hurled at the other constituted skillful wartime propaganda. Indeed, the seventeenth-century press used all of these images to fight a proxy civil war. These ideas, however, were not mere wartime propaganda but appealed to deeply held beliefs of the English majority. The question to ask is not whether Charles abused his authority but why so many people thought he was God's appointed.

It is not a coincidence that it was William Lilly, the mythmaker, and not Ireton or Cromwell who provided Parliament with its best propaganda. And yet despite the fact that Lilly was more than able to present the revolution's legal and political case before the public, mythic images and not reasoned political argument crowded his pages. Similarly, royalist inter-preters of ancient prophecy might have argued politics. Instead they chose myth because it confronts the powerful fear of change more clearly than Parliament's lists of grievances. In other words, even those who might have made an influential case based upon all the factors historians usually use to explain the civil war spoke in terms of enchantment. And despite Lilly's best efforts, centuries of imagery gave an absent king an advantage over Parliament in possessing whatever power there was to be had.

There were few pamphlets about the New Model Army, Cromwell, or Ireton. James Hind was much admired and Ludwig Muggleton was not. Seventeen publications told about the royalist thief who made laws for no one and judged no one and yet enjoyed a greater popular following than members of Parliament, committee men, and the other "caterpillars of the times." Moreover, the pamphleteers did not see Hind merely as an example of all the immoral Cavalier qualities Puritanism detested; the last publications about him converted this royalist thief into a semidivine lawgiver.

Puritans may have won the Whitehall and Putney debates, but the pam-phlets discussed in this volume demonstrate very clearly that the revolu-tion lost the battle for the English mind. Englishmen wanted a king, believed there should be a king, and were very happy when they had one again. They did not appreciate Parliament's efforts to chase whores off the streets, to close down alehouses, and to limit the production of strong ale.

For most people in seventeenth-century England life was not a crusade for religious reform. They may have hated abuses, but they wanted conti-nuity and stability, not change. Indeed, the desire for stability is the most important dimension to the publications discussed in this volume. Almost every publication dealt with here, whether about monsters, popular heroes, evil Catholics, or the preservation of strong ale, was conservative and saw change as a threat.

Revolutionary attempts to change England's monarchy met with resis-tance, as a reader of these pamphlets might have predicted. After every-thing, the stability of 1640 was preferable to revolutionary experimentation. Indeed, the widespread skepticism reflected in these pamphlets may explain why powerful individuals with rational grievances against monar-chy failed to bring about change. Other than subsequent scholars, it would seem that few people were at all convinced that Puritans could bring about anything beneficial. Even with a power base in Parliament itself and with the best army in the land, in the end, the revolution could not impose a new order. Rather, it gave way to a man with neither personal experience at governance nor many personal prospects for a bright future. But Charles II did have one striking asset: he was a king.

By 1660 England again had strong ale and a divine king. And people danced in the streets.

Notes

NOTES TO PREFACE

1. Norman Hamson, "The Two French Revolutions," *The New York Review of Books* 36, no. 6, p. 11.

2. The literature concerning the civil wars and the interregnum is very great indeed. For a summary of recent schools of thought, see R. C. Richardson, *The Debate on the English Revolution Revisited*, 2nd ed. (London: Routledge and Kegan Paul, 1989). A good general account of diverse areas of study from economics to music to ecclesiastical and legal affairs is Godfrey Davies, *The Early Stuarts, 1603-1660*, 2nd ed. (Oxford: Clarendon Press, 1959). The bibliography on pages 416-443 is very helpful. John S. Morrill's excellent bibliography, *Seventeenth-Century Britain, 1603-1714* (Kent: Dawson/Archon Press, 1980), is a fine place to begin an investigation of any subject or issue of the age.

During the last fifty years, scholars have attempted to widen the constituencies studied and thereby better understand the views of many groups apart from those wielding power. Some recent scholars have indicated that most Englishmen were not caught up in the frenzy of optimistic change and have attempted to assess town-level grievances. The titles of their works themselves tell much of the story: J. S. Morrill, *The Revolt of the Provinces* (London: Allen & Unwin, 1976); Brian Manning, *The English People and the English Revolution* (London: Heineman Books, 1976); Roger Manning, *Village Revolts: Social Protest and Popular Disturbances in England, 1509-1640* (Oxford: Clarendon Press, 1988); Keith Lindley, *Fenland Riots and the English Revolution* (London: Heineman Books, 1982); D. Underdown, *Revel, Riot and Rebellion* (Oxford: Clarendeon Press, 1985); and Buchanan Sharp, *In Contempt of All Authority* (Berkeley: University of California Press, 1980).

Popular religion and revolutionary radical ideas are nicely described by Christoper Hill, *The World Turned Upside Down: Radical Ideas During the English Revolution* (London: Viking Press, 1972); F. D. Dow, *Radicalism in the English Revolution, 1640-1660* (London: Basil Blackwell, 1985); Frank J. McGregor and Barry Raey, *Radical Religion in the English Revolution* (Oxford: Clarendon Press, 1984); Jerome Friedman, *Blasphemy, Immorality and Anarchy: The Ranters and the English Revolution* (Athens: Ohio University Press, 1987). Information on individual radicals can be located in Richard L. Greaves and R. L. Zaller, *A Biographical Dictionary of British Radicals in the Seventeenth Century*, 3 vols. (Brighton: Harvester Press, 1982-84). For additional sources of relevant aspects of the revolution and popular religion, see the notes to subsequent chapters.

3. See the following catalogues: G. K. Fortescue, ed., *Catalogue of the Pamphlets, Books, Newspapers, and Manuscripts Relating to the Civil War, the*

Comonwealth, and the Restoration, Collected by GeorgeNThomason, 1640-1661, 2 vols. (London: British Museum, 1908); *The Thomason Tracts, 1640-1660,* parts I and II (Ann Arbor, MI: University Microfilms, 1981); C. R. Gillett, ed., *Catalogue of the McAlpine Collection of British History and Theology,* 5 vols. (New York: Union Theological Seminary, 1927-1930); J. Kennedy, W. A. Smith, and A. L. Johnson, eds., *Dictionary of Anonymous and Pseudonymous English Literature,* 7 vols. (Edinburgh: University Press, 1926-1934); A. W. Pollard and G. R. Redgrave, eds., *A Short Title Catalogue of Books Printed in England, Scotland, and Ireland, 1475-1640* (London: Bibliographical Society, 1906: reprinted 1969); Donald Wing, ed., *A Short Title Catalogue of Books Printed in England, Scotland, and Ireland, 1641-1700,* 3 vols. (New York: Columbia University Press, 1945-1951)

NOTES TO CHAPTER 1

1. For the history of English printing, please consult the following: William M. Clyde, *The Struggle for Freedom of the Press From Caxton to Cromwell* (Oxford: Oxford University Press, 1934; reprinted New York: Burt Franklin, 1970); Elizabeth Eisenstein, *The Printing Press as an Agent of Change* (Cambridge: Cambridge University Press, 1979); Eisenstein, *The Printing Revolution in Early Modern Europe* (Cambridge: Cambridge University Press, 1983); C. R. Gillett, *Burned Books: Neglected Chapters in British History and Literature* (New York: Columbia University Press, 1932); W. W. Greg, *Some Aspects and Problems of London Publishing Between 1550 and 1650* (Oxford: Clarendon Press, 1956); P. M. Handover, *Printing in London from 1476 to Modern Times* (London: Allen & Unwin, 1960); Leona Rostenberg, *Literary, Political, Scientific and Legal Publishing, Printing and Bookselling in England, 1551-1700* (New York: Franklin, 1965); F. S. Siebert, *Freedom of the Press in England, 1476-1776* (Urbana: University of Illinois Press, 1952); H. S. Bennett, *English Books and Readers, 1475-1557,* 2nd ed. (Cambridge: Cambridge University Press, 1969); Bennett, *English Books and Readers, 1558-1603, Being a Study of the History of the Book Trade in the Reign of Elizabeth I* (Cambridge: Cambridge University Press, 1965); Bennett, *English Books and Readers, 1603-1640, Being a Study of the History of the Book Trade in the Reign of James I and Charles I* (Cambridge: Cambridge University Press, 1965); P. M. Handover, *Printing in London from 1476 to Modern Times* (Cambridge, MA: Harvard University Press, 1960); Christopher Small, *The Printed Word: An Instrument of Popularity* (Aberdeen, SD: Aberdeen University Press, 1982); Roger Chantier, ed., *The Culture of Print and the Uses of Print in Early Modern Europe,* tranlated by Lydia Cochran (Princeton: Princeton University Press, 1989).

2. See D. M. Loades, "The Theory and Practice of Censorship in Sixteenth-Century England," *Transactions of the Royal Historical Society,* 5th series, 14 (1974): 141-157; Annabel Patterson, *Censorship and Interpretation: The Condition of Writing and Reading in Early Modern England* (Madison: University of Wisconsin Press, 1985); Oliver Thomson, *Mass Persuasion in History: An Historical Analysis of the Development of Propaganda Techniques* (New York: Crane & Russak, 1977).

3. See Cyprian Blagden, *The Stationers Company: A History, 1407-1959* (Stanford: Stanford University Press, 1960) and Edward Arber, ed. *A Transcript of* the *Registers of the Company of Stationers in London, 1554-1640,* 5 vols. (London, 1875-94; reprinted Gloucester, MA: P. Smith, 1967).

4. Sandra Clark, *The Elizabethan Pamphleteers: Popular Moralistic Pamphlets, 1580-1640* (Rutherford, NJ: Associated Universities Press, 1983), p. 26.

5. Joseph Frank, *The Beginnings of the English Newspapers, 1620-1660* (Cambridge, MA: Harvard University Press, 1961), p. 162.

6. Concerning the early newspaper, see Siebert, *Freedom of the Press in England*; Geoffrey A. Cranfield, *The Press and Society: From Caxton to Northcliffe* (London: Longman, 1978); Richmond P. Bond, ed., *Studies in the Early English Periodical* (Chapel Hill: University Of North Carolina Press, 1957); F. Dahl, *Dutch Corantos, 1618-1650* (The Hague: Koninklijke, 1946); Joseph Frank, *The Beginnings of the English Newspaper, 1620-1660* (Cambridge, MA: Harvard University Press, 1961); Peter Fraser, *The Intelligence of Secretaries of State and Their Monopoly of Licensed News, 1600-1688* (Cambridge: Cambridge University Press, 1956); Matthias A. Shaaber, *Some Forerunners of the Newspaper in England* (Philadelphia: University of Pennsylvania Press, 1929).

7. See Cranfield, *The Press and Society,* p. 14ff.

8. Frederick W. Bateson, ed., *Cambridge Bibliography of English Literature,* 5 vols. (Cambridge: Cambridge University Press, 1940-1957), vol. 1, pp. 736-763. The most available source of English newspapers is the 300 reels of the University Microfilm Thomason Collection. See G. K. Fortesque, ed., *Catalogue of the Pamphlets, Newspapers, and Manuscripts Relating to the Civil War, the Common-wealth and Restoration Collected by George Thomason, 1640-1661,* vol. 2, part II (London: British Museum, 1908), pp. 371-440. Other useful guides and lists are the following: D. C. Collins, *A Handlist of News Pamphlets, 1590-1610* (London: SW Essex Technical College, 1943); Fortesque, *Catalogue,* pp. 447-767; J. L. Harner, *English Renaissance Prose Fiction, 1500-1660* (London: G. Prior, 1978); James T. Henke, *Gutter Life and Language in the Early Street Literature of England: A Glossary of Terms and Topics, Chiefly of the Sixteenth and Seventeenth Centuries* (West Cornwall, CT: Locust Hill Press, 1988).

9. For these numbers, see the introduction to Fortesque, *Catalogue,* p. xx; Siebert, *Freedom of the Press in England,* p. 191, arrives at slightly greater figures.

10. Margerie Plant, *English Book Trade: An Economic History of the Making and Selling of Books* (London: Allen & Unwin, 1965, 1974).

11. Cranfield, *The Press and Society,* p. 20.

12. Concerning Muddiman, see P. Frazer, *The Intelligence of the Secretaries of State and Their Monopoly of Licensed News, 1660-1688* (Cambridge: Cambridge University Press, 1956); J. G. Muddiman, *The King's Journalist, 1659-1689* (London: Bodley Head, 1923).

13. See Lawrence Stone, ed., *Schooling and Society* (Baltimore: John Hopkins University Press, 1976); Stone,"The Educational Revolution in England, 1560-1640," *Past and Present* 28 (1964): 41-80; Stone, "Literacy and Education in England, 1640-1900," *Past and Present* 42 (1969): 69-139; Margaret Spufford, *Small Books and Pleasant Histories* (Athens: University Of Georgia Press, 1981), chapter 2; W. A. L. Vincent, *The State and School Education 1640-1660* (London: SPCK, 1950).

14. R. S. Scofield, "The Measurement of Literacy in Pre-Industrial England," in J. Gooch, ed., *Literacy in Traditional Societies* (Cambridge: Cambridge University Press, 1968), p. 311-325; Kenneth A. Lockridge, *Literacy in Colonial New England* (New York: Norton, 1974).

15. See, for instance, Michael Van Cleave Alexander, *The Growth of English Education 1348-1648: A Social and Cultural History* (University Park: Penn State Press, 1990); Joan H. Moran, *The Growth of English Schooling, 1340-1548* (Madison: University of Wisconsin Press, 1985); David Cressy, *Literacy and the Social Order: Reading and Writing in Tudor and Stuart England* (Cambridge: Cambridge University Press, 1980); R. A. Houston, *Literacy in Early Modern Europe, 1500-1800* (London: Longman, 1988); W. A. L. Vincent, *The State and School Education.*

16. See Keith Wrightson and David Levine, *Poverty and Piety in an English Village: Terling, 1525-1700* (New York: Academic Press, 1979), p. 150.

17. Thomas Nashe, *Works,* ed. R. B. McKerrow and F. P. Wilson, (Oxford: B. Blackwell, 1958), p. 23, cited in Bernard Capp, "Popular Literature," in Barry Reay, ed, *Popular Culture in Seventeenth Century England* (New York: St. Martin's Press, 1985), p. 203; See also Stephen S. Hilliard, *The Singularity of Thomas Nashe* (Lincoln: University of Nebraska Press, 1986); Peter Clark, "The Alehouse and the Alternative Society," in D. Penning and K. Thomas, eds., *Puritans and Revolutionaries* (Oxford: Clarendon Press, 1978), pp. 47-72. Also see H. A. Moncton, *A History of the English Public House* (London: Bodley Head, 1969).

18. Concerning the radical publisher Giles Calvert, see Altha E. Terry, *Giles Calvert: Mid-17th Century English Bookseller and Publisher* (New York: Columbia University Press, 1937). Lawrence Clarkson described how he was introduced to Abiezer Coppe, the leader of London's Ranter community, through Giles Calvert at an alehouse where the radical preacher Mary Lake held forth. See Clarkson's *Lost Sheep Found* (London, 1660), p. 25. An exact facsimile reprint was published by the Scolar Press in Ilkley, Yorkshire, in 1974. On the hawkers of books in general, the best available is Felix Folio, *The Hawkers and Street Dealers of the North of England Manufacturing Districts: Their Dealings, Dodgings, and Doings,* 2nd ed. (Manchester: Abel Haywood, 1858). Also, R. B. McKerrow, ed., *Dictionary of Printers and Booksellers, 1557-1640* (London: Bibliographical Society, 1910); H. R. Plomer, ed., *Dictionary of Printers and Booksellers, 1557-1775* (London: Bibliographical Society, 1977).

19. Joseph Frank, *The Beginnings of the English Newspaper,* pp. 235, 240, 259-60, 271.

20. Concerning London during this period, see A. L. Beier and Roger Finlay, eds., *London 1500-1700, The Making of a Metropolis* (London: Longman, 1986). The demographic changes taking place at this time are described in E. A. Wrigley and P. S. Schofield, *The Population History of England, 1541-1871* (Cambridge, MA: Harvard University Press, 1981); Leonard Cantor, *The Changing English Countryside, 1400-1700* (New York: Methuen, 1987); Peter Clark and Paul Slack, *Crisis and Order in English Towns, 1500-1700: Essays in Urban History* (London: Routledge & Kegan Paul, 1972).

21. See H. Herd, *The March of Journalism* (London: Allen and Unwin, 1952), p. 21.

22. *The Faithfull Scout*, no. 188, July 14-21, 1654, p. 1492. On London's importance, see H. V. Routh, "London and the Development of Popular Literature," *Cambridge History of English Literature* 7 (1911): 316-63. London would continue to dominate news reporting until the emergence of provincial presses in about 1700. Even then, these regional presses remained very dependent upon London. See G. A. Cranfield, *The Development of the Provincial Newspaper* (Oxford: Clarendon Press, 1962).

23. For a very short but comprehensive overview of seventeenth-century popular literature, see Bernard Capp's chapter on the subject in Barry Reay, ed., *Popular Culture in Seventeenth Century England*. For more in-depth analyses, please consult the following: George Boas, *Vox Populi* (Baltimore: John Hopkins University Press, 1969); Leo Lowenthal, *Literature, Popular Culture and Society* (Englewood Cliffs, NJ: Prentice Hall, 1961); Charles C. Mish, *Short Fiction of the Seventeenth Century* (New York: New York University Press, 1963); Victor E. Neuberg, *Popular Literature: A History and a Guide* (London: Penguin Books, 1977); H. E. Rollins, *A Pepysian Garland* (Cambridge: Cambridge University Press, 1922); Leslie Shepard, *The History of Street Literature* (Newton Abbot: David & Charles, 1973); Spufford, *Small Books and Pleasant Histories*; Roger Thompson, ed., *Samuel Pepys' Penny Merriments* (London: Constable Press, 1976); Thompson, *Unfit for Modest Ears* (London: Macmillan, 1979); Thompson, "Popular Reading and Humour in Restoration England," *Journal of Popular Culture* (1976); L. B. Wright, *Middle-Class Culture in Elizabethan England* (Chapel Hill: University Of North Carolina Press, 1935); F. P. Wilson, "The English Jestbooks of the Sixteenth and Seventeenth Centuries," *Huntington Library Quarterly* 2 (1938-9); R. Thompson, "Popular Reading and Humor in Restoration England," *Journal of Popular Culture* 9 (1976); John Wardroper, ed., *Jest Upon Jest: A Selection from the Jestbooks and Collections of Merry Tales Published from the Reign of Richard III to George III* (London: Routledge & Kegan Paul, 1970); Sandra Clark, *The Elizabethan Pamphleteers: Popular Moralistic Pamphlets, 1580-1640* (Rutherford, NJ: Farleigh Dickinson University Press, 1983); Frederick O. Waage, *Thomas Dekker's Pamphlets, 1603-1609, and Jacobin Popular Literature* (Salzburg, Austria: Institute for English Literature, 1977); Tessa Watt, *Cheap Print and Popular Piety 1550-1640* (Cambridge: Cambridge University Press, 1991).

24. C. Blagden, "The Distribution of Almanacs in the Second Half of the Seventeenth Century," *Studies in Bibliography* 10 (1958); Bernard S. Capp, *English Almanacs, 1500-1800: Astrology and the Popular Press* (Ithaca: Cornell University

Press, 1979), p. 44; Gene Boll,me, *Les Almanacs Populaires au 17e et 18e Siècles* (Paris: Mouton, 1969); D. C. Allen *The Star-Crossed Renaissance* (Durham, NC: University of North Carolina Press, 1941), chapter 5; E. F. Bosanquet, "English Seventeenth-Century Almanacs," *The Library,* 4th ser., 10 (1929-1930): 361-97; Carroll Camden, "Elizabethan Almanacs and Prognostication," *Transactions of the Bibliographical Society,* 2nd ser., 17 (London, 1932).

25. David C. Fowler, *A Literary History of the Popular Ballad* (Durham, NC: Duke University Press, 1968); C. Gerould, *The Ballad of Tradition* (Oxford: Oxford University Press, 1957); Francis J. Child, ed., *The English and Scottish Popular Ballads* (New York: Cooper Square, 1965); Hyder E. Rollins, *An Analytical Index to the Ballad Entries (1557-1709) in the Register of the Company of Stationers in London* (Chapel Hill: University of North Carolina Press, 1924); Rollins, "The Black-Letter Broadside Ballad," *Publications of the Modern Language Association* 34 (1919); Rollins, *Cavalier and Puritan, Ballads and Broadsides . . . 1640-1660* (New York: New York University Press, 1923); C. M. Simpson, *The British Broadside Ballad and Its Music* (New Brunswick, NJ: Rutgers University Press, 1966); Natascha Würzbach, *The Rise of the English Street Ballads,* trans. Gayna Walls (Cambridge: Cambridge University Press, 1990).

26. Gene Bollême, ed., *La Bibliothèque Bleue* (Paris: Gallimard Julliard, 1971); Spufford, *Small Books and Pleasant Histories.*

27. See the *Dictionary of National Biography* (Oxford: Oxford University Press, 1917-) for each: Thomas Deloney, V:777; Martin's Parker, XV:262-254; John Taylor, XIX:431-438. Also Rollins, *Black-Letter Broadside,* pp. 296-306; W. Hunt, *The Puritan Moment* (Cambridge, MA: Harvard University Press, 1983); McKerrow, ed., *Dictionary of Printers and Booksellers, 1557-1640;* Plomer, ed., *Dictionary of Printers and Booksellers, 1557-1775.*

28. Spufford, *Small Books and Pleasant Histories,* chapter 4.

29. Spufford writes that the pamphlets in Pepys's collection were wholly non-political; *Small Books and Pleasant Histories,* p. 219. This is correct only in the sense that most commoners probably did not identify with the standard political factions one might find in Parliament, and therefore pamphlets were rarely openly partisan. In fact, chapbooks were largely consumed with the civil war. When the appearance of monsters and terrible natural disasters is attributed to one side of the conflict or the other, it is difficult to maintain that pamphlets were nonpolitical.

30. Spufford, *Small Books and Pleasant Histories,* pp. 72-75, 225-37, 245-49. Also, *The Life of Long Meg of Westminster* (1620) in Mish, *Short Fiction;* F. O. Mann, *The Works of Thomas Deloney* (Oxford: Clarendon Press, 1912), pp. 1-272.

31. *The Penitent Murderer,* p. 9. The other pamphlets published about this murder are *Blood Washed Away By Tears of Repentance; Heavens Cry Against Murder; A Full and the Truest Narrative of the Most Horrid, Barbarous and Unparalleled Murder.* All of the above can be located in the Thomason Collection.

Several contemporary pamphlets about murders have been collected by Joseph H. Marshburn and Alan R. Velie in *Blood and Knavery* (Rutherford, NJ: Farleigh Dickinson University Press, 1973) and Joseph H. Marshburn, *Murder and Witchcraft in England, 1550-1640* (Norman: University of Oklahoma Press, 1971).

For secondary sources dealing with murder, please consult the following: J. A. Sharp, "Domestic Homicide in Early Modern England," *The Historical Journal* 24 (1981): 29-48; James B. Given, *Society and Homicide in 13th Century England* (Stanford, CA: Stanford University Press, 1977); Clare Gittings, *Death, Burial and the Individual in Early Modern England* (London: Croon Helm, 1984).

Concerning crime at this time, the reader might turn to the following: J. S. Cockburn, ed., *Crime in England, 1550-1800* (Princeton, NJ: Princeton University Press, 1977); J. A. Sharp, *Crime in Seventeenth-Century England* (Cambridge: Cambridge University Press, 1983); Sharp, *Crime in Early Modern England 1500-1750* (London: Longman, 1984); Michael Weisser, *Crime and Punishment in Early Modern Europe* (Atlantic Heights, NJ: Humanities Press, 1979); Leanore Lublein, "The Context of Murder in English Domestic Plays, 1590-1610," *Studies in English Literature* 23 (Spring 1983): 181-96.

32. See, for instance, Mitchell Stephens, "Sensationalism and Moralizing in Sixteenth- and Seventeenth-Century Newsbooks and News Ballads," *Journalism History* 12 (Autumn/Winter 1985); Sandra Clark, *The Elizabethan Pamphleteers: Popular Moralistic Pamphlets, 1580-1640* (Rutherford, NJ: Farleigh Dickinson University Press, 1983); Tessa Watt, *Cheap Print and Popular Piety, 1550-1640* (Cambridge: Cambridge University Press, 1991); Benjamin Boyles, *The Polemic Character, 1640-1660: A Chapter in English Literary History* (Lincoln: University of Nebraska Press, 1955).

33. S. Gardiner, ed., *The Constitutional Documents of the Puritan Revolution 1625-1660* (Oxford: Clarendon Press, 1906), p. 139.

NOTES TO CHAPTER 2

1. See chapter 1 in Keith Thomas's *Religion and the Decline of Magic* (London: Weidenfeld and Nicholson, 1971); P. Laslett, *The World We Have Lost* (London: Methuen, 1965); Herbert Leventhal, *In the Shadow of the Enlightenment* (New York: New York University Press, 1976).

2. Lynn Thorndike, *A History of Magic and Experimental Science,* 4 vols. (New York: Macmillan, 1923-1958); James G. Frazer, *The Golden Bough* (New York: Macmillan, 1900). For rural Italian peasant systems of religious belief, see Carlo Ginzburg, *The Night Battles: Witchcraft and Agrarian Cults in the Sixteenth and Seventeenth Centuries* (Baltimore: Johns Hopkins University Press, 1980); Richard Keickhefer, *Magic in the Middle Ages* (Cambridge: Cambridge University Press, 1990).

3. Concerning saints and their role in popular belief, see C. J. Loomis, *White Magic: An Introduction to the Folklore of Christian Legend* (Cambridge, MA: Harvard University Press, 1948). The best discussion of the superstitious understanding of the sacraments remains J.-B. Thiers, *Traité des Superstitions qui regardent les*

Sacremens (1679; 5th ed., Paris, 1741). Also, Aron Gurevitch, *Medieval Popular Culture: Problems of Belief and Perception* (Cambridge: Cambridge University Pres, 1988).

4. Joshua Trachtenberg, *Jewish Magic and Superstition* (New York: Berhman, 1939; reprinted New York: Atheneum, 1970).

5. The literature concerning witchcraft is very extensive. The general reader might start with Thomas, *Religion and the Decline of Magic.* The following accounts should prove useful in providing a fundamental appreciation of the modern historiography of the subject: Brian P. Levack, *The Witch-Hunt in Early Modern Europe* (London: Longman, 1987); Joseph Klaits, *The Servants of Satan: The Age of the Witch Hunts* (Bloomington: Indiana University Press, 1985); Christina Larner, *Witchcraft and Religion: The Politics of Popular Belief* (New York: B. Blackwell, 1986). Also, see chapter 9, note 2.

6. The thaumaturgic character of monarchy is discussed by Marc Bloch, *Les Rose thaumaturges: étude sur le caractère surnaturel attribué " puissance royale, particulièrement en France et en Angleterre* (Strasbourg: Bibliothèque de la Faculté, 1924); Raymond Crawford, *The King's Evil* (Oxford: Oxford University Press, 1911). More recent studies of theories of kingship and related issues include: Samuel H. Hooke, *Myth, Ritual and Kingship: Essays on the Theory and Practice of Kingship* (Oxford: Clarendon Press, 1958); John L. Miller, *Bourbon and Stuart: Kings and Kingship in France and England in the Seventeenth Century* (New York: F. Watts, 1987); Ernst H. Kantorowicz, *The King's Two Bodies: A Study in Medieval Political Theology* (Princton: Princeton University Press, 1957); Fritz Kern, *Kingship and the Law in the Middle Ages, I: The Divine Right of Kings* (Oxford: B. Blackwell, 1939); Franklin L. Baumer, *The Early Tudor Theory of Kingship* (New York: Russell and Russell, 1900).

NOTES TO CHAPTER 3

1. The literature on the subject of apparitions is quite extensive. Interested readers might refer to the following for a discussion of apparitions and monsters during the medieval period and then during the Reformation, when the appearance of these phenomena was again important: Jacques LeGoff, "The Marvelous in the Medieval West," *The Medieval Imagination,* trans. Arthur Goldhammer (Chicago: University Of Chicago Press, 1988); Claude Kappler, *Monstres, demons, et merveilles a la fin du Moyen Age* (Paris: Payot, 1980); Michel Meslin, ed. *Le Merveilleux: L'imaginaire et les croyances en Occident* (Paris: Bordas, 1984); Daniel Poiron, *Le Merveilleux dans la litterature francaise du Moyen Age* (Paris: Presses Universitaires de France, 1982); Rudolf Schenda, "Die protestantisch-katholische Legendpolemik," *Archiv für Kulturgeschichte* 52 (1970); Schenda, "Hieronymus Rauscher und die protestantisch-katholische Legendpolemik," in Wolfgang BrHckner, ed., *Volkerz hlung und Reformation* (Berlin, E. Schmidt, 1971); Philip M. Soergal, "From Legends to Lies: Protestant Attacks on Catholic Miracles in Late Reformation Germany," *Fides et Historia* 21, no. 2 (June 1989): 21-29. For seventeenth-century England, in addition to Keith Thomas, *Religion and the Decline of Magic* (London: Weidenfeld and Nicholson, 1971), the reader will find the following useful: Chris

Durston, "Signs and Wonders and the English Civil War," *History Today* 38 (October 1987); Norman R. Smith, "Portent Lore and Medieval Popular Culture," *Journal of Popular Culture* 14 (Summer 1980); Rudolf Wittkower, *Allegory and the Migration of Symbols* (Boulder, CO: Westview Press, 1977); Llewellyn H. Buell, "Elizabethan Portents: Superstition or Doctrine?" *Essays Critical and Historical Dedicated to Lily B. Campbell* (Berkeley: University Of California Press, 1950), pp. 25-41. Other than the publications mentioned in the text, the interested reader might also read Thomas Bromhall's *A Treatise of Specters, or, An History of Apparitions, Oracles, Prophecies and Predictions* (1658). The 367-page text was originally written in French but was translated into English by T. B. for this publication.

Monsters have received less scholarly attention. Other than as literary themes, very little has been published about monsters, yet Joseph Frank, *The Beginnings of the English Newspapers, 1620-1660* (Cambridge, MA: Harvard University Press, 1961), p. 302, note 85, maintains that 10 percent of newspaper stories published during the interregnum concerned accounts of monsters. See Claude Lecouteux, *Les Monstres dans la litterature allemande du Moyen Age*, 3 vols. (Göttingen: Kümmerle Verlag, 1982); Rudolf Schenda, "Die Französische Prodigienliteratur in der zweiten Hälfte des 16. Jahrhunderts," *Münchner Romanistische Arbeiten* 16 (1961); Schenda, "Die deutschen Prodigiensammlungen des 16. und 17. Jahrhunderts," *Archiv für Geschichte des Buchwesens* 4 (1963). For England, in addition to Thomas's *Religion and the Decline of Magic*, an excellent place to start is Katharine Park and Lorraine J. Datson, "Unnatural Conceptions: The Study of Monsters in Sixteenth and Seventheenth Century France and England," *Past and Present* 92 (1981): 20-54. Also helpful are Ronald Westrum, "A Note on Monsters," *Journal of Popular Culture* (Summer 1980); C. J. S. Thompson, *The Mystery and Lore of Monsters, with Accounts of some Giants, Dwarfs and Prodigies* (New York: Bell Publishing Co., 1958); Rudolph Wittkower, "Marvels in the East: A Study in the History of Monsters," *The Journal of Warburg and Courtould Institutes* 5 (1942): 159-97.

As in so many other areas, the ridiculous and the sublime move in the same circles. The popularity of circus monsters and the serious study of physical anomaly were intricately involved. Sailors and travelers from abroad brought to Europe a variety of animals and stories of strange-looking peoples with equally strange habits. In turn, the popular press disseminated illustrations of strange beings and described where and how monsters had been discovered all over the foreign world. Even serious intellectuals expressed an avid curiosity into the realm of the biologically feasible, as is amply demonstrated by the 200-page study *Anthropologie abstracted, or, the Idea of Human nature Reflected in Brief Philosophical and Anatomical Collections* (1655) or the even more ponderous tome *Anthropometamorphosis: Man Transformed, or the Changeling* (1653). This 559-page study is subtitled "A treatise on the practices of various peoples in adorning or deforming the body" and presents many dozens of illustrations of alleged tribesmen from Asia, Africa, and America. Both works emphasized that foreigners did not look human like Europeans. These, of course, were not chapbooks, were not read in taverns, and were not sung like ballads, but there can be little doubt that they reflected the interest all classes shared in human oddity. Moreover, their illustrations are terrific.

By 1600 monsters were on public display at Bartholomew Fair in London, and they often traveled a circuit of public houses and taverns, where people could see them for a small fee. The range of monsters on display depended on what was available at the moment, but deformed births such as Siamese twins, sheep with two heads, and cats with extra tails and paws were always popular. Grotesque human adults were more rare, more popular, and more valuable.

The increased availability of monsters and the anatomical discoveries from autopsies provided nontheological conceptions of monstrosity so that by the end of the seventeenth century unusual births were understood as medical pathologies rather than as divine punishments. At the beginning of the century, however, opinion understood monsters as divine prodigies. The confusion and bitterness of the civil war did not favor a rapid change in ideas. People still perceived monsters as prodigies—the results of God's curse—and each side in the civil war found monsters useful in characterizing their opponents and demonstrating God's ever-present interest in the propagation of their particular viewpoint. Many spokesman for God delighted in reminding their parishioners of sin and damnation and were probably angered by the idea that monstrous births were chance medical pathologies since this lessened God's importance in the world and his hatred for their opponents.

2. See *Dictionary of National Biography* (Oxford: Oxford University Press, 1917-) 11: 1137-1141. William Lilly will be treated in depth in the next chapter.

3. See *Dictionary of National Biography* 13: 285-288. Merlin will be treated in depth in the next chapter.

NOTES TO CHAPTER 4

1. Prophecy, astrology, and the apocalyptic tradition are vast interrelated subjects with immense bibliographies. Yet each is different; this chapter will concentrate only upon prophecies. More than its cousin astrology, prophecy captured the common Englishman's imagination and provided the revolution with a set of powerful images to justify Parliament's rule. The following should prove helpful in coping with the more narrow field of medieval prophecy: Marjorie Reeves, *The Influence of Prophecy in the Middle Ages* (Oxford: Clarendon Press, 1969); Reeves, *Joachim of Fiore and the Prophetic Future* (London: SPCK, 1976); Reeves, "History and Prophecy in Medieval Thought," *Mediaevalia et Humanistica* 5 (1974): 51-75; John J. I. von Döllinger, *Prophecies and the Prophetic Spirit in the Christian Era* (London: Rivingtons, 1873, reprinted 1980); Michael Barkun, *Disaster and the Millennium* (New Haven: Yale University Press, 1974); Norman Cohn, *The Pursuit of the Millennium,* rev. ed. (New York: Oxford University Press, 1970); Dietrich Kurze, "Prophecy and History," *Journal of the Warburg and Courtould Institutes* 21 (1958): 63-85; Robert E. Lerner, "Medieval Prophecy and Religious Dissent," *Past and Present* 72 (1976): 3-24; Patrick Curry, *Prophecy and Power: Astrology in Early Modern Europe* (Princeton: Princeton University Press, 1989).

2. The best source for Reformation-age prophecy is George Williams, *The Radical Reformation* (Philadelphia: Westminster Press, 1962). For Servetus, see Jerome Friedman, *Michael Servetus: A Case Study in Total Heresy* (Geneva: Droz Press, 1978).

3. On Merlin, see *Dictionary of National Biography* (Oxford: Oxford University Press, 1917-) 13: 285-288. Also, see the following: E. Anwyl, "Merlin," in

J. Hastings, ed., *Encyclopedia of Religion and Ethics* (Edinburgh: T & T Clark, 1908-1926), vol. 8 and pages 565-70; W. E. Mead, "Introduction," in M. B. Wheatly, ed., *Merlin, or the Early History of King Arthur* (London: EETS, 1899); John S. P. Tatlock, *The Legendary History of Britain* (Berkeley: University of California Press, 1950, reprinted New York: Gordin Press, 1974). Concerning Geoffrey of Momouth, see Ernest Jones, *Geoffrey of Monmouth, 1648-1800* (Berkeley: University Of California Press, 1944; reprinted Folcroft, PA: Folcroft Library, 1974; Norwood, PA: Norwood Press, 1977); Laura M. Keeler, *Geoffrey of Monmouth and the Late Latin Chroniclers, 1300-1500* (Berkeley: University of California Press, 1946; reprinted Milwood, NY: Kraus Reprints, 1976); Paul Zumthor, *Merlin le Prophète* (Lausanne: Imprimerie Reunies, 1943; reprinted Geneva: Slatlin Reprints, 1973).

4. A good introduction to English prophecy is Keith Thomas, *Religion and the Decline of Magic* (London: Weidenfeld and Nicholson, 1971), pp. 389-432. For more complete discussion see Rupert Taylor, *The Political Prophecy in England* (New York: Columbia University Press, 1911; reprinted New York: AMS Press, 1967). For the civil war period, see Harry Rusche, "Prophecy and Propaganda, 1641 to 1651," *English Historical Review* 84 (1969): 752-70; Rusche, "Merlini Anglici: Astrology and Propaganda from 1641 to 1651," *English Historical Review* 80 (1965): 322-33. Also, M. H. Dodds, "Political Prophecies in the Reign of Henry VIII," *Modern Language Review* 11 (1916); W. C. Previté-Orton, "An Elizabethan Prophecy," *History* 11 (1918). See also Carroll Camden, "Elizabethan Almanacs and Prognostication," *Transactions of the Bibliographical Society*, 2nd ser., 17 (London, 1932). See also C. A. Patrides and Joseph Wittreich, eds., *The Apocalypse in English Renaissance Thought and Literature* (Ithaca, NY: Cornell University Press, 1984); Folke Dahl, "King Charles Gustavus and the Astrologers William Lilly and John Gadbury," *Lyenos* (1937): 161-186.

5. Rusche, "Prophecy and Propaganda," pp. 754-55, note 2.

6. See *Dictionary of National Biography* 18:119-20. Also, Richard Head, *The Life and Death of Mother Shipton* (London: W. Onley for J. Back, 1697; reprinted London, 1871). For the impact of her prophecies in later centuries, see William H. Harrison, *Mother Shipton Investigated* (London: Wm. Harrison, 1881; reprinted Norwood, PA: Norwood Press, 1976 and 1978). Citations in the text are taken from *Twelve Strange Prophecies* (1642) but the Shipton text is identical in all publications.

7. See *Dictionary of National Biography* 11: 1137-41. Also, Bernard S. Capp, *English Almanacs 1500-1800: Astrology and the Popular Press* (Ithaca, NY: Cornell University Press, 1979), pp. 44, 48-9, 57-8, 73-86; F. S. Siebert, *Freedom of the Press in England, 1474-1776* (Urbana: University of Illinois Press, 1952), pp. 179-302; Derek Parker, *Familiar to All: William Lillly and Astrology in the Seventeenth Century* (London: Jonathan Cape, 1975); Patrick Curry, *Prophecy and Power*. Lilly wrote, among other works, *Merlinus Anglicus Junior* (1644); *Prophecie of the White King* (1644); *England's Prophetical Merline* (1644); *Collection of Prophecies* (1645); *Anglicus* (1646); *The World's Catastrophe* (1647); *A Peculiar Prognostication* (1649); *English Ephemeris for 1650* (1650); *Monarchy or No Monarchy* (1651); and *Annus Tennebrosus* (1652). He also wrote an autobiography entitled *William Lilly's History* *of His Life and Times from the Year 1602.* It was written in 1648, when Lilly was forty-six, but remained unpublished until 1715, when it was printed by J. Roberts. It was reprinted in London by C. Baldwin in 1822 and again in 1829 by Whittacher, Trucker, and Arnot.

8. Peter Helwyn, *Cyprianus Anglicis: Life of William, Lord Archbishop of Canterbury* (London, 1671) p. 138, cited in Rusche, "Prophecies and Propaganda," p. 757.

9. *Mr. William Lilly's History of King James the First and King Charles the First* (London, 1651), p. 81. Pages 77 to 105 provide a prophetic background to the revolution as a whole. Just a few years earlier Lilly had argued that it was proper to oppose Charles because he had usurped English liberties. In the *White King* he wrote, "The times require that I speak the truth . . . for if his Majesty labor the subversion of this present Parliament and call those whom we have entrusted with our lives and fortunes rebells, and labor with his sword to conquer us and bring upon us the barbarous and bloody Irish . . . then I say he hath left the protection of us" (p. A4b). As for Parliament's authority, Lilly wrote, "We have the liberty to defend our selves, our laws, religion, liberty and all the reason in the world to stand firm to our Parliament, which is ordained by God to break the neck of oppression and correct the errors of Monarchy." Lilly was aware that should monarchy return, he may have placed himself in as dangerous position, "and run myself upon a rock and made myself irreconcilable to his Majesty." Lilly was prepared to pay for his views, and it is out of this confidence that he could write "Let what will come of it, truth is truth." Truth seemed somewhat less obvious when Charles II returned to London and Lilly found himself in the awkward position of having to swear loyalty to that monarch.

10. Rusche, "Merlini Anglici," p. 322-33. See also Thomas, *Religion and the Decline of Magic,* p. 413, citing Lilly's *Autobiography,* p. 106; H. R. Plomer, A Printer's Bill in the Seventeenth Century," *The Library,* new series, 7 (1906).

11. According to Thomas, *Religion and the Decline of Magic,* pp. 344-47, both Anglican and Presbyterian authorities remained dubious of astrological forecasting, and both regularly censored almanacs. See also Capp, *English Almanacs;* D. C. Allen, *The Star-Crossed Renaissance. The Quarrel About Astrology and Its Influence in England* (Durham, NC: University of North Carolina Press, 1941); and T. O. Wedel, *The Medieval Attitude Towards Astrology, Particularly in England* (New Haven: Yale University Press, 1920).

12. Taylor, *Political Prophecy,* p. 83.

13. See William Lilly, *Supernatural Sights and Apparitions* (1644) pp. 47-48; *The Starry Messanger* (1645), p. 23; *An Astrological Prediction of the Occurrences in England* (1648), p. 17; *Annus Tenebrosus* (1652), p. 40.

14. Rusche, "Merlini Anglici," pp. 325, 332.

15. David Underdown, *Prides Purge* (Oxford: Oxford University Press, 1971), p. 183.

16. Nostradamus remains popular and in print. See Edgar Leoni, *Nostradamus: Life and Literature* (New York: Esposition Press, 1961); Henry Robert, ed., *The Complete Prophecies of Nostradamus* (Great Neck, NY: Nostradamus Press, 1973).

NOTES TO CHAPTER 5

1. Christopher Hill, *The World Turned Upside Down: Radical Ideas During the English Revolution* (London: Maurice T. Smith, 1972) is the best source for revolutionary-age radical sects. Also, Frank J. McGregor and Barry Reay, *Radical Religion in the English Revolution* (Oxford; Oxford University Press, 1984). F. D. Dow, *Radicalism in the English Revolution 1640-1660* (Oxford: Basil Blackwell, 1985). For a broader perspective, see the excellent bibliography in Michael Mullet, *Radical Religious Movements in Early Modern Europe* (London: Allen & Unwin, 1980).

2. Thomas Edwards, *Gangraena: or, a Catalogue of Many of the Errours, Heresies, and Pernicious Practices of the Sectaries of This Time, Part I,* published in February 1646; Part II published in May 1646; Part III published in December 1646; Ephraim Pagitt, *Heresiography; or, a description of the Heretics and Sectaries of the Latter Times,* published in May 1645.

3. Double supralapsarianism was the view of predestination favored by Calvin's successor, Theodore Beza, and the the Belgian Conference of 1561. It maintains that God predetermined both the elect and the reprobate (hence, *double*) before (hence, *supra*) the beginning of time. Or, that in God's wisdom, Adam and Eve were predestined to fall so that He would be able to punish the wicked of the future. Some found this doctrine quite awesome and held to the more tolerant single infralapsarian predestination, which maintained that God predeterminbed only the elect and did so within time, after the fall. Hence, God permitted some individuals to work their way into heaven through good works. This position, often considered that of the Roman Catholic church, was rejected by most Protestants who, because of their own notions of original sin, rejected the possibility of good works. Those Calvinists who rejected the Catholic position but could not accept the strident double form mentioned above might accept a middle position such as double infralapsarian predestination, which argued that God predestined both the elect and damned but did so within time, after the fall in Eden. At least this position did not make God the mainspring of evil in the world. These issues came to a head in early-seventeenth-century Holland at the Council of Dort, where the TULIP formula, an acronym for five axioms of belief, finally settled the issue for orthodox Calvinists. This declaration affirmed (1) Total depravity of mankind (because of original sin); (2) Unconditional grace (that is, unmerited for the elect); (3) Limited atonement (only the elect could atone, but obviously did not need to); (4) Irresistable grace (even the most evil person can not resist grace if he is predestined for election); (5) Perservarance of the saints only (or, that only God's elect can stay the course of righteousness, even if they commit evil sins while the reprobate can never merit forgiveness).

For more information concerning predestination and related themes, the reader might consult Charles D. Cremeans, *The Reception of Calvinist Thought in England* (Urbana: University of Illinois Press, 1949); and M. Walzer, *The Revolution of the Saints* (Cambridge, MA: Harvard University Press, 1965).

4. The Ranters will be discussed in detail later. For additional information about Clarkson, see the *Dictionary of National Biography* 4:461-463, and Jereome Friedman, *Blasphemy, Immorality and Anarchy: The Ranters and the English Revolution* (Athens, OH: Ohio University Press, 1988), pp. 96-122.

5. The best biography of Servetus remains Roland Bainton's *Hunted Heretic: The Life and Death of Michael Servetus* (Boston: Beacon, 1953). For an in-depth analysis of Servetus's eclectic theological system, see Jerome Friedman, *Michael Servetus: A Case Study in Total Heresy* (Geneva: Droz, 1978).

6. Readers can consult the following for additional information about these sects: Concerning the Familists, the two most recent studies are Jean D. Moss, *"Godded with God": Hendrik Niclaes and His Family of Love* (Philadelphia: American Philosohpical Society, 1981); Alastair Hamilton, *The Family of Love* (Cambridge: James Clark, 1981); Rufus M. Jones's older studies on mystical and spiritual religion remain of value for his insights, humanity, and clean prose. Among other works, see his *Studies in Mystical Religion* (London: Macmilan, 1923).

Concerning the Ranters, the most recent study is Friedman, *Blasphemy, Immorality and Anarchy*; and from very different orientations, J. C. Davies, *Fear, Myth and History: The Ranters and the Historians* (Cambridge: Cambridge University Press, 1986); Norman Cohn, *The Pursuit of the Millennium* (New York: Harper Torchbooks, 1961); Christopher Hill, *The World Turned Upside Down,* chapter 9 tells us about "Seekers and Ranters" and chapter 10 about "Ranters and Quakers." G. F. S. Ellens, "The Ranters Ranting: Reflections on a Ranting Counter Culture," *Church History* 40, no. 3 (1971), pp. 91-107. Ellens compares the Ranters to recent counterculture hippies. Frank J. McGregor, "The Ranters," B.Litt. degree thesis, University of Oxford, November 1968, n. 1434; McGregor, "Seekers and Ranters," in J. F. McGregor and B. Raey, eds., *Radical Religion in the English Revolution* (Oxford: Oxford University Press, 1984. A. L. Morton, *The World of the Ranters* (London: Lawrence and Wisehart, 1970). More of a collection of general essays than a true analysis of Rantism, this volume has one general chapter on Ranters and one on Clarkson, with the remaining five chapters devoted to aspects of Leveller democratic thought. Nigel Smith, ed., *A Collection of Ranter Writings* (London: Junction Books, 1983) features selections by Coppe, Clarkson, Salmon, and Bauthumley as well as a good introduction by Smith.

Concerning the Muggletonians, first cousins to the above, see Christopher Hill, *The World Turned Upside Down* and Christopher Hill, Barry Reay, and William M. Lamont, *The World of the Muggletonians* (London: Temple Smith, 1983). Since publication, two of these authors have disagreed concerning the primacy of Reeve and/or Muggleton. See Lamont's "The Muggletonians, 1652-1979. A Vertical Approach," *Past and Present,* no. 99 (May 1983), pp 22-40. Hill's rejoinder and Lamont's subsequent rebuttal are: Hill, "The Muggletonians," *Past and Present,* no. 104 (August l984), pp. 153-58; W. Lamont, "A Rejoinder," *Past and Present,* no. 104 (August 1984), pp. 159-63.

Concerning the Quakers, consult Robert Barclay, *The Inner Life of the Religious Societies of the Commonwealth* (London: Hodder and Stoughton, 1876); W. C. Braithwaite, *The Beginnings of Quakerism,* 2nd ed. (Cambridge: Cambridge University Press, 1955) and *The Second Period of Quakerism,* 2nd ed. (Cambridge:

Cambridge University Press, 1961); the following by Rufus Jones: *Studies in Mystical Religion; Spiritual Reformers in the 16th and 17th Centuries* (London: Macmillan, 1914); *The Quakers in the American Colonies* (New York: Macmillan, 1923); *The Later Periods of Quakerism* (London: Macmillan, 1921); and more recently, Hugh Barbour, *The Quakers in Puritan England* (New Haven: Yale University Press, 1964) and Barry Raey, *The Quakers and the English Revolution* (London: Temple Smith, 1985).

7. Robert M. Grant, *Gnosticism and Early Christianity* (New York: Harper Torchbooks, 1966), p. 200.

8. See Cohn, *The Pursuit of the Millennium.* For an opposing point of view, see Robert Lerner, *The Heresy of the Free Spirit in the Later Middle Ages* (Los Angeles: University of California Press, 1972).

9. Henry C. Lea, *A History of the Inquisition in Spain,* 4 vols. (New York: Macmillan, 1906-7). This study remains the English language standard for scholars studying the Alumbrados.

10. See for instance, John Calvin, *Treatises Against the Anabaptists and Against the Libertines,* trans. Benjamin W. Farley (Grand Rapids, MI: Baker Books, 1982). Luther's views and tirades against the "enthusiasts" are by now legendary.

11. Albert Henry Newman, "Adam Pastor, Antitrinitarian Antipaedobaptist," *American Society for Church History,* 2nd ser., 5 (1914): 75-99.

12. Lerner, *The Heresy of the Free Spirit,* pp. 39-40, 121-3; and Steven Runciman, *The Medieval Manichee: A Study in the Christian Dualist Heresy* (Cambridge: Cambridge University Press, 1947).

13. For a complete discussion of anti-Ranter literature, see Friedman, *Blasphemy, Immorality and Anarchy,* pp. 251-310. For a good analysis of how the popular press of the day could create a Ranter frenzy, see Davis, *Fear, Myth, and History.*

14. George Fox, *Journals,* 2 vols. (London: Headly Brothers, 1902), vol. 1, p. 47.

15. *Encyclopaedia Britannica,* 11th ed. (New York: Cambridge University Press, 1910-1911), vol. 22, p. 895.

16. Jones, *Studies in Mystical Religion,* p. 467.

17. Concerning Arthington, see Keith Thomas, *Religion and the Decline of Magic* (London: Weidenfeld and Nicholson, 1971), pp. 134ff.

18. Concerning Abiezzer Coppe, see the *Distionary of National Biography* 4:1115 and for a discussion of all his religious writings and ideas see Friedman, *Blasphemy, Immorality and Anarchy,* pp. 75-95.

19. See H. Scobell, *A Collection of Acts and Ordinances . . . London* (1658), part 2, pp. 124-26.

20. Concerning the Diggers, consult the following: Lewis H. Berens, *The Digger Movement in the Days of the Commonwealth* (London: Simkin, 1906; reprinted London: Holland and Merlin Press, 1961); T. Wilson Hayes, *Winstanley the Digger* (Cambridge, MA: Harvard University Press, 1979); W. H. G. Armytage, *Heavens Below: Utopian Experiments in England, 1560-1960* (London: Routledge & Kegan Paul, 1961); and Christopher Hill, *The Religion of Gerrard Winstanley,* Past and Present Supplement, vol. 5, Oxford, 1978.

21. Concerning Richard Coppin see the *Dictionary of National Biography* 4:1116-1118, and for a discussion of his religious writings and ideas, see Friedman, *Blasphemy, Immorality and Anarchy,* pp. 17-58.

22. Concerning Joseph Salmon, see Friedman, *Blasphemy, Immorality and Anarchy,* pp. 141-55, for a discussion of his religious writings and ideas.

NOTES TO CHAPTER 6

1. Historians are often squeamish about discussing religious charlatans for fear that some were indeed sincere or represented some larger political or economic orientation of importance. Also, some phenomena frowned upon today, such as faith healing, were accepted in the seventeenth century. Even George Fox, the famous Quaker leader, claimed to have healed over 150 people of terrible maladies. But it is a mistake to include charlatanism within the parameters of legitimate spiritual religion much as it would be a mistake to include magic within the proper study of physics or to confuse the illusory appearance of anything with its reality. Hence, this chapter will assume that those claiming to be Jesus Christ and possessing the ability to perform miracles but who then make their way into someone's bed or wallet were less part of a prophetic tradition than participants in a long tradition of confidence operators. Those claiming to be some biblical personality, even if at times they were quite humorous, should be recognized for the frauds they were. Scholars have a responsibility to study the voices of the past but are under no obligation to be fooled or conned by them. Confusing charlatanism with religious enthusiasm is a disservice to both and is probably predicated upon an appreciation or an understanding of neither. Some of the material presented here is available in earlier form in Jerome Friedman, "Their Name was God: Religious Charlatans in the Seventeenth-Century Popular Press," *Journal of Popular Culture* 25 (Summer, 1991): 55-66, and Friedman, *Blasphemy, Immorality and Anarchy: The Ranters and the English Revolution* (Athens, OH: Ohio University Press, 1988).

2. The literature on these individuals is terribly sparse. For additional information about Elizabethan messianic pretenders, see Keith Thomas, *Religion and the Decline of Magic* (London: Weidenfeld and Nicholson, 1971), pp. 133-6ff; and R. Matthews, *English Messiahs* (London: Methuen, 1936). The *Dictionary of National Biography* writes of Wightman (21:195-6), and another source of information is Richard L. Greaves and R. L. Zalern, *A Biographical Dictionary of British Radicals in the Seventeenth Century,* 3 vols. (Brighton: Harvester Press, 1982-84).

3. *See the Dictionary of National Biography* 8:864-5.

4. See Raymond Klibansky et al., *Saturn and Melancholy* (London: Nelson, 1964), p. 94. Christopher Hill, *The World Turned Upside Down: Radical Ideas During the English Revolution* (London: Maurice Smith, 1972) makes the point that insanity was often an assumed cover for the expression of radical ideas. There is considerable merit to this "king's-fool" view of those who actually proposed radical solutions to social ills but then claimed to be insane to avoid prosecution. On the other hand, most charlatans claiming to be Jesus, Mary or the reincarnation of Aaron the High Priest rarely had anything more radical to propose than their own aggrandizement. It is always unfortunate when scholars can not distinguish between the insane and the radical. See note 1.

5. See Friedman, *Blasphemy, Immorality and Anarchy,* pp. 167-191.

6. Concerning John Pordage and Thomas Webb, see Friedman, *Blasphemy, Immorality and Anarchy,* chapters 15 and 16, as well as *Dictionary of National Biography* 16:150-1.

7. Concerning Naylor, see the *Dictionary of National Biography* 14:130-133, and Hill, *The World Turned Upside Down,* pp. 241-258 et passim. Also, Greaves and Zallern, *Dictionary of British Radicals,* and Barry Raey, *The Quakers and the English Revolution* (London: Temple Smith, 1985) and W. C. Braithwaite, *The Beginnings of Quakerism,* 2nd ed. (Cambridge: Cambridge University Press, 1955).

8. For more on these individuals, see Friedman, *Blasphemy, Immorality and Anarchy*; Hill, *The World Turned Upside Down*; and, of course, Greaves and Zallern, *Dictionary of British Radicals.*

9. Robins's followers held peculiar views. Tydford's notion that Cain was a member of the trinity is reminiscent of the views of the Bogomils and other earlier dualists who also subscribed to the idea that Jesus and Satan, like Cain and Abel, were dualist representations of worldly powers and were both sons of God within the trinity. Unfortunately, it is impossible to know how they came upon such esoteric opinions. See Steven Runciman, *The Medieval Manichee: A Study of the Christian Dualist Heresy* (Cambridge: Cambridge University Press, 1947); F. C. Burkitt, *The Religion of the Manichees* (Cambridge: Cambridge University Press, 1925).

10. See Robert M. Grant, *Gnosticism and Early Christianity,* rev. ed. (New York: Harper & Row, 1966), pp. 70-97, and Hans Jonas, *The Gnostic Religion,* 2nd ed. (Boston: Beacon, 1963).

11. For more information about Puritan morality laws, see Keith Thomas, "The Puritans and Adultery: The Act of 1650 Reconsidered," in Donald Pennington and Keith Thomas, eds., *Puritans and Revolutionaries* (Oxford: Clarendon Press, 1978), pp. 257-82; Cynthia B. Herrup, "Law and Morality in Seventeenth-Century England," *Past and Present,* no. 106, (1985): 102-23.

12. Friedman, *Blasphemy, Immorality and Anarchy,* pp. 96-120.

13. The full development of Clarkson's ideas on this theme are more complex than the treatment here would suggest. The reader might wish to consult Friedman, *Blasphemy, Immorality and Anarchy,* pp. 96-120, where this subject is discussed in full from the vantage point of all of Clarkson's writings. As a concept, redemption through evil is one of the most fascinating notions of salvation because it argues that the very evil deeds constituting sin and perversion also provide holiness, sanctification and salvation. Human degeneracy is both the source of the believer's fall from grace as well as the pathway back to God. For the broader application of these ideas in Christianity, see Jerome Friedman, "Christ's Descent Into Hell and Redemption Through Evil: A Radical Reformation Perspective," *Archiv für Reformationsgeschichte* 76 (1985): 217-230. For a similar type of argument on this same theme in Judaism, see the chapter "Redemption Through Sin," in Gershom Scholem, *The Messianic Idea in Judaism* (New York: Schocken Books, 1971).

14. Concerning Muggleton and the sect named after him, see Christopher Hill, *The World Turned Upside Down,* and Christopher Hill, Barry Reay, and William Lamont, *The World of the Muggletonians* (London: Temple Smith, 1983). Since publication, these authors have disagreed concerning the primacy of Reeve and/or Muggleton. See Lamont's "The Muggletonians, 1652-1979: A Vertical Approach," *Past and Present* 99 (May 1983): 22-40. Hill's rejoinder and Lamont's subsequent rebuttal are: Hill, "The Muggletonians," *Past and Present* 104 (August l984): 153-58; W. Lamont, "A Rejoinder," *Past and Present* 104 (August 1984): 159-163. See note 1.

NOTES TO CHAPTER 7

1. Catholics had been vilified in the press for decades. See Joseph Frank, *The Beginnings of the English Newspapers, 1620-1660* (Cambridge, MA: Harvard University Press, 1961), pp. 24 and 26 for coverage of Catholics in the early press and page 77 for the rumor that Charles I was a Catholic. Sandra Clark's *The Elizabethan Pamphleteers: Popular Moralistic Pamphlets, 1580-1640* (Teaneck, NJ: Fairleigh Dickinson University Press, 1983), p. 189, details anti-Catholic animus for the period before the outbreak of the civil war. For the civil war years, Thomas, *Religion and the Decline of Magic* (London: Weidenfeld and Nicholson, 1971), p. 543, cites the very worthwhile unpublished doctoral dissertation by Robin Clifton, "The Fear Of Catholics in England, 1637-1645," Oxford, 1967. Also see B. Magee, "Popish Plots in the Seventeenth Century: The Great Panic of 1641," *The Month* 175 (1940). Also, Brian Manning, "The Outbreak of the English Civil War," in R. H. Parry , ed., *The English Civil War and After, 1642-1658* (Berkeley: University of California Press, 1970), pp. 4, 7; and Michael G. Finlayson, *Historians, Puritanism and the English Revolution: The Religious Factor in England Before and After the Interregnum* (Toronto: Toronto University Press, 1987); R. W. Harris, *Clarendon and the English Revolution* (London: Hogarth Press, 1983); George Miller, *Edward Hyde, Earl of Clarendon* (Boston: Twayne, 1983).

2. The standard work on the Christian image of Islam is Richard W. Southern, *Western Views of Islam in the Middle Ages* (Cambridge, MA: Harvard University Press, 1962). More recently, Norman Daniel, *Islam and the West: The Making of an Image* (Edinburgh: Edinburgh University Press, 1966); and Daniel, *Islam, Europe and Empire* (Edinburgh: Edinburgh University Press, 1966).

3. Concerning the readmission of Jews to England, the following should prove helpful: David S. Katz, *Philosemitism and the Readmission of Jews to England* (Oxford: Oxford University Press, 1982); Mel Scult, *Millennial Expectation and Jewish Liberties* (Leiden: Brill, 1978); Cecil Roth, *A History of the Jews in England* (Oxford: Clarendon Press, 1941); H. S. Q. Henriques, *The Return of the Jews to England* (London: Macmillan, 1905). The curious relationship that developed between Cromwell and Mennasseh ben Israel, the spokesman for Dutch Jewry who conducted negotiations with the English government, is described in Roth, *The Life of Mennasseh ben Israel* (Philadelphia: Jewish Publication Society, 1934); Lucien Wolf, *Mennasseh ben Israel's Mission to Oliver Cromwell* (London: Macmillan, 1901); and most recently and from a very different point of view, Joseph Kaplan, Henry Méchoulan, and Richard Popkin, eds., *Menasseh ben Israel and His World* (Leiden: Brill, 1989).

4. There are many fine general works on anti-Semitism, but the enchanted and magical view of the Jew as a semidemon is best captured by Joshua Trachtenberg, *The Devil and the Jews* (Philadelphia: The Jewish Publication Society, 1943) and most recently, R. Po-Chia Hsia, *The Myth of Ritual Murder: Jews and Magic in Reformation Germany* (New Haven: Yale University Press, 1988). And from a slightly different perspective, Alan H. Cutler, *The Jew as an Ally of the Muslim: Medeival Roots of Antisemitism* (Notre Dame, IN: University of Notre Dame Press, 1986).

5. Identifying New Christians has been an historically complex issue but a good introduction to the subject and the role New Christians played in early modern European economic and cultural life is Jerome Friedman, "Jewish Conversion and the Spanish Pure Blood Laws," *Sixteenth Century Journal* 18 (1987): 4-29. The best general understanding of how mercantilism and trade fostered greater toleration of Jews is Jonathan Israel's excellent study, *European Jewry in the Age of Mercantilism, 1550-1750* (Oxford: Oxford University Press, 1985). Also, see Norma Perry's "Anglo-Jewry, the Law, Religious Conviction and Self Interest, 1655-1753," *Journal of European Studies* (1984): 1-23.

6. The reader might consult the following regarding the Fifth Monarchists and the English apocalyptic tradition: Paul K. Christianson, *Reformers in Babylon: Apocalyptic Visions from the Reformation to the Eve of the Civil War* (Toronto: University of Toronto Press, 1978); Bryan W. Ball, *A Great Expectation: Eschatological Thought in English Protestantism to 1660* (Leiden: Brill, 1975); Louise F. Brown, *The Political Activities of the Baptists and Fifth Monarchy Men in England during the Interregnum* (Washington, D.C.: American Historical Association, 1912); B. S. Capp, *The Fifth Monarchy Men: A Study in 17th Century Millenarianism* (London: Bowman and Littlefield, 1972); Katharine R. Firth, *The Apocalyptic Tradition in Reformation Britain, 1530-1645* (Oxford: Oxford University Press, 1979); William M. Lamont, *Godly Rule: Politics and Religion 1603-1660* (London: Macmillan, 1969); and Philip G. Rogers, *The Fifth Monarchy Men* (Oxford: Oxford University Press, 1966).

7. On the importance of 1656 see Christopher Hill, "Till the Conversion of the Jews," *The Collected Essays of Christopher Hill,* 2 vols. (Amherst, 1986), vol. 2, pp. 296-300.

8. See, for instance, Richard H. Popkin, "The Lost Tribes, the Caraties, and the English Millenarians," *Journal of Jewish Studies* 37 (1986): 213-22.

9. See Peter Toon, ed., *Puritans, the Millenium, and the Future of Israel: Puritan Eschatology 1600-1660* (Cambridge: James Clarke, 1970), pp. 20-6; also, J. Fines, "'Judaising' in the Period of the English Reformation—The Case of Richard Bruern," *Transactions of the Jewish Historical Society* 21 (1962-67): 323-6; H. E. I. Phillips, "An Early Stuart Judaising Sect," *Transactions of the Jewish Historical Society* 15 (1939-45).

10. Joseph Cotton believed it possible to introduce the Mosaic code into the colonies. See Capp, *Fifth Monarchy Men*, p. 170.

11. For additional information about these individuals, see Jerome Friedman, *Blasphemy, Immorality and Anarchy: The Ranters and the English Revolution* (Athens, OH: Ohio University Press, 1988). For George Foster, see pages 127-40; John Robins, pp. 156-60; Thomas Tany, pp. 167-90.

12. For additional information regarding this interesting fable, see George K. Anderson, *The Legend of the Wandering Jew* (Providence, RI: Brown University Press, 1963; reissued, 1991); C. Schoebel, *La Légend de Juif Errant* (Paris: Maisonneuve, 1877).

NOTES TO CHAPTER 8

1. For the Puritan ethic and seventeenth-century sexual morality, see: Jean Mather, "The Moral Code of the English Civil War and Interregnum," *The Historian* 12 (1985): 92-95; Keith Thomas, "The Puritans and Adultery: The Act of 1650 Reconsidered," in Donald Pennington and Keith Thomas, eds., *Puritans and Revolutionaries* (Oxford: Clarendon Press, 1978), pp. 257-82; Cynthia B. Herrup, "Law and Morality in Seventeenth-Century England," *Past and Present*, no. 106, (1985) 102-23; William E. Monter, *Enforcing Morality in Early Modern Europe* (London: Variorum, 1987). The following will provide background material: F. G. Emmison, *Elizabethan Life and Morals and the Church Courts* (Chelmsford: Essex County Council, 1963); Martin Ingram, *Church Courts, Sex, and Marriage in England, 1570-1640* (Cambridge: Cambridge University Press, 1988). For subquent developments see Dudley W. R. Bahlman, *The Moral Revolution of 1688* (New Haven: Yale University Press, 1957).

2. *A Speech of the Honorable Nathanael Feines* (London, 1641), p. 12.

3. For a good discussion of how the single parish attempted to cope with sin and immorality, see John Addy, *Sin and Society in the Seventeenth Century* (London: Routledge, 1989); Ronald A. Marchant, *Puritans and the Church Courts in the Diocese of York, 1560-1640* (London: Longmans, 1960).

4. For a discussion of how members of Parliament generally viewed attempts to provide for personal morality, see J. R. Kent, "Attitudes of Members of the House of Commons to the Regulation of 'Personal Conduct' in Late Elizabethan and Early Stuart England," *Bulletin of the Institute of Historical Research* 46 (1973).

5. C. H. Firth and R. S. Rait, *Acts and Ordinances of the Interrugnum, 1642-1660*, 3 vols. (London: H. M. Stationery Office, printed by Wyman and Sons, 1911), vol. 2, pp. 387-9.

6. Peter Clark, "The Alehouse and the Alternative Society," in Donald Pennington and Keith Thomas, eds., *Puritans and Revolutionaries*, p. 55. This is an extremely readable article. Also see Clark, *The English Alehouse: A Social History* (London: Longman, 1983) for a more complete treatment. Also, H. A. Monckton, *A History of the English Public House* (London: Bodley Head, 1969); Monckton, *A History of English Ale and Beer* (London: Bodley Head, 1966); H. G. Husdon, *Social Regulation in England Under James I and Charles I: Drink and Tobacco* (Chicago: University of Chicago Press, 1933); R. F. Bretherton, "Country Inns and Alehouses," in Reginald V. Lennard, ed., *Englishmen at Rest and Play* (Oxford: Clarendon Press, 1931). And for something more humorous, see Douglas Sutherland, *Raise Your Glasses: A Light Hearted History of Drinking* (London: MacDonald, 1969).

7. Clark, "The Alehouse and the Alternative Society," p. 59. For an alternate view, see Tessa Watt, *Cheap Print and Popular Piety, 1550-1640* (Cambridge: University Press, 1991).

8. Clark, "The Alehouse and the Alternative Society," p. 57.

9. *Teratalogia, or a Discovery of God's Wonders* (London, 1650), p. A3a.

10. *A Preparative to Study, or, The Virtues of Sack* (London, 1641), p. 1.

11. Clark, "The Alehouse and the Alternative Society," p. 50.

12. Ibid., p. 48.

13. Concerning church-ales, see T. G. Barnes, "County Politics and a Puritan Cause Celebre: Sommerset Church-ales, 1633," *Transactions of the Royal Historical Society*, 5th ser., 9 (1959): 108-10.

14. Addy, *Sin and Society*, p. 108.

15. These statistics are taken from Keith Thomas, *Religion and the Decline of Magic* (London: Weidenfeld and Nicholson, 1971), p. 20. For more on this subject the reader might consult the following: C. M. MacInnes, *The Early English Tobacco Trade* (London: K. Paul, Trench and Trubner, 1926); A. Rive, "The Consumption of Tobacco Since 1600," *Economic History* 1 (1926); J. E. Brooks, *The Mighty Leaf: Tobacco Through the Centuries* (Boston: Little Brown, 1952); H. G. Hudson, *Social Regulations In England.*

16. Some readers may believe Harry the Hangman wrote in jest since few people now find as many uses for human excrement. Those readers might wish to see

John G. Burke, *Scatological Rites of All Nations* (1891; reprinted New York: Johnson Reprint, 1968), especially pp. 277-338 for more on these curious practices.

17. Samuel Pepys, *The Diary of Samuel Pepys,* ed. Robert Latham and William Mathews, 9 vols. (Berkeley: University of California Press, 1970-1983), vol. 5, p. 78.

NOTES TO CHAPTER 9

1. The most comprehensive single-volume study of women in the seventeenth century is Antonia Fraser, *The Weaker Vessel* (New York: Vintage Books, 1985). Other important works include the following, with yet other titles in notes below: Mary Prior, ed., *Women and Wives in English Society 1500-1800* (London: Methuen, 1985); Simon Shepherd, ed., *The Women's Sharp Revenge: Five Women's Pamphlets from the Renaissance* (New York: St. Martin's Press, 1985); Susan D. Amussen, *An Orderly Society: Gender and Class in Early Modern England* (New York: B. Blackwell, 1988); G. R. Quaife, *Wanton Wenches and Wayward Wives* (London: Croom Helm, 1979); Carroll Camden, *The Elizabethan Women* (Houston: Elsevier Press, 1952); Mary W. Chapman and A. Beatrice W. Chapman, *The Status of Women under the English Law* (London: Routledge, 1909); Alice Clark, ed., *Working Life of Women in the Seventeenth Century* (New York: Dutton, 1919; reissued London: Routledge & Kegan Paul, 1982); Jean Donnison, *Midwives to Medical Men: A History of Inter-Prefessional Rivalries and Women's Rights* (New York: Schocken Press, 1977); G. E. and K. R. Fussell, *The English Countrywoman: A Farmhouse Social History* (London: A. Melrose, 1953); Dorothy Gardiner, *English Girlhood at School: A Study of Women's Education through Twelve Centuries* (Oxford: Oxford University Press, 1929); Margaret George, "From Goodwife to Mistress: The Transformation of the Female in Bourgeois Culture," *Science and Society* 37 (1973); Wallace Notestein, "The English Women, 1580-1650," in J. H. Plumb, ed., *Studies in Social History* (London: Longman, 1955); Myra Reynolds, *The Learned Lady in England 1650-1760* (Boston: Houghton Mifflin, 1920); D. M. Stenton, *The English Woman in History* (London: Macmillan, 1957); Roger Thompson, *Women in Stuart England and America* (London: Routledge & Kegan Paul, 1974). For the romantic view of Puritan love, see Keith Thomas, "The Puritans and Adultery: The Act of 1650 Reconsidered," in Donald Pennington and Keith Thomas, eds., *Puritans and Revolutionaries* (Oxford: Clarendon Press, 1978), p. 259; J. T. Johnson, *A Society Ordained by God: English Puritan Marriage Doctrine in the First Half of the Seventeenth Century* (Nashville, NY: Abingdon Press, 1970); W. and M. Haller, "The Puritan Art of Loving," *Huntington Library Quarterly* 5 (1941-42); R. M. Frye, "The Teachings of Classical Puritanism on Conjugal Love," *Studies in the Renaissance* 2 (1955).

2. The literature concerning witchcraft is very large. The general reader might start with Keith Thomas, *Religion and the Decline of Magic* (London: Weidenfeld and Nicholson, 1971), and the following accounts are very useful in providing a fundamental appreciation of the modern historiography of the subject: Brian P. Levack, *The Witch-Hunt in Early Modern Europe* (London: Longman, 1987); Joseph Klaits, *The Servants of Satan: The Age of the Witch Hunts* (Bloomington: Indiana University Press, 1985); Christina Larner, *Witchcraft and Religion: The Politics of Popular Belief* (New York: B. Blackwell, 1985); Christina Larner,

Enemies of God: The Witch-hunt in Scotland (London: Chatto & Windus, 1981). For a broader perspective, the reader might consult: J. Caro-Baroja, *The World of the Witches* (Chicago: University of Chicago Press, 1964); R. Kieckhefer, *European Witch-trials: Their Foundations in Popular and Learned Culture, 1300-1500* (London: Routledge & Kegan Paul, 1976); A. Macfarlane, *Witchcraft in Tudor and Stuart England* (London: Routledge & Kegan Paul, 1970); Macfarlane, *Witchcraft and Religion: The Politics of Popular Belief* (Oxford: B. Blackwell, 1984); H. C. E. Middelfort, *Witch Hunting in Southwest Germany, 1562-1684* (Stanford: Stanford Univ.ersity Press, 1972); E. W. Monter, *Witchcraft in France and Switzerland* (Ithaca: Cornell University Press, 1976); Monter, ed., *European Witchcraft* (New York: John Wiley, 1969); Jeffrey Burton Russell, *Witchcraft in the Middle Ages* (Ithaca: Cornell University Press, 1972); H. R. Trevor-Roper, *The European Witch-Craze* (Harmondsworth: Penguin, 1969); Norman Cohn, *Europe's Inner Demons* (New York: Basic Books, 1975).

3. Concerning herbal poisions, see L. H. Pammel, *A Manual of Poisonous Plants* (Cedar Rapids, IA: The Torch Press, 1957); and J. M. Arena and James W. Hardin, *Human Poisoning from Native and Cultivated Plants* (Durham, NC: Duke University Press, 1974).

4. Several contemporary pamphlets about murders have been collected by Joseph H. Marshburn and Alan R. Velie in *Blood and Knavery* (Rutherford, NJ: Fairleigh Dickinson University Press, 1973); and Joseph H. Marshburn, *Murder and Witchcraft in England, 1550-1640* (Norman: University of Oklahoma Press, 1971). For secondary sources dealing with murder, please consult the following: J. A. Sharp, "Domestic Homicide in Early Modern England," *The Historical Journal* 24 (1981): 29-48; James B. Given, *Society and Homicide in 13th Century England* (Stanford: Stanford University Press, 1977); Leanore Lublein, "The Context of Murder in English Domestic Plays, 1590-1610," *Studies in English Literature* 23 (Spring 1983): 181-96; Clare Gittings, *Death, Burial and the Individual in Early Modern England* (London: Croom Helm, 1984). Murder is also treated in more general studies of crime, such as the following: J. S. Cockburn, ed., *Crime in England, 1550-1800* (Princeton: Princeton University Press, 1977); J. A. Sharp, *Crime in Seventeenth-Century England* (Cambridge: Cambridge University Press, 1983); Sharp, *Crime in Early Modern England 1500-1750* (London: Longman, 1984); Michael Weisser, *Crime and Punishment in Early Modern Europe* (Atlantic Heights, NJ: Humanities Press, 1979).

5. The important role played by women in revolutionary-period sects has not received the amount of scholarship it deserves. Still, there are some very good works that provide a staring point. Mabel R. Brailsford, *Quaker Women 1640-1690* (London: Duckworth, 1915); Isabel Ross, *Margaret Fell: Mother of Quakerism* (London: Longman, 1949); M. P. Higgins, "Women in the English Civil War," M.A. thesis, University of Manchester, 1965; Keith Thomas, "Women and the Civil War Sects," *Past and Present* 13, 1958; David Weigall, "Women Militants in the English Civil War," *History Today* (June 1972); E. M. Williams, "Women Preachers in the English Civil War," *Journal of Modern History* 1 (1929).

6. Concerning pornography, see Roger Thompson, *Unfit for Modest Ears: A Study of Pornographic, Obscene, and Bawdy Works Written and Published in*

England in the Second Half of the Seventeenth Century (Totowa, NJ: Rowan and Littlefield, 1979); H. C. Allen and R. Thompson, eds., *Contrast and Connection* (Athens, Ohio: Ohio University Press, 1976), chapter 2; David Foxon, *Libertine Literature in England, 1660-1745* (New Hyde Park, NY: University Books, 1965); A. V. Judges, ed., *The Elizabethan Underworld: A Collection of Tudor and Early Stuart Tracts and Ballads* (London: E. P. Dutton, 1930; reissued, London: Routledge & Kegan Paul, 1965); G. Salgado, ed., *Cony-Catchers and Bawdy Baskets: An Anthology of Elizabethan Lowlife* (Harmondsworth: Penguin, 1972); G. Legman, *The Horn Book: Studies in Erotic Folklore and Bibliography* (New York: University Books, 1964); E. J. Burford, *Bawdy Verse: A Pleasant Collection* (New York: Penguin, 1982).

7. Concerning prostitution, see: E. J. Burford, *Bawds and Lodgings: A History of the London Bankside Brothels from 100-1675* (London: Owen, 1976); E. J. Burford, *The Orrible Synne: A Look at London Lechery from Roman to Cromwellian Times* (London: Calder & Boyars, 1973); Lydia L. Otis, *Prostitution in Medieval Society: The History of an Urban Institution in Languedoc* (Chicago: University of Chicago Press, 1985); Paul Hair, ed., *Before the Bawdy Court: Selections for Church Court and Other Records Relating to the Correction of Moral Offences in England, Scotland, and New England, 1300-1800* (London: B. Elek, 1972); Carol Weiner, "Sex Roles and Crime in Late Elizabethan Herfordshire," *Journal of Social History* 8 (Summer 1975): 38-60. A wealth of information about prostitution and illicit sex can be gleaned from the following: James T. Henke, *Gutter Life and Language in the Early Street Literature of England: A Glossary of Terms and Topics Chiefly of the Sixteenth and Seventeenth Centuries* (West Cornwall, CT: Locust Hill Press, 1988); Eric Partridge, *A Dictionary of Slang and Uncoventional English,* 8th ed., ed. Paul Beal (New York: Macmillan, 1984); Partridge, *A Dictionary of the Underworld* (London: Routledge & Kegan Paul, 1964); Phillip Pinkus, *Grub Street Stripp'd Bare* (London: Constable, 1968).

8. Luke Own Pike, *A History of Crime in England,* 2nd ser. (London: Smith Elder, 1873-76), p. 183; Peter Clark "The Alehouse and the Alternative Society," in Donald Pennington and Keith Thomas, eds., *Puritans and Revolutionaries* (Oxford: Clarendon Press, 1978), p. 60, notes the additional consideration that bastards posed a problem for inheritance.

9. Burford, *Bawds and Lodgings.*

10. Sex in Venice was more interesting. See Guido Ruggiero, *Boundaries of Eros: Sex Crime and Sexuality on Renaissance Venice* (Oxford: Oxford University Press, 1985).

11. On this subject, see: C. Bingham, "Seventeenth Century Attitudes Towards Deviant Sexuality," *Journal of Interdisciplinary History* 1 (1970): 447-69; D. O. Frantz, "Lewd Priapians and Renaissance Pornography," *Studies in English Literature* 12 (1972): 157-72; John G. Bourke, Scatological Rites of All Nations (1891; reissued New York: Johnson Reprint, 1968).

12. See the very interesting volume by Stanislaw Andreski, *Syphilis, Puritanism, and Witchhunts* (New York: St. Martin's Press, 1990). Also, L. Clarkson,

Death, Disease and Famine (London: Gill & MacMillan, 1975), pp. 1-40. The subject remained of interest in this period. See, for instance, J. Joynel's *Treatise of the French Disease* (1670); Bismoorth's *New Discovery of the French Disease* (1682); Gideon Harvey, *Little Venus Unmasked* (1670).

13. Samuel Pepys, *The Diary of Samuel Pepys,* 9 vols., ed. Robert Latham and William Matthews (Berkeley: University of California Press, 1970-1983), vol. 2, p. 170.

14. Henke, *Gutter Life and Language,* p. 257.

15. L. Stone, *The Crisis of the Aristocracy, 1558-1641* (Oxford: Clarendon Press, 1966), p. 620.

NOTES TO CHAPTER 10

1. Concerning bandits as popular heroes, see: Eric J. Hobsbawm, *Bandits* (New York: Pantheon Books, 1981); Hobsbawm, *Primitive Rebels* (Manchester: Manchester University Press, 1971); Maurice Keen, *Outlaws of Medieval Legend* (London: Routledge & Kegan Paul, 1961); Frank W. Chandler, *The Literature of Roguery,* 2 vols. (London: Houghton Mifflin, 1907, 1981); W. H. Bonner, *Pirate Laureate: the Life and Legends of Captain Kidd* (New Brunswick, NJ: Rutgers University Press, 1947).

2. A complete listing of newsbooks about James Hind can be found in G. J. Gray, *A General Index to Hazlitt's Handbook* (London: B. Quaritch, 1893).

3. J. A. Sharp, "Last Dying Speeches: Religion, Ideology and Public Execution in Seventeenth-Century England," *Past and Present,* no. 107 (May 1985): 144-67.

4. Highwaymen were of great interest to contemporaries. Two early works describing crime and evildoing in early modern England are Thomas Dekker's *The Belman of London: Bringing to Light the Most Notorious Villainies That Are Now Practiced in the Kingdom* (London, 1608), and Thomas Harmon's *Fraternity of Vagabond* (London, 1575). See also Captain Alexander Smith, *A Complete History of the Lives and Robberies of the Most Notorious Highwaymen, Footpads, Shopslifts and Cheats of Both Sexes,* 5th ed., ed. Arthur L. Haywood (New York: Brentano, 1926); Charles Johnson, *A General History of the Lives and Adventures of the Most Famous Highwaymen, Murderers, Street-Robbers and Et Cetera* (London, 1734); Related to these, see A. L. Beier, "Vagrants and the Social Order in Elizabethan England," *Past and Present,* no. 64, (August 1974): 3-29; F. Aydelotte, *Elizabethan Rogues and Vagabonds* (Oxford: Clarendon Press, 1913; reprinted London: F. Cass, 1967); Max Beloff, *Public Order and Popular Disturbances, 1660-1714* (London: F. Cass, 1963); Jean Jules Jusserand, *English Wayfaring Life in the Middle Ages,* trans. Lucy Toulmin Smith, 4th ed. (London: Benn, 1950). Concerning crime in early modern England, the following should prove helpful: J. S. Cockburn, *Crime in England, 1500-1800* (Princeton: Princeton University Press, 1977); John L. McMullan, *The Canting Crew: London's Criminal Underworld 1550-1700* (New Brunswick, NJ: Rutgers University Press, 1984); Gamini Salgado, *The Elizabethan Underworld*

(Totowa, NJ: Rowman and Littlefield, 1977); John A. Sharpe, *Crime in Early Modern England 1550-1750* (New York: Longman, 1984); Michael R. Weiser, *Crime and Punishment in Early Modern Europe* (Atlantic Heights, NJ: Humanities Press, 1979); L. O. Pike, *A History of Crime in England,* 2 vols. (London: Smith, Elder & Co., 1873-76), vol. 2.

5. C. H. Firth, *Cromwell's Army: A History of the English Soldier During the Civil Wars, the Commonwealth and the Protectorate,* 4th ed. (London: Methuen, 1962); L. F. Solt, *Saints in Arms, Puritanism and Democracy in Cromwell's Army* (Stanford: Stanford University Press, 1959); Bernard Capp, *Cromwell's Navy: The Fleet and the English Revolution 1648-1660* (Oxford: Clarendon Press, 1989); M. A. Kishlansky, *The Rise of the New Model Army* (Cambridge: Cambridge University Press, 1979).

6. For biographical information about Hind, see the *Dictionary of National Biography* (Oxford: Oxford University Press, 1937-) 9:803.

7. There is a long literary tradition of male cross-dressing. See Winfried Schleiner, "Male Cross-Dressing and Transvestism in Renaissance Romances," *Sixteenth Century Journal* 19, no. 4 (Winter 1988): 605-20.

8. See the *Dictionary of National Biography* 8:1187 for biographical details of Hannam's life and exploits.

9. Curiously, Robin Hood had been virtually forgotten but was rediscovered in the sixteenth and seventeenth centuries. See Keen, *Outlaws,* p. 99. Also, R. H. Hilton, "The Origins of Robin Hood," *Past and Present,* no. 14 (November 1958): 30-44; J. H. Holt, "The Origins and Audience of the Ballads of Robin Hood," *Past and Present,* no. 18 (November 1960): 898-110. On the theme of royal propaganda, see Carole Levin, *Propaganda in the English Reformation: Heroic and Villanous Images of King John* (Lewiston, NY: Edwin Mellen Press, 1988).

NOTES TO CHAPTER 11

1. For the details of Wharton's life, see *Dictionary of National Biography* (Oxford: Oxford University Press, 1937-) 20:1313-15. Also, Harry Rusche, *"Merlini Anglici*: Astrology and Propaganda from 1641 to 1651," *English Historical Revue* 80 (1965): 322ff. Wharton's writings have been collected in *The Works of George Wharton,* ed. John Gadbury (London, 1683).

2. Rusche, *"Merlini Anglici,"* p. 324.

3. C. Syms, *The White King Raised* (1647), p. 7.

4. For the details of William Sedgwick's life, see *Dictionary of National Biography* 17:1123. In 1647 Sedgwick gave Charles I a volume of his poems entitled *Leaves of the Tree of Life.* After reading part of the book, Charles returned it, saying he believed "the author stands in need of some sleep."

5. Concerning Paul Grebner, see Keith Thomas, *Religion and the Decline of Magic* (London: Weidenfeld and Nicholson, 1971); and Harry Rusche, "Prophecies and Propaganda, 1641 to 1651," *English Historical Revue* 84 (1969): 765ff.

6. For the details of Arise Evans's life, see *Dictionary of National Biography* 6:934.

7. Thomas Edwards, *Gangreana* (1646), vol. 2, p. 173.

8. John Aubrey, *Miscellanies* (1857), p. 128. See also John Brown's *Basilicon* (1684), p. 162.

9. Arise Evans, *The Voice of King Charles* (1655) p. 41.

10. For details of Gadbury's life, see *Dictionary of National Biography* 7:785-86. Also, Folke Dahl, "King Charles Gustavus and the Astrologers William Lilly and John Gadbury," *Lyenos* (1937): 161-86.

11. For details of Coppe's life, see *Dictionary of National Biography* 4:1115. For an analysis of his views, see Jerome Friedman, *Blasphemy, Immorality and Anarchy: The Ranters and the English Revolution* (Athens, OH: Ohio University Press, 1987), pp. 75-95.

NOTES TO CHAPTER 12

1. Sir Roger L'Estange, *The Intelligencer,* August 31, 1663.

2. See Geoffrey Cranfield, *The Press in Society: From Caxton to Northcliffe* (London: Longman, 1978), p. 16, for a complete list of these publications. Unfortunately, no analysis of this undoubtedly very funny literature exists.

3. Roger Thompson, *Unfit for Modest Ears* (London: Macmillan, 1979), p. 42. Roger Howell, "'The Devil Can Not Match Him'; The Image of Cromwell in Restoration Drama," *Cromwelliana,* Cromwell Association, Gloucester, England (1982-3).

4. G. Kitchin, *Sir Roger L'Estrange* (London: K. Paul, Trench, Trubner & Co., 1913), p. 267.

5. Godfrey Davies, *The Early Stuarts,* 2nd ed. (Oxford: Oxford University Press, 1959), p. 172; Peter Laslett, *Family Life and Illicit Love in Earlier Generations* (Cambridge: Cambridge University Press, 1977), chapter 3; G. E. Aylmer, *The State's Servants: The Civil Service of the English Republic, 1649-1660* (London: Routledge & Kegan Paul, 1973), p. 307.

6. Restoration "immorality" is a literary commonplace. See, for instance, Roger Thompson, "Two Early Editions of Restoration Erotica," *The Library,* 5th ser., 32 (1977); G. S. Alleman, "Matrimonial Law and the Materials of Restoration Comedy," Ph.D. diss., University of Pennyslvania, 1942, available on University Microfilms, Ann Arbor, MI; V. de S. Pinto, *Sir Charles Sedley* (London: Constable, 1927); and the following by J. H. Wilson: *A Rake and His Times* (London: Muller, 1927); *The Court Wits of the Restoration* (Princeton: Princeton University Press, 1948); *Nell Gwyn* (London: Muller, 1952); *All the King's Ladies* (Chicago: University of Chicago Press, 1958).

7. Reported by Sir Roger L'Estrange, *Observator,* February 4, 1682. Cited in Thompson, *Unfit For Modest Ears,* p. 40.

8. Raymond Crawford, *The King's Evil* (Oxford: Oxford University Press, 1911), pp. 105-112.

9. See D. Underhill, *Revel, Riot and Rebellion* (Oxford: Clarendon Press, 1985), p. 284. Also, Dudley W. R. Bahlman, *The Moral Revolution of 1688* (New Haven: Yale University Press, 1957).

NOTES TO CONCLUSION

1. Carlo M. Cipolla, *Faith, Reason and the Plague in Seventeenth-Century Tuscany* (New York: Norton Press, 1981).

2. See R. Po-Chia Hsia, *The Myth of Ritual Murder: Jews and Magic in Reformation Germany* (New Haven: Yale University Press, 1988).

3. See, for instance, R. C. Richardson, *The Debate on the English Revolution Revisited,* 2nd ed. (London: Routledge & Kegan Paul, 1989).

4. For instance, John Morrill, ed., *Reactions to the English Civil War 1642-1649* (New York: St. Martin's Press, 1982).

5. As an example consider the excellent volume by Sandra L. Zimdars-Swartz, *Encountering Mary: From La Salette to Medjugorje* (Princeton, NJ: Princeton University Press, 1991).

6. Peter Laslett, *The World We Have Lost: England Before the Industrial Age* (New York: Charles Scribner's, 1965).

Alphabetical Title Listing of Pamphlets Cited in this Study

The following alphabetical listing of titles of pamphlets cited in this volume can be located in the Wing listings, the Short title Catalogue, and the index of the George Thomason Tract Collection of the British Library. Almost all are available on microfilm as part of the Thomason Tract Series from University Microfilms of Ann Arbor, Michigan.

The Age of Wonders, or, Miracles Are Not Ceased (1660).
An Alarum of War, Given to the Army (1649).
Ale Ale-vated into the Ale-titude (1653).
Americans No Jews, or, Improbabilities That the Americans Are of That Race (1651).
Anglicus (1646).
Annus Tennebrosus (1652).
Anthropologie Abstracted, or, the Idea of Human Nature Reflected in Brief Philosophical and Anatomical Collections (1655).
Anthropometamorphosis: Man Transformed, or the Changeling (1653).
The Apprentice's Warning Piece, Being a Confession of Peter Moore (1641).
The Arraignment, Trial, Conviction and Confession of Francis Deane (1643).
The Arraignment and Trial of the Ranters, with a Declaration (1650).
Arsy Versy, or, the Second Martyrdom of the Rump (1660).
Astrological Judgment Upon His Majesties Present March (1645).
An Astrological Prediction of the Occurrences in England (1648).

Babylon's Beauty (1644).
Basilicon (1684).
The Beacon Quenched (1652).
A Beacon Set on Fire . . . Concerning the Vigilance of the Jesuits, A Second Beacon Fired (1652).
The Belman of London: Bringing to Light the Most Notorious Villainies That Are Now Practiced in the Kingdom (1608).
The Bespotted Jesuit Whose Gospel is Full of Blasphemy (1641).
Beware of False Prophets (1644).
The Black Box of Rome (1641).
The Black and Terrible Warning Piece (1653).
A Blazing Star Seen in the West (1642).
Blood Washed Away By Tears of Repentance (1657).
Bloody News From Dover (1646).
Bloody News From the North (1650).
A Bosom Opened to the Jews (1656).
A Brief Anatomy of Women (1653).
A Brief Answer . . . Against the Coming of the Jews (1656).
A Brief Description and Character of the Religion and Manners of the Phantastiques in General, Especially Anabaptists, Independents, Brownists, Enthusiasts, Levellers, Quakers, Seekers, Fifth Monarchy Men and Dippers (1660).
A Brief Description of the Future History of Europe From anno 1650 to 1710 (1588).
Brightman's Predictions and Prophecies (1641).

Britain's Royal Star (1661).
British and Outlandish Prophecies (1657).
The Brothers of the Blade, Answerable to The Sisters of the Scabard (1641).
A Brown Dozen of Drunkards, alias, Drink-Hards (1648).

Calvers' Royall Vision (1648).
Camilton's Discovery of the Devilish Designs . . . of the Society of Jesus (1641).
A Catalogue of the Several Sects and Opinions (1647).
Certain Prophecies Presented Before the Kings Majesty by Scholars of Trinity College (1642).
The Character of a Rump (1660).
Chocolate, or, an Indian Drink (1651).
A Collection of Ancient and Modern Prophesies Concerning these Present Times with Modest Observations Thereon (1645).
Concerning the Restraint Lately Set Forth Against Drinking, Potting and Piping on the Sabbath Day (1641).
The Confession of a Papist Priest (1641).
Confidence Dismantled (1651).
Cromwell's Bloody Slaughter-House (1660).
Cromwell's Conspiracy (1660).
Counterblaste to Tobacco (1604).
A Curse Against Parliament Ale (1649).
The Curtain-Drawer of the World (1612).
Cyprianus Anglicis: Life of William, Lord Archbishop of Canterbury (London, 1671).

Declaration of Arise Evans (1653-4).
The Declaration of Captain James Hind (1651).
The Declaration of John Robins (1651).
A Declaration of a Strange and Wonderful Monster, Born in Kirkham Parish in Leicestershire (1645).
A Declaration and Vindication of the Nobility, Gentry and Others of the County of Kent, That They Had No Hand in the Murther of Our King (1660).
A Description of a Sect Called Family of Love (1641).
The Devil Incarnate (1660).
The Devil in Kent or His Strange Delusions at Sandwitch (1647).
The Devil's Reign Upon Earth (1655).
A Dialogue Between Mistris Macquerella, A Suburban Bawd, Ms. Scolopendra, a Noted Courtezan and Mr. Pimpinello, an Usher (1650).
A Discoursive Probleme Concerning Prophecies (1588).
The Discovery of the Jesuit's Trumpery (1641).
A Discovery of the Most Dangerous and Damnable Tenets That Have Been Spread Within This Few Years (1647).
A Discovery of Twenty Nine Sects Here in London (1641).
The Discovery of Witches (1647).
The Divine Dreamer (1641).
A Divine Potion to Preserve Spiritual Health (1648).
Doomesday, or, The Great Day of the Lord's Judgment (1647).
The Drunkard's Character (1646).

The Eighth Liberal Science, or, the New Found Art and Order of Drinking (1650).
*An Endeavor After the Reconcilement of That Difference Between Presbyterians and
Independents About Church Government in a Discourse Touching the Jews
Synogogue* (1648).
England's Black Tribunal (1660).
England's Genius Pleading for King Charles (1660).
England's Jubilee, Britania Rediviva (1660).
England's Prophetical Merline Foretelling to All Nations of Europe until 1663 (1644).
England's Warning Piece (1660).
The English Devil, or Cromwell (1660).
English Ephemeris for 1650 (1650).
The English Gusman, or, The History of That Unparalleled Thief, James Hind (1652).
*The English Villain, or, The Grand Thief The Witty Rogue Arraigned, Condemned
and Executed, or, The History of that Incomparable Thief, Richard Hannam* (1656).
The Ex-ale-tation of Ale, the Ancient Liquor of This Realm (1642).
*The Examination, Confession, Trial and Execution of Joan Williford, Joan Cariden
and Jane Holt* (1645).
An Excellent Comedy Called, The Prince of Priggs Revels (1651).
Extraordinary News From Constantinople (1641).

*A False Jew, or, a Wonderful Discovery of a Scot, Baptized at London for a
Christian, Circumcised at Rome to Act a Jew but Rebaptized at Hexham for a
Believer but Found Out At Newcastle to be a Cheat* (1654).
False Prophets Discovered (1642).
*The Fanatick History, or, An Exact Relation of the Old Anabaptists and
New Quakers* (1660).
The Fifteen Real Comforts of Matrimony (1681).
Fortunate Uprising, or, The Rump Upward (1660).
Four Severall Strange Prophecies (1642).
Fourteen Strange Prophecies (1649).
Fraternity of Vagabond (1575).
*A Full and The Truest Narrative of the Most Horrid, Barbarous and
Unparalleled Murder* (1657).

*Gangraena, or, a Catalogue of Many of the Errours, Heresies, and Pernicious
Practices of the Sectaries of This Time,* Part I, published in February 1646; Part II
published in May 1646; Part III published in December 1646.
*A General History of the Lives and Adventures of the Most Famous Highwaymen,
Murderers, Street-Robbers and Et Cetera* (1734).
God Save the King (1660).
The Good Angel of Stamford (1659).
Good News From Oxford (1642).
The Great and Bloody Vision (1654).
*The Great Memorial, or, a List of Those Pretended Judges Who Sentenced Our Late
King* (1660).
The Great Sins of Drunkenness and Gluttony Set Forth in the Proper Colors (1656).
The Great Turke's Letter Sent unto the Prince of Transylvania (1645).
Hannam's Last Farewell to the World (1656).

Harry Hangman's Honor (1655).
A Health to All Vintners, Beer-Brewers and Ale Tonners (1642).
Heaven's Cry Against Murder (1657).
The Hebrews' Deliverance At Hand (1651).
Hell Broke Loose (1646).
Henry Marten's Familiar Letters to his Lady of Delight (1662).
Heresiography; or, a Description of the Heretics and Sectaries of the Latter Times
    (1645).
Here's Jack in the Box (1656).
Hind's Elder Brother, or, The Master Thief Discovered (1652).
Hind's Ramble (1651).
A History of the Second Death of the Rump (1660).
The Hope of Israel by Menasseh ben Israel, Whereunto Are Added Some Discourses
    Upon the Point of The Conversion of the Jews (1651).
The Horn Exalted, or, Room for Cuckolds, with an Appendix Concerning Women
    and Jealousy (1660).
A Hue and Cry After the High Court of Injustice . . . Who Condemned the Late
    King's Majesty to Death, with a Perfect List of All Their Names (1660).
Hymnus Tobaci, A Poem in Honor of Tobacco (1651).

Ignatius His Prophecy Concerning These Times (1642).
Immortality in Mortality Magnified (1647).
The Impudence of the Romish Whore (1644).
Innocency Appearing Through the Mists of Pretended Guilt (1655).
Ireland's Amazement, or, The Heaven's Armada (1641).
Israel's Condition and Cause Pleaded (1656).

The Jesuit's Character (1642).
The Jesuit's Creed (1642).
Jews in America, or, Probabilities that the Americans are of That Race (1650).
The Jovial Crew, or, The Devil Turned Ranter (1651).
Joyful Newes for All Christendom, Being a Happy Prophecy (1661).
The Just Devil of Woodstock, or, A Narrative of the Several Apparitions, the Frights
    and Punishments Inflicted upon the Rumpish Commissioners (1660).
Justices of the Peace of Westminister (1651).

The Key to Prophecy (1659).
King Charles I: His Imitation of Christ, or, the Parallel Lines of Our Saviour's and
    Our King's Suffering (1660).
King Charles, His Star (1654).

The Ladies Champion, Confounding the Author of the Wandering Whore (1660).
The Lamentable Complaints of Nick Froth the Tapster and Rulerost the Cook: A
    Vindication of Strong Beer and Ale (1647).
The Last Will and Testament of James Hind, Highway Lawyer (1651).
Laudensium Apostasia, or, a dialogue in Which Is Shewen . . . the Greatness of the
    Late Archbishop (1660).
The Life and Death of John Atherton (1641).

The Life and Death Of King Charles the Martyr, Paralleled with Our Saviour (1650).

Lilly Lash't With His Own Rod, or, An Epigram on the Quaint Skill of that Arch Temporizing Astrologer, Mr. William Lilly (1660).

The Lineage of Lucusts, or, the Pope's Pedigree The Papist's Petition in England (1642).

Look About You, or . . . Take Heed of the Jesuits (1647).

A Looking Glass for a Drunkard, or, A Drunkard Defined (1652).

A Looking Glass for Traytors (1660).

The Lord Merlin's Prophecy Concerning the King of Scots (1651).

The Lord Osmond's Overthrow, Which was the Chief Commander of the Rebels (1642).

The Lord's Loud Call to England (1660).

The Lost Sheep Found (1660).

Lues Venerea, or, A Perfect Cure of the French Pox (1660).

The Lying Wonders, or Rather, the Wonderful Lies (1660).

Maiestis Irradiant, or, The Splendor Displayed of Our Soveraigne King Charles (1660).

The Marine Mercury, or, A True Relation of the Strange Appearance of a Man-Fish. . . Having a Musket in One Hand and a Petition in the Other (1642).

The Mathematical Divine (1642).

The Melancholy Knight (1615).

Merlinus Anglicis (1652).

Merlinus Anglicus Junior (1644).

A Miracle of Miracles Wrought by the Blood of King Charles the First (1650).

Mistriss Rump Brought to Bed of a Monster (1660).

Monarchy and No Monarchy in England (1651).

More Warning Yet, Being a True Relation of a Strange and Most Dreadful Apparition (1654).

The Most Strange and Wonderful Apparitions of Blood (1645).

The Most Strange and Wonderfull Apparition of Blood in a Pool at Garreton (1647).

The Most Wonderful and True Relation of Master John Macklin (1657).

Mr. Pryn's Letter and Proposals to King Charles (1637).

Mr. William Lilly's History of King James the First and King Charles the First (1651).

Murder, Murder, or, A Bloody Relation of how Anne Hamton . . . Murdered Her Dear Husband (1641).

Mutatis Polemo, The Horrible Strategems of the Jesuits (1650).

Mutatus Polemo Revisited (1650).

Mysteries of Love and Eloquence (1658).

The Mystery of Prophecies Revealed (1660).

A Narrative of the Proceedings of a Great Council of Jews Assembled in the Plains of Ageda in Hungaria, to Examine the Scriptures Concerning Christ (1655).

A Nest Of Serpents Discovered . . . Called Adamites (1641).

Newes From the Dead, or, A True and Exact Narration of the Miraculous Deliverance of Anne Greene (1650).

New News and Strange News from Babylon (1641).

A New Proclamation (1653).

The New Years Wonder (1642).

Newes From the Great Turke (1645).

Newes From the New Exchange, or, The Commonwealth of Ladies (1649).

Newes From Rome (1641).
Newes From Whitehall (1654).
News From Holland (1647, 1655).
Nine Notable Prophecies (1644).

The Old Anabaptists Grand Plot Discovered (1660).
Oliver Cromwell, The Late Great Tirant (1660).
Organon Salutis: An Instrument to Cleanse the Stomach (1657).

Panacea, or, The Universal Medicine, Being a Discovery of the Wonderful Virtues of Tobacco (1659).
The Parliament of Women (1646, 1656).
A Peculiar Prognostication (1649).
The Penitent Death of a Woeful Sinner (1641).
The Penitent Murderer (1657).
A Perfect Narrative of the Phantastique Wonders Seen in the West of England (1660).
Philastrogus' Knavery Epitomised with a Vindication of Mr. Culpepper, Mr. Lilly, and the rest of the Students in that Noble Art (1651).
A Pill to Purge Melancholy, or, Merry News from Newgate (1652).
The Plot Discovered and Counter Plotted (1641).
The Plots of Jesuits (1653).
The Plotters Unmasked: Murderers, No Saints (1660).
Poesis Rediviva (1655).
The Poor Man's Plain Path-way to Heaven (1603).
The Pope's Proclamation, The Pope's Benediction (1641).
The Practical Part of Love (1660).
A Preparative to Study, or, The Virtue of Sack (1641).
The Presbyterian Lash, or, Noctroff's Maid Whipt (1661).
A Profitable and Necessary Booke of Observations and a Brief and Necessary Treatise Touching the Cure of the Disease Now Usually Called Lues Venera (1596).
The Prophecy of David Upan (1651).
A Prophecy Lately Found Amongst the Collection of the Famous Mr. John Selden (1659).
The Prophecy of Mother Shipton (1641).
Prophecy of the Scottish Sybill (1651).
The Prophecy of a White King of Brittaine (1643).
The Prophecy of the White King And Dreadfull Dead-man Explained (1644).
The Prophecy of the White King Explained (1648).
Pseudo-Astrologus, The Spurious Prognosticator Unmasked (1659).

The Quaker-Jesuite, or, Popery in Quakerisme (1660).

The Ranter's Bible (1650).
The Ranter's Declaration (1650).
The Ranter's Last Sermon (1654).
The Ranter's Monster (1652).
The Ranter's Principle and Deceits Discovered (1655).
The Ranter's Ranting (1650).

The Ranter's Recantation (1650).
The Ranter's Religion (1650).
A Relation of a Terrible Monster Taken by a Fisherman near Wollage (1642).
Religion's Lottery, or, The Church's Amazement (1642).
A Remedy for Uncleanness (1658).
Resident at Constantinople (1642).
The Resurrection of Dead Bones, or, The Conversion of the Jews (1655).
Reverend Mr. Brightman's Judgments (1642).
Robin Hood and His Crew of Soldiers, A Comedy Acted at Nottingham on the Day of His Sacred Majesties' Coronation (1661).
Rome's ABC (1641).
The Routing of the Ranters (1650).
The Royal Joy (1660).
The Royal Martyrs ... The State Martyrology (1660).
The Rump Dock't (1660).
Rump Enough (1660).
The Rump Served in With a Grant Sallet (1660).
The Rump Ululant (1660).
The Rump's Despairing (1660).
The Rump's Last Will and Testament (1660).

Sad News From the Eastern Parts (1642).
A Second Discovery of Hind's Exploits (1651).
Select City Quaeries (1660).
The Serpent's Subtlety Discovered (1656).
Seven Arguments Plainly Proving That Papists Are Traitorous Subjects (1641).
Seven Severall Strange Prophecies (1643).
Several Apparitions Seen in the Air at the Hague (1642).
Several Observations on the Life and Death of King Charles I (1651).
A Short Demurrer to the Jews Remitter into England (1656).
A Sign from Heaven, or, A Fearful and Terrible Noise Heard in the Air (1642).
Signs From Heaven, or, Several Apparitions Seen and Heard in the Air in the Counties of Cambridge and Norfolk (1642).
Signs and Wonders From Heaven with a True Relation of a Monster Born in Ratcliffe Highway (1645).
A Single Eye (1650).
The Sisters of the Scabard's Holiday (1641).
Speculum Impietis (1644).
The Speech and Confession and Richard Hannam (1656).
A Speech of the Honorable Nathanael Feines (1641).
The Spiritual Madman (1648).
The Starry Messenger, or, An Interpretation of Strange Apparitions (1644).
A Strange Apparition in an Ale-house (1641).
Strange and Fearful News From Plaisto in the Parish of Westham (1645).
A Strange and Lamentable Accident That Happened Lately at Mears Ashby in Northamptonshire (1642).
Strange and Miraculous News From Turkie, Sent to Our English Ambassador A True and Wonderful Relation of a Whale (1645).
Strange Newes From Scotland (1647).

Strange News From Newgate, or, A True Relation of the False Prophet (1647).
Strange News From Newgate and the Old Bailey (1650).
Strange News From the North (1650).
Strange News From Warwick (1642).
A Strange and True Conference Between Two Notorious Bawds, Damrose Page and Pris Fotheringham (1660).
Strange and True News from Gloucester (1660).
A Strange and Wonderful Example of God's Judgments (1645).
The Strange and Wonderfull Prophecy of David Cardinal of France (1660).
A Strange and Wonderful Relation of the Burying of Joan Bridges of Rochester (1646).
A Strange Wonder, or, The City's Amazement (1641).
A Strange Wonder, or, A Wonder in a Woman (1642).
Supernatural Sights and Apparitions Seen in London June 3 1644 (1644).
A Swarm of Sectaries and Schismatiques (1641).
The Sword's Apology (1644).

Take Warning Before It Be Too Late . . . to Take Heed of Sectaries (1648).
Teratalogia, or a Discovery of God's Wonders (1650).
A Testimony Against the People Called Ranters (1659).
To The Lord General Cromwell and His Council (1653-4).
A Total Rout, or a Brave Discovery of a Pack of Knaves and Drabs (1653).
A Treatise of Specters; or, An History of Apparitions, Oracles, Prophecies and Predictions (1658).
The Trial of Captain James Hind (1651).
Trial of Traytors (1660).
The Troubled Spirited Man's Departing (1653).
A True Copy of a Prophecy Which Was Found in an Old Ancient House... Where Unto Is Added Mother Shipton's Prophecies (1642).
A True and Exact Relation of the Several . . . Late Witches . . . at Chelmesford (1645).
A True and Perfect Picture of Our Present Reformation (1648).
The True and Perfect Relation of the Taking of Captain James Hind (1651).
A True Relation of the Most Horrid and Barbarous Murders, Committed by Abigail Hill (1658).
A True Relation of the Strange Apparitions Seen in the Air on Monday, February 25, 1649 (1649).
The True Relation of Two Wonderfull Sleepers (1646).
Truth Appearing Through the Clouds of Undeserved Scandal (1654).
Twelve Strange Prophecies (1648).
Two Strange Prophecies (1642).

A Vindication of the Roman Catholics of the English Nation (1660).
A Vindication of Those . . . Called Diggers (1649).
A Vision (1648).
The Voice of King Charles (1655).
Vox Infantis, or, The Prophetical Child (1649).
The Wandering Jew (1656).
The Wandering Whore (1660).
A Warning Piece to the World (1655).
We Have Brought Our Hoggs to a Fair Market, or Strange News From Newgate (1652).

A Whip for a Drunkard and a Curb for Prophaness (1646).

The White King Raised and the Dreadful Deadman Revived (1647).

The Whore's Rhetoric (1681).

William Lilly, Student in Astrology, His Past and Present Opinion Touching Monarchy in These Nations (1660).

William Lilly's History of His Life and Times from the Year 1602 (1648, 1715).

The Wiltshire Rant (1652).

Wine and Women (1646).

The Witch of Wapping (1652).

The Witches of Huntingdon (1646).

Wit's Interpreter (1656).

A Wonder in Staffordshire, or, A Staffordshire Wonder (1660).

A Wonder of Wonders (1650).

Wonderfull News, or, a True Relation of a Churchwarden in the Town of Toscester (1642).

A Wonderful Plot, or, A Mystery Of State Discovered (1647).

The Wonderful Works of God Declared by a Strange Prophecie (1641).

The Wonderfull Works of God Declared by a Strange Prophecy of a Maid (1641).

The World's Catastrophe or Europe's Many Mutations until 1666 (1647).

The World Turned Upside Down, or, A Brief Description of the Ridiculous Fashions of These Distracted Times (1647).

Index